Reader's Digest

The Countryside Detective

Reader's Digest

The Countryside Detective

Published by The Reader's Digest Association Limited • London • New York • Sydney • Montreal

Consultant Dr David Bellamy OBE
Experts Dr Frances Dipper, Jonathan Elphick, Mont Hirons, Peter Marren, Dr Peter Moore, Dr Pat Morris, Chris O'Toole, Pat Wisniewski
Writers David Burnie, Robert Burton, Dennis Furnell, Rob Hume, Peter Marren
Photographer Jason Smalley
Additional photography Heather Angel, Guy Edwardes, Andrea Jones
Illustrators Represented by Wildlife Art Ltd: Stuart Carter, Mike Langman, Peter David Scott, Simon Turvey
Digital Illustrator Ian Atkinson
Maps PC Graphics (UK) Ltd
Indexer Laura Hicks

The Countryside Detective
was edited and designed by
The Reader's Digest Association Limited, London

If you have any comments or suggestions about this book, e-mail us at:
gbeditorial@readersdigest.co.uk

Reprinted with amendments 2000

The typefaces used in this book are Bembo and Frutiger
Printed in Belgium
ISBN 0 276 42438 7

Reader's Digest editorial team
Editor Brenda Houghton
Art Editor Julie Bennett
Deputy Editor Neil Thomson
Assistant Editors Alison Candlin, Celia Coyne, Cecile Landau
Senior Designer Jane McKenna
Designers Keith Miller, Dominic Zwemmer
Editorial Assistant Rachel Weaver
Picture Researcher Martin Smith
Proofreader Barry Gage

Reader's Digest General Books
Editorial Director Cortina Butler
Art Director Nick Clark
Executive Editor Julian Browne
Development Editor Ruth Binney
Publishing Projects Manager Alastair Holmes
Picture Research Editor Martin Smith
Style Editor Ron Pankhurst

Part of my upbringing

Foreword by Dr David Bellamy OBE

'I am often asked which is my favourite country and, although I have seen much of the world, the answer is always, 'The British Isles'. Why? Because the sights, sounds and smells of our countryside are part of my upbringing. I can even put names to many of the common wild flowers and the wildlife that I see. I also know a little bit about many of them – which sting or bite, which taste or smell nice or nasty, which are the baddies and the goodies. Each new experience is the start of an adventure of discovery. There is never a dull moment.

Though born and brought up in London, I spent my spare time in the green spaces between the buildings and, as soon as I could, got on my bike and discovered the country and the seaside. I found diverse, exciting landscapes overflowing with wild flowers, birds and insects, and rural people – farmers, shepherds, labourers and gamekeepers – who were only too willing to share their knowledge and their love of the natural history of their locality.

In those days I would give my mum a bunch of wild flowers for her birthday and she would help me to find out their proper names. As Boy Scouts we paid for our campsites by helping the farmers to coppice woodlands and to clear out the weeds and silt that rapidly filled the farm and village ponds, clogging the only water supply available to their horses and cattle and myriad plants and other animals.

'In those days I would give my mum a bunch of **wild flowers** for her birthday and she would help me to find out their **proper names**.'

I learned about the wild places and wild things of Britain by watching, listening and exploring. So I was delighted to be asked to head the team putting together *The Countryside Detective*, because its aim is to help all who read it to share my boyhood experience and to find out more about the wildlife of our islands.

I must confess I was a bit worried at first, because experts can be the most boring people on earth, but the team of master detectives that Reader's Digest gathered together to create this book are anything but that. You have in your hands the knowledge of the Poirots, Marples and Morses of the natural history world, enlivened with a little humour.

This isn't one of those books with only the Latin names of mammals or birds, and pictures that you could only see through a high-powered telescope on a clear day. It is an all-action detective story that takes you outdoors hunting for the clues and hard evidence that will help you to understand what you see, hear and smell all around you. Just like people, plants and animals live in communities, each with an important job to do in the society of nature. So once you have managed to get the first clue in sight, you'll see the rest of the whodunnit? unfold before your very eyes.

Clues galore make every outing a challenging adventure whatever the time of year. Who lost the feather and why? What made the hole in the cow pat? Who set fire to the heath? What did the barn owl have for dinner last night? Who killed cock robin?

As I write this foreword, it is 40 years to the day that a group of enthusiasts first met on Box Hill in Surrey to help to manage a bit of our countryside back into biodiverse working order, so that the orchids that had inspired Charles Darwin could live on. I am just off to join them once again to celebrate 40 years of partnership with all the other conservation bodies, and many local communities, caring for our wilder places.

With the help of *The Countryside Detective*, I hope you will set out to discover and enjoy the countryside the way I did as a boy. The more you understand our plants and animals – how and why they live where and as they do, and the most intricate details of their ecology – the more you will appreciate the importance of maintaining a blooming, buzzing biodiversity. And then I hope you will join our campaign to achieve it!'

Starting an investigation: Setting the scene

This book is designed to help you to get more pleasure from the beautiful countryside of Britain by showing you how to find the clues that guide you to the wildlife you've never seen before. You will learn to spot the signs that open the door to all the excitement of the natural world, and discover how to interpret each find so that it leads you on to another. When you understand the story behind the landscape and the wildlife in it, every walk in the country will be a richer experience.

Six different worlds

Landscape gives you clues about the history of the land, while flora and fauna add the spice of living things. In the following pages we show you how the two dovetail together.

The book is divided into six different habitats, because the animals, birds, plants and insects that you can hope to find in woodland, for instance, are quite different from those that you might see by the coast.

Climate also plays its part: for example, the harsh conditions of the uplands govern what plants can grow there and these, in turn, dictate which animals can live in these desolate places.

The countryside also changes as the year progresses. The hedgerow that is studded with flowers in spring will be laden with berries when autumn comes, and with birds and mammals feeding on them. So every habitat is visited in spring, summer, autumn and winter to highlight the special features to hunt for season by season.

Grassland & Farmland

This first section takes you through hay meadows and fields grazed by stock, studies what is living among the crops and in water meadows, explores chalk downs and gentle valleys and investigates hedgerows and verges. This sort of land is often crossed by footpaths where it is easy to walk and discover the world about you.

Woodland

Next the book goes into the greenwood to uncover the architecture of the trees and find out how they can reveal the wood's history.

This section tracks down the carpets of flowers that transform ancient woods in spring, explores mountain woods bent into weird shapes by the wind, penetrates damp western woodlands smothered in soft moss and hanging lichens and peers down the regimented rows of conifer plantations in search of their shy inhabitants.

Waterside

The third section investigates life in the water and along the bank. Here are the clues to watch out for as you walk along a towpath or the banks of a stream, the busy creatures around you when you are boating quietly along a canal or on the Broads, and the wildfowl and fish eaters to search for in lakes and rivers. It peers into the little world of the pond, and reveals the wealth of bird life that is colonising reservoirs and old gravel pits on the fringes of our cities.

Moor & Mountain

The book now moves on to the windswept uplands where only the sturdiest plants and creatures can find a hold. It travels into the mountains to find the clues that lead to our rarest birds, such as the turkey-like capercaille and the golden eagle, and mammals such as the winter-white mountain hare.

It explores the rare blanket bogs and fragile limestone pavements to find their very special inhabitants, and encompasses sandy lowland heaths, such as those in the New Forest, with their mixture of scrub, heather and woodland.

Where the rain falls *The persistent patter of rain makes Britain green. The highest annual rainfall is in the west, where you will find mossy woods, great lakes and ground that is too wet for agriculture, so rich in wildlife.*

Spring in stages *Spring comes early in the south and on low ground. Higher up and farther north, the average March temperature is several degrees lower, and you will have to time your hunt for spring flowers and early birds for a few weeks later.*

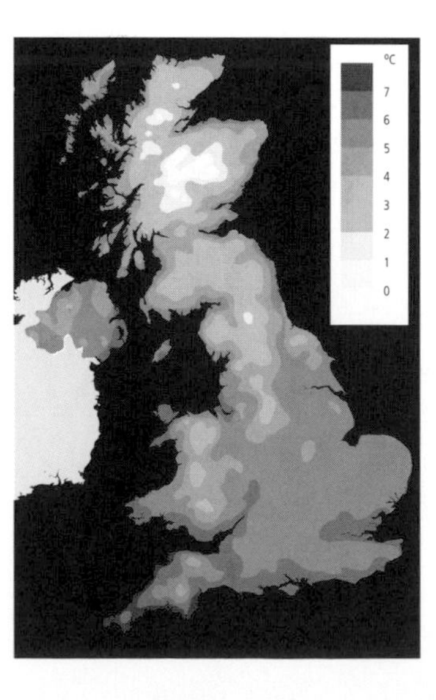

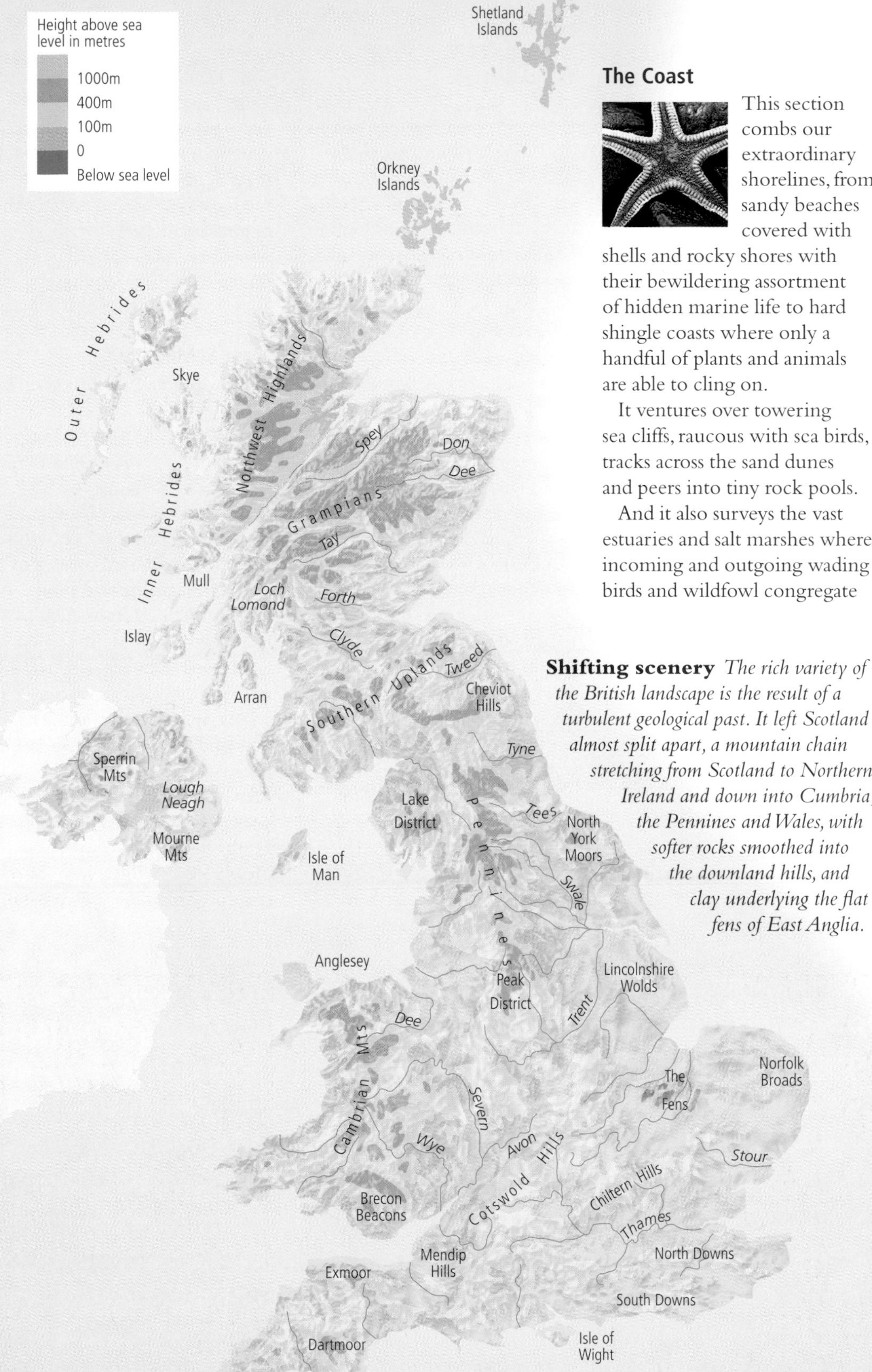

Shifting scenery *The rich variety of the British landscape is the result of a turbulent geological past. It left Scotland almost split apart, a mountain chain stretching from Scotland to Northern Ireland and down into Cumbria, the Pennines and Wales, with softer rocks smoothed into the downland hills, and clay underlying the flat fens of East Anglia.*

The Coast

This section combs our extraordinary shorelines, from sandy beaches covered with shells and rocky shores with their bewildering assortment of hidden marine life to hard shingle coasts where only a handful of plants and animals are able to cling on.

It ventures over towering sea cliffs, raucous with sea birds, tracks across the sand dunes and peers into tiny rock pools.

And it also surveys the vast estuaries and salt marshes where incoming and outgoing wading birds and wildfowl congregate in their thousands, turning these often deserted shorelines into dramatic natural theatres.

Towns & Cities

The final section comes close to home to investigate the mammals, birds, plants and insects that have managed to make their homes in suburbia. In cities, towns and villages, public parks and private gardens, even on sewage works and rubbish tips there are hundreds of wild things to discover and enjoy once you have the clues that tell you where to look.

Moors and heaths
Compare this map with the weather and relief maps (left and opposite page) and see how most moors and heaths (the darker areas) lie on the old hard rocks of the north and west uplands, and where moist Atlantic winds create boggy ground.

The initial
Lines of enquiry

Establish your position

The first step towards being a countryside detective is to think about where you are. If you are walking through a grassy field, you can expect to find different plants, birds and animals than if you were making your way up a mountainside.

And because there are many variations within each habitat, this book reveals the 'indicator' plants that tell you, for example, whether the land you are walking across lies on chalk or granite, because the type of rock dictates which plants will grow.

Once you realise that if you see old man's beard (traveller's-joy) in the hedgerows it means you are on chalk, then you can start to search the surrounding meadowland in the hope of finding a blue butterfly.

If you realise you are punting your boat alongside a reed bed, you will know that you might come across a harvest mouse or a reed warbler nesting in the reeds, or see a marsh harrier quartering the sky above.

Stalking deer *A field edge close to shelter offers the chance of seeing fallow deer, like this fawn. Keep watch at dawn or dusk, when they emerge to feed. If you hear a sharp bark, is means the doe is near, has sensed your presence and is warning her offspring.*

Narrow the search

Knowing which are the likeliest places to find animals, or evidence of their presence, gives you the best chance of detecting them. For instance, your best chance of finding an otter's spraint, or scent marking, is under a bridge across a stream. If you are on the beach looking for signs of life, lift up some seaweed, because that's where rock pool animals are most likely to be – keeping moist while the tide is out.

A sheet of corrugated iron lying on the ground or propped up against a wall, attracts small mammals to the sheltered conditions beneath. Lift it up and you might find a bank vole, field vole, shrew or yellow-necked mouse. And if the sheet is in a sunny position, you may surprise a grass snake or other cold-blooded reptile enjoying the warmth.

Try to tap into sources of special knowledge: ask local people such as farmers, foresters, gamekeepers, police, rangers and road sweepers for advice. They can help you to concentrate your field of search.

Be realistic

Do not expect to see too much at first. Most mammals are small or nocturnal or both, and are hard to find. Animals that have long been hunted by man, such as badgers, foxes, otters and hares, can be particularly wary and hard to track down.

Mammals tend to spend more time on the ground than birds, and often reveal signs of recent activity by leaving droppings or footprints, or by digging holes. Generally, therefore, you can expect to find more signs of their presence and in relatively accessible places. With practice, you will find that you are discovering more and more.

Pick your moment

Every season of the year offers different sights and sounds for the countryside detective. Creatures that mate out of sight in the heart of the woods in spring may emerge into the open in summer, when they are searching for food for their ravenous young. In autumn, when these youngsters set out on their own, they offer you more chances to view them.

Birds are easiest to trace in spring when you can hear them singing for a mate or to scare others off their territory and can try to track the song back to the singer. You get a second chance to find your local birds in late spring and summer when the eggs hatch. Then you can listen for the piping calls of the hungry youngsters in the nest.

Rhythms of the year

Plants, too, bud and blossom, fruit and shed their leaves at different times of the year. Plants on sand dunes, for instance, are almost all early flowering and then die down in the summer drought. Wetland plants, on the other hand, suffer no lack of water in summer and can flower later and stay green for longer.

So if you are on the hunt for particular plants, time your visit to their habitats for the right season. This will give you many chances to find and identify them, and to look for signs of the insects, birds and small mammals that depend on them for food and shelter.

Always be ready to seize an opportunity. If you spot a flock of birds mobbing a patch of hedgerow, tiptoe over and take a closer look. You will probably find that they have spotted a stoat or other predator, enjoying its daytime rest.

Brave the cold

Don't just be a fair weather detective. Many landscape features, and particularly the underlying geological structure, become more visible in winter. Equally, the architecture of a wood is more easily seen when the leaves have fallen and the structure and arrangement of the trees is exposed.

Buried roads through the fields, which might be old drove roads to long-closed markets, are often picked out by frost where summer crops would hide them.

And the bird's nest you should not go near in spring and summer, when it is occupied, is easily found in winter and can be explored without any harm.

Listen and sniff

We human beings rely on our sight more than any other sense. But to be a true countryside detective you need to use your other senses as well.

Hearing will help you to detect many more birds than sight. Learn to distinguish some of the common bird calls and songs and next time you walk through the woods you will be able to name the songsters.

Mammals and reptiles make noises too – listen for the yelp of a fox in winter, the puffing of a courting hedgehog in early summer or the rustle of a snake in the undergrowth in spring.

With practice, you can also cultivate a sharper sense of smell. For instance, carnivores are generally more 'smelly' than herbivores, so if you are not sure if a burrow belongs to a rabbit or a fox, sniff the entrance. A strong musky smell tells you a fox lives there.

Smell is also a good way to identify certain plants, such as bog myrtle, which smells like cough medicine; scented mayweed, whose crushed leaves smell of pineapple; water mint, whose powerful scent was used as an early form of smelling salts; or the stinkhorn fungus, which smells like rotting flesh. Taste, too, can be useful: it isn't always easy to tell the various grasses apart, but if you chew a stem of sweet vernal grass you will find that it tastes of almonds.

Spotting a kingfisher
A riverbank overhung with trees to perch on is the place to hunt the elusive kingfisher. Summer is time to start your search as a breeding pair have to flash in and out of the water catching 100 or more fish a day for their chicks.

On the trail of
Clues and signals

When you first arrive at a likely spot, scan the site for any obvious signs. Molehills and rabbit burrows, for example, are fairly easy to see. Try to work out how the animal would behave: it would use a hedgerow as a corridor from one denser patch of cover, such as a wood, to another, so look along the bottom for tracks or hair. Walk over to any prominent feature, such as a gatepost or tree stump, and check it for territorial markings such as droppings.

If you see a sunny south-facing bank with exposures of bare earth, look for tiny holes made by nesting mining bees and wasps. If you find a pile of dead wood, try lifting off some loose bark to see if you can discover some wood-boring beetles, a spider sleeping after a night-time of hunting prey, or shiny brownish yellow centipedes, resting after wreaking carnage among small insects and wood lice.

One clue may lead you to another. For instance, if you find a distinctive footprint, look for other signs such as droppings, fur or feathers nearby to confirm your identification. Nocturnal mammals such as badgers tend to be most active at dusk or dawn, so that is the time to look for them. And the signs they leave behind at night will be more fresh at dawn than midday, so get up early to search for droppings and tracks.

The place *If you think you have found a fox's earth (above) look for signs nearby to clinch it such as a paw print (below left), some hairs caught on a fence (below), or the animal's droppings (below right).*

Tracks

Always examine patches of muddy ground where you may find the imprint of a paw, hoof or a bird track. If the prints are fresh, you may be able to follow them for some distance and discover the animal's living quarters.

Sand dunes and bunkers on golf courses are other great places for footprints. On snowy days, nothing can move about without leaving tracks and you will be amazed at how much activity is revealed.

Remember, however, that most of the tracks you find in the countryside will have been made by domestic animals, particularly sheep, cattle, horses and dogs. Learn to recognise these common prints so that you can discount them. For more about tracks, see page 284.

Fox footprints

Trails

A trail will form where a passing animal disturbs or flattens the vegetation, especially if it tends to follow the same path regularly. This can lead you to a worthwhile discovery. For instance, badgers leave prominent trails from their setts to their feeding grounds so you may be able to follow one and find the sett. More temporary trails may be made in the early morning dew by passing animals. In dense grass, field voles often create a maze of tiny runways.

Remember that most wild mammals are much smaller than we are and so the trail they make may lead under a fence or through the bottom of a hedge. A disappearing trail will suggest to the detective that it is not a human path. Look around for confirming evidence, such as a tuft of fur caught on wire or snagged on brambles.

Fox hair

Toothmarks

Examining the vegetation for signs of grazing can tell you about the nature of the animal that has eaten it. Grass has a pointed tip, so a straight top means something has bitten it. Look around and see if you can spot the culprit. Rabbits nibble plants close with sharp teeth, producing a finely cropped finish: you can see this clearly on heather. Deer tug at vegetation, often leaving tears in the stems and leaves, easy to see on heathland bushes.

Droppings

Wherever there are animals there will be droppings. They are one of the most common countryside clues and they can tell you a great

The vigil *Go back at night to the area where you found the fox's earth, when the fox will be out on the hunt. Keep very quiet and still and try to catch a glimpse of this nocturnal hunter as it searches for its prey.*

FURTHER INVESTIGATIONS

When you have found something interesting in the countryside, try to go back again at a different time of year to discover what has happened since your last visit. Where have the fledglings gone that you heard chirruping in spring? Has the flower you saw last year succeeded in spreading to a new place this summer? Is the badger whose footprint you saw in the winter snow still in its sett the following summer – can you track down its signals? Trees are particularly rewarding to revisit, since they stay where you found them, and you can study how they change over many years.

Plot the next move Don't just keep a score of how many species you have found; start to study their behaviour too. For instance, if you discover a bat roost in a nearby house, sit and watch the bats flying against the skyline. Try to work out how many there are, where they go to forage for insects, what landscape features act as flightlines and what time they usually return to the roost.

Check it out When you discover a new and interesting plant, bird or any other creature, make a note of it on the spot, with a sketch or details of any distinguishing features. Then when you get home, check your notes with a good field guide, such as the *Reader's Digest Nature Lovers' Library* (see page 339 for details).

Collect the evidence Consider starting a small natural history 'museum' of your own. Bring back a leaf, a feather, a toadstool or a piece of seaweed that has a particular meaning for you: this book will tell you how to preserve it.

Learn from others Many organisations exist to encourage you to learn more about our wildlife, or to help you to study a favourite group, such as birds, mammals or wild flowers. For a list of addresses, see page 341.

deal about what animals are living in a neighbourhood so you can start to search for them.

Even if you cannot recognise the droppings of individual species, you can appreciate how they fall into categories.

Carnivores such as foxes, tend to produce a single, sausage-shaped dropping, often twisted and usually with bits of feather, fur or bone visible.

Herbivores like rabbits and sheep, eat large quantities of vegetation and produce a lot of droppings. These tend to be spherical or oval shaped, fall in clusters and have a fairly uniform texture.

Insectivores such as shrews, mostly leave droppings too small to find, but hedgehogs leave droppings about half the size of your little finger, grey or black and studded with beetle remains.

Fox droppings

Burrows

The easiest time to uncover a burrow is in autumn or winter when there is less vegetation to screen it. However, you are more likely to see activity at the burrow in spring when the young emerge. You can get an idea of the occupant by the burrow's size:

Ping-pong ball Burrows this size are home to mice or voles.

Tennis ball A burrow this big probably belongs to a mole, water vole or rat.

Fist Burrows that are the size of a clenched fist are usually dug by rabbits.

Football Burrows that are as big as a football include the fox's earth and a badger's sett. For holes in the riverbank, see page 142; for holes in the ground made by insects, see page 166.

Bird pellets

These are the indigestible remains of food – fur, feather, bones etc – that some birds regurgitate. They tell you which birds are in the vicinity and what local animals they are preying on. Pellets look quite similar to droppings. Study the examples in this book and learn to tell the difference.

Solitary oak

Oak puzzle

If you come across something unusual, try to work out what has occurred. For instance, if you come across an oak seedling out in the open, far from a mature oak tree, ask yourself how it could have travelled so far from its parent? The answer is that a jay is responsible: it has carried an acorn there and dropped it, or buried it for later attention, and then forgotten where it was.

Using the
Best techniques

Stalking your quarry

When you want to see the animals of the countryside, going out on your own is best, as groups can be noisy.

When you are looking for evidence, several people are often more effective than one: they can discuss, calculate and offer alternative interpretations.

Dusk and dawn are the best times to watch most mammal species and the early part of the day is best for most species of birds.

When you are moving, do so slowly and quietly. Do not make sudden movements: the snap of a twig will sound deafening to a small animal.

When you are standing still, camouflage yourself against your background: stand in the shadows or peer from behind a tree or wall.

If you sense there is something on the path ahead, take the bend on the inside and keep close to the vegetation: you may see it before it sees you.

Keep to the paths for the sake of the resident creatures – and for your own safety when you are in isolated places.

Maintain surveillance: spend time waiting and watching in likely places, such as on a riverbank, at the edge of a wood or close to a hedge. Listen for a splash in the river, the call of a hidden bird, a soft rustle in the grass.

Camouflage gear

Wear clothes that are dark or muted in colour: waterproofs are often best.

Try to be as quiet as you can: avoid wearing or carrying anything that might creak, rustle or jangle.

Most mammals have a keener sense of smell than humans, so don't wear perfume or aftershave and try to keep the wind in your face.

Handling the evidence

If you move anything to see what is beneath, put it back carefully exactly where you found it. Remember this is some animal's home.

Mind where you put your feet: plants are important too.

Only approach a bird's nest in autumn or winter, when the birds have gone.

Never take birds' eggs – it is an offence under the Wildlife and Countryside Act.

Do not pick wild flowers, though you might allow a small child to pick a few common ones to encourage their interest in nature. Digging up wild flowers is an offence under the Wildlife and Countryside Act.

Tools of the trade

This is what a countryside detective ought to carry:

Binoculars – especially for detecting birds (see box).

Compass – to detect which aspect a bank or wall faces.

Magnifying glass – to get a close-up picture of tiny plants, plant parts, bird pellets, insects and footprints.

Notebook and pencil – to record things you want to investigate further.

Torch – to look into holes, under logs and so on, with a red filter for night-time observation.

Mirror – to look under things without moving them, such as the gills on the underside of a mushroom cap.

Small plastic container – to temporarily house insects or small water animals for close examination.

CHOOSING BINOCULARS

A good pair of binoculars is an important tool for the countryside detective. Binoculars are rated by two numbers, such as 7x50 or 9x40. The first number is the magnification, the second the diameter in millimetres of the larger lenses. Choose a magnification between 7 and 10. Lower than that means you won't see distant animals clearly; higher means the binoculars will be big and heavy and really need a tripod. The best lens size for bird watching, and most other uses, is between 30 and 50mm.

Focusing To adjust the setting, focus on something detailed, such as a car number plate. Close your right eye and turn the focusing wheel in the centre until the image is sharp. Then close the left eye and turn the focusing wheel on the eyepiece (not the central wheel) until this image is also sharp. From now on you should only need to adjust the central focusing wheel.

Using Don't keep your binoculars in their case – if you have to fumble to open it when an animal appears, you may miss it. When you see a bird or other animal, keep it in view – don't look down for your binoculars – and raise the binoculars, focusing as quickly as possible. Hold them steady, near the far end. It may help to tuck your elbows into your sides, or to steady yourself against something solid, like a tree.

If you wear glasses, you may lose the edge of the view through your binoculars, because your eyes are too far from the eyepieces. It is better to remove your glasses – practice taking them off while raising your binoculars in one smooth motion. Or buy binoculars designed for spectacle wearers – look for a 'B' in the manufacturer's code.

FOLLOW THE COUNTRYSIDE CODE

Fasten gates A loose farm animal may damage itself or others. If it escapes onto a road it may cause an accident.

Keep dogs under control Dogs are permitted on public paths. But a farmer may demand that a dog be kept on a lead, and is entitled to shoot a dog caught worrying animals, and to claim for losses.

Keep to public paths It is trespass to walk across farmland. If necessary, walk in single file to avoid trampling crops and grassland.

Use gates and stiles Climbing over walls or forcing a way through hedges and fences causes damage, which may be expensive to repair, and there are strict laws of trespass.

Leave plants alone Don't pick or root up flowers or break off branches. Plants and other wildlife are interdependent and long-term abuse will upset the natural ecological balance.

Keep water clean Most of the water used in Britain comes from country streams and reservoirs. Don't pollute them with rubbish and waste food, or use them as lavatories.

Take litter home Empty cans and broken glass can injure livestock and trap small animals. Plastic wrappings, dirty paper or leftovers may cause harm if eaten, and the plastic links on cans of drink can trap birds.

Be careful of fire Fires can cause irreparable damage to wildlife and their natural habitats. Do not throw away glass objects, or drop lighted matches or cigarettes.

Take care on country roads Where there is no pavement, walk in single file on the right-hand side to face oncoming traffic. Drive slowly on country roads where livestock may stray or be moved between fields.

... AND AT THE SEASHORE

Put it back Lift rocks carefully and replace any you may have moved the same way up – there are animals underneath which need them for shelter.

Be gentle Take care when touching soft-bodied animals – they are very delicate. Leave animals where you find them.

Mind your feet Don't trample through rock pools.

Collect with care If you want to take shells home, make sure they are empty first. Leave attached seaweed in place – there is plenty lying loose on the strand line.

Don't shop Don't buy curios such as coral, starfish or sea urchins – they would almost certainly have been alive when collected.

Make safety a priority Check tide times to avoid being cut off. Keep away from soft sand and mud – it is easy to get stuck. Don't climb cliffs: it is dangerous, and may disturb the plants and animals that live on them. Tell someone where you are going and when you expect to return.

Drifts of wild flowers through fresh grass

Winter's bare grey fields vanish under a surge of growth

Spring brings great changes to the fields as the warmth and light of longer days sees winter's washed-out shades replaced by the vibrant colours of wild flowers and fresh grass. For grazing animals, this surge of growth provides the nourishing early bite they need after the rigours of the previous months and before the females give birth. Many fields are an unvarying, if lush, sea of green – the result of regular reseeding with one or two varieties of grass, but it is still possible to find areas of old pasture. In places like the Yorkshire Dales and the open expanses of the South Downs, there are meadows that have never been ploughed or artificially fertilised. Here profusions of wild flowers bloom in the grass each spring.

Pasture patchwork

Around Springfield Farm in the Yorkshire Dales National Park (above), old stone walls crisscross the land, containing the livestock in some fields and excluding it from others needed for hay. Where uncut grass is left to grow, buttercups, self-heal, knapweed and other wild flowers bloom.

Hawthorn trees grow around the edges of the fields – their creamy white blossom providing a rich source of nectar for hover flies and honeybees. In the undergrowth queen bumblebees, recently emerged from hibernation, clamber through the vegetation in search of a disused mouse hole or other place to nest.

Other insect survivors from the previous autumn which you might see include three species of butterflies that hibernate, and so are the first to appear each spring. Look out

for the false eyes on a peacock butterfly's wings as it basks on a flower – markings that deter hungry birds. The small tortoiseshell butterfly has orange-and-black wings, but it is the blue half-moon pattern on the edges that will catch your eye first. The yellow wings of the brimstone are easy to spot when it flies, but it keeps them closed when settled and blends in with the vegetation.

When swallows perch you can distinguish the sexes. The male bird (left) has longer tail feathers than the female. The longer and more even these 'streamers' are, the better his chances of winning a mate.

Rolling, open downland

The chalk uplands of southern England were home to Britain's first farms, and sheep have grazed on slopes around Hambledon Hill, Dorset (above), for some 4000 years.

On such open slopes and hilltops, the constant nibbling of sheep and rabbits has created a short springy turf threaded with ground-hugging flowers that is a delight to walk on. The warm, dry soil that overlies the chalk rock supports a host of wild herbs like thyme, marjoram and lady's bedstraw, filling the air with a Mediterranean fragrance. On warmer south-facing slopes there is a chance of spotting the clouded yellow butterfly, a migrant from across the Channel, and leaf-eating and predatory insects – grasshoppers, crickets, beetles and wasps – can also be seen. April showers bring out Roman snails, the largest type of snail to be found in Britain, and one which lives only in the comparatively warm chalk and limestone areas of southern England.

Sunny banks and ant hills are good places to watch for adders and lizards, basking in the weak spring sunshine to warm-up their cold-blooded bodies. With few trees, bird life is less varied, but skylarks and meadow pipits can often be seen and heard.

If you look at cowslips you will see that the pollen-bearing stamens are above the stigma or female part of the flower on some plants and below it on others. This ensures that insects always fertilise one plant with pollen from another.

As the days lengthen, spring sees migrant birds on the wing – inward or outward bound. The open fields are a good place to 'read' this arrival and departure board, with flocks of bramblings, fieldfares and redwings, which wintered in Britain to escape harsher weather farther north, starting the return trip to their summer territories. Replacing them, you can expect to see waves of immigrants arriving over several weeks. Warblers fly in from southern Europe, and swallows, house martins and swifts end their long haul from Southern Africa.

Songbirds in fine voice

Spring is by far the best time of year to hear birds singing. Although in many species male and female birds sound identical, you can usually be reasonably sure that it is males you are listening to, as they have to sing to advertise their territories and attract a mate. The robin, however, is one exception to this rule – the female birds often being just as vociferous as the males.

Many types of bird perch on a 'songpost', such as a bush, to sing. Once the location of one of these is known, it is usually possible to watch the spot and listen to the resident songster.

Melodies mark maturity

As your ears become more practised, listen to the songs of birds of the same species. With some – chaffinches and great tits, for example – you can sometimes pick out individuals whose songs are more elaborate and melodious. These are older male birds. Their more sophisticated repertoires are probably a signal to females that they are proven providers, having survived longer than less tuneful rivals.

Secretive songsters

Among the most evocative of spring bird calls are those of the cuckoo and turtle dove – birds more often heard than seen.

The cuckoo, which records show is most often heard for the first time on April 25, calls when on the wing. If you hear one, scan the sky for a hawk-like grey bird, possibly marked by a mob of small birds chasing it away from their nests.

Overhead wires are one place to look if you hear the purring *courr-courr* of a turtle dove. When it flies away, this smallest of pigeons – hardly bigger than a blackbird – can be identified by the chevron pattern of its white and dark tail feathers.

Hairy diet *If you spot a cuckoo on a bush, search the leaves for hairy caterpillars. Unlike most birds, cuckoos eat these, then regurgitate the hairs in pellets.*

THE OPEN SKY FOR A STAGE

Birds that breed and nest in open country where there are few trees and bushes to perch on and use as songposts often have conspicuous song flights: delivering their territorial challenges and nuptial advances from the wing. By studying these flights (how high they go, how long they last, how wide an area of sky is covered) you can tell what sort of bird you are watching – even in the case of those that look similar, such as the meadow pipit and skylark. With a bird like the lapwing, where identification is easy, you can simply enjoy watching and listening to one of the most spectacular nuptial performances in the world of birds.

FOOD CHAIN REACTION As soon as wild flowers open in the fields, insects appear to gorge on the nectar. Some, like the **orange tip butterfly** feeding on lady's smock (main picture, below) have emerged from chrysalises in which they metamorphosed from caterpillars over winter. Others, like the **tawny mining bee** on the dandelion (inset) have just come out of winter hibernation.

Mating quickly follows feeding, so soon there is a flying, crawling, living larder for birds. Find an inconspicuous spot from which to watch a patch of wild flowers in a field and you will see wagtails, tits and other birds with nestlings coming to feed, fluttering up to catch beakfuls of insects.

VANISHING SPECK If you hear a warbling song coming from the sky, but cannot see a bird, it is probably the song of an ascending **skylark** (right). This small bird's song flight takes it to a height of 100m (330ft) or more, where it is a mere speck or even invisible.

At the start **[1]** the skylark flutters steeply up into the wind, then starts to sing. Its wing beats increase to 12 a second as it ascends vertically **[2]**, hovering for periods, but singing all the time. At the zenith of its flight **[3]**, the skylark drifts in an arc. The descent **[4]** resembles the climb until the skylark is 5-10m (15-30ft) above the ground, when it falls silent and drops like a stone. A foot or so above the grass, the bird recovers itself, skims forward and lands close to where it began.

AEROBATIC VIRTUOSO The nuptial flight of the **lapwing** (below) starts with a slow, lumbering take-off, but after a few moments the bird has accelerated **[1]** into a swerving low-level display **[2]**, making sudden, tumbling swoops during which the throb of its wing beats are clearly audible at close range **[3]**. The bird also utters a hoarse ***peerr-willup-o-weep*** a whooping, undulating version of its usual '***pee-wit***' call. At the climax of the display, the bird soars up and dives down in a series of three or four twisting roller-coaster loops. These end with a final flourish when the lapwing soars upwards **[4]**, levels out **[5]**, then rolls onto its back **[6]** and dives towards the ground before levelling out at the last moment and hitting the ground at a run.

RAISING THE TEMPO Listen for the increasing frequency of its ***pheet pheet*** call as a **meadow pipit** (left and inset) climbs steeply **[1]** to a height of about 30m (100ft). This small bird then changes its tune for a slower, more melodious one before descending in a series of slow swoops **[2]** – its wings pointing upward and its tail spread out to catch the air and act as a parachute. On landing, it rounds off its short song flight with a trilling call.

Caught on the wire *If you see sheep's wool snagged on barbed wire, look out for blue tits and other birds collecting it for their nests.*

This nest is occupied

When birds have paired up, they start building nests. Pigeons and crows ferrying twigs for their simple platforms are easy to spot, and the noisy scufflings of blackbirds and thrushes as they rummage along the bottoms of hedges for dry grass are another easily detected sign of nest-building. You could also try watching likely sources of building material to see if birds are making collections – for example, muddy riverbanks are visited by swallows and house martins. If you know where there are free-range poultry, you might see long-tailed tits collecting beakfuls of small feathers with which to line their nests.

By April, many of the warblers will be starting to arrive from their wintering grounds in Africa. With the trees not yet fully in leaf, this time of year gives the birdwatcher the best chance of seeing these elusive, often sombre-plumaged birds as they sing from branches and perform short, fluttering courtship flights.

Within a few weeks dense foliage will clothe the trees and the only evidence that warblers are in the vicinity will be a tantalising glimpse as they flit behind foliage, or the sound of their fine songs coming from the leafy depths of a thicket. Willow warblers and chiffchaffs, two pale, greenish yellow birds, are the first of the warblers to arrive. Much more conspicuous is the male blackcap, whose crown of dusky feathers make him the most distinctive of this family of songsters, especially when he raises them in a crest.

Focus and identify

Because most warblers tend to look fairly similar, a pair of binoculars is useful to help you to distinguish them while listening to their songs. The garden warbler and whitethroat, for example, have similar pale underparts, but in closer focus through the field glasses, the whitethroat's brown wings, as well as the conspicuous colouring from which it gets its name, stand out more clearly.

CLOSE COUSINS Two birds to listen and look out for in the hedgerows are the **yellowhammer** (left) and its close cousin the **corn bunting** (below). They are among the first species to start staking out their territories in spring, singing from a tree, bush, fencepost or overhead wire. The yellowhammer's call is a repetitive and persistent ***chiz-iz-iz-iz-izee*** while the corn bunting's metallic ***chi-chi-chi*** sounds like a bunch of keys being shaken. With its canary-yellow head and breast, chestnut rump and white outer tail feathers, the yellowhammer is colourful and unmistakable, but the unobtrusive corn bunting's streaky brown plumage makes it difficult to spot.

Like many other birds these two switch from a winter diet of seeds to one of insects when spring arrives. If you return to the spot where you heard it singing a few weeks before, you will probably see one of them again. This time it may be pausing on a familiar perch to check for danger before flying down to the nest – built on the ground or low down in a bush. If you spot a grub or insect in its beak, it means the chicks have hatched.

Q **I saw one bird feeding another, which did not look like a fledgling. What was going on?**

A It was probably courtship feeding, which is common among many birds. The male presents his mate with food, strengthening the bond between them.

EGGSHELLS ON THE GROUND – Piecing together the evidence

Only about half the eggs laid by small birds result in fledged young, ready to leave the nest. There are numerous reasons for such high losses of eggs and chicks – a predator robs the nest, a storm washes it away, a sudden cold spell leaves the parents starving and forces them to abandon the nest.

Pieces of shell found on the ground often provide evidence of whether the chicks hatched normally or something else intervened first.

SAFELY HATCHED A neatly topped shell, such as this **rook egg**, is a sign of a normal hatching. The chick uses its egg tooth, a bony projection on the tip of its beak, to chip around one end of the shell from inside. It then lifts the loose portion, like a lid. If it has not dried or been scavenged, you will see the thin membrane lining the shell.

DISCARDED BY ADULT Once you've identified the shell as the remains from a hatching, you can confidently tell how it got there. Parent birds like this **starling** carry the empty shells away from their nests, usually dropping them some distance away. This ensures the shells don't reveal the whereabouts of the nest and chicks to a predator such as a cat.

ROBBED EGG Nest robbers such as magpies, foxes, hedgehogs and stoats smash eggs such as this **pheasant egg** from the outside. Their teeth or beaks leave jagged puncture holes, with the broken edges of the shell deflected inwards by the force of the attack. Once they have broken through the shell, predators devour the entire contents of the egg – lining membrane as well as albumen and yolk, or unhatched chick. The inside of the shell is left clean and shiny, as though it had never contained anything.

MOST AT RISK Tread carefully if you find the remains of an egg eaten by a predator, because there's a good chance it could have come from the clutch of a ground-nesting bird. These nests are the most vulnerable because foxes, stoats and other mammal predators, can get at them, as well as birds like the **magpie** pictured by this pheasant's nest.

UNBROKEN EGG If you find a whole egg, its colour will help you to work out where it has come from. This **dunnock's egg**, could be the work of a cuckoo chick. But a bright blue egg in the grass usually turns out to be a starling's. One starling will often lay in the nest of another, making room for it by removing one of the nest-owner's clutch.

CUCKOO'S WORK Take care where you step if you find a speckled reddish brown egg on the ground, it may belong to a meadow pipit – a ground-nester. The cuckoo often uses the pipit as a host. When the **cuckoo chick** hatches, it rolls the host's eggs out of the nest.

Close-up on
The rabbit

This is a good season to look for rabbits, or for signs that they are about. Brought to Britain as fur and meat animals about 800 years ago, rabbits soon escaped into the countryside and have become one of our most common wild mammals. Over the centuries their grazing habits have had an enormous effect on the landscape – the short springy turf of the South Downs, for example, is the result of sustained nibbling by rabbits and sheep.

If you see a rabbit, the warren will be nearby, probably within about 50m (55yd) or so. Frequent ploughing restricts warrens to strips of ground around the edges of fields, but on swathes of open grassland, such as parts of the chalk downs and some clifftop areas, where the land has not been cultivated for years, long-established warrens with many burrows occupy wide patches of ground.

Rabbits are choosy feeders, so prominent patches of plants they avoid, such as gorse, ragwort, thistle, mouse-ear chickweed, forget-me-not and bracken, are good indications that they are around. Look out too for beds of nettles and elderberry bushes – plants that thrive on the nitrogen-rich soil created by rabbit droppings and urine.

WHO'S AT HOME? If you disturb a hare, look for its **form** (inset) – a shallow, grass-lined depression in which the animal lies up for much of the day. One that has been recently vacated will be imprinted with the animal's shape and may still be warm. A form can also contain a young hare – a female keeps each of her litter of two or three leverets in a separate one. The entrance to a rabbit's **burrow** (arrowed) will be worn smooth if it is in use; once abandoned, vegetation soon grows up and obscures a burrow from view. You might also come across a blocked burrow. This is likely to be a stop – a blind burrow containing young, which the doe earths up for their protection. Don't disturb it.

SMELLY MARKERS Often, the first sign of rabbits is piles of **droppings** (inset right). They use **communal latrines** (right) around the edge of the warren as territorial markers and often select a prominent place such as an ant hill or tree stump.

Demanding diet If you've ever had a pet rabbit, you will know that they eat their own droppings. It may seem like an unsavoury habit, but refection, to give it the scientific name, is essential to rabbits, ensuring that they break down the cellulose in grass and other vegetation and extract the maximum nutrition from their diet.

The first droppings, which are fairly soft and still have a high nutritional value, are usually passed inside the burrows and then eaten again. The hard, dry-looking pellets you see on the ground outside are the second, more concentrated waste product. Hares and some other herbivorous rodents also tackle their food in this way, but cattle, deer and other ruminants regurgitate semi-digested food, or cud, for a second chewing.

DIPS IN THE GROUND Shallow holes, known as **scrapes** (left), are also territorial markers. They are especially common where there are warrens about, so that the ground along the boundary may be pockmarked with small excavations. Rabbits make similar holes in winter and spring, when their usual sources of food are in short supply and they need to dig for roots to eat.

FURRY FINDS Rabbits often leave bits of fur along their runs – snagged on bramble and gorse bushes, or caught on the bottom strands of fences that they squeeze under. Birds are quick to seize on them as nesting material. In spring, if you find bigger tufts of fur on the ground, they show where two buck rabbits have been fighting, or perhaps where a cat, fox or other predator has made a kill.

REGULAR ROUTES
Conspicuous narrow paths across the short turf around a warren, or lines of flattened vegetation in longer grass, reveal the **runs**, worn by rabbits as they move between their burrows and feeding grounds. They're worth following for the things you sometimes find on them: clumps of fur, where a fox has lain beside the run and killed a passing rabbit; perhaps even the prey's hind feet – discarded because they are tough to eat.

SPOT THE DIFFERENCE

RABBIT OR HARE? Distinguishing a **rabbit** (left) from a **hare** (right) can be difficult, especially at a distance, but if the animal is running away and you can see a white 'scut' of fur on the underside of its tail, it is a rabbit, flashing this warning sign to others in the colony. Hares are normally solitary and have no need to signal danger, so they keep their tails down as they run, and flatten their long ears too.

If the animal stays in view long enough, watch how it runs. Rabbits move in jerky, bouncing hops. Hares have longer, more powerful hind legs, which they extend far forwards to launch themselves into a fast, bounding run.

In spring, both animals can be so distracted by rivalry and courtship that they will ignore a quiet observer. Then you may get close enough to notice that rabbits are grey-brown, with short, rounded, untipped ears, while hares have distinctively ginger fur and long, black-tipped ears. Rabbits also have dark brown eyes, while the hare's are a lighter, golden brown.

Verges burst into bloom

The verges lining thousands of miles of roadside are one of the great joys of the British countryside. For many people – country-dwellers as well as those who live in towns – it is the blossoming of the verges more than any other event that signals the arrival of spring. Where roadside vegetation is regularly cut short, or a harsh local climate keeps a cap on exuberant growth, delicate wild flowers like fumitory and harebells put on discreet shows. But in many places wild parsley and hawthorn blossom crowd along the edges of lanes and roads in a heady spring show of creamy white flowers and fresh foliage.

Wait for the may *The saying 'ne'er cast a clout 'til may is out' refers to the hawthorn blossom, the traditional name of which is may. Don't take off your winter woollies until the blossom opens, the proverb advises.*

There seems to be a warm day every spring when a wave of cow parsley, also called Queen Anne's lace, suddenly foams along the verges, attracting millions of insects to its blooms.

To the casual observer, cow parsley seems to flower from May to September, but a closer look reveals that it is just the first of many umbellifers – plants with flat, umbrella-like heads of flowers – that bloom through the summer and attract a wide range of insects. They include the giant hogweed, which grows up to 4m (13ft) tall with a thick, blotchy stem. Although fairly rare on verges, it's worth being able to recognise this plant because it can cause a nasty skin rash if you touch it, especially during hot weather.

THORNY ISSUE SOLVED

Although hawthorn is the better known old hedgerow tree, the blackthorn or sloe is also often seen. Both bear white spring blossom but they can be told apart by their different flowering times and whether or not there are leaves with the blossom.

Blackthorn flowers on bare branches in March, providing, along with pussy willow, an important early source of nectar for insects. The hawthorn does not blossom until May, after the tree has come into leaf.

Profusion of parsleys *Cow parsley* **[1]** *is the most common of the white hedgerow parsleys, as well as the earliest to flower. Sweet cicely* **[2]**, *whose leaves smell strongly of aniseed when crushed, is more widespread in the north than the south. Angelica* **[3]**, *with its pink-tinged flowers, and hemlock* **[4]**, *a poisonous plant with blotchy stalks, often grows in roadside ditches. Alexanders* **[5]** *are more usually found on verges near the coast.*

FUNGI THAT FRUIT IN THE SPRING

Autumn is the traditional season for mushroom hunting, but the two varieties pictured can be found in the spring, especially on old grassland overlying chalk and limestone. Like most fungi, both disappear from fields treated with chemical fertilisers.

Triggering an explosion The most impressive spring fungus is the **morel** (right). It is easily recognised by the sponge-like yellow-brown cap and its thick, pale stalk. Morels eject their spores upwards in a small explosion, rather than dropping them from hanging gills like the field mushroom does. If you find a morel, try fanning the air above it with your hand: this will sometimes encourage the fungus to fire off its spores with an audible 'pop'. A moment later you will see the smoky wisp of the thousands of microscopic spores as they drift away on the air. Make sure you don't strike the stalk when you try this experiment: it is very brittle and snaps easily.

Smell of oatmeal The stocky **St George's mushrooms** (left) first appear around the saint's day on April 23, but it is more usual to come across this – the most common of the spring fungi – in May. The mushrooms, which are edible, smell distinctly like fresh oatmeal and commonly grow in rings. The larger the ring, the longer the hair-like underground mycelium, from which the mushrooms grow, has been in the soil.

RICH SITES FOR STUDY

Places where nettles grow are always worth investigating. These plants like ground which has been enriched by animal droppings or human activities. High clumps of nettles often obscure a badger set, signpost a rabbit warren or mark a tumbledown building.

Most of the nettles you see will be the common perennial type, which grows to about 1.5m (5ft), but look out for the small annual nettle, which reaches only 30cm (1ft).

Patches of nettles are feeding and breeding grounds for several species of butterflies, including the red admiral, peacock and comma. Examine the crowns of nettles for any leaves with edges drawn and held together by silken threads. These little 'tents' are the distinctive shelters of red admiral caterpillars, while what look like shrivelled leaves dangling from the stems could be the chrysalises of comma or peacock caterpillars. Don't attempt to unravel any of these structures as the larvae inside are easily damaged. Instead, make a note of the spot and return there periodically until you're rewarded with the sight of the adult butterflies.

Grasping the nettle

It's true that a nettle won't sting if you grasp it firmly: the brittle poison-filled hairs, which snap and act like small hypodermic needles when just brushed against, bend back harmlessly under firm pressure.

When you are stung, try the traditional remedy of rubbing the skin with a dock leaf. The dock leaf contains an antidote to the inflammation and this is released as you crush the leaf by rubbing. Usefully, docks often grow beside nettles.

SPOT THE DIFFERENCE

STINGING NETTLE OR DEAD NETTLE? The leaves of stinging nettles and dead nettles are a similar shape making them hard to tell apart at a glance, but **stinging nettles** (above left) have round stems whereas the stems of **dead nettles** (above right) are square. Dead nettles, which do not sting, also bear colourful flowers in place of the greenish catkins of stinging nettles.

Silk shelter *These small tortoiseshell caterpillars look as if they are caught in a spider's web. In fact, it is a protective canopy of their own making, a distasteful wrapper between themselves and predatory birds. The caterpillars of peacock butterflies spin a similar covering.*

Banks full of beetles

Hedge banks have long provided homes for ground-nesting birds like partridges and whitethroats, and small mammals such as mice, voles and shrews. They also support many insects – some beneficial, others damaging to crops. Where hedges have been grubbed out, however, predatory beetles that help to control pest numbers no longer have the ability to range across the huge new fields created, and farmers have had to find ways of replacing their lost bases.

If you notice a series of ridges about 40cm (16in) high and 2m (6ft 6in) wide running at intervals across a very large arable field, you're probably looking at beetle banks. These have been created by farmers to provide the ideal over-wintering habitat for insects that prey on aphids and other crop pests.

The banks are planted with cocksfoot and timothy, tussocky grasses that shelter insects, small mammals, and invertebrates, including ladybirds, wasps and harvestmen. But the metallic-sheened ground beetles, devil's coach horse and other rove beetles do most to keep down pests. In this way they reduce the amount of insecticide that needs to be sprayed on crops – benefiting the farmer and consumer – and it is for them that banks are being created by selective ploughing.

Beetle banks are also providing a home for other animals that used to inhabit the field margins. Harvest mice, for instance, are finding the strong upright flowering stems of the tussock grass the ideal support for their nests in late summer.

Chemical victim Field edges are good places to search for four-leaved clovers, traditionally thought to bring good luck. But if you find a large number, they may have been affected by herbicides (weed-killing chemicals) blown on the breeze. Look out, too, for other oddities, such as square-centred daisies and strangely twisted thistles.

IDENTITY PARADE – Beetles on the bank

Beetle banks such as this, on a farm in Loddington, Leicestershire, offer quarters to beneficial beetles that will prey on any invertebrates eating the nearby crop. To see this nocturnal army, lift a stone or loose clod, trying not to let light flood underneath, and take a peep. Some beetles will scurry down small holes, but others will freeze on the spot.

Cereal killer Violet ground beetles are common among cereal crops, where they prey on many of the insects – adults and larvae – that attack grain.

Night hunter The glossy black ground beetle's long legs enable it to dart across the soil and between stems to catch other insects in the dark.

Chemical defence The devil's coach horse eats caterpillars and earwigs. When it is threatened, the beetle raises its tail and squirts a nauseous fluid.

MASTER MIMICS

If a flying insect appears at face-level, as though inspecting you, then silently darts away faster than the eye can follow, it is probably a hover fly. The males, like those of many species of insects, including gnats and mayflies, take up station in the air and wait for a passing female to mate with. They regard you as a large intruder in their territory.

Look at hover flies on flowers and you will see that while they have the characteristically large eyes of flies, they mimic bees and wasps by possessing similar colour bandings – a warning signal that discourages birds from eating them.

Hover flies further confuse potential predators by settling on cow parsley and other flowers alongside the insects they mimic, making it difficult for birds to tell them apart.

Twice as nice *Hover flies feed on the honeydew secreted by clusters of aphids. As larvae they prey on the aphids themselves.*

Mate or intruder? *A fox will see off an interloper, but if you see one fox chasing another in the spring, it's more likely to be a dog and vixen pairing up. The dog fox holds his tail out stiff and straight, while the vixen arches her back, tucks her tail between her legs and scurries in front of him.*

FOXES STALKING IN FIELDS

Spring is the best time of year to see foxes in the open during daylight as this is the season when they stalk the field boundaries for mice, voles and rabbits to feed their young. If you see or smell a fox – you don't need a keen sense of smell to recognise its strong, 'doggy' scent – stand absolutely still. The animal may be so intent on listening for rustlings in the grass or looking for movements that give away the presence of prey that it won't sense you.

Characteristic pounce

When a fox 'fixes' small prey, it pounces with a characteristic 'mouse-jump' – leaping into the air and coming down with its forepaws on the victim, then seizing it with its teeth.

You may also be surprised to see a fox walking past a rabbit or pheasant without taking any notice of what seems to be an easy meal. This is probably because the vulnerable animal has shown that it is aware of the fox's presence. Both animals know the element of surprise has been lost and a chase will be a waste of energy.

Q **I found a dead shrew lying on the path. It appeared to be uninjured. How did it die?**

A According to folklore, the bodies of shrews turn up on paths because the noise and vibration of passing feet give the tiny animals a mortal shock. In fact, they are dropped by cats and foxes – animals which often use pavements and paths, and catch prey in adjoining verges. The shrews are dropped because they secrete an evil-tasting substance from glands in the skin. This works as a defence against small predators, but when a cat or fox pounces the shrew is often killed or fatally injured before its repellent taste can save it. As long as the shrew does not look fly-blown, examine the corpse without picking it up. The chances are you will find the needle-like puncture marks inflicted by the teeth of a predator, perhaps marked by a small bloodstain. Now search through the adjoining undergrowth – you may find more dead shrews.

Close-up on
Grass

Chewing the cud *Grass contains a combination of cellulose and the abrasive mineral silica, making it one of the toughest diets to digest. That's why cattle, like many other hoofed mammals, including sheep and deer, are ruminants: after the first chewing, they regurgitate the semi-digested grass or cud and give it a second grinding before swallowing it again. They usually lie down to do this, their jaws working methodically.*

The last thing you may notice while walking over the fields is the grass beneath your feet and beside the path, yet it would be difficult to exaggerate its importance. The new leaves of most plants grow from the tips, but with grass they grow from the base. This means that the tops can be removed by grazing (or mowing) and the grass keeps growing.

You can see this if you pull up a few stems of grass and examine them. You will notice small shoots, or tillers, growing from the main stems, and swollen joints called nodes (see below right) from which the grass leaves sprout, all along the stems. At first, the leaves wrap tightly around the stalks, but then they open into the long, flat blades we usually think of as 'grass'. Grass has another useful attribute: if the stem is flattened, the nodes on the underside grow more quickly, so it springs upright again.

stem node and leaf

Clue to the habitat

You can tell one type of grass from another if it has been left to flower; look for ungrazed patches around the edges if the field has been grazed. Grass flowers are very small and inconspicuous, so carry a magnifying glass as well as a field guide. Recognising what sort of grass is growing in the fields tells you a great deal about the richness of a habitat.

GRAZERS' NEEDS

Cattle need long grass because they wrap their long, raspy tongues around it and pull it into their mouths. Among the grasses you can expect to find on cattle pastures are small meadow grass **[1]**, which grows in a wide range of soils and meadow fescue – at its best in damp meadows, where it will grow up to 1.2m (4ft) tall if left to flower.

Sheep and rabbits nibble the grass much closer to the ground to produce a short turf. Sheep's fescue is the traditional grass found in sheep pasture, especially in the chalk and limestone downlands and dales where England's medieval wool industry has its roots. It grows in dense tufts with fine, stiff, almost bristle-like leaves, and the delicate flowering heads are violet-tinged.

Egg-shaped

You are also likely to find stands of quaking grass **[2]** where animals are grazing. This species of grass has clusters of egg-shaped, purplish brown flowers which vibrate in a breeze – giving the plant its common name. Quaking grass survives because livestock finds it too bitter to eat. Where grass is left to grow for hay on chalk downland, look for upright brome **[3]**, whose purplish flowers have orange-red anthers.

1

2

3

tiny florets on stem

Poised for release *Many grasses have minute flowers, so it's worth while carrying a magnifying glass to appreciate them to the full. By using one, you will be able to see the anthers of sheep's fescue (right), which are poised on such delicate filaments that pollen is released by the slightest draught.*

Q **What is in the large, round, black plastic bags that can be seen lying on newly cut fields in spring?**

A They contain cut grass which will rapidly ferment into silage and be used as winter fodder, or fed to animals kept permanently in sheds. On many farms the grass is not bagged, but unloaded into a pit or clamp, then covered in plastic sheeting and weighed down with old tyres. For the farmer, a major advantage of cutting silage over haymaking is that it does not rely on dry weather.

Pincer movement *Like many other hoofed mammals, sheep have incisor teeth on the lower jaw and a bony pad on the upper one. Both teeth and pad are steeply angled forward, so sheep can use them like pincers, gripping and nipping off grass far closer to the ground than most grazers. Because the bony pad is especially hard, sheep can also browse on tough plants such as heather and gorse.*

FIELDS OF CHANGE

The wide variety of grasses and other plants found in old meadows that have never been ploughed provides the richest sort of grassland environment. Livestock, however, grazes such pasture very selectively, so permanent meadows have to a large extent been replaced by leys – fields that are regularly ploughed and reseeded with a very limited range of grasses.

Inaccessible ground

Nowadays, old, plant-rich meadows are increasingly restricted to nature reserves and waterlogged or steep ground where farm machinery cannot be used.

Sometimes improved versions of rye grass, a tough-stalked species with flat, dark green flowers, will be the only species you find in a field. But it is often mixed with timothy grass **[1]**, also called cat's-tail because of its long, cylindrical head of tightly packed florets. These are tinged pink or white.

Feathery heads

Two grasses that indicate the field is an old, permanent meadow are cocksfoot **[2]** and Yorkshire fog **[3]**. Cocksfoot has dark grey-green leaves and lilac-tinted flowers. Yorkshire fog has feathery pink flower heads, whitening as they grow older to make fields appear clothed with fog.

Flowers seize their chance in the woods

Colour covers the woodland floor as the sun breaks through

Woodland in springtime is a pageant of renewal. The sap is rising from the roots, surging through the microscopic plumbing beneath the bark to burst into the unfurling buds. Flowers open on the woodland floor and for the first time in months you can see queen bumblebees and butterflies, just emerged from hibernation, at the blossom of sallows and blackthorn, and hear the full song of early birds like the blackbird, wren and great tit. The very word spring comes from woodland. It originally meant the sprays of fresh green shoots that appear as days lengthen. To a woodsman, it referred specifically to the new shoots sprouting from the hazel stump he had cut the previous autumn.

An individual carpet

Different woodlands have different springs. The most colourful are the old parish woods of oak, ash and hazel on the stiff clay soils of middle England. These are woods of primroses (the prima rosa or first flower), violets and celandines, perhaps the closest to the springtime of our mind's eye. Better-drained woods on the steep upper slopes of the chalk downs, and on sandy soils, are often awash with bluebells, perfuming the air with that faint ethereal honey-scent.

In the shady wet woods of Wales and western Scotland, mosses cover earth, stone, stump and the trees themselves in a thick green carpet. The ash woods of the limestone dales enjoy a late spring, since ash is usually the last tree to spring into leaf, and dog's mercury, archangel and wood forget-me-not grow knee high under its open

fretwork. Farther north still, it is the turpentine scent of resin that announces spring's arrival in the high pine and birch forests of Scotland, where spring bursts almost overnight as the sap runs and the buds crack.

For woodland flowers, like the lesser celandines in this Hertfordshire wood (above left), survival means winning the race to bloom and set seed before the trees come into leaf and block out the light. If you walked blindfold through the wood at Cressbrookdale in Derbyshire (above centre), the smell given off by crushed leaves would instantly betray the ramsons, or wild garlic, underfoot. Bluebells flourish in the conditions offered by a coppiced wood in Aversley, Cambridgeshire (above right). They are not flowers of deep shade but thrive in dappled sunlight.

Twenty picturesque bluebell woods

1. **Queen Elizabeth Forest Park** Stirling
2. **The Falls of Clyde** nr New Lanark, South Lanarkshire
3. **Cree and Castramon** Dumfries and Galloway
4. **Portglenone Forest** Portglenone, Co. Antrim
5. **Castle Eden Dene** nr Hartlepool, Northumbria
6. **Forge Valley Woods** nr Scarborough, North Yorkshire
7. **Treswell Wood** nr Retford, Nottinghamshire
8. **Rigsby Wood** nr Alford, Lincolnshire
9. **Coed Aberartro** nr Harlech, Gwynedd
10. **Saltwells Wood** nr Dudley, West Midlands
11. **Martinshaw Wood** Leicestershire
12. **Foxley Wood** nr Reepham, Norfolk
13. **Bradfield Woods** nr Bury St Edmunds, Suffolk
14. **Castle Woods** Carmarthenshire
15. **Ebbor Gorge** nr Wells, Somerset
16. **Warburg Reserve** nr Henley-on-Thames, Oxfordshire
17. **Wormley Wood** nr Cuffley, Hertfordshire
18. **Kew Gardens** London
19. **The Mens** nr Petworth, Sussex
20. **Denge Wood** nr Canterbury, Kent

Almost every parish has its own much-loved bluebell wood. Here are some of the most exceptional woodlands open to view, packed with bluebells and other spring wild flowers.

Floral signposts to the past

Did you find your local wood carpeted with wild flowers in spring? The answer will tell you something of its history because it has been found that certain wild flowers are almost always associated with old woods and are called indicators (see list below). Although there are other reasons why one indicator species might be present, the more you find, the more likely it is that your wood is several hundred years old.

Why is it that certain flowers are found mainly in older woods? One clue is the way they grow. Flowers like bluebells, wood anemone and sweet woodruff usually occur not singly but in masses. This is a sign that they grow and reproduce from bulbs or creeping stems, rather than from germinating seeds.

Flowers that hang on

Next, look at the leaves of some woodland flowers, or the fronds of woodland ferns. You will realise they are often broad and spreading, forming a dense mass of greenery that enables them to catch as much sunlight as possible when the canopy starts to cast dense shade over them. This dense growth means there is little room for young seedlings to germinate.

Flowers that live and spread in this way tend to be good at hanging on, but bad at moving to other places. Hence they persist in old woods, maybe for hundreds of years, but do not readily colonise newly planted ones unless they are situated right next door and don't have to cross any intervening fields or roads in order to spread.

Newly planted woods, on the other hand, are colonised by plants such as cleavers and willowherbs, which produce masses of seed and spread quickly through the habitat. But dense conifer woods usually have no carpets of flowers, because the evergreen trees cast a permanent shade and also shed needles all the time into a thick layer where few plants can grow.

FLOWER STRATEGIES

In some ways, woodlands can be a fertile habitat for plants. Their soils are rich in humus and rarely dry out, while competition from grasses and other aggressive plants, such as buttercups, is restricted. On the other hand, woodland plants have to cope with deep shade in summer and difficult conditions for seed dispersal. Looking carefully at the characters of plants provides clues as to how they are able to survive.

Making an early start

Many woodland plants flower early, before the trees are in leaf. For most, this flying start involves drawing on food stored underground from the previous year. Search the patch of wood anemone for its thick, pale brown rhizomes (creeping stems) packed with nutrients just beneath the surface. Bluebells and wild daffodils use food from bulbs; the lesser celandine and the early purple orchid have root tubers to sustain them and primrose and oxlip, long-lived plants, develop root systems that store food.

Attracting visitors

Wood anemones may look pretty, but smell them and you will find they are almost scentless. Neither do they have any nectar. Despite this, they are visited by flies, bees and beetles. Why? Because their pollen is edible, and while feasting on it, some pollen will brush off onto their backs and be transferred to the next plant they visit.

Notice that most of the flowers in a patch face towards the sun. This enables each one to receive the maximum amount of sunlight, thus warming the flower, which is helpful in supplying energy to its cold-blooded insect pollinators. Violets, on the

WILD FLOWERS that indicate ancient woods

Barren strawberry	Pendulous sedge	Wood anemone
Bluebell	Pignut	Wood goldilocks
Butcher's broom	Primrose	Wood horsetail
Cow-wheat	Ramsons or wild garlic	Wood melick
Dog's mercury	Sanicle	Wood sorrel
Early dog violet	Solomon's seal	Wood speedwell
Great woodrush	Stinking iris	Wood spurge
Herb Paris	Sweet woodruff	Wood vetch
Lily of the valley	Three-veined sandwort	Yellow archangel
Moschatel	Toothwort	Yellow pimpernel
Nettle-leaved bellflower	Violet helleborine	Yellow star-of-Bethlehem
Oxlip	Wild daffodil	

Hot and smelly The wild arum, or cuckoopint, turns kidnapper to achieve pollination. The flowers lie around the base of a poker-shaped structure called the spadix. This becomes hot: try touching it – you will feel something akin to a mild electric shock! The heat vapourises compounds which smell like rotting flesh and this attracts flies. They crawl down the spadix in search of carrion and are trapped among the flowers by a ring of hairs.

The flies then become dusted with pollen from the flowers, which they carry to other cuckoopints when the spadix withers.

Hard at work *A bee fly sups from a primrose (above) and a hover fly enjoys wild garlic (left). Insects visiting flowers in spring pay for their meals by carrying pollen from flower to flower.*

other hand, secrete their nectar in a small spur at the back of the flower. Only long-tongued insects like bees, which happen to be the best pollinators, can reach into the spur and get at its contents.

Look at orchids and you will see that they, too, have spurs. In some cases, these are so deep that only butterflies and moths can reach into them and obtain the elusive nectar.

Double protection

The primrose ensures cross-pollination by having two kinds of flowers. Peer closely into a few primroses and see if you can find some with a dot in the middle like the head of a pin. This pin is the female part, the stigma, and these are known as pin-eyed primroses. Others have a cluster of pointed structures, composed of the male parts, or stamens, and these are called thrum-eyed (thrum is an old name for a frayed thread).

This arrangement means that a bee, poking its long tongue down the flower tube to reach the nectar, will brush pollen on to itself from the thrum-eyed flowers and then, when it visits a pin-eyed one, transfer the pollen to the stigma. This preserves the genetic diversity in the primrose and prevents harmful inbreeding – at least in theory. In practice, tiny beetles eat a lot of the pollen. You will probably catch them in the act if you cut a flower in half.

ENLISTING HELP

Although woodland flowers produce plenty of seed, if you look at the dense mass of flowers it is hard to imagine how their seedlings could establish themselves – there isn't room. But some species have evolved ingenious ways of distributing their seeds to more favourable sites.

When they have finished flowering, search among violet leaves for their seed capsules. If the capsules are ripe, they will explode, scattering the tiny seeds into the air. Examine a seed through a magnifying glass and you may detect an oil body, a translucent bump, at one end. This attracts ants, which carry the seeds off to their nest as food, frequently dropping some on the way. Try following an ants' trail and noting whether violets flower more prolifically along it than elsewhere.

Dog's mercury also has seed that seems attractive to ants. If you find their relatively heavy seeds on the ground around the parent plant, they will have little chance of germinating since dog's mercury grows in a dense mass. Instead, it seems to rely on ants to transport the seeds to a better site. The insect's reward is the nutritious oil that exudes from the seeds.

Indebted to ants *Dog's mercury (right) and the common dog violet (below) both draw on the services of ants to help spread their seeds to a patch of bare ground where there is space for them to germinate. These spring flowers need special help with seed dispersal because they grow in such dense mats across the woodland floor, their seeds cannot find a foothold nearby and need to be transported to a more favourable site.*

Trees burst into flower

You can walk through a wood in early spring and hardly notice that the trees are in flower as native species often have insignificant, greenish blossoms. Trees must flower, be pollinated and set seed to produce a new generation, but most woodland trees are wind-pollinated so they don't need to waste energy producing showy flowers and nectar to attract insects. As a rule, if a flower is standing up from the branch, it relies on insects for pollination; if it dangles down, it scatters its pollen to the wind.

Wind-pollinated flowers have an advantage over those pollinated by insects: they can flower early in the year when few insects are about but when winds are often strong and the release of their pollen is not impeded by leafy growth. One type of flower to look out for on many trees is the catkin, which consists of a large number of flowers massed together on a flexible stalk.

The first trees you are likely to see in flower are hazel and alder, which flower in February and March. Their tight, bud-like male catkins are produced by the trees the previous year and triggered to mature by lengthening daylight hours. Hazel catkins look like lamb's tails, twisting and turning in the slightest breeze and spilling clouds of golden-yellow pollen. Reddish purple alder catkins are less familiar, as they normally grow high up out of sight.

Later on, in April and May, many of the tall forest trees come into flower. Ash, beech, birch, elm and oak are all wind-pollinated. The height of these trees assures that their pollen will travel a long distance. But where does this pollen land, and how is fertilisation achieved? All these trees share a similar trick: they have both male and female flowers. While the male ones are large and dangling, the females are tiny, looking like sticky buds or tufts of hair. They trap pollen floating in the wind, which then fertilises the ovules inside the female flower.

The chances of the pollen landing in the right place are very small, but trees can reduce the odds by self-pollination, where pollen from male catkins can fertilise female flowers on the same tree. One reason why some female flowers are so small is that the trees produce only a few large seeds per flower, so the females contain only a few ovules for the pollen to fertilise.

One tree, two flowers *Some trees, such as the oak, carry different flowers on the same branch. The long dangling male flowers produce pollen; the tiny bud-like flowers (inset) are female and after being pollinated, will ripen into acorns. Feel them and you will find they are sticky, so that pollen blown on to them stays put.*

Q How do trees cause hay fever?

A Wind-pollinated trees must release great quantities of pollen (like this alder, right) as much of it is wasted by landing in unsuitable places. It is this mass of drifting pollen that can trigger hay fever in spring.
The most potent pollen in early spring comes from alder, elm, hazel and poplar. In late spring and early summer, pollen from birch, oak, plane and poplar causes problems.

Blossom year *Beech trees bear tuft-like male and female catkins which look rather alike, but don't be surprised if you can't find any. Beech blossoms only once every two or three years, and even less often in the north.*

BRIGHT CATKINS FOR HUNGRY INSECTS

The willow family, which includes sallows (which are broad-leaved willows) and poplars, are pollinated by both wind and insects. Their catkins contain nectar, which attracts insects such as the **brimstone butterfly** (right) at a time of year when food is scarce. And because they need to attract insects, they produce showy catkins.

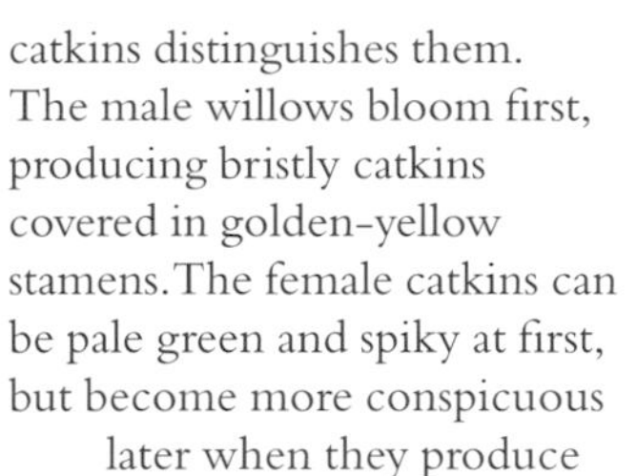

Eye-catching males

Most willows have male and female catkins on separate trees and it is easy to tell them apart in spring when the look of the catkins distinguishes them. The male willows bloom first, producing bristly catkins covered in golden-yellow stamens. The female catkins can be pale green and spiky at first, but become more conspicuous later when they produce white down.

Poplars have a similar pollination mechanism: female trees produce green catkins and male trees catkins whose mass of red anthers make them look rather like fat red caterpillars. In aspens, the poplar most often found in mature woods, the fluffy male catkins are flecked with yellow pollen when ripe while the female catkin is green.

Which sex? *Study the catkin and you can tell whether a pussy willow is male or female. Female catkins (left) have downy hairs that give the tree its name. The male tree (below) has gold-tipped catkins: the colour attracts insects.*

PRETTY FOR A PURPOSE

Trees that produce more conventional nectar-bearing flowers, such as field maple, lime and sycamore, tend to flower later than those that produce catkins. This enables them to take advantage of the increasing numbers of insects flying about in May and June. These flowers are scented to attract their insect pollinators and they are not distinguished by sex.

First flowers The blackthorn (left) is unusual because it flowers so early. If you spot a mass of white flowers in March, on bare twigs that appear almost black by contrast, this is the blackthorn. It sometimes flowers prolifically in a cold spell, known as a blackthorn winter. The blackthorn belongs to the rose family, which includes crab apple, hawthorn, rowan, whitebeam and wild cherry; they all have prominent scented white or pinkish blossom to attract insects.

Broad appeal Wild cherry (right) has open, rather flat single flowers that seem to be designed for insects, like this hover fly, whose short tongues cannot reach very far inside the flower.

Fly table Many of the later-flowering trees, such as rowan (left), have wide massed flowers. These act as platforms where slow-moving pollinators like beetles and some flies can crawl about in comfort, feasting on nectar and being dusted with pollen.

Watching as buds open

Hidden inside a tree's buds are the leaves, flowers and stalks for next year's growth. The buds are formed in autumn and are protected from winter frost and drought with a seal of hard bud scales. If you collect a twig with buds just before bud-burst in spring, and put it into water in a warm place, you can watch these hard scales separate as the bud swells and the tender leaves unfurl and grow. Horse chestnut performs particularly well in a milk bottle on a windowsill.

Trees do not come into leaf all at the same time. Generally the first hint of green you will see in early spring is in the hedgerow, when hawthorn is bursting bud, and in thickets of willow and poplar when the twigs turn a startling red or yellow.

The principal forest trees come into leaf in April. Birch and elm are early, followed by oak, beech and finally ash – on which the buds rarely open before the beginning of May.

Much depends on the location, however. You will find trees in warm, well-lit places coming into leaf earlier than the same trees on north-facing slopes, in frost pockets or in dense woodland. The timing of the opening of the buds also depends on the height of a tree. Bushes and saplings come into leaf earlier than older trees, and very tall trees come into leaf in stages, the lower branches first, the topmost ones last. This means that a wood with different layers of vegetation will turn green in instalments.

The opening of the buds will also vary from year to year, and in different parts of the country. In the mild sea air around Bristol, for example, the leaves start to open about nine days earlier than on the windy downs at Marlborough, though they are on roughly the same latitude.

To discover when each tree comes into leaf in your area, keep a nature diary, recording the times when most buds are breaking. Do trees on opposite sides of a valley leaf at the same time? Does the side of a tree which gets most sunshine come into leaf before the other side? A nature diary will reveal all.

Shaped by circumstance *Trees that grow in well-lit but often windy situations have small leaf blades on flexible stalks that are more or less wind-proof, like the opening* ***rowan leaves*** *(below). Woodland trees must modify their shape to fit the available space, which is why trees growing in the open, like the* ***beech tree*** *coming into leaf (bottom), are relatively broad while most woodland trees are taller, narrower and more irregular. If you find a spreading tree in woodland, it is a clue that the tree was there first and the wood has grown up around it.*

The ground Many plants on the woodland floor flower early in spring, attracting pollinating insects to their bright blooms before the trees come into leaf and cast them into dense shade.

The canopy Broadly speaking, the taller the tree, the later it comes into leaf. This helps an understorey to co-exist with a taller canopy layer and early flowers to flourish. Oak and beech are fairly late coming into leaf, and ash is usually the last of all.

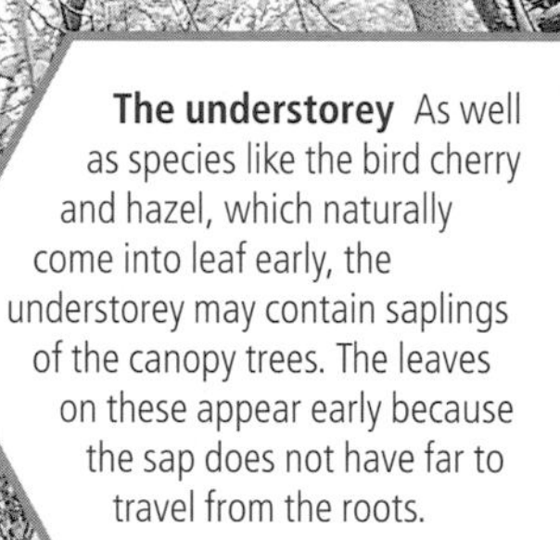

The understorey As well as species like the bird cherry and hazel, which naturally come into leaf early, the understorey may contain saplings of the canopy trees. The leaves on these appear early because the sap does not have far to travel from the roots.

PALE AND INTERESTING The remarkable-looking **toothwort** (above) flourishes without the aid of leaves or sunlight. This woodland flower has found an unorthodox way of surviving once the canopy starts to cast its shade, by becoming a parasite. The toothwort manages without chlorophyll by tapping into the roots of trees such as elm or hazel for food.

LEAF SHAPE

Why should the leaves of trees come in so many shapes and sizes, and why do shape and size matter? Forest trees, in competition for growing space, need big broad leaves to capture as much sunlight as possible. This is why you'll see that beech, lime, hazel and, to a lesser extent, oak have a dense mass of leaves, which filters out most of the sunlight and casts a dense shade.

Study the leaves of woodland trees and you will notice that many, such as those of the lime, wych elm and hazel have a pointed end. This helps to disperse raindrops and prevent water remaining on foliage, which can encourage fungal and bacterial plant diseases.

Trees adapted to dry places like the chalk downs often have hairy leaves, which create a thin protective envelope of cool moist air to minimise water loss. The wayfaring tree, for instance, not only has hairy leaves, but also hairy twigs. Its old country name, hoarwithy, comes from 'hoar' meaning white and refers to the frosted look given to it by its silky hairs. Toothed leaves or leaf hairs may also give the leaves some defence against being eaten by caterpillars and other insects.

Conifers avoid many of the problems of broad-leaved trees by having narrow needles, which in most species are evergreen (though larch sheds its leaves in autumn). Although needles are less efficient at manufacturing food than wide flat leaves, they are resistant to drought, relatively snow-proof, and do not need replacing every year. This means the tree can put more of its energy into growth.

Tipped to drip *The leaves of the hazel (left) are shaped so that rain is rapidly channelled along the midrib and off the tip. This keeps the foliage dry, so helping to prevent fungi from developing on the leaves.*

Modified leaves *To stop the whitebeam's leaves (left) from drying out, they have a coating of hairs on the underside; these are so dense, the foliage flickers silver in the wind. The yew's narrow leaves (right) enable the tree to survive in dry places because their small surface area reduces water loss.*

WHO MADE THESE MARKS – BADGER OR DEER? Badgers may betray their presence by leaving scratch marks (below right) on dead wood or the bark of trees – usually on elder, but also on oak and elm. They make them with their strong front claws, up to 1m (3ft) from the ground. Badgers probably scratch to remove mud from their claws after a night's digging, not to sharpen them. Scratching nearly always takes place before the badger returns to the sett at dawn, and is most obvious where the soil is heavy and clinging. A badger may also scratch when it marks its territory with scent exuded from a gland at the base of the tail. Nearer the ground, look for indistinct hind-feet marks.

Fallow deer bite tree bark to supplement their diet at the end of winter, leaving teeth marks such as the ones on this holly (left).

Close-up on

The badger

A pile of old straw, bracken or dried grass dumped outside a woodland hole in spring is a telltale sign of a badger sett. Nearby, you may also notice ferns uprooted and their leaves bitten off where badgers have gathered bedding to keep their suckling cubs warm. In neighbouring pastures, overturned cow pats with pits excavated beside or underneath them are signs that hungry badgers have been foraging for dung beetles.

Badgers live all over Britain, although they are rare in northern Scotland, but they are most common in the south-west and Wales. They usually make their setts where woodland and pasture meet, where food – particularly earthworms – and bedding material are plentiful, and often on well-drained, easily dug slopes. Badgers also try to ensure that each entrance to their sett provides cover so they can emerge unseen, though on moorland the entrance may be in the open.

Elder and blackberry often grow near setts. Badgers eat the fruit and the seeds germinate after passing through their intestines. Nettles also thrive in the newly disrupted soil enriched with badger dung found near badger setts.

WHOSE DROPPINGS – BADGER OR FOX?
Badgers often leave their droppings (right) in funnel-shaped latrines that they have excavated within about 20m (65ft) of their sett. But you may also see badger dung in pits dug in open pastures where badgers have been foraging for worms and beetles. Most droppings are soft, about 7.5cm (3in) long, and often with conspicuous remains of undigested insects attached to them.

Fox droppings (left) are deposited on open ground, not in pits. They are always twisted, and tapered at one end, and they may be darker or paler in colour, depending on what the animal was eating and how long has elapsed since the droppings were deposited.

WHOSE HAIRS ON THE WIRE – BADGER OR SHEEP? Look for stiff **badger hairs** (below) on barbed wire near badger setts or on the paths that the badgers frequent on their night-time foray. If the badger ducked under the fence, the hairs will have come from its back and they will be 5-7.5cm (2-3in) long,white with a black zone near the pointed end. If it went over the fence, the hairs will be from its belly and usually be all black. **Sheep's wool** (right), is a soft white or grey fleece with no wiry hairs.

Out and about *A three-month-old badger cub (right) joins a group of adults foraging at night. The offspring remain in family groups, called clans, for several years.*

WHOSE HOME IS THIS – BADGER OR FOX? The typical entrance to a **badger sett** (left) is at least 25cm (10in) and often up to 35cm (14in) across. A newly excavated hole has rough edges which become smoother with use. In spring you may see a pile of discarded straw outside. Look out, too, for heaps of earth, which badgers kick out with their powerful hind legs: on slopes these may build up into a platform. If, in spring, a heap of earth outside a well-used entrance is flattened, this is a clue that cubs have begun to make forays outside.

A fox hole (right) often has the remains of a meal left outside. Rather than dig a hole, foxes will enlarge rabbit holes or move into unoccupied badger setts. Fox holes are usually free of ejected earth and have a distinctive musty smell.

WHO WALKED HERE – BADGER OR DOG? On patches of mud near the sett or along the sparse but well-worn paths to and from their latrines and sources of food and water, you may detect **badger footprints**. The print of the fore foot (near left) with its five clear pads and claws, is broader than it is long. The print of the hind foot (far left) is smaller than that of the fore foot and often overlaps it, so that the tracks of a single walking badger are sometimes mistaken for those of a female badger with her cub.

The footprints of a dog out on a country walk (right), made by its front and hind feet, have four thick, blunt claw marks. Try to trace the outline of the soft main pad: it is concave on the front foot and convex on the back one.

HOW TO WATCH BADGERS

Seeing live badgers is thrilling, but patience, persistence and the motivation to stay awake through the hours of darkness are needed if you are to observe them first hand.

Ideally, the sett you select to watch should be in regular use with well-defined, well-worn paths leading to and from it. Get to know the setts in your vicinity and choose one that does not have too many entrances – say three or four rather than ten. Make sure you are in place by sunset, at the very latest, or two hours before dawn. Dress warmly and position yourself downwind from the sett entrance. If you are taking a torch, use one with a red filter, which is less disturbing to animals.

You may hear the badgers scratching before you see them. They often groom vigorously when they first emerge from 12 or more hours of underground confinement. Listen, too, for snuffling as they suck in air to 'test' the outside world for smells. If you are lucky the emerging badgers will linger near the sett entrance and visit their latrines before moving off to forage for the earthworms, beetles, small mammals, fruit and cereals that largely compose their diet.

Songbirds in the wood

Male birds have two ways of attracting a mate – with song or a flight display, or sometimes both. But under the enclosing canopy of the springtime wood, their options are confined to singing, which is why this is the best habitat in which to listen to birdsong. Approaching dawn is heralded by a chorus of song, but as the sun rises this ebbs away and the birds go about their daily business of finding food, building nests and raising young. There is often a second chorus towards dusk, and you can hear individual birds singing throughout the day and, in the case of the nightingale, for much of the night too.

Why do male birds sing? For two reasons: to attract a mate and to stake out and hang on to a territory. Hence they sing best when there are rivals within earshot. While female birds tend to be far less vocal, there are exceptions: hen robins, for instance, can often be heard in autumn and winter.

If you know something about the habits of a bird, you will have a better idea of where to look when you hear one. Some birds, such as the song thrush and wood warbler, sing from high perches, so scan the treetops for them. Others, such as the robins and marsh tits, sing from lower down, and the chiffchaff tends to sing from inside dense cover.

Some birds have definite woodland habitat preferences, which can help to narrow down the possibilities when you are trying to identify a bird by its song. It is unlikely that the bird you are hearing is a redstart, for example, unless there are mature trees in the wood.

If you are in a wood with tall oaks and a rather bare floor, typical of many hillside woods in the west, listen out for the wood warbler as this is just the kind of habitat it likes. The garden warbler, by contrast, prefers a dense understorey, and the tree pipit an open wood with large clearings. And while most of our woodland birds live in deciduous woods, several, like the coal tit and tiny goldcrest, feed more often in the branches of conifers.

Trio of specialists

The capercaillie, Scottish crossbill and crested tit are the most specialised woodland birds. You are unlikely to hear them outside Scotland's native pine forests. The crossbill and capercaillie feed on pine needles and seeds; the crested tit excavates its nest in tree stumps and the soft wood of pine is ideal for this purpose.

RUNNING CHORUS

For a real birdsong experience, try visiting a well-established wood before dawn on a quiet morning in late April or May. Some birds, like the cuckoo, wake up while it is still dark and can be heard first. Next listen for the short repeated phrases, such as ***did-he-do-it? did-he-do-it?***, of the song thrush. The mistle thrush's loud, abrupt song has shorter pauses and lacks the repetition of the song thrush.

With the glimmer of dawn, the voices build up. Most people can pick out the rook, wood pigeon and pheasant, and the great spotted woodpecker's hollow drumming.

The marsh tit,

Hunt the singer

The marsh tit **[1]** *and the garden warbler* **[2]** *are elusive birds as they prefer to sing from the dense understorey. The likeliest place to glimpse a wood warbler* **[3]***, is on a perch high up in the tree canopy, especially in oak woods, and the redstart* **[4]** *sings in the open, on trees such as alder, birch or rowan.*

Pine lovers *The Scottish crossbill* **[1]** *and the capercaillie* **[2]** *can only be heard in the Scots pine forests of the Highlands. The tiny goldcrest* **[3]**, *Britain's smallest bird, and the coal tit* **[4]**, *live on a more widespread variety of conifers.*

THRILLING SOUND IN THE DARK

The song everyone wants to hear is that of the **nightingale** (below). Despite its name, the nightingale sings by day, too, to deter rival males and claim a territory. But the quiet of late evening, when it sings more complex songs to attract a female, is the best time to hear one, especially if several males compete to out-sing one another. The song is easy to recognise but varied, with short loud phrases, usually alternating a churring ***jug jug*** with a crescendo of clear, sad notes – try counting different song-phrases you hear.

Nightingales are strictly woodland birds, frequenting native woods with dense, tangled cover. Their traditional habitat was formerly hazel coppice; now they are more often heard among bramble and other cover growing alongside rides and glades, or in willow thickets in river valleys. Many good nightingale woods are nature reserves, and local Wildlife Trusts often run 'nightingale evenings' where you will be guided to a likely place.

Hearing a nightingale is one thing, seeing it is another, although you sometimes spot this robin-sized bird silhouetted against the dusk. In Britain, it normally sings from deep cover, crouched low on a branch. Use binoculars to search for the part of the bird in motion – the beak, which snaps open and shut like a pair of scissors – and watch as it seems to sing with its whole body and soul.

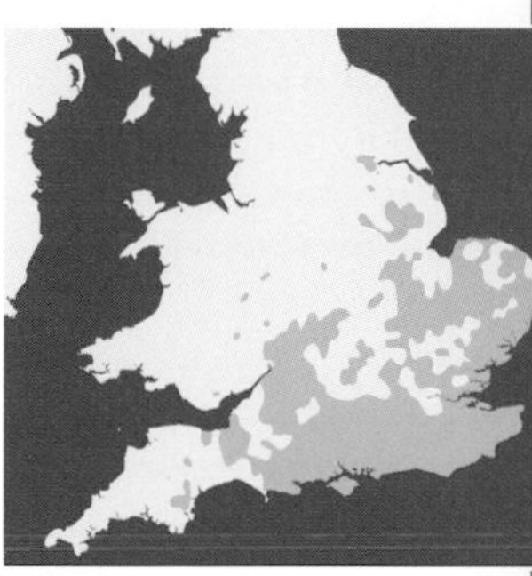

Silent nights You won't hear a nightingale in many parts of Britain: these summer visitors settle only in the areas shaded dark on the map above.

which despite its name prefers woodland to wet, utters a characteristic, sneezing *pitch-ou*. The woodlark seems to pronounce the letter 'l' in its sweet, liquid call *too-loo-eet*.

Song is particularly important in distinguishing the different warblers – important to them as well as to those listening to them. Though they look almost alike, the lovely descending cadence of ***swee-swee-sweetou*** notes of the willow warbler forms a complete contrast to the monotonous two-tone song of the chiffchaff. Their close relative, the wood warbler, sings the same ***stip-stip-stip*** notes faster and faster, ending in a trill.

The two that are hardest to separate by song are the garden warbler and blackcap. It takes practice to separate the mellow, even song of the garden warbler from the scratches and whistles of the histrionic blackcap.

Close scrutiny

Once you know the main songs and call-notes of the common woodland birds, the next step is to recognise individuals. Try taking the same walk each morning over several weeks, noting the regular singing places of each bird, and mark each one on a large-scale map.

A bird sings in spring to attract a mate and, all being well, will nest nearby, so by charting the singers, you will be able to build up a census of what birds are present, and where, in your local wood.

AN EERIE FLIGHT You hear an intense, high-pitched ***twisk*** in damp, open woods in the evening. What is it? See if you can spot a mottled brown bird circling above the trees with slow wing beats, its long bill pointing downwards, and listen for a grating ***kwar, kwar***, more like a croaking frog than a bird. What you are witnessing is the display flight, or roding, of the woodcock as it searches the ground for a mate.

Close-up on
Birds on trees

The nuthatch is a reckless, sharp-billed bird a little bigger than a house sparrow. Find it by listening out for its ringing ***chwit*** call-note, and shrill piping ***tui, tui, tui*** song, which carries a long way on a calm day.

Woodpeckers, along with the nuthatch and the treecreeper, share a gravity-defying life on tree trunks. They use their strong claws to hang on, even upside-down, and their broad, stiff tails as props to balance themselves. Woodpecker activity is at its height in spring when the birds are more vocal than usual, and when male and female great spotted woodpeckers indulge in aerial chases through the wood.

The three British woodpeckers, the green, great spotted and lesser spotted, are all shy birds. The green woodpecker gives its presence away by the loud laughing call-note ***keu-keu-keu***, known as a yaffle. It is the largest of the three – about the size of a pigeon – and unmistakable with its olive-green wings, yellow rump and red crown. It has a characteristic bounding flight. If you hear a hollow drumming sound, look out for a spotted woodpecker. Both great spotted and lesser spotted males deliver rapid blows to a bough with their bill, producing a noise that acts as a warning to other males and an advertisement for females.

The most likely place to look for woodpeckers is in mature woods and in parks that contain old trees. Woodpeckers feed in most types of mature woodland and can exploit a range of plant foods like hazelnuts, pine seeds and berries as well as insect larvae. Stand quietly and study the woodpecker as it climbs a tree in a series of jerky hops using its tail for support. If it senses your presence, it will disappear round the back of the trunk, but stay still and it may emerge and allow you a better look. With binoculars you will see that woodpeckers have specialised feet that are modified for climbing by having two toes facing forward and two backward to give a balanced grip.

Clues to identification

The nuthatch and treecreeper trust to their natural agility and scuttle about the trunks and branches on ordinary forward-facing toes. Nuthatches are particularly enjoyable to watch as they can run down trees (something woodpeckers and treecreepers can't do) with a flash of white and chestnut. Treecreepers spiral in a jerky mouse-like fashion up one tree then fly down to the base of the next tree and repeat the process.

LISTEN THEN LOOK If you have heard the unmistakable sound of a woodpecker and want to try and locate it, start by checking nearby trees for signs of damage. They are sedentary birds and are likely to be feeding and displaying somewhere close to where you heard them.

Marks on the bark Woodpeckers and nuthatches have long powerful bills which they use to hack holes in trunks or branches (below) or to chip away at loose bark looking for grubs, and to smash open nutshells to extract the kernel – their padded skull structure prevents brain damage. Where an over-mature tree shows bits of missing bark, examine it closely: a woodpecker's bill leaves marks like converging dashes.

Stump workshop Woodpeckers often use a favourite stump or tree as a workshop (above right): you can detect one by the pile of nutshells or stripped cones at its base. If you look at a damaged pine or spruce cone, you can tell if it is the work of a great spotted woodpecker by the dishevelled look. The bird pulls them apart to get at the seeds and sometimes the scales of the cone are split lengthways.

Jammed in Nuthatches like to jam hazelnuts into a fissure in the bark (right) and hack out a more or less circular hole, leaving half-moon shaped marks in the bark. The great spotted woodpecker shares this habit but, being more powerful, hammers at nuts and acorns lengthways to split them, leaving a chisel mark like a long diamond in the bark.

The great spotted woodpecker (left) may be heard drumming up to half a mile away in spring. The **lesser spotted** (right) is the most elusive woodpecker and spends most of its life high up in the trees moving restlessly about, and pecking at the wood like a sewing machine. It is easiest to detect from its call-note, a shrill ***pee-pee-pee***, and quieter, more rattling drumming, lasting several seconds.

HOME MARKERS A litter of wood chips below a tree is a good sign of a nesting woodpecker. Another clue, in June, is the sound of the young chirping or squeaking. Follow the sound and you might be able to trace the hole, but withdraw if the birds show signs of distress.
The place to look for the nest hole of a **green woodpecker** (right) or the great spotted, is 2-6m (6-20ft) up the trunk of a mature tree. Contrary to common belief, it need not be hollow as woodpeckers can bore holes in solid wood to the soft wood beneath. The lesser spotted woodpecker usually makes its nest hole in a branch, often on trees that have soft wood, like alder or willow.
The nuthatch's nest hole (right) is very difficult to spot. The bird plugs most of the hole with mud, which dries to almost the same colour as the bark, leaving only a tiny space as an entrance.

The treecreeper is slightly smaller than the nuthatch, with a slender, slightly curved bill which it uses to probe for beetle grubs and insects. It is unobtrusive, so it is worth learning its song: a thin high-pitched ***tsee-tsee-tissi-sissi-tsee***.

ANTS AND DROPPINGS Unlike other woodpeckers, the green woodpecker often feeds on the ground, particularly on ants. Giveaway signs characteristic of woodpecker damage to look for around wood ant nests are chunks torn from the **nest mound** (below) and even shallow tunnels drilled into the ants' nest. In such places, or nearby, you may find the bird's **droppings** (below right). These appear to be wrapped in ash-grey paper, rather like fat cigarette butts, and if you break them open you will discover that they contain the undigested remains of ants and other insects.

Spring sunshine brings icy waters back to life

Warmth and extra daylight set the current of life surging

Rivers and ponds still feel cold to the touch in early spring but for wildlife that lives in and around water the worst is past. The rise in temperature of just a few degrees signals that winter is over and the busiest time of year is about to begin.

The increasing length of days is just as important as the extra warmth. It triggers the growth of waterside trees such as alders and willows, and of a rich variety of plants along the banks and in the shallows. Fish feed on the growing numbers of aquatic insects and other invertebrates as breeding time nears.

On the bank, look and listen for signs of herons and kingfishers, water voles and toads as they each start their annual search for a mate.

Clear, calm waters

The sparkling River Test at Stourbridge, in Hampshire (above), is typical of streams and rivers which are fed by rain falling on the chalk downs of the south of England. The porous rock works as a huge natural filter, screening out the particles of soil and grit that make other lowland rivers murky, before feeding the rainwater into the clear streams at the base of the chalk some weeks or even months later.

Chalk has another effect which is easy to see. Rainwater soaks quickly into the rock at the surface and seeps gradually through, so chalk rivers and streams are not affected by sudden floods or torrents caused by heavy rain rushing straight off the land into the river. As a result, plants like the water crowfoot can grow, trailing gently in the current, without being swept away. By late

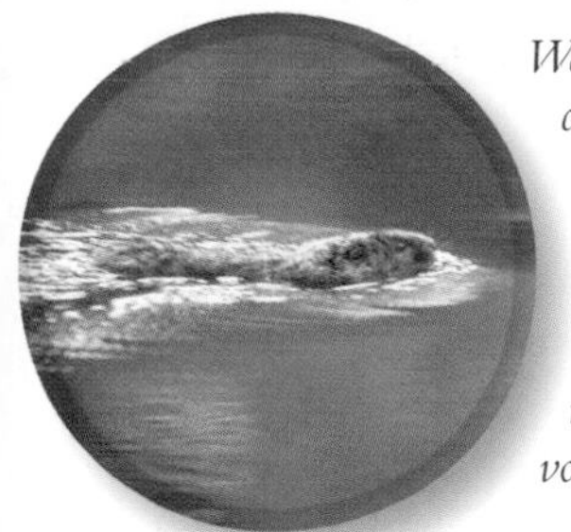

Watch the surface of a chalk stream and you may see the bow wave made by a water vole's snout. Unlike the rats they are often mistaken for, water voles prefer clean water.

April its green tresses are covered with white flowers, held on stalks just above the water's surface. Such plants provide cover for the creatures that move in the transparent world below the surface.

Look into the clear waters of a chalk stream, and you might spot the dark fleeting shape of a brown trout or a freshwater crayfish – a creature which depends on the calcium in the water to construct its shell.

Soggy under foot

Sweat Mere in Shropshire (above), is an old alder carr, a type of swampy woodland that most walkers will avoid. The clusters of trunks show that the alder trees were once coppiced (see page 115) to make charcoal. The trees are also extremely beneficial to wildlife: at least 140 species of insects feed on the leaves, including the caterpillars of the alder kitten moth, alder sawflies and several types of leaf beetle.

In March, before the alders come into leaf, the soggy ground is studded with marsh marigolds, also known as king-cups. Their burnished flowers stand out against the smooth, dark mud, on the surface of which you might find the footprints of birds. Look for the trails left by coots, with their long, unwebbed feet and distinctive scalloped flaps along each toe.

Regularly flooded carrs like this are usually very fertile, but alders will thrive even in poor ground. They have special swellings on their roots which contain millions of bacteria. These bacteria can collect or 'fix' nitrogen from the air, turning it into a natural fertiliser which the trees can use. The nobbly masses of root nodules are sometimes as big as a cricket ball – look for them where the roots of trees have been exposed.

As early as March, the pollen-covered stamens of marsh marigolds begin to attract insects such as this reed beetle, with its glossy, metallic sheen.

Standing at the water's edge

Melting snow and heavy rain in winter and early spring often cause rivers to burst their banks. Long after these floods have subsided, you can discover how high they rose by looking for dead vegetation and rubbish, left high and dry by the falling water. The best places to look for such jetsam are where there is an obstruction in the river. The branches of a tree, bowing down into the current, can act as a small dam, also a fence, continued into the water to discourage livestock wading around it, can trap mounds of flood-borne debris.

It is crucial for waterside plants to develop defence mechanisms that can help to prevent them being swept away by floods. Many, such as the water dock, have strong root systems to hold them in the ground.

Alders and willows have the same feature. Look where the river has undercut the trees and you can see it at work in the muscular knots of roots holding them firm in the mud.

Often riverside trees lean over so far that their lower branches dip into the water. Yet the roots still anchor them firmly to the land – keeping the tree alive and slowing erosion of the bank.

Breathing under water

Willows are the quintessential waterside tree. Their roots can take up oxygen from the water, allowing them to survive in wet soils where other trees would drown. They also absorb nutrients from the water and can considerably reduce the levels of nitrates and phosphates in polluted rivers and streams.

Harvest of branches

Willows can grow to over 20m (65ft), but many are stunted by being pollarded to produce a crown of flexible young branches, or osiers, which can be woven into baskets and used in furniture making.

Regular pollarding extends the life of trees, as their restricted size keeps their nutritional needs low. Even a willow a hundred years old is not considered ancient.

Aged pollarded willows, with their thick stumpy trunks and dense sheaf of crowning branches, are especially valuable to other wildlife. Lichens and mosses spread slowly across the bark and the caterpillars of more than 150 species of large moth feed on the leaves.

In spring, willow catkins provide a valuable early source of pollen and nectar for insects. Pussy, or goat willow, catkins emerge so early in March that they are out even before the tree comes into leaf.

All in a row

You often see willows growing in a straggling line beside the water, especially where a river flows through low-lying farmland. This is because broken twigs washed downstream readily root when they become lodged against the bank.

One willow, the crack willow (below), is particularly good at spreading in this way because its twigs are very brittle and break off easily in the wind.

If a line of trees has catkins on them and they are all the same sort, either all male or all female, then it is likely that the trees are all self-rooted 'cuttings' from a single parent willow growing upstream.

Fishing for flotsam Overhanging trees often catch debris floating downstream during a flood. This can get stuck, particularly in forked branches, and left behind when the flood waters subside.

Sign of flood The water dock has a deep and strong root system which helps to prevent it from being swept away in floods and high water. The mud and tangled vegetation twisted around this water dock's tall stems indicate that it has recently been submerged by flood water but has survived.

Male or female?

Willow catkins are either male or female but they usually grow on separate trees and are easy to tell apart. These catkins are from the crack willow, but their distinguishing characteristics are common to other species of willow, too. The female flowers (above left) are a silvery green whereas the male catkins (left) are yellow, and bear pollen.

BRIEF ORGY On calm spring evenings beside clean, unpolluted rivers and other bodies of water, look out for clouds of mating mayflies – brown-bodied insects about 5cm (2in) long. After hatching from eggs, mayflies live in the water as aquatic larvae, or nymphs, for between one and three years, but their lives as adult insects are brief. Some species live as long as two or three days as adults, unless a leaping fish makes a meal of them first, but others survive for only a few hours.

If you come across a **mayfly swarm** (bottom) in the early afternoon, it is likely that you can find more of the insects on the ground, shedding their armour-like larval skins. Look among the grass and other vegetation along the water's edge for the emerging adults, unfolding their wings in preparation for their mating flight.

Within a few hours, **floating masses** of dead bodies (right) can be seen on the surface of the water. After mating, the females drop their fertilised eggs into the water and then both sexes die.

Fish beneath the ripples

The dark shadows of brown trout hanging in a deep pool or the hint of a pike lurking along a bank are not easy to detect, let alone identify. But you can learn to spot clues from a river that will tell you what might live there. Where there is weed growing thickly on the bottom, predators such as perch and pike are likely to skulk, waiting to dart out and seize their prey of fish, frogs or even chicks. Other fish, such as chub, prefer the open waters of clear streams where they hunt small fry.

Home territory *Trout (top) are highly active fish, so they need the plentiful supply of oxygen found in clean, fast-flowing water. A gravel bottom is typical of this kind of stream, because the current carries along the particles of mud rather than depositing them on the riverbed. In contrast, carp (above) cannot breed unless the temperature is higher than 17°C, and so thrive only in the warmth of shallow, slow-flowing waters.*

If you know how to interpret them, the splashes and ripples made by fish at the surface are as informative as the tracks made by animals on land.

If there are swarms of insects over the water, watch and listen for the single 'plop' of a jumping fish. But a sudden volley of small splashes in a clear lake or fast stream could be made by a shoal of minnows or other small fish panicked by a trout.

In a slower-moving river the splashes might indicate a frenzy caused by the approach of a pike. Scan the edge of the reeds to see if you can pick out the fast-moving wake of this voracious predator as it lunges towards its prey.

Wake watching

Other creatures also create wakes as they cut through the water. The grass snake, which skulks in ditches and ponds, holds its head above the surface and leaves a sinuous trail behind it. The water vole nudges a path through the water, holding just its snout high and dry.

SPOT THE DIFFERENCE

WHAT MADE THE RIPPLES?
When **dimples** appear on top of the water, there will be fish swimming just below the surface. It may be that shoals of young dace or other small fish are feeding on insects that are floating on the water. Carp also agitate the surface as they run upriver to spawn, so that the shallows almost seem to boil.

If you hear a plop or a **splash** on an otherwise still pool or lake, study the pattern of ripples the fish has left behind. A jumping salmon, trout, bleak, chub or dace will make a characteristic spreading set of concentric ripples when it splashes back into the water after leaping to catch an insect. Keep watching the spot where you saw the ripples; if the fish jumps again in the same place, it is probably a trout.

Swirls of **bubbles** close to the bank are usually made by a shoal of bottom-feeding fish such as carp or bream in the shallows. The tench stays out of sight as it nuzzles through the mud of ponds and sluggish stretches of river searching for worms, but you can trace its movements by watching the trail of bubbles it makes as they break the surface.

SECRETS OF THE STICKLEBACK

Sticklebacks live in most fresh waters, so if you push a net through the weeds and between stones you should be able to catch one. To see them in the water, look in clear, shallow streams or drainage ditches.

If the water is very clear, you might be able to make out the spines that give the fish its name. These jab into the mouths of predators, making them spit the stickleback out.

Private lives

In spring, you might be lucky enough to witness a stage in the stickleback's fascinating love life. This is when the male develops his courtship colours – a bright red underside and blue eyes. He then builds a nest of algae and weed, like a small green dome on the silty bottom. The nest, like the fish, is about the length of your middle finger.

Your best chance of seeing the male is when he is guarding the nest, because he is dogged in his duty. Even if he spots you and darts away, he will soon return to his post.

The fry hatch after about eight days and the male tends them for another two weeks, protecting them from predators and keeping them near the nest. Once the cycle is complete, he starts again, raising several broods in the breeding season.

Q **Will sticklebacks survive if they are caught with a net, put in a jam jar and taken home?**

A No. The change in water temperature and oxygen level when they are removed from the river will eventually be fatal. Also, sticklebacks feed on small freshwater animals, and giving them waterweed or fish food will not keep them alive. Enjoy looking at them in your jam jar then carefully put them back into the water.

Attentive father *Once the male stickleback has enticed a female into his nest with his zigzag mating dance, he nudges her tail (top left) to stimulate spawning. Then he chases her away, enters the nest and fertilises the eggs. He guards the nest (centre left) as the eggs develop, fanning the water around it with his fins (bottom left) to keep oxygen circulating until the young hatch.*

Elusive eels and nocturnal newts

Between January and June, but especially in May, Britain's rivers and estuaries offer a glimpse of one of the world's most remarkable migrations – that of the eel. The eel larvae hatch in the Sargasso Sea in the mid Atlantic and drift more than 2500 miles eastwards on the Gulf Stream ocean current. Their journey takes up to three years and on the way they develop into elvers – transparent, pencil-thin, young eels. But even at the British coast, their journey is not yet over.

On the move *If you want to see eels, try taking out a torch on a moonless night when the rivers are high. Wait near a weir or other obstacle, and you might see eels slithering around them through the wet grass.*

If you see raucous flocks of gulls and terns thronging around estuaries, on low-lying ground, or lining the banks of a river or stream in spring, go and investigate. The hungry birds are probably gathering to feast on elvers as they collect in their thousands before swimming upstream, and you may be able to see the groups of these baby eels on the move in the muddy water (inset, below right).

The great eel runs, in which millions of elvers congregate each spring, are the Severn estuary, The Wash and the Solway Firth, but you could see them in any estuary, lowland river, drainage ditch or fen.

Fish on dry land

Some eels swim many miles inland to ancestral stretches of river where they will mature, and even make slithery journeys overland to reach a particular pond or lake imprinted on their migratory 'memory'.

Eels have a slimy, mucus covering. This enables them to leave the water and wriggle across land without drying out, so they can make their way around obstacles in a river, such as weirs and sluice gates.

This is not their only technique for survival on land: eels can absorb oxygen through their skin and are unusual among fish in also being able to 'breathe' air through their gills when out of water.

As the young eels mature, their backs turn brown and their undersides yellow – perfect camouflage for their life on the river bottom. There, they lie in wait and prey on water snails, frogs, freshwater crayfish and smaller food such as tadpoles and fish eggs.

Returning to the sea

The eels grow to maturity in fresh water – most in their ancestral river. Then, after a period of anything from seven to 19 years, the adults set off to retrace their original route back to the Sargasso Sea, where they spawn and die.

If you see eels during these mass late summer and autumn migrations, you will notice that they are now grey-backed and silver-bellied, for ocean camouflage. Your torch might pick out their enlarged eyes, which are thought to help them navigate on their long journey.

Eel spotting *A leaf gives an idea how small elvers are (inset) but adult eels are easier to see. They are often caught in traps (left) on rivers.*

Water dragon The great crested newt is the least common of the three British species of newt. It has a grainy-looking skin but its most distinctive feature is the male's dragon-like crest. In water it stands up impressively but on land the colour fades, the crest droops and it is ultimately absorbed by the newt's body.

Great crested newts are rare because of the dwindling number of large fish-free ponds that are their habitat. They are protected by law, so if you see one, inform your local Wildlife Trust (see Gazetteer). If you do find newts in a pond, they are more likely to be either common newts or palmate newts (see below).

Precious parcel *Female newts, like this great crested one, lay their gelatinous eggs on the leaves of water plants such as pondweed. They place one egg on each leaf and then fold it. The stickiness of the egg glues the leaf's edges together to make a protective envelope.*

ELUSIVE AMPHIBIANS

Almost everyone will have seen a frog at some time, even just in the back garden. But, although they also spend much of their adult life on land, newts are far more reclusive. They hide in damp places by day and feed under cover of darkness.

Your best chance of spotting a newt comes in spring and early summer, when the adults return to water to breed. Look for a pond with submerged water plants, where the females can lay their eggs, and where there are few fish to prey on the tadpoles and adult newts.

When you find a likely pond, watch quietly from the edge on a sunny day. If there are newts, you may spot one basking near the surface. Look for the bright orange or straw-coloured flash of its belly as the newt turns to swim away from you.

SPOT THE DIFFERENCE

WHOSE TADPOLE? From the time they hatch, **newt** tadpoles (above) have their distinctive long, thin shape. They develop their front legs first whereas in the tadpoles of **frogs** (below) and toads, the back legs appear first. Newt tadpoles also keep their feathery gills until they are mature enough to leave the water.

Native newts *The common, or smooth, newt (top), is the most numerous of the three British species of newt and the only one found in Northern Ireland. The palmate newt (above), so called because its hind feet are noticeably webbed, is found throughout Britain, and at high altitudes, such as on moorlands and heaths, is more common than the smooth newt.*

Clinging on *The force that creates the invisible skin on water – surface tension – also gives drops of water their shape. It allows them to defy gravity by hanging from a branch but, as the water collects and the droplet grows, its weight will eventually become too great and the surface tension will be broken.*

Life on the surface

From a distance, the unruffled surface of a pond appears the picture of peace. But look closer and you will discover a battle zone, where the air meets the water, full of insects and other water creatures preying on one another. For some, the water's surface is a place to soak up sunlight or to collect oxygen. For others, it is a trap that snares unlucky victims and makes them easy to attack. Even small ditches and cattle troughs can give you a glimpse into this world, where killers may lurk just beneath the surface, or run brazenly across it to seize their prey.

A force called surface tension stretches an invisible 'skin' across the surface of water, giving insects such as pond skaters a floor to walk on. You can test the existence of surface tension by very gently lowering a pin onto a cup of water with no traces of soap: if your hand is steady, the pin will float.

Most creatures would step straight through this magic layer, making walking on water impossible, but some insects have dense, water-repellant hairs on their legs, which help to stop them breaking the surface.

Many water creatures, such as the raft spider, use this skin to sense vibrations on the surface and locate their prey. Stretches of calm, still water are essential for this technique, so ponds are perfect places to see these hunters in action.

Skimming the surface Look for loose groups of pond skaters on a pond's surface and watch how these predators move. They 'row' over the water, using their middle pair of legs to propel them, the back ones to steer and the short front pair to seize dead or dying insects.

TAKE A DIP IN THE POND

Seeing the insects and other small creatures that live in a pond is not just a case of peering in and even if the water is clear, most water creatures will dive out of sight if they sense you standing at the edge. With a net you will be able to explore a little of this underwater world by fishing in spring when there is not too much weed. To take a closer look, tip your catch into a glass jar containing some pond water.

If you are interested in beetles, pond skaters, water boatmen and water mites, drag your net across the surface of the pond. To pick out tadpoles, snails, mayfly nymphs or damselfly nymphs, sweep your net through clumps of pondweed (go back to the pond in summer to see the adult flies). And for bottom dwellers such as flat worms, bloodworms and caddisfly cases, gently skim the mud at the bottom with your net.

Scorpion snorkel A sleek insect with a pointed 'tail' is a water scorpion, but it is not a true scorpion. It preys on insects, tadpoles and small fish and clings to weeds in stagnant ponds so that its 'tail' (a breathing tube) breaks the surface.

Ready for action Look for small patches of 'dust' floating on the surface – these are groups of springtails, each no longer than the thickness of a coin. Stir the water, and they will release their coiled, spring-like tails and flick themselves into the air.

Water dodgems Small, shiny black 'speed boats' zooming around in circles on the surface of a pond are whirligig beetles. Their eyes are divided into two parts, one section for looking over the surface and the other for seeing under the water.

Lone hunter The solitary water measurer moves slowly, feeding on animals on and just below the surface. It has a slender body, like a stick insect, and two long antennae that look like a fourth pair of legs.

Upside down The backswimmer, also called the greater waterboatman, preys on small fish and tadpoles. It looks very similar to a lesser waterboatman but you can easily tell them apart: the lesser waterboatman swims the right way up; the backswimmer, on its back. Both can also fly. If you catch one, tip it gently onto the bank and once it is dry it will take to the air, drumming its wings.

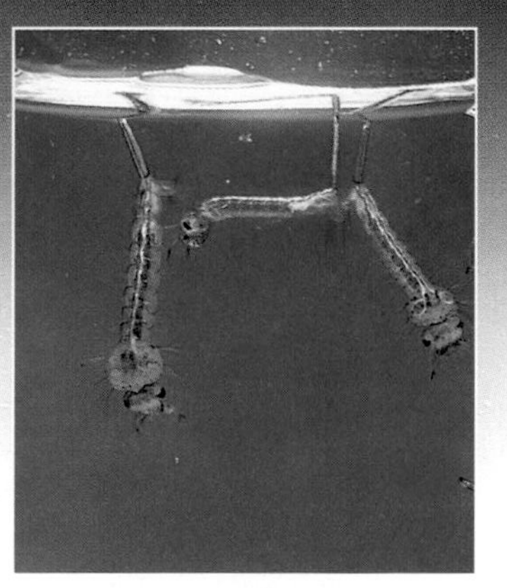

Juvenile forms The larvae of biting gnats (above) and mosquitoes hang, head down, from the surface of the water drawing in air from a short tube near their back end. If the pond is stagnant, and you scoop up mud from the bottom, you might find bloodworms, the larvae of non-biting midges.

MINIATURE DIVING BELLS

As you peer in from the water's edge, you might spy a silvery bubble hidden among the pond-weed – too fragile to survive being pulled out of the water. This is an oxygen bell belonging to a **water spider** (right).

The spider traps air in its body hair, then swims down and stores it in the underwater 'balloons' made of silk, which are anchored to the weed. The spider can then breathe this air instead of always going back to the surface, but it is also a valuable supply for the spider's young, which hatch from eggs laid in the bells.

Another water insect that traps air to breathe under water is the great diving beetle. This big, dark beetle, as long as a paperclip, is unmistakable. It is an underwater hunter which packs the air it needs to survive below its wing-cases but this makes it very buoyant and the beetle has to cling to weeds or swim vigorously to stop itself floating up to the surface. Its larvae are almost twice the size – 5cm (2in) carnivores, each with two breathing holes at the tip of its abdomen.

Sitting ducklings *A newly hatched brood of mallards (left) will number about a dozen. But if you see the brood regularly you may notice how its numbers are reduced by predators and bad weather. Only the toughest and luckiest ducklings survive into summer – as a rule, only two or three of the original dozen.*

Close-up on Water birds and their chicks

The first task facing a newly hatched duckling is to find food. Parent ducks do not feed their young but, if the mother was forced to nest away from the water's edge because she could not find a suitable site, you might see her in spring leading her small, fluffy charges to the waterside where they can forage before they starve. When they reach their destination, the new chicks will face the routine dangers that confront all water birds in their first few weeks of life – dying in sudden cold, wet snaps, or being eaten by a predator such as a fox or a pike.

Camouflage plays a part in protecting the young birds from predators. Mallard ducklings, which spend a lot of time on open water, have a pale creamy underside, making it difficult for predatory fish watching from below the surface to see them. By contrast, young tufted ducks tend to stay among vegetation, where their overall dark colouring helps to make them inconspicuous to predators lurking on the land as well as those beneath the surface of the water.

Family resemblance

Many young water birds bear little resemblance to their adult form and the easiest way to identify a chick is to look around for the parent bird, which is unlikely to be far away. As the chick matures, its downy plumage is replaced by 'contour' feathers, which give the bird a more streamlined shape and enable it to fly. A young bird does not develop its full adult colouring until it is ready to breed – usually during its second spring. This helps to protect it from breeding adults, which might see it as a rival and attack it. Swans will chase off their cygnets as soon as they turn completely white.

Desirable location *Many water birds, such as the great crested grebe (right) build floating nests, or anchor them to reeds, to be safe from bankside predators. The tufted duck (below) and other ducks prefer to nest on dry land.*

Decoy duck Some adult ducks, particularly the mallard, will feign injury, such as a broken wing, to distract the attentions of a predator from their young. Although many ducks nest on land, they are usually close enough to the water to escape from cats and foxes.

Floating refuge *Young mute swans, standing out in their grey-brown juvenile plumage, take refuge from danger by climbing aboard a parent's back. By gripping the adult bird's feathers with their beaks, the cygnets can even stay in place when the parent up-ends for food. When startled, young grebes can be seen doing the same thing.*

SPOT THE DIFFERENCE

COOT OR MOORHEN? Adult coots and moorhens are quite distinct but their chicks can be confused. Adult coots (above left) have a white 'face', or shield, and beak. Adult moorhens (above right) have a red shield and yellow-tipped beak.

The young coot (below left) has a red beak and shield like a moorhen, that fades as it matures. The long spiky feathers on its head and breast are orange and white with red tips.

The moorhen chick (below right) also has a red beak and shield, and a patch of reddish skin shows through on the back of its almost bald head. Overall, it is a darker, much sleeker bird than the young coot.

Babysitting duty In late spring you may see newly hatched moorhens being tended by dull brown birds, quite unlike the dark glossy adults you might expect. These are the chicks' older brothers and sisters. Most ducks hatch only one clutch each year but moorhens produce two or even three broods during a season and older chicks are enlisted to help with new arrivals.

Finding a meal in the stream

One of the pleasures of walking beside a river in spring is watching out for small birds hunting for food in the water or on the bank. Often all you get is a brief glimpse as they flash past, but these freshwater feeders share a useful trait for the countryside detective: they tend to keep to the same territory. If you catch sight of a kingfisher, it is likely to return. If you disturb a bird on the bank, it will fly only a short distance before stopping, giving you a second chance to study it.

Although they are widespread along slow-flowing, lowland rivers and even city-centre canals, kingfishers fly so fast that all you usually see is a flash of turquoise as one speeds past.

If you've never seen a kingfisher before, you may be surprised at how small it is when you do encounter one. They also blend into the background remarkably well, given the vibrancy of their plumage.

Instead of hoping to spot a kingfisher as it speeds past, look out for its perch. If you can locate this, you're much more likely to see the bird itself.

How to spot a fishing perch

Although a kingfisher will sometimes hover as it searches for fish, it usually watches the water from a favourite perch, such as a branch hanging low over the current. In time, this perch will become splashed with white droppings, making it easy to spot.

When you identify a likely perch, wait patiently for the bird to take up its post scanning the water's surface for ripples made by small fish. You may see it plunge into the water, but the dive happens so suddenly that you are more likely to hear just the splash. Wait for it to emerge and, if it has been successful, you will see it using the perch as a board on which to batter its thrashing catch.

Heads or tails?

Watch what it does next. If the fish is for itself, the kingfisher will dexterously spin the meal in its beak to swallow it headfirst so that the scales can't catch in its throat. In spring it is likely to juggle the fish until it has it by the tail, before flying off to present it, headfirst, to its mate or nestlings.

Expert angler
Kingfishers stay under water for only a few seconds before emerging (left), perhaps with a fish. If the bird perches, then grips the fish so that the head protrudes from its beak (right), it's a sign that the catch is intended for its mate or young.

Varied techniques *Dippers perch on rocks, plunge their heads into the current and even 'fly' under water in search of their insect prey.*

Q How do dippers see under water?

A The dipper's eyes have very powerful lenses, which enable it to see as well under water as in the air. Like all birds, it also has a third eyelid, which sweeps away any grit that gets into its eye. Using binoculars, you can see the milky white colour when it blinks.

BIRD UNDER WATER

A spring stroll beside a fast-flowing stream in northern or western Britain is the best time and place to see the dipper, a bird with the ability to walk under water.

Diving for a living

Dippers eat the small insect larvae that live among the stones on the riverbed. To get at them, a dipper swims below the surface, angling its wings back against the current, so that the pressure of the water prevents it from bobbing to the surface. It also uses its legs under water, running along the riverbed.

You may make out a blackish brown back as the dipper streaks past, low over the water, but the best way of distinguishing the bird is by its bright white bib. You cannot mistake it, waving like a handkerchief as the bird repeatedly curtsies from a rock in the middle of the stream.

If you can get close enough, you will see that it looks like a large wren, with a rotund body and short, pert tail. It also makes a loud wren-like *zit-zit-zit* call. If it is unaware of you, a dipper will feed in the shallows or hop boldly into the current and disappear on a foraging trip.

Knowing its limits

A dipper will not fly ahead of you for long: once it reaches the end of its territory, it turns back and flashes past. This means you can estimate the range of a breeding pair in spring and go back to the area in the autumn, after the young have flown, to search for the vacant nest. Look for a dome of moss under a bridge, in a rocky cleft or behind a waterfall, but don't remove it.

WATERSIDE WAGTAIL

While you are searching for a dipper, you may encounter a grey wagtail, as both birds favour the same turbulent streams.

The wagtail has a very long tail compared with the dipper, which it raises and spreads like a fan when it alights. Look for its contrasting black-and-white tail feathers as the bird makes short flights, stopping and starting just ahead of you, and listen for its sharp *tiz-zit* call as it flies.

River dances

At fist glance the wagtail and dipper seem to move in a similar way. But wagtails bob, wagging their tail and rump, whereas dippers make dainty curtsies.

By the beakful *Look out for grey wagtails paddling in the shallows at the edge of a fast-flowing stream or collecting beakfuls of insects and larvae from the riverbed. You might also see them hawking for insects underneath overhanging trees.*

Hidden chorus *The bittern (bottom left) and reed warbler (above) are well camouflaged in dense reed beds. The water rail (top left), with its red beak, grey underside and pinkish legs, is more distinctive but it crouches low to the ground, showing its speckled brown back, that blends with the reeds.*

Sounds of birds in the reeds

Reed beds are perfect hideaways for birds. Mallards, coots and moorhens are common at the edges, but there are many more birds that are elusive and hardly ever venture into the open. Here, a pair of ears finely tuned to springtime calls can be more useful to you than binoculars, as calls are often the only clues to a bird's presence. Two of these recluses, the water rail and the bittern, are rare but they have loud, unmistakable calls which carry over considerable distances, and sometimes presage their appearance from the reeds.

If you are stopped in your tracks on a walk beside a reed bed by what sounds like a pig grunting and squealing among the reeds, don't expect a porker to come crashing out. What you are hearing is the amazing vocal display, or 'sharming', of a water rail. For variation, the male also has a rhythmic hammering song. You are most likely to hear a water rail at dusk, when the bird is at its most active.

This shy relative of the moorhen occurs over most of the British Isles, although it is less common than it once was. Seen through the reeds you might easily mistake the movement of a water rail for a rat because its narrow body, flattened from side to side, allows it to slip easily between the plants.

Long-distance call

One of the most unearthly bird calls you can hear – stranger than that of any owl – is the booming of a bittern. The eerie sound is like a lowing cow or a foghorn and it can carry over the swaying heads of the reeds for more than two miles.

Only the fact that the bittern can be heard over such a distance allows any chance of tracking one down. It is very rare, breeding in only a handful of reserves, including Minsmere in Suffolk, Leighton Moss in Lancashire and Lee Valley Park – a green corridor stretching into north-east London.

At about 75cm (30in) from beak to tail, the bittern is only a little smaller than a grey heron, but stands erect and well hidden among the reeds. The bird is easy to identify in the air; it flies with its head and neck tucked in but with legs trailing, like a heron. Its wings are broad, mottled and barred like an owl's.

Repeated song

The strident calls of the water rail and bittern carry above the sound of the sighing reeds around them. But the reed warbler's flowing ***churr-churr-churr...chirruc-chirruc-chirruc*** would probably be lost to the wind if it were not so insistently repeated all day long.

The reed warbler arrives in Britain from Africa in mid April or May. You are most likely to hear this late migrant in East Anglia or the south-east of England, although the bird can occur as far north as a line from the Humber Estuary to Morecambe Bay.

When you do hear a reed warbler, stop and scan the tops of the reeds. It is rare to catch more than a very fleeting glimpse of this sparrow-sized, thin-billed, pale-breasted brown bird as it flutters up to catch a passing insect, but you may be able to pinpoint its position in the reeds by singling out the stems that are flexing as the bird sidles up and down them.

COASTAL BIRDS THAT FLOCK ON INLAND WATERS

Some water birds are firmly attached to freshwater sites and others to the sea: it would be extremely rare to come across a moorhen in sea water or a puffin inland. But not all birds are this particular. In spring, reservoirs, flooded gravel pits and sewage farms are populated by flocks of sea birds that seem to have turned their backs on the coast and come to live around areas of fresh water to mate and raise their young.

Angry mobs

Two of these, the black-headed gull and the common tern, are noisy and quarrelsome. In the breeding season, they can be confused at first glance because they both have red bills and black heads, but their distinctive ways of flying and feeding quickly enable you to tell them apart (see panel below).

If you see either of these birds in spring, keep an eye on them as you walk. They are very protective parents, and will mob you if you approach too close to their nest.

Return of the osprey On large Scottish lochs, April sees the arrival of the osprey: Britain's only freshwater bird of prey. Although they breed solely in Scotland, you might find ospreys in unexpected places as they make brief 'refuelling stops' at reservoirs in southern England on their way from Africa and the Mediterranean. They have dark backs and shoulders, a dark stripe across their white heads in line with their eyes, and pale undersides.

Needle-sharp talons enable an osprey to catch fish with its feet, and spiny scales on its toes give it a grip on its slippery prey. The bird flaps slowly over the water, then suddenly plummets from about 30m (100ft), often completely submerging. When it resurfaces, with its catch slung beneath its body, the osprey flies off to a perch to feed.

SPOT THE DIFFERENCE

TERN OR GULL?
A jerky flapping action characterises the flight of the **common tern** (top right). The bird moves through the air, rising and dipping, showing the long forked tail which has earned it the alternative name of sea swallow.

The **black-headed gull** (bottom right) is an expert glider, only flapping its wings when it changes course or needs to fly into a head wind. Black-headed gulls (far right) usually land on the water's surface to feed, but terns splash down to snatch food from the water and take off straight away.

First signs of new life on uplands and heaths

Spring comes grudgingly to high and exposed places

Snow and squally showers linger on the moorland and mountains of Scotland, the Pennines and north Wales. The bleak landscape remains cloaked in the winter browns of rushes and coarse grass, but look and listen closely and you will be surprised how many signs of spring you can find. Small mammals, birds and insects have been foraging all winter on fruits and seeds left over from the abundant autumn harvest. What they have missed now have a chance to germinate.

A patchwork of colours indicates heather of different ages. You may come across black, smouldering patches – not an accident but evidence of a deliberate management technique: rotational burning stimulates new growth.

Mountain heights

A swift stream like this, in the An Teallach buttresses (above) in the Scottish Highlands, is ideal for the dipper, a bird with the ability to submerge itself as it searches for food on the stream bed (see page 57). Look out for it as it bobs up for air. If you see one you can be sure that the water is clean, as the dipper is very sensitive to pollutants.

Red grouse challenge rivals for territory or mate with reverberating calls, ending with a guttural ***back, back, back-go-back***. If you hear a call, look for other birds on nearby hillocks. Ravens dive and tumble, calling in deep croaks – look for their long heads and bills, long, angled wings and diamond-shaped tails – and on clear days, peregrines soar in pairs above crags, searching for nesting sites. This is also the time of year to see mountain hares. They are usually

Mountain hares moult from white to brown in spring. When the snow has melted but the hares are still white in patches, they are quite visible against the dark moor.

nocturnal but are active by day in spring while mating. Their tracks in spring reveal their broad, widely-spaced hind feet still heavily furred for winter to keep them from sinking into snow.

Red deer graze on open ground. You are unlikely to see a mixed herd as males, whose velvety antlers are starting to bud, stay in small separate groups until autumn, when they fight for dominance of harems of hinds.

On gentler slopes

At lower altitudes, such as in the Carneddau Mountains of Snowdonia (above), gorse is in flower. Rocks and walls support lichens, and spiders and wheatears nest in cracks. Swathes of bluebells on open hills reveal that there was once a wood there, but the flowers are vulnerable to grazing and cannot survive on high ground, where they suffer from frost.

'Kissing's out of season when the gorse is out of bloom,' goes the saying, and with three native species of gorse in Britain, one will nearly always be in flower. But the chief glory of a gorse-covered moor comes in April and May, when the black-green bushes of common gorse, which grows head-high on sheltered slopes, are swathed in yellow flowers and the air is filled with the blooms' coconut-like scent. On sunny days in April and May listen out for the tiny but distinct popping sound made by the ripe seed pods of the gorse as they explode and scatter their contents.

Listen for the linnet's sweet twittering, interspersed with harsh twanging notes and the brief warbling of the whinchat, mixed with pauses and dry, metallic sounds. When alarmed, the whinchat's call resembles that of its close relative the stonechat – a sound resembling two stones struck together.

The spiky gorse offers protection for the nests of Dartford warblers, linnets and whinchats, which feed on the abundant insects attracted by the richly scented blossom.

SPOT THE DIFFERENCE

GORSE OR BROOM? Gorse is a spiny evergreen. Its yellow flowers have five petals, two of them joined together to form a 'keel', and at the base of each flower is a fleshy yellow tube, the calyx, which outlasts the blooms. Common gorse (below left) flowers in spring. On acid western moors you will find western gorse, low and compact, flowering in autumn. Look for lesser gorse in the New Forest: it lies flat and flowers from August to October. **Broom** (below right) is most widespread on slopes with acid soil, where it makes a vibrant display in May and June, after the best of the gorse. Broom's stalks are smooth, not spiny; the plant has long, whippy stems with short, broad leaves, arranged in threes, which it sheds in winter. The flowers are larger than those of gorse and sometimes have a tinge of red.

The three key moorland plants

Three plants form the basis of habitats for a wide range of insects, birds and animals on heaths and moors. One is gorse, sometimes called furze or whin, which covers large areas but is vulnerable to exposure in wide open places. It can be difficult at a distance to distinguish between gorse and broom: both dark green bushes bearing yellow 'peaflowers'. Gorse often rises in clumps above wide expanses of heather, another of the main moorland plants. The third is bracken, whose delicate young fronds belie its invasive nature.

On moorland which is managed by rotational burning, gorse thrives in thickets between strips of shorter heather. Its deep roots and woody stems can survive the annual fires, giving the gorse a headstart in the following months, before the rest of the vegetation regenerates. Rabbits do the bushes more damage for where they graze, gorse suffers.

In a landscape which is otherwise bleak, the highly scented flowers of gorse attract a variety of insects. Look for the fawn, hairless caterpillar of the grayling butterfly, easy to recognise with its dark stripe down each side. The large brown adult butterflies fly over moors in summer.

On ripe seedpods you might find gorse shield bugs. They hibernate in the litter beneath gorse bushes in winter and move onto the plant to feed in spring. Look closely at the stalks and you might find the web of a gorse orb weaver spider (below left) or the spider itself, sitting in a silken saucer in the centre. It must repair its work constantly, as the web is torn by struggling prey and loses its vital stickiness after a day or two.

Strange 'fruit' *On the tip of a gorse stem you might see what looks like a crinkled fruit or seed. If you watch carefully and for long enough, you might be able to detect it slowly moving – this is the gorse orb weaver spider.*

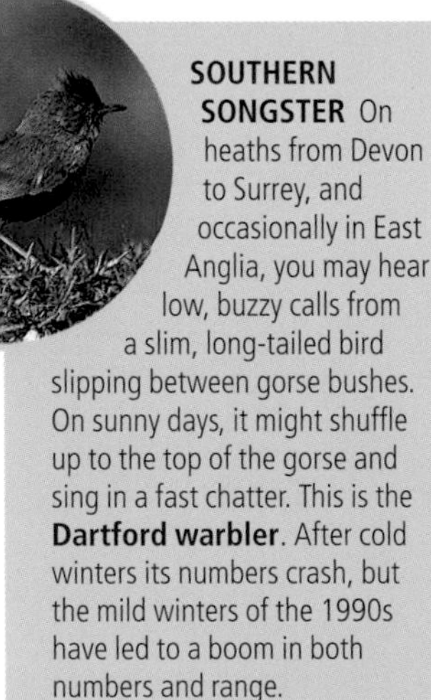

SOUTHERN SONGSTER On heaths from Devon to Surrey, and occasionally in East Anglia, you may hear low, buzzy calls from a slim, long-tailed bird slipping between gorse bushes. On sunny days, it might shuffle up to the top of the gorse and sing in a fast chatter. This is the **Dartford warbler**. After cold winters its numbers crash, but the mild winters of the 1990s have led to a boom in both numbers and range.

A DOMINANT SURVIVOR

Bracken is poised to take over wherever heather is burned too harshly and overgrazing reduces the extent of gorse. It spreads uncontrollably on low heaths with light, acid soils such as the Brecon Beacons. However, it is vulnerable to frost, so wise campers should pitch their tents on bracken slopes, which are likely to be frost-free at dawn.

In early spring, you walk ankle-deep in brittle, orange litter, which by late summer will make green stands as tall as a man. Look out for ants, which are attracted to bracken by the sugary liquid that oozes from nectaries at the base of fronds.

The thin underground stems branch from thicker shoots perhaps a metre deep, where they are safe from fires, and the bracken soon becomes so

MOORLAND SNAKES Springtime sun on heathland brings adders into the open where they bask on ant hills and beside bramble thickets and heather tussocks. Smooth snakes are found on southern lowland heaths, where they burrow in soft soil near mature heather and dwarf gorse. Male adders can appear to 'dance' in spring, swaying their heads in a challenge to other males as they vie for territory or a mate. A disturbed adder may hiss, but by nature they are shy and rarely seen. However, sit quietly and you might hear the soft rustling of an adder in dry undergrowth as it searches for its prey of mice, shrews, voles and lizards.

Adders are short fat snakes, about 60cm (2ft) long, with small, square heads. They are yellow, brown or olive, with an unmistakable 'V' behind the head and a black zigzag running along the back. The males have deep red eyes and the females orange, with a vertical slit for a pupil. Both sexes are venomous and a bite requires urgent hospital treatment but is rarely fatal to humans.

Smooth snakes are grey-brown or olive with two rows of dark spots, a dark stripe on the side of the face and a dark band across the back of the head. Both sexes grow to about the same length as an adder. They will often bite, with needle-sharp teeth, but are not poisonous.

Empty skin Snakes periodically shed or 'slough' their skin as they grow. The adder (far right) often uses the spines on gorse to help it to shrug off an old skin, so if you look on gorse bushes you might be lucky enough to come across the discarded skin of an adder (right). Even after it is shed, the skin remains clearly imprinted with the snake's small scales and the zigzag pattern which runs down its back.

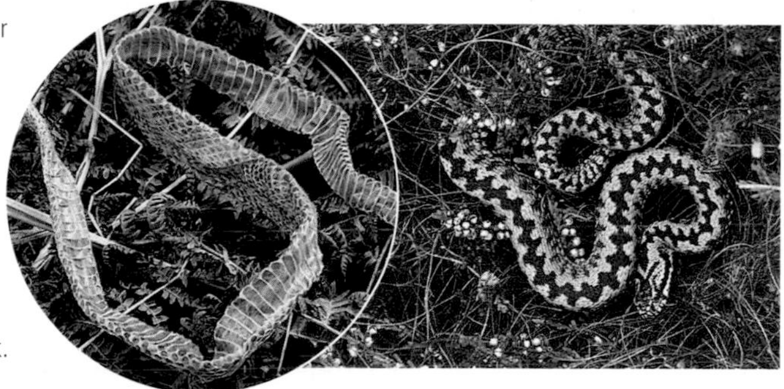

Newly hatched *On heather-covered moors in April, emperor moths emerge from their cocoons. The cocoon is closed tightly around the moth, leaving only a narrow opening, so that the moth can push out from the inside, but enemies cannot get in.*

dominant that few other plants can survive in the deep shade beneath a dense patch.

One of the reasons for bracken's success is that its fronds contain cyanide, so it is not heavily grazed. It is damaged by trampling, especially by cattle, which break the stem and crush young shoots. Sheep tread more lightly, and where they graze, the plant can thrive.

Tender shoots *From April onwards, look among the bracken litter for the first new shoots pushing up in curled fronds.*

INSECTS IN THE VEGETATION

On sunny days in April and May moths fly fast and low over heather-covered heaths and moors. If you see a moth in the daytime, you can be sure that it is a male: females only fly at night and lay their eggs in late spring, a few weeks after they are most visible on the wing.

As you walk on bell heather, look for a silky silver-grey pouch spun between the stems. Peek inside and you could be face to face with the large-eyed jumping spider, a carnivore waiting for passing flies and beetles. Silken tubes spreading over dry heaths and extending up to an arm's length below ground help the purse-web spider to catch its prey of caterpillars, beetles and flies.

In late spring, too, you might see bumblebees with orange rear ends lumbering heavily among the mountain and moor vegetation as they seek out early sources of nectar and pollen.

Sheep shape the landscape

Well-managed heather moors are burned periodically to stimulate the growth of new shoots. This burning must be carefully controlled to destroy other plants and keep trees at bay without damaging the roots of the heather. But grazing animals such as sheep, cattle and ponies also play an important part in maintaining the balance of plants on moors. Without them, seedlings and scrub would soon take hold, and trees such as the fast-growing birch would turn the moor into woodland. But the balance is delicate, and too many sheep can also change the moor.

Sheep graze mainly on grass, and browse on leaves and new seedlings, allowing woody plants, such as bracken, gorse and heather to flourish.

If you see a patch of recently burned ground massed with sheep you might be witnessing the start of a change of scene. The sheep will devour the newly-emerging shoots, leaving bare ground that is soon colonised by mosses and lichens.

On wet moors, purple moor grass follows the mosses, growing in dense, waist-high tussocks. On well-drained soil, clumps of bristly mat-grass take hold (below left).

In Victorian times, tough old castrated rams, or 'wethers', grazed the mat-grass. But the softer-mouthed ewes and lambs of today's hill flocks avoid it, allowing it to take root and replace the original moor and mountain vegetation.

Hill top survivors

Mountain sheep are bred locally for different habitats, but all are agile and self-reliant. Lowland sheep are more productive but less hardy, and cross-breeding is common to develop good all-round varieties. But on the highest slopes, where hardiness is essential, you might still see

ROUGH GRASS Tussocks of **mat-grass** on moors (left) are home to the **fox moth caterpillar** (inset). Be careful not to touch the caterpillar as its hairs can irritate the skin. **Welsh mountain sheep** (below) graze around these clumps of mat-grass as they are wiry and unpalatable, allowing the fox moth to develop into its adult form. The insect pupates in March or April in upright silky cocoons at the base of the grass or half-buried in moss, and emerges as an adult moth in May, to reveal pale-banded orange wings.

Q I found this lamb separated from its mother – what should I do?

A Leave it alone. Its mother will almost certainly come back – many birds and animals leave their young temporarily to feed and she could even be waiting nearby for you to go. You will only distress or harm the young animal by carrying it away. Only tell the farmer if it is injured. If it has strayed onto a road or other dangerous place, move it to safety or watch from a distance while someone tells the farmer.

one of the older, local breeds, such as the Rough Fell, Cheviot or Whitefaced Dartmoor.

The most common breed of mountain sheep in Britain is the Scottish blackface. You will recognise one by its curved horns, black face, and the long fleece which hangs around it like a skirt. If you see black lambs in the Lake District, they are probably Herdwicks, the hardiest of all the hill breeds. The fleece of a Herdwick sheep turns light brown then grey as the animal matures.

WHO'S BEEN GRAZING HERE?

Sheep are not the only animals that graze on the heather moors. Wild red deer (bottom), the species most common on moors and mountains, also feed off young heather shoots. They begin to move uphill in late spring, to avoid the biting flies on lower slopes and to take advantage of the new plant growth, but sometimes descend again to richer grazing at night.

If you find evidence of grazing on plants, try to identify the animals responsible, then look out for them in the surrounding land. An obvious sign of sheep is their wool, which they leave caught on fences and brambles or stuck to their droppings. Red deer hair is harder to spot, being brown, and is rarely left behind as evidence except on barbed wire. Droppings and tracks are also helpful clues.

CALLING CARDS Droppings make excellent clues when trying to distinguish between the presence of sheep and red deer. Both animals are vegetarian and must eat large quantities of plant matter each day in order to meet their nutritional needs, so their droppings are abundant and easy to find. **Red deer droppings** (left) are separate and acorn shaped: blunt at one end and tapered at the other. **Sheep droppings** (inset left) are rounder and more clustered.

FOLLOW THE TRAIL Other clues to look for are tracks in the muddy ground in lanes and around gateposts. If you are out on a morning following a late fall of snow, the tracks will be even clearer. Cloven-hoofed animals such as deer and sheep leave twin 'slots', one made by each 'toe'. Red deer and sheep slots are similar in size, at 5-7.5cm (2-3in) long, but **deer prints** (left) have a distinctive symmetrical curve each side towards a narrow tip. The two halves of **sheep prints** (inset left) are narrower, the tips rounded but not as broad and the outer edges straighter.

SPRING SNACK Sheep need an 'early bite' in spring: nutritious foliage available early in the year to help them to recover from the hard winter. In the Pennines, in particular, this is provided by **hare's tail cotton sedge** (above). Look for it growing in tussocks, each stem with a single white flower head which develops as the seeds ripen. Don't confuse it with broad-leaved or common cotton grass, both of which grow evenly with clusters of nodding, cottony flower heads.

Close-up on
Stone walls

Next time you approach a stile over a dry-stone wall, don't just climb over, but stop and study the surface of the stones and the gaps between them. These intricate structures are like miniature mountains: the tops are usually dry and exposed, the bases damp with dripping rainwater, and any south-facing side will be heated by the sun. These contrasts are strongest in the south, where the summers tend to be warmer than in the north.

Walls are built partly to use up pieces of stone scattered in fields but also because in some fields, the soil is too poor to support a hedge and so, both on and around the wall, the environment is a tough one for plants and animals. For evidence of life, you must look in the crevices and shady places, on the north-facing or cooler side of the wall, or at the base among the vegetation, where it is more likely to remain dark and damp.

Lichens are among the most common living things on walls, and form colourful crusts over the rocks. They are one of the most basic life forms, consisting of an alga embedded within a fungus. Because they live on the food created by the alga from sunlight, look for them in sunny places. Some lichens are sensitive to atmospheric pollution so their abundance may indicate that the air is clean.

Birds bring life to the rocks

Lichens, algae and ferns thrive wherever plentiful bird droppings make the wall fertile. If you discover a large clump of vegetation on the stones, it often indicates that the spot is a regular perch, so look out or listen for the resident bird. Most rest only for a short time on walls, but wheatears and pied wagtails sometimes nest in the deeper cavities and nuthatches and treecreepers hunt along the cracks for insects. Seeds deposited in bird droppings occasionally germinate in crevices, which is why you may find garden plants such as candy tuft, campanulas and wallflowers, growing out of the wall.

PRIMITIVE LIFE On limestone walls look for the lichen, ***Caloplaca heppiana*** (left). Lichens are long-lived and slow-growing – many increase by a mere 1-2mm in a year with a few large 'leafy' types achieving 10mm (3/8in) – so if you find one 20cm (8in) across it could be 200 years old. Lichens can tolerate frost, drought and hot sun – though they won't increase in size in extreme weather. Once conditions improve, however, they start growing again.

The colours of lichens vary greatly – the pigments have long been used as dyes – but orange is the most common. Another example, *Xanthoria parietina*, is an indicator of acid rocks. The coloured spots which dot the surface of many lichens are fruiting bodies, which produce spores.

UNDER THE LENS The **springtail** (right) is among the few insects that feed on the lichens and mosses of stone walls, but these primitive plants do support mites and microscopic invertebrates such as nematodes and tardigrades and these are eaten by the other insects living on the wall.

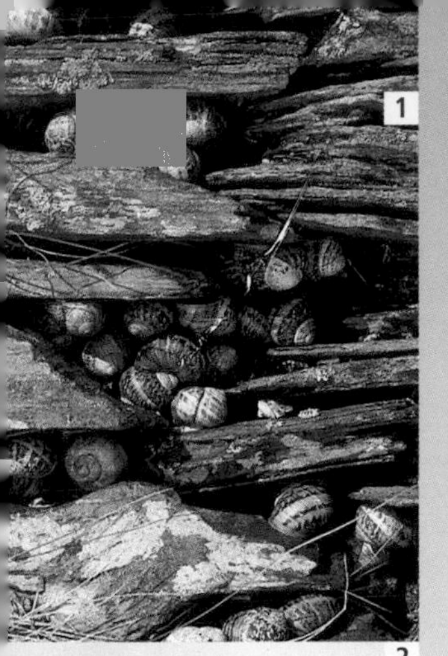

HIGH-RISE LIVING

As spring warms the stones, woodlice move up from the frost-free cavities at the base of the wall where they clustered for winter. They live on plant debris, and where there are woodlice you will probably find their enemy, the centipede.

On limestone walls, where there is the calcium they need for their shells, snails shelter in damp crevices **[1]**. Bumblebees also nest in crevices, especially in areas where foxgloves abound.

Spider cities

Walls provide refuge for more than 60 kinds of spider. The most common is the fat-bodied zebra spider **[2]**, a jumping spider with four large, forward-facing eyes. It does not spin a web but stalks prey, catching it with a sudden leap. Wolf spiders are also plentiful, emerging in direct sunlight to patrol the wall and adjacent vegetation for prey.

A common wall inhabitant is the eight-legged harvestman, a distant relative of the spider. The harvestman's long legs are its main means of detecting food: its two eyes look sideways and see little more than light and shade. Without venom or a web, the nocturnal harvestman crawls about feeling for woodlice, snails and other harvestmen to eat.

Reptile retreat

Common lizards **[3]** come out of hibernation in spring to bask on walls. The bare rock warms quickly in the sun and helps these cold-blooded creatures to heat their body. The crevices provide secure retreats and an abundance of insect prey.

Few mammals find enough food to make them stay on the wall. Voles, mice and shrews nest at the base, where grass provides warmth and shelter, and live on plants and seeds or prey on spiders and insects.

Lithe stoats and sometimes a weasel **[4]** may dodge in and out between the stones hunting for mice and voles. If you see a stoat disappearing, wait and watch. Stoats are deeply curious and a tiny pointed face will almost certainly soon reappear. Try coaxing it out by sucking it the back of your hand to make a squeaking noise.

LEAFY FRONDS The delicate-looking, triangular fronds of the **maidenhair spleenwort** (right) are typical of most ferns. Look for its long, tapered rows of 30-40 pairs of toothed leaflets draping from a wiry blackish leaf stalk, or 'petiole'. The **rusty-back fern** (inset, below left) is quite different. It has long leathery leaves with wavy lobes along their sides, and scales on the undersides that turn from silver to a rust colour as the frond matures.

All ferns need moisture – they spring out of shady crevices where damp earth collects, particularly on light-coloured limestone walls – but rusty-back ferns cannot survive either harsh winters or hot summers and are most common in the mild south and west. In a drought, the fern shrivels up as if dead but comes back to life again once it rains.

CUSHIONING THE ROCK Long, silvery 'hairs' and brown spore cases pointing upright on straight stems belong to ***Tortula muralis*** (right). This is a specialist wall moss – a mural, true to its name – but not the only moss found on stone walls. On northern walls look for ***Homalothecium sericeum*** (inset left), which forms mats of silky leaves. Mosses grow best in moist places where they are not dried out by wind and sun, so look for them at the base of stone walls or in crevices, but look on the top of a limestone wall and you might find an exception to this rule. *Grimmia pulvinata* grows on the driest, hottest parts of a wall, in soft cushions of grey-green, pointed leaves, each ending in a silvery hair.

Most birds choose a mate in spring and together they defend a territory which accommodates the adult birds and satisfies the needs of their growing family. Song is a crucial part of this defence and time spent listening on heaths and moors in spring will be amply rewarded with a concert of calls. Look up into the sky when you hear a song: there are very few places on open land for birds to perch, so you may witness the song flights – often incorporating aerobatic displays – that some species have developed to mark out their domain and attract a mate.

Song and dance routines

Drumming bird Male snipe perform a switchback display flight, and with each downward plunge, vibrate their stiff, widely fanned outer tail feathers in the rushing wind to create an extraordinary bleating or humming sound – a technique known as 'drumming'. If you hear a short, buzzing hum, scan the sky for a male snipe in mid display.

Ploughing the land *The curlews' wetland habit of probing for worms in mud with their down-curved bills can be seen on moors in ridges and furrows, where the birds have turned over the vegetation while foraging for insect larvae.*

In earliest spring, particularly in Wales and Ireland, look out for flocks of fieldfares and redwings gathering in fields on the edges of the moor. These cousins of the song thrush winter in Britain from continental Europe and regroup in March and April before returning north.

The first migrants you are likely to notice on the moors are the wading birds – curlews, lapwings, snipe and golden plovers. They return to this high land to nest after a winter spent at lower altitude in wetlands and along the coast.

Curlews trace simple, rising and falling flights over moors and trill ecstatic, bubbling songs in spring but they can also be heard throughout the year repeatedly calling their name, *coor-li*. Look for them along farm tracks where the ground has been churned up by tractor tyres, making it soft enough to probe with their beaks.

Snipe leave less evidence of their hunting, since they probe straight down into soft mud, feeling for worms. Their very long, straight bills have sensitive tips that can open and close around their prey underground.

CLOSE TO THE GROUND

Breeding birds on mountains have fewer resources than those at lower altitudes: rocks offer some shelter but there is little nest-building material. Some species, such as wheatears, use holes lined with a few twists of grass and some sheep's wool.

Waders keep their eggs in a shallow scrape in the earth, but their chicks hatch with a coat of warm down and are ready to leave the 'nest' almost as soon as they are dry, so a soft lining is an unnecessary luxury.

Living on the ground, these birds rely heavily on camouflage for their safety. Curlews, golden plovers and snipe have complex feather patterns that help them to blend into the background. You might nearly step on a snipe before it flies away from you with a hoarse *schaaap*, but curlews and golden plovers will call out as you approach.

If you are on the southern downlands from mid March, or farther north from the end of the month, you may see a bird with a bright white rump and strong black tail feathers jerking up and down. This is a wheatear.

On high ground they nest in the crevices of stone walls; lower down they often use abandoned rabbit burrows. Look for them wherever heavy farm machinery has exposed stones and earth.

Danger signal The flash of its white rump as a wheatear takes flight warns of approaching danger, but these birds mostly remain on the ground, perching on boulders and hopping through short grass to feed on insects.

Peak conditions

Don't be surprised if you see seagulls on mountaintops, such as the summit of Snowdon. These scavengers are attracted by the scraps left by visitors, but may also take the eggs or chicks of ground-nesting birds.

On the very highest peaks of northern Scotland, intrepid climbers might be surprised by a ptarmigan, scuttling away over the rocks. In spring, the male of this high-altitude relative of the red grouse moults from winter white to patchy grey, white and black. The female develops a brownish 'pepper-and-salt' pattern, so that both sexes are well camouflaged against the rocks, gravel, mosses and lichens of their bleak habitat.

A rare sight *A 'lek' is where black grouse perform their courtship dance. You are unlikely to witness a display but you might come across a promising patch of bare, trampled earth. Search for dropped feathers to confirm your suspicions.*

ALL FOR SHOW

Some birds don't sing to seduce a female, but stage mock battles in early spring to impress watching females with their fitness as a potential mate.

Groups of the game birds black grouse and capercaillie gather at traditional sites to 'lek' in spectacular dawn rituals. Since they are too heavy to display in flight, the black grouse fan out their lyre-shaped tails and act out show-fights, jumping and kicking as they make explosive 'sneezing' calls.

The best time to see them is in the brightening light after dawn. Scan the hillsides for open spaces where the large, black males will be clearly visible.

Rocky bay

As the spring tide retreats from this rocky bay at Faraid Head in northern Scotland (above left), sea caves, sometimes coated with glistening jewel-like sea anemones, are drained of water. Living features such as this forest of kelp also lie exposed to the air.

Kelp is the largest seaweed found around Britain's coast. Its underwater forests are rich in shorelife such as blue-rayed limpets, sea urchins and sponges, while pipefish and wrasse hide among its waving fronds. In the air the branched kelp fronds, which sway gently when under water, droop from their stalks, but their slimy surface prevents them from drying out in the few hours before the tide returns. Walking on these slippery kelp beds is hazardous: better to peer into a deep pool nearby or wait for summer and snorkel over them when the tide is in.

Techniques for living on a shifting shore

Coastal life finds a hold in the teeth of wind and tides

On the coast, spring is both a time of year and a type of tide, and both have enormous effects on the plants and animals that live along the shore. Spring tides occur once a fortnight throughout the year, when the earth, sun and moon are aligned at each full and new moon. Then, because of the combined gravity of the sun and moon, the sea rises higher and retreats farther than it normally does. Twice a year the largest tides of all take place, at the spring and autumn equinoxes. As these extreme tides retreat parts of the lower shore that are not exposed at other times are revealed, giving you the opportunity to explore areas that are normally submerged. You might even come across a wreck.

Sand and dunes

Look for colour on the clifftops and among the dunes as spring flowers unfurl their petals. Among the first to appear will be annuals such as blue-flowered speedwells and white-flowered chickweeds, which gain a flying start by germinating the previous autumn. By April, gorse and broom make a glorious yellow show on some dunes, followed by the lilac blooms of sea rocket along the strandline, where the sea meets the land at high tide. Shingle beaches are often white with the blossom of sea campion.

Along some parts of the coast, sand has been blown inland to form dunes – banks at the back of the beach. But if the sand is light enough to be blown about on a landward breeze, why is it that these dunes rarely spread more than a few hundred metres inland? The answer is that the sand becomes fixed by vegetation. That is, it becomes bound up in a meshwork of plant roots and creeping stems.

Marram grass (as seen at Formby Sands in Lancashire, above) has the ability to grow through fresh sand after being buried. However, you will not see marram grass on the beach as it is killed by too much exposure to saltwater.

Behind the dunes you may find 'slacks', depressions where the sand is damp or even where there are shallow pools. Mounds of creeping willow, patches of rushes and carpets of moss cover much of the ground. You may see marsh orchids, too, pink flowers massed on leafy stalks, each with a nectar-filled spur at the back. Only long-tongued insects such as butterflies can reach this nectar from the perching platform on the lower lip of the flower.

Dunes to visit

These sand dunes are all rich with wildlife and many are SSSIs. In Scotland, machairs are coastal lowlands similar to dunes. To protect sand dunes, stick to board walks when they are provided.

The sand dune habitat is very like a desert – dry, at least near the surface, and poor in nutrients. Any rain percolates quickly through the sand, while the salt-laden wind blowing off the sea increases the problems of drought. Moreover, the unstable surface makes it difficult for seedlings to secure a foothold. So how do some plants manage to survive in the dunes? The answers are revealed when you study them closely.

How plants tame the dunes

Try walking inland from the beach over a well-developed dune system and observe how the vegetation changes as you move away from the sea.

Nearest the sea, the first plants you find may be growing on the strandline just within reach of high spring tides. The bits of rotting seaweed and other debris brought here by the tide provide just enough humus for some of the hardiest seashore plants to grow. Sea rocket, with its lilac flowers and divided fleshy leaves is common here. Break open a leaf and notice how moist it is inside. Like many dune plants, sea rocket stores water in its leaves.

Holding water *Up in the dunes, the succulent leaves of sea spurge hold on to precious moisture. Break open a leaf or stem and white latex will ooze out – this has a burning taste which rabbits avoid.*

THE DUNE FIXER

If sand is light enough to be blown on the breeze, why does it spread only a few hundred metres inland? The answer is that the sand becomes fixed by vegetation, bound up in a mesh of plant roots and buried stems that holds it firmly in place.

The most important dune-fixing plant is **marram grass**. Look at the bottom of a clump and you will find a tuft of dead leaf-bases formed in previous years. Grasses grow from the base not from the tips like other plants (see page 28) and in marram grass this enables the shoots to push upwards through sand – even when they have been buried – from regular points along its stems, at up to a metre a year. The covering of sand may even help to protect the new growth from the sun.

On the west coast, strong winds from the Atlantic carrying sand produce marram-fixed dunes up to 30m (100ft) high. If you could remove all this sand, leaving just the marram grass, you would discover a vast network of dead stems and roots representing decades of upward growth.

The build up of marram Over many years, as the clump of marram grass is repeatedly buried and regrows again, it builds an ever-taller sand dune around it (below). Its deep and extensive root system takes advantage of the porous nature of the sand: during the day, the sun heats up the surface layers and, since hot air rises, this effectively sucks up cooler, damper air from farther down in the dune. At night the moisture in the air condenses and the plant obtains most of its water from droplets formed in the sand.

STEP 1 Tufts of sea lyme grass (above) and sand couch grass have a distinctly bluish tinge and distinguish the **foredunes**, which lie between the tidal shore and the taller yellow dunes. These grasses have a waxy coating on their leaves, enabling them to tolerate drought. They fix sand with their roots, but as the dune grows in height, the more aggressive marram grass invades and out competes them.

STEP 2 Beyond the foredunes lie steeper, more dramatic dunes covered with marram grass. They are often called **yellow dunes** since most of the surface is still loose, open sand. If you look at a marram leaf in dry weather you will see it is tightly rolled. In this way the grass protects its vulnerable pores (stomata) through which water is lost, while exposing the tougher side of the leaf, with its thick waxy cuticle. If you go out after a shower of rain, you will discover that the leaves have unrolled in the moist air.

STEP 3 Behind the crests of the yellow dunes you may find a sheltered, completely contrasting area on the leeside. It is colonised mainly by mosses and greyish coloured lichens, like the cladonias and dog lichen, which give this zone its name: the **grey dunes**.

The lichens and mosses receive much of their water from dew, especially in spring and autumn when warm humid days give way to cold nights. But how do they survive in hot, dry weather? They deactivate, or shut down their life processes throughout the dry periods and appear as shrivelled-up scraps of vegetation, manufacturing food and growing again only when moister conditions return.

Early start *Sea mouse-ear germinates in autumn so it is ready to flower in early spring. The seeds then lie dormant through the dry summer.*

Dew drinker *Many lichens, such as this species of the genus* Cladonia, *can survive the arid conditions found in sand dunes by absorbing moisture from dew.*

STEP 4 Moisture is less of a problem in the next zone in your journey through the dunes: the **dune slacks**. Look for the hollows between the dunes which may be marshy or even contain shallow pools of fresh water. How can pools form in sand? Because the flat bottoms of these depressions lie close to the local water table. Look for mounds of creeping willow and carpets of mosses to confirm the presence of underground water; you may even find rushes and sedges in the hollows.

STEP 5 The final stage of the journey inland brings you to **stabilised dunes** behind the slacks. Here the dying vegetation of the slacks has built up a thick layer of humus and so the land can now support pasture grasses and bushes of flowering plants such as hawthorn. This last zone is often destined to become a golf course, reclaimed farmland, heathland or plantations of salt-tolerant trees such as the Corsican pine.

Seaside residence *Look out for rabbits on the dunes, particularly sunbathing in the morning. They often dig their warrens here as the sand is easy to excavate. Any tall plants you see near a warren are likely to be those that rabbits find unpalatable, such as sea spurge (opposite page), but their droppings provide essential nutrients for dune plants.*

How animals tame the dunes

On the first truly warm days of the year the dunes come to life as bees, butterflies and other insects pollinate the first flush of flowers. Toads spawn in pools in the dune slacks, and on some pebbly beaches terns begin to set up territory above the high-tide mark. For the full-time residents of the dunes, life's two most pressing problems are securing a relatively moist place out of the sun and finding enough food. The first is easily solved by burrowing into the sand. Getting enough to eat, however, calls for clever foraging or hunting techniques.

SOAKING UP THE SUN Be careful how you tread in the dunes, because you might come across sand lizards and snakes basking in the sunshine. They need to spend time in the sun to warm up their cold-blooded bodies.

Sand lizards (inset below) are often found sunbathing on top of a tussock of grass; the tussock offers the lizard good camouflage and also gives it a panoramic view of approaching predators such as snakes, foxes or weasels. Another advantage of grassy tussocks is that they elevate the lizard off the scorching sand when the sun is at its hottest. Watch how a lizard on hot stone or sand lifts its feet one at a time to give them some respite from the blistering heat.

For the best chance of spotting basking lizards or snakes go out to the dunes in the morning, before the sun gets too hot, or in the early evening. Both creatures tend to return to their dens from noon until about 6pm.

Adders wait out the warmth of the midday sun in abandoned rabbit burrows or cool crevices. A female (below) can be distinguished by her colouring: a dull brown with poorly defined zigzag markings, as opposed to the strongly contrasting pale grey and black of the male's markings. A female adder bears live young – a dozen or more at a time – but leaves them almost immediately to fend for themselves.

Finding insects in sand dunes is difficult, since most are good at hiding themselves away. You will need to look for clues associated with the way they live. If you spot half-moon shaped sections missing from the leaves of a dune plant, it is likely to be the work of the coastal leaf-cutter bee. Look around for a dark bee slightly larger than a honeybee. It is the female that cuts out neat pieces of leaf with her large mandibles to construct the nest. The bee's favourite plant is water mint, so the place to start your search is in the wet dune slacks where this plant grows.

Tiring work *A coastal female leaf-cutter bee takes a break from cutting leaves with its strong mandibles to drink some sugary nectar from a restharrow flower. If you come across one of these small bees carrying a piece of leaf curled up under its body, follow it carefully and it may lead you to its nest hole in the dunes.*

Agile hunters

Should you see a small, silvery grey or black-and-red wasp dragging a spider along the sand, it is likely to be a female spider-hunting wasp. It is taking its live prey (paralysed by its sting) to a nest chamber in a burrow somewhere nearby. The spider will be food for a single wasp larva. There are many other hunting wasps, some of which emerge later in the year.

The black-and-yellow field digger wasp resembles a garden wasp, but has a more delicate body and flattened abdomen. It hunts flies and carries its prey beneath its body. If you follow it you may see it reach its nest-burrow, which is often on the side of a hollow or sandpit.

Double take

If you see what appears to be a double insect flying low over the dunes or hovering at the entrance to a nest hole, you are most likely to have found *Oxybelus uniglumis*. This striking wasp has a dumpy, triangular body, marked with zebra stripes of black and white. It carries its prey impaled behind on its sting, like a cocktail sausage. The paralysed fly, which is often larger than the wasp, is always carried upside-down with its legs in the air.

Where to look for beetles

Some distinctive beetles inhabit the dunes in spring, and can be found fairly easily if you know where to look. On short turf containing bedstraw you may see the black-humped form of the bloody-nosed beetle bumbling along. The 'blood' is a red defensive fluid the beetle sometimes exudes from its

Take-away meals *The sand digger wasp (above) specialises in hunting non-hairy caterpillars. It can be attracted to picnic food, but do not panic – in spite of its black and orange markings it is harmless to humans. Like the spider-hunting wasp (left), it drags the paralysed prey into its burrow as food for its developing larvae.*

DUNE AMPHIBIAN April to June is a good time to spot the rare **natterjack toad**, now found more often in dunes than anywhere else, especially in north-west England, south-west Scotland and East Anglia. Look for it in its breeding areas: the shallow pools of dune slacks, preferably on open sandy ground with little vegetation. If you visit a likely pool in the late evening you may hear the loud croaking chorus of males. Natterjacks are smaller and less warty than common toads, with compact bodies and a prominent yellow stripe running down their backs. They survive the arid dune environment by secreting mucus from glands in their skins to keep them moist. They are good diggers and can disappear beneath the sand in a few seconds. During the day they hide in these burrows, often made on a steep bank, emerging just before dusk.

Any dead tadpoles you find at the bottom of a dried-out pool are casualties of the natterjack's high-risk breeding strategy. The toad lays its strings of eggs in shallow pools and these can quickly dry out in a spell of hot weather. Well-meaning conservationists have sometimes deepened spawning pools to prevent this, but with disastrous results. Not only is the natterjack toad a surprisingly poor swimmer, but deep pools soon acquire predators, as well as common toads with which the natterjack seems unable to compete.

The natterjack is a protected species, which must not be caught or disturbed, but you can visit their ponds by torchlight, and watch them spawn, the male tightly clinging to the larger female with his darkly pigmented nuptial pads.

mouth if it senses danger. If you look closely you will see that its wing-cases are fused, making it unable to fly.

Above the strandline, or in the dune slacks, is where you will find *Broscus cephalotes*. This black, shiny ground beetle with prominent hooked jaws builds a burrow where it lies in wait for its prey. You can sometimes find it by lifting stones in places where rotting seaweed has blown up from the shore. One of the creatures it preys upon is the coastal bristletail, which forages along the strandline. Look for a rapidly moving insect like a silverfish, with three long tails and even longer antennae.

Keeping watch... *When her eggs are nearly ready to hatch the female nursery web spider (right) places her egg sac in a protective silken tent tethered to a plant in the dune slacks. She then stands on guard until the spiderlings emerge.*

How to spot spiders

You may see dune spiders running fast over the strandline and other places where small insects congregate. The grey speckled dune wolf spider is visible when it is on the move, but virtually impossible to spot against the sand when at rest. The effect is of a spider becoming alternately visible and invisible. Another good place to look is among tufts of marram grass, whose interiors are cooler and slightly more humid than the surrounding air. Some species of spider live only in this microhabitat.

Close-up on
Rock pools

On a warm spring day a rock pool may seem a peaceful natural aquarium. But rock pool life is not always tranquil: at low tide the water may heat up and become oxygen deficient (oxygen is absorbed more effectively by cold water), or the pool may be picked over by gulls and other sea birds. And as the tide turns and waves roll over the pool, what was once a placid environment becomes a swirling Jacuzzi. How do plants and animals survive in such challenging conditions? And what prevents the tide from washing everything away?

The demands of rock pool living differ according to where on the shore the pool is situated. Pools near the top of the beach are left exposed by the outgoing tide for longer periods than those farther down. They may then be diluted by rain, or become more saline as the sea water evaporates in the sun. Their temperature also fluctuates with the weather and the time of day. Only a handful of plants and animals can survive in such extreme conditions.

Pools at the bottom of the beach, however, are more like lagoons and may stay in contact with the sea even at low tide. Because they are more stable, the life they support is more abundant and varied.

What you can expect to find living in a rock pool also depends on the strength of the twice-daily wave action it receives. You'll discover that a rock pool on a fairly level shore experiences gentle waves and so has a richer flora and fauna than a pool on a steep shore where the incoming tide hits the rocks with a smack that sweeps away anything that is not firmly attached.

STAYING PUT All except the most sheltered rock pools are scoured by the tide. Yet if you revisit a pool after the next tide, you generally find it much as you left it. Why don't the seaweeds and animals get flushed away? Because they cling fast or hide in crannies.

Seaweeds are a sort of algae. Some of the most common red seaweeds escape the pull of the current by lining the pool as a flat carpet or crust. A pink and white coating on the rocks is likely to be either ***Lithothamnion*** (inset left) or *Lithophyllum*.

Forming a fringe around the edge of a rock pool, you may see tufts of the delicate lilac-coloured seaweed ***Corallina*** (inset below right). Rub a frond between your finger and thumb and it will feel gritty. Through a hand lens you will be able to see that this is because of its coral-like skeleton of calcium carbonate. Though it can cope with changes in salinity of water, *Corallina* cannot withstand exposure to the air. When it dies, the white calcium carbonate skeleton remains – look for it at the bottom of the pool.

Sea anemones hang on to rocks by suction. The species you are most likely to see is the **beadlet sea anemone** (above). Some, like the one on the left in picture, will have unfurled their tentacles to sting and capture food. Others, like the one on right in picture and any exposed to the air, will be closed. The snakelocks anemone cannot survive in air and you will only see it in pools that never empty. In shallow pools where light penetrates, the tentacles of this naturally brown anemone are coloured green by algae that help the creature to manufacture food by photosynthesis.

HOW SHAPE PROTECTS

Lift a clump of seaweed or peek under a rock and you may find a crab. Its flattened body enables it to scuttle into shady crevices to avoid the tidal currents or to hide when it feels threatened. Sometimes when two crabs meet they will fight – stay quiet and you can watch their gladiatorial combat.

The crab you are most likely to see around a rock pool is the common shore crab. Unlike other crabs, the shore crab can live in diluted sea water in pools high up the beach by altering the salt balance of its own body. It does swim, but its legs are better adapted for walking and you may see one scuttling across the rocks.

If you see a periwinkle or a whelk that appears to be moving on legs over rocks and seaweed, you have discovered a hermit crab. It lives in the empty shell of another creature because it lacks a complete shell of its own. Look to see if there is anything unusual attached to it: the shells are sometimes covered with small sea anemones or sea firs.

These hitchhiking sea anemones offer the protection of their stinging tentacles, while taking some of the food of the hermit crab in return.

Beachcombers Both the shore crab (above) and hermit crab (right) are great scavengers. The shore crab will eat anything of a suitable size, dead or alive, but the hermit crab only eats dead organic matter.

FISHY ADAPTATIONS You may be surprised how many fish you can find in a rock pool. Most will dash for cover if they see you but if you can make yourself less obvious, by lying down on a rock, they will often reappear. Some, like the shanny, can be tempted out with morsels of food such as small snails or sea slaters (see page 80).

The fish best adapted to life in rock pools often have the ability to cling tightly to the rocks with the aid of a sucker. Gently lift up a stone and you may find a warty **lumpfish** (right) clinging on using the sucker on its belly.

Fish marooned in an isolated rock pool often have excellent camouflage to protect them from predatory sea birds. The **shanny** (right) changes colour to match its surroundings and can disappear from view in the blink of an eye.

An eel-like shape enables species such as the **butterfish** (inset left) to hide in tight crevices and between or under rocks. This yellowy brown fish also has slimy skin like an eel, enabling it to slip easily from the jaws of a predator or escape between the fingers of someone fishing in the pool.

Entering the tidal zone

The coastline of Britain is strongly influenced by the tides. Between the sea and dry land there is a section of beach – the intertidal zone – that is covered by water at high tide, but increasingly exposed to the air as the tide goes out. On rocky shores you will find much of this zone covered by what appears to be a uniform layer of seaweed. Taker a closer look and you will find that several different species of seaweed are arranged in broad bands across the beach.

What creates the colours? *Cliff headlands shelter a beach composed of rocks and sand in this Cornish cove. As the tide goes out, black channelled wrack and green sea lettuces are seen clinging to the exposed rocks, while a thick blackish band of lichen marks the splash zone along the cliff face.*

Along the top of the beach, where the sea hardly touches the land, you will find very few plants growing. This is known as the splash zone, the most inhospitable region of all – too salty for most land plants and too dry for seaweeds. You may occasionally see patches of thrift or samphire which establish themselves here, protected by their waxy, succulent leaves. But the only plants that really thrive in this region are lichens.

Spot different lichens

Lichens are exceptionally hardy and adapted to growing on bare substrates like rock. The absence of other plants on this part of the shore gives lichens their chance to take hold. There are three common species, with contrasting colours. You will often find them in bands, like the layers of a sponge cake, because their tolerance to salt varies. The black *Verrucaria maura* grows nearest to the sea and can be mistaken for tar stains; above it you may see an orange band of *Caloplaca*, and farther up still a yellow band of *Xanthoria*, often merging into greenish *Ramalina siliquosa* and grey *Lecanora*.

Below the splash zone lies the upper shore, which is covered by sea water at high tide only. Everything that lives here must be able to cope with exposure to the air for most of the day. Even so, the rocks are often plastered with seaweed.

Why is seaweed slimy?

Anyone who has tried to walk across seaweed will be familiar with its slimy surface. This not only saves the seaweed from drying out but also prevents other plants from growing on it.

The most common species found at the top of the shore is channelled wrack, a small, dark-coloured seaweed, divided into narrow fronds, each with a moisture-retaining channel. If you part the mass of weed you

Just add sea water *Channelled wrack is able to withstand exposure to the air. Out of the water it is brittle and black but turns browny green (left) when wetted by the sea.*

will be able to see how it sticks itself to the rocks with a cluster of branches known as a holdfast.

Roughly in the middle of the shore you will see bladder wrack and flat, or spiral wrack. Both seaweeds have flat fronds which cover the rock; those of flat wrack have a smooth edge while the fronds of bladder wrack have a wavy edge and air bladders on either side of a midrib.

Closer to the sea the rocks are the home of serrated wrack. This seaweed does not have bladders and its edges are toothed, as its name implies. It is not found farther up the beach because it cannot survive lengthy periods out of water. You can usually see it hanging in dense masses from rocks at low tide. Look out too for tangled lengths of another lower shore seaweed, known as mermaid's tresses (*Chorda filum*), and the button-like beginnings of thongweed, which later sprouts two strap-like fronds.

LOOK IN CALMER WATERS On the shores of sheltered bays you may come across a large, yellowish brown seaweed with single air bladders, the size of a thumbnail, forming knots along a narrow frond. This is **knotted wrack**. It is too bulky and easily damaged to survive the heavy wave action of exposed beaches. But unlike some of its relatives it can tolerate the muddy conditions of estuaries.

Signs of a forest *After a storm look for loose kelp fronds washed up on the beach. These indicate that there is an underwater kelp forest nearby. Go back after a spring tide and you may see the kelp beds exposed. Kelp casts off an old frond and grows a new one every year, but the stem is perennial and long-lived. By cutting across the stalk of a piece of kelp cast on the shore you can count the annual growth rings, like those on a tree trunk.*

Beach bands *There are many types of seaweed on the beach. Bladder* **[1]** *and spiral wrack* **[2]** *are found mainly around the mid tide zone, while serrated wrack* **[3]** *grows closer to the low-tide mark.*

Surviving until the sea returns

Turn over the masses of seaweed and examine the crannies of rocks and you will be surprised at how many different types of animal you can find living there. Most have hard shells which prevent them from drying out at low tide, as well as protecting them from predators. Many are secured firmly to the rocks and you will not be able to remove them – they need this strong anchorage to survive the scouring action of the waves.

You have to search carefully in the cracks to find any animals in the splash zone as only those that can find shelter in the rocks or tiny pools can survive in this harsh environment. At the top of the beach you may come across the small periwinkle, its tiny shell covered in a grape-like bloom. It survives here because it can feed on land, as long as it is slightly damp, and in the open air, although it still needs the sea to breed. But what do these creatures gain by living in such a hostile place? Probably two things: there is plenty of food to be found among the tidal debris and relative freedom from competition and predators.

After sunset
As dusk approaches sea slaters – creatures resembling large flat wood lice – scuttle across damp rocks in the splash zone.

Another common inhabitant of the upper shore is the acorn barnacle. The rocks are often covered with them, their hinged plates shut tight when the water recedes. Barnacles start feeding as soon as the incoming tide covers them, when their hinged plates open and they use their legs (cirri) to filter plankton and organic debris for food. You might be able to see them in action underwater on a calm day if you lean carefully over a sea wall or pier to which barnacles are attached.

Secret of the limpet's grip

Limpets, too, are able to hug tight to the rock using a muscular foot shaped like a suction pad. Grasp a limpet with your hand and you will feel the muscle go into action. They wait out the low tide with their shells clamped down, fitting neatly into a groove worn into the rock. Only when the tide is in do they move about, browsing on algae from the rock surface. Another grazer characteristic of this region of the beach is the rough periwinkle (its shell feels rough to the touch). The hard 'door' at the entrance to the shell is there to seal in moisture.

While searching for barnacles and periwinkles, you may come across a strange purplish, translucent film stretched over rocks. This is *Porphyra umbilicalis*, an edible seaweed.

Closer to the sea

Walk down to the middle of the beach and you will notice that the signs of life become more abundant. Animals and plants living here are nearer the sea and so suffer less from drying out, although they have to withstand the onslaught of marine predators such as starfish. Some of the force of the waves is cushioned by the masses of seaweed found here.

One easy-to-find resident of the middle shore is the common

A limpet comes unstuck Springtails gather to feed on an upturned limpet. These tiny bluish grey creatures scavenge for dead organic matter along the strandline and in isolated pools, helping to clear the beach of debris.

Parking place Grooves in the rock show where limpets travel – up to 1m (3ft) – in search of food at high tide. They always return to clamp tightly to the same spot and because they can live for 16 years, this eventually wears away a small depression.

or edible periwinkle, a robust species with concentric dark lines on its shell. It lives both on rocks and seaweed.

Delicate seaweeds

Closer still to the sea, you will come across the red seaweeds, perhaps the most beautiful plants to be found on the lower shore. Many are difficult to identify but a deep red, narrow-branched seaweed that looks like a little leafless shrub is probably *Ceramium rubrum*. Another, dulse – which is sometimes gathered for food – has flat, lobed blades of purplish red.

You may also see tufts of carragheen or irish moss, a dark red seaweed with flat, branching fronds. This produces a vegetable gelatin that is often used for thickening ice cream and sauces. Most red seaweeds, however, are confined to deeper pools or grow only below the low-water mark, because they are too delicate to withstand drying or direct sunlight.

HOW TO PRESERVE SEAWEEDS

Seaweeds, especially the smaller red and green ones, can easily be pressed to make a collection, which is an excellent way of learning to identify them. Even if you can't reach the lower shore, where most of the red species grow, you can usually find a few pieces washed up in the strandline. Only collect small amounts since seaweed does not keep well. Carry your specimens in a plastic bag to prevent them from drying out, and press them as soon as possible.

You will need the following equipment: watercolour paper, a shallow dish or bowl, a small paintbrush, a pencil, some gauze (or nappy liners) and lots of newspaper.

Step 1 Label a sheet of watercolour paper in pencil, stating where and when you found the seaweed. Float the seaweed in a tray of water and slip the watercolour paper underneath it.

Step 2 Using the paintbrush, gently spread out the fronds. Then carefully drain off the water.

Step 3 Cover the seaweed with gauze, or a nappy liner, and place it between sheets of newspaper.

Step 4 Weigh the pressing down with books. Change the newspaper every day to aid drying and after a week the seaweed should be ready for display. Exhibit the pressing in a protective clear plastic wallet, or frame it.

Bladder match The flat periwinkle is often found on bladder wrack, its smooth flattish shape resembling the seaweed's bladders and so providing camouflage. It comes in a variety of colours, including yellow and olive green (above).

Frond find Examine the fronds of wrack and kelp and you may see the small white tubes of *Spirorbis borealis*, a filter-feeding worm. If the wrack is under water, use a hand lens to see if you can spot the worms' tiny tentacles protruding from the tubes.

Early spring ends suburban hibernation

Grey streets transformed as trees burst into blossom

Spring arrives early in the city. Traffic, street lights and centrally heated buildings all pump out heat, raising the temperature in large cities to several degrees higher than in the surrounding countryside. In streets, parks and gardens, and on wasteland, native trees and shrubs such as dogwood, hawthorn, oak and rowan come into leaf or begin to flower, and hibernating animals such as the hedgehog emerge from their winter sleep some weeks earlier than their rural relatives. The milder climate also allows cultivated plant species from warmer regions of the world to flourish in Britain's suburban gardens and municipal parkland, particularly in southern cities where severe frosts are rare.

New trees for old

Among the most popular spring-flowering trees are the cherries (above), introduced to Britain from Japan. The cherry has few animal visitors, but some insects take its flower nectar and aphids feast on the new leaves. You may see ants climbing cherry trees to milk the aphids of their honeydew.

Another common street tree is the London plane. This was widely planted in the early 20th century upon the realisation that it can resist soot by shedding slabs of dirty bark to expose a fresh layer beneath.

Now that the reduction in coal-burning has made this characteristic less important, a wider range of trees is planted in our streets. Species such as alder, aspen, field maple, hornbeam, lime, mountain ash, silver birch, whitebeam, white poplar and the native bird cherry all support insects, plants and fungi.

The caterpillars of the brown-tail moth are voracious feeders and are capable of stripping the leaves from cherry trees, lime, buckthorn, hawthorn and plum.

These in turn, attract other wildlife, so that a diverse, thriving natural community develops, based on the street tree.

The false acacia, originally from North America, is another useful urban tree. It grows rapidly in the city environment, and this, plus its ability to add nitrogen to the soil, has led to it being planted on land scarred by old industry. You can also see grey squirrels feeding on its bark in early spring.

Flower displays

Parks are the best place to see the showy spires of horse chestnut flowers in spring (above). The sticky buds and leaves are insect-repellent, but the flowers have a pattern, visible in ultra-violet light, which can be seen by bees and butterflies but not by humans. When a flower is fertilised, the spots change colour, telling the bees to look for nectar in a fresh flower and thus ensuring pollination of as many flowers as possible.

The more modest white blossom of hawthorn is most often seen in roadside and garden hedges. It is a typical hedgerow plant and it often indicates where an old country hedge has been incorporated as the town spread outwards. Hawthorn gives refuge to nesting birds in spring, such as the magpie, which weaves its ball-shaped nest within the protection of the spines.

Check in urban hedges for other hedgerow shrubs such as blackthorn, dogwood, guelder rose and spindle – easy to identify by their spring blossom – and for trees such as elm, field maple and oak, whose presence may indicate an ancient rural boundary. These remnants of a past landscape make ideal wildlife corridors: watch out for hedgehogs in early evening. Give them some tinned cat food and water and you might be rewarded with a sighting of a litter in late spring.

Blue tits forage on the flowers and fresh leaves of horse chestnuts for insects, a useful source of food at the start of the breeding season.

The buzzing of the bees

The springtime explosion of blossom has just one purpose: to attract insects so that they will distribute the plants' pollen. This is essential to ensure that flowers are fertilised and will fruit and set seed to produce next year's young plants. As you walk through any park or garden in spring you will notice it is humming with insect pollinators: bumblebees, honeybees and solitary bees are particularly effective. Pollinating insects are also a source of food for birds, helping to maintain the ecological balance of the urban environment.

The first bees you see in any number will probably be honeybees, which have lived through the winter feeding on their reserves of honey. Colonies of bumblebees die out at the end of summer and only the new queens, full of fertilised eggs, hibernate. In early spring you may see a large new queen meandering through the garden in solitary flight. After feeding on nectar she begins searching for a new nest site. Watch her hover along hedge bottoms and grassy banks – she is looking for a suitable hole or disused burrow.

Apart from honeybees and bumblebees, most of the 250 species of British bees live solitary lives, although some nest so close to one another that they appear to be members of a colony. The first species of solitary bees to appear in spring will have survived the winter in their natal nest.

Hole searcher The red mason bee makes its nest in cavities in brick walls, hollow stems and even keyholes, using mud to seal in its grubs.

Tireless workers? *The image of bumblebees as expert pollinators is not true of the males: since they only need to feed themselves, they often loiter for hours at a time at a single flower.*

WASP WATCHING

Should you find an unusually large wasp in your garden in early spring, it is likely to be a queen of the common wasp. She will be looking for a nest site for her first batch of eggs.

A good place to look for wasp nests is in a hole in the ground or in the corner of a shed or loft. It is best to be cautious as you approach, as wasps will fiercely defend their nests.

TAKING A CUTTING Neat semi-circular sections cut out of the leaves of your roses is evidence of the **leaf-cutter bee**. This bee uses the leaf segments to make nest cells. The female glues 10-15 pieces of leaf together to make a thimble-sized well which she packs with pollen and nectar and then lays an egg on top.

WASPS IN THE HOUSE Wasps often make their **communal nests** in lofts (inset below). These intricate constructions are made from chewed wood.

A **queen wasp** (below) gathers dead wood from a fence to make her nest. She chews it into a pulp to make into thin papery sheets and spreads these layer upon layer to build the nest. You can hear the scraping sound made by a wasp as it collects wood from a yard away. The pale patches of newly exposed timber also reveal where wasps have been collecting nest material.

Though wasps visit flowers for nectar, they more usually live as carnivores. They prey on insects, some of which are classed as pests, and feed on carrion, thus helping to clean up the garden.

Sting alert

When you are investigating bees and wasps, don't get too close as honeybees and wasps both sting. They inject a venom that contains pheromones, powerful scents that incite other members of the colony to also attack. So if a bee or wasp stings you, move well away or go inside before any others join in.

The sting of most honeybees is barbed and gets hooked into the skin with the poison sac and muscle still attached, pumping in the venom. As the bee flies off, part of its abdomen is torn away with the sting, and the bee dies.

A wasp has an unbarbed sting, which it can use repeatedly. The same is true of queen honeybees and bumblebee workers and queens, although bees are generally less aggressive than wasps. The strength of a bumblebee's sting depends on the species. However, the stings of solitary species of bees and wasps are generally too weak even to penetrate human skin.

There are other insects that resemble small wasps or bees, but are completely harmless to humans. These include hover flies and conopid flies.

Prolific hunters *Wasps live by feeding on other insects: this one is devouring a hover fly, whose colours mimic those of the wasp for camouflage. It may fool birds, but a wasp is not deceived.*

First flutters of spring

One of the most delightful indications of spring in the urban landscape is your first sighting of a butterfly on the wing. Butterflies lay their eggs in neglected parkland, overgrown cemeteries, roadside verges and inaccessible corners of gardens, where caterpillars emerge in the spring sunshine to feed on succulent young leaves. The caterpillars, in turn, attract the attention of hungry birds, which are constantly burning up energy as they look for mates and build their nests.

The first butterflies to look out for in spring are those that hibernate through the winter as adults and are tempted out by the warmth of the spring sunshine. Two species, the peacock and small tortoiseshell, spend the winter in the shelter of garden sheds and garages. If you venture in for the mower early in the season, you may find them fluttering among the cobwebs and crashing against the windows, trying to escape towards the sunlight.

Once in the open, they use their sense of smell to find the particular food plant their caterpillars will need: look for them flying upwind in search of the newly unfurling leaves. Peacocks and small tortoiseshells head for patches of nettles on which to lay their eggs. If you find the caterpillars, look on the stems of the plant for a tiny, wasp-like insect. This is an ichneumon wasp: it lays its eggs on or in the caterpillars and when its grubs hatch, they eat their helpless hosts.

Year-round butterfly

The yellow brimstone is the only British butterfly you may see all year round, but it is most obvious in spring when it is looking for a mate and for a buckthorn or alder buckthorn bush to lay its eggs on.

After a sudden chill, you may notice that all the brimstones have disappeared. This is because their tiny green larvae will eat only buckthorn leaves, so if there is a drop in temperature, the brimstones go back into semi-hibernation to wait

SAFETY IN NUMBERS The eggs of the **small tortoiseshell butterfly** (inset below) hatch into spiny black-and-yellow caterpillars, which live in clusters (right). If you disturb them you will see the caterpillars start a synchronised head-waving movement, evolved to deter predators.

HIDDEN IN THE LEAVES You will have to look hard to spot a **brimstone butterfly** (inset right) resting in ivy: the veins on the underside of their wings hide them well. Their green caterpillars (below) are also perfectly camouflaged against the leaves of host plants.

HOLLY AND IVY In spring, the first **holly blue butterflies** (inset right) feed on holly and lay their eggs on the leaves. But when, by late summer, the caterpillars (right) have developed into a second generation of butterflies, the females choose ivy as the plant on which to lay their eggs.

for better weather when the bush will be in full leaf and egg-laying can resume.

Visitor to the vegetable patch

The sight of tiny white eggs on the leaves of an allotment cabbage will make a gardener's heart sink. They will hatch into caterpillars that will feed on the crop. The caterpillars become small white butterflies, which are the most abundant species found in vegetable patches. You can see the first small whites flying between March and May.

MASTER OF DISGUISE To protect itself from predation, the **comma butterfly** has developed a cunning disguise for each stage of its life cycle. The solitary caterpillar looks like a bird dropping; the pupa (above) resembles a furled leaf; and the adult butterfly – when at rest or in hibernation – uses its ragged-edged, brown wings to mimic a dead leaf.

EARLY BIRDS

The first songster you hear in town as winter turns to spring is likely to be the mistle thrush. It begins singing in the harsh weather of January and seems to delight in trying to out-do the noise of the traffic. This handsome bird stands very upright and is larger than a song thrush, with pale edges to its wing feathers and white corners to its tail feathers.

The tiny warbler, the chiffchaff, turns up in March. Most are newly arrived from North Africa and the Mediterranean, but small numbers overwinter in Britain, especially in the warmer urban areas, feeding at bird tables.

Red nets preferred

Redpolls and siskins are other relative newcomers to Britain which can be seen in our gardens in late winter and early spring. Redpolls usually visit in small groups; they are brown and streaked, with a red forehead. Siskins are small, green-and-yellow treaked finches and descend on gardens in ones and twos. They particularly like to feed on peanuts slung from plastic nets by the bird table, seeming to prefer red nets, and often hang upside-down to feed.

Watch out for male siskins courting: they perform a series of acrobatics that shows off their brilliant yellow plumage.

Car-park cafeteria

The pied wagtail has also learnt to benefit from the human environment. If you see a two-tone bird with a long tail walking around your local car park, its tail wagging up and down, head moving backwards and forwards, it is a pied wagtail. This species finds easy pickings foraging under vehicles for frazzled insects which fall off car radiators, and may even flutter up inside the engine bay to pick off insects stuck to the radiator.

Q **I saw a bird that looked like a white blackbird. What was it?**

A Occasionally a bird is born without the normal pigment in some of its plumage. Some are completely white, with pink eyes, but often the condition is partial. It is commonly seen in blackbirds (below) and crows, especially in towns. This may be because the white colouring, which makes it an easy target for predators in open countryside, is less of a handicap in built-up areas. But even if such a bird survives and breeds, its offspring will not necessarily show the trait.

On track *The pied wagtail settles on railway lines and roads to gather dead insects.*

In a flap *The male dunnock, a small brown bird, similar in size to a house sparrow, is galvanised into frantic, aggressive wing-flapping should another male invade his territory. The dunnock will even peck out a rival's sperm from a female before he mates with her himself.*

Close-up on

The dawn chorus

As winter retreats, nothing lifts the spirits of the city-dweller more than hearing the melodious chorus of early morning birdsong, which can begin at 4am in the South. Although the pavements are still grey, and the parks and gardens bare and muddy, just before dawn first one male bird and then another sings at the top of his voice to attract a female to join him and to warn off rivals.

City birds sing rather than show off in some other way – such as performing dramatic display flights – since most of the small birds that have found a home here once lived in woodland and scrub. Such birds are generally subdued in colour and depend on the strength of their voice to find a mate because activities such as display flights are impossible in the woodland canopy.

The chorus starts at dawn for practical reasons. One is that the light is not yet strong enough to allow predators to pinpoint the whereabouts of the singer. An early start also means that the chorus does not cut into valuable feeding time. Most songbirds are primarily insect-eaters, at least in the breeding season, and they find it hard to detect their prey when the light is poor. Low temperatures also mean few insects are active. The air at dawn is often still so their songs carry far and wide.

Song thrush A variety of short phrases are repeated in a loud, clear voice, such as ***Did he do it? Did he do it? Philip, philip, philip*** and ***quick, quick, quick***.

Robin The passionate cascade of liquid warbling mixed with shriller notes and abrupt changes in pitch and tempo come from the robin. It is exceptional as it sings all year round, with both sexes using their voices.

Blackbird The rich melodious song of the blackbird has a flute-like quality. Various phrases are performed, without the repetition that typifies a song thrush.

SINGING IN TURNS

No two dawn choruses are ever quite the same: which birds take part and the order in which they begin to sing will vary, but the blackbird is usually the first voice you will hear, followed by the song thrush, perched high up in the trees or on a TV aerial. Next come the robin and the surprisingly loud warble of little wrens. The dunnock likes to sing its clear high notes from the protection of a hedge or shrub and it is easy to recognise the soft cooing of the wood pigeon. You will know if a mistle thrush has joined in from the top of its tree because its wild disjointed song is particularly noisy.

Gradually the chorus intensifies with the thin trill of a bluetit in flight, the shrill ***tea-cher tea-cher*** call of a great tit and the cheerful song of a chaffinch. Less easy on the ear is the call of the house sparrow. Not known for the quality of their 'song', house sparrows make up for it in enthusiasm and volume.

A tawny owl may join in with a series of quavering hoots, and on the edge of town you might hear a pheasant; its distinctive double crow accompanied by the rattling of its wing quills.

TUNING IN

To help you pick out each song, listen to a good-quality recording at home, preferably one that begins with a full dawn chorus then isolates the individual birds. There are some excellent recordings on the market or you may be able to borrow them from the library (the sound is clearest on CD). Listen to the recording several times, then go out in the garden and see if you can pick out which bird is which.

Remember that some species, such as the chaffinch and blackbird, sing in regional dialects and may not match the recording exactly.

Find a good spot
The best place for city-dwellers to hear the dawn chorus is where there are some trees and plenty of scrubby bushes – in back gardens, squares or parks. Cemeteries are particularly good places to listen because churchyard yews and gravestones provide the birds with song posts. Go an hour before sunrise to make sure you are in position before the start of the chorus, which should last at least half an hour.

Wildlife trusts and the RSPB provide information about local outings to hear the dawn chorus at its best in late April and May (see page 339 for telephone numbers).

Q In the words of the song, could I hear a nightingale sing in Berkeley Square?

A No, you won't find a nightingale in town because this shy bird lives in woodland, where cover is provided by dense undergrowth. A bird singing at night in the city is probably a blackbird or a robin. These birds take advantage of street lighting to continue singing late into the night, proclaiming their territories and warning off potential rivals.

Dunnock A cheerful, high-pitched, hurried-sounding series of broken warbling phrases comes from the dunnock.

Mistle thrush If you hear a bird in full song during rain, it is likely to be the mistle thrush, also known as the storm cock. Its loud song is wilder than a blackbird's, with broken phrases consisting of three to six short notes followed by a pause.

Wood pigeon This bird makes a throaty muffled call of five notes, ***woo coooo coo, coo-coo***, emphasising the second note.

Wren Listen for its low ***tic tic*** calls before an explosion of clear, high-pitched warbling notes mixed with (and usually ending on) intense, rattling trills.

Late call The spring migrants rise later than the permanent residents and the first to join in is often the chiffchaff, soon followed by a wistful, rippling cascade of sound from the willow warbler (right).

If you think you heard a lapwing, curlew or golden oriole in the city, you've probably just been duped by a starling. These common town birds are excellent mimics.

Take a look at park life

Ornamental lakes and ponds in towns and cities, designed to please the human eye, have become the homes of water birds, particularly ducks, swans and geese. On the outskirts of most cities there are also reservoirs or flooded sandpits and clay workings – dug to provide building materials for the town as it grew – and these offer further habitats for all kinds of water birds. For many city youngsters feeding the ducks in the park is their earliest close contact with wildlife.

What could be a better way of studying ducks than feeding them at the local park? Urban ducks are tame and trusting of people – some will take food from the hand – unlike rural ducks, which are more wary of human contact. Although you will see park ducks fighting for the scraps of bread and biscuits you throw to them, this is not their natural diet. Left to forage on their own, they are keen grazers, eating grass, algae (microscopic green plants that grow as slime on ponds), some insects and seeds, and even tadpoles and spawn.

Study your local ducks and you'll notice they have different ways of finding their food. Dabbling ducks, such as the mallard, carry their tails high out of the water and have long necks which enable them to lower their heads to feed, filtering water and mud to sieve out tiny food particles with their broad, flattened bills. Where the bottom is deeper, they 'up-end', with just their tails sticking up out of the water and stretch their long necks to reach the food below, paddling with their webbed feet to stay in position.

Q **I saw a duck wandering around a supermarket car park. What was it doing?**

A On rainy days ducks can sometimes be found wandering round car parks, confused by the reflection from the wet tarmac into thinking it is water – often with fatal results.

You won't see the tail of a diving duck, such as the tufted duck, up-ended in this fashion because it submerges and swims under water to feed. It is more streamlined, with a shorter neck than a dabbling duck. Diving ducks plunge to the bottom of ponds and lakes to pick up weed and algae, or to fish for frogs, spawn, small fish and insects.

Having a dabble *The bill of the shoveler (above) is lined with tiny spines which trap insects and seeds as water is filtered. A jet-black stern with a white streak (left), tells you that the up-ended duck is a male mallard, feeding on the bottom; curly black feathers confirm it. A greyish tail on a black stern indicates a male gadwall.*

ON TRIAL If you see a female mallard flying with one or more drakes in spring, you're watching a nuptial flight test, which she conducts to find the fittest male to father her brood. The one demonstrating the best aeronautical skills will be allowed to follow her to the nest site. Mallards are ungainly birds on land, but superb fliers, with wings so powerful they can take off almost vertically from the water.

Three's a crowd When a female duck leaves her nest to feed you may see her being mobbed by a number of drakes. She may even be drowned in the mêlée. This happens because there are fewer females than males, since many females are taken by predators while incubating eggs. Even when he has failed the flying test, you can still see a drake without a partner chasing a female, trying to separate her from her mate.

WHY DO PEACOCKS WAIL?

Nobody forgets the first time they hear a peacock. The raucous call, which sounds like a very loud mewing wail, is made by the male to proclaim his territory and you are most likely to hear it early in the morning or late in the evening. If you can't see the bird, look up: peafowl are not confined to the ground and often roost in trees.

You'll find it harder to spot the peahen. Although she is almost as big as a goose, her dull green and grey plumage offers excellent camouflage, even in urban areas, and your best chance of seeing one is to keep an eye on the male bird in the hope that you might spot a female nearby.

All for show *The best time to see a peacock displaying his stunning plumage is during the breeding season, which lasts from spring to early summer.*

Wild living

The peacocks you see in urban parkland are semi-wild and self-sufficient. They may be fed on grain, but will eat park vegetation and insects.

Peacocks frequently escape into the wild and have managed to adapt well to the British environment. However, they are prone to losing chicks in wet British summers, and usually manage to raise only one, or sometimes two, broods.

WHAT IS THAT EXOTIC BIRD?

A vivid flash of colour glimpsed out of the corner of your eye, or an extraordinary squawk, might draw your attention to a tree and a bright, tropical bird in its branches. A parrot in the park? Your first instinct might be to call someone to try to rescue it, but don't be alarmed – it probably isn't a newly escaped pet but a bird that has adapted to life in the semi-wild of suburbia.

In the 1960s a number of ring-necked parakeets, also known as rose-ringed parakeets, escaped or were released. The first records of them breeding in the wild were made in Kent, although they have been sighted in Manchester and Merseyside.

Parakeets are seed-eaters and are ideally suited to urban life, where bird tables and park visitors provide them with food. They nest in cavities in trees, including the disused holes of the green woodpecker, and in special nest boxes. The main threat they face comes from those birds of prey, such as the kestrel, that are returning to cities (see page 192).

Pretty polly *A parakeet looks oddly conspicuous in a British setting, but its colourful plumage only rarely incites attacks from other birds.*

Going back to nature

The minute any part of the man-made environment is neglected, nature races in to seize it back. Abandoned airfields become quiet habitats for rabbits and hares; disused railway lines offer obscurity where foxes and badgers can thrive and every inch of abandoned earth is speedily populated by those great opportunists, the weeds. Their brightly coloured flowers are quickly discovered by nectar-hunting bees and butterflies, while the ground disturbed by burrowing animals provides an excellent nesting and foraging environment for solitary hunting wasps and bees.

Time flies *If you have ever blown on a dandelion clock to 'tell the time', you will know how easily the seeds travel. This dispersal mechanism is part of the plant's success in urban areas. The parachute-assisted seeds are carried to new sites over great distances on the turbulent air produced by traffic on roads and railway lines.*

Whenever you find a stretch of neglected urban land you will see a dandelion. Why is this? The dandelion triumphs because it has a whole range of survival strategies. It can develop its seeds without the need for insect pollinators so it can reproduce in barren places; its seeds are wind-blown and it can germinate on poor soil.

Staying put

Once established, a dandelion seedling puts down deep, well-anchored roots that survive any damage to the foliage above ground. The leaves produce a bitter, narcotic latex which deters browsing animals, and the flat leaf rosette allows it to withstand mowing or the heavy tread of a human or animal. And the dandelion's sturdiness has a knock-on effect: its nectar supports early bumblebees and butterflies that could otherwise not live in the wasteland.

You will often find the daisy-like flowers of mayweed and feverfew on waste ground, too. They flourish because they produce many small seeds which are able to germinate in very poor soil and in tiny crevices.

SPOT THE DIFFERENCE

WHICH ONE IS A DANDELION? In spring, when almost every wild flower seems to be yellow, it is easy to confuse the **dandelion [1]** with its many lookalikes. Here are a few of the common impostors.

Coltsfoot [2] is easy to recognise because the flowers, borne at the top of reddish brown scaly stems, come out before the large flat leaves develop. For this reason, one old country name for it is 'son before father', but it gets its more common name from the leaves, shaped like the imprint of a hoof.

Cat's ear [3] has ragged-edged leaves that are not very cat-like. Hairs on the leaves help to protect the plant from being eaten. The flowers are held on green stems that also bear small, scale-like bracts near the top.

Common groundsel [4] can be distinguished from the dandelion because its flowerheads are much smaller and can be seen all year round. Groundsel's lightweight floating seeds carry far and wide, enabling it to spread into all sorts of distant sites.

CITY LOW-LIFE

We may not like the idea, but rats tend to follow people around, living off their waste. If you catch sight of a rat on a patch of waste ground, it indicates that the site was once built upon, even though the old buildings may be demolished.

In a city you are often no more than 3m (10ft) away from a rat. There are brown and black rats in Britain, but the black rat is rare and hangs on mainly in dockland areas. Brown rats are more widespread because they are so adaptable, making their homes in every human habitat.

They can be found wherever there is food (be it a rubbish tip or a grain store), shelter and a supply of water. They thrive in towns, using sewers and gardens as thoroughfares. And although they foul food stores and can spread disease, they are a food source for urban predators such as foxes and owls.

Making a mark *If you suspect there are rats nearby, look for their droppings, which are shaped like jelly beans (inset). Or check if there is a dark greasy mark low down on a wall (left), made where the rat has brushed by, leaving a scent trail.*

Rats in residence

Often the first sign that there is a rat in your garden is when it climbs onto the bird table, sometimes in broad daylight, to pick up food. If you regularly put waste food on a compost heap, rats may soon appear.

If you think you may have a brown rat for a neighbour, look for a burrow in a quiet area of your garden. The entrance will be a little smaller than the diameter of a half-pint mug and you will see earth thrown around the hole. Check, too, for rat droppings (see left) near trails through vegetation: the trail may lead to the rat's burrow.

Survival instinct *Rats can colonise the most unpromising sites because they are able to consume both vegetable waste and meat.*

Tough invaders *Common chickweed (below left) persists through the winter months, giving it a head start in spring. The seeds of pineapple weed (below right) can 'hitchhike' their way to new sites in the rubber tread of car tyres. Both plants are commonly seen on waste ground.*

Toad tunnel An underpass for toads, built under a road, helps them to get to their spring mating ponds in safety.

Close-up on
Frogs and toads

The first clue that frogs have decided to invade your garden pond may well be the sound of the males' gentle croaking: if there are a lot of frogs in the pond, the sound will carry some distance. If the visitors are toads you may hear them chirp or yap like a small dog – not croak – a noise made by males to ward off other males who try to mount them or steal their mates.

Finding frogs or toads squashed on roads and railway tracks is another sign that these amphibians are on the move. In spring, both frogs and toads set out to mate and lay their eggs in the pond where they were born. Toads will travel up to a mile, often following routes that were in use long before the road or railway was built. Frogs are less specific, however, and may choose to spawn in the first pond they come across.

If you catch a glimpse of a frog or toad, the simplest way to tell them apart is by their gait: frogs hop or leap while toads usually walk. If you can get closer, you will see that a frog has long, muscular hind legs for jumping and strongly webbed feet. The head is narrow, with the eyes set high on the skull. The skin is moist and smooth, ranging from greenish brown with dark blotches to yellow or orange. Toads are rounder with short, stocky legs. The head is broad and they have captivating eyes with a golden iris. The skin is dry, warty and usually brown.

Mating frenzy Over-eager frogs will cluster around one female, gripping her legs or anything that comes within their grasp and occasionally drowning her. If you see a fish in the garden pond being pursued by a frog, it is because there are no female frogs available, and a desperate male is opting for the next best thing.

Long embrace When frogs pair up, the mating clinch, known as amplexus, can last for two days.

SPOT THE DIFFERENCE

FROG OR TOAD SPAWN

Frogs and toads lay their eggs in a transparent jelly that protects them from physical damage and insulates them in the cold water, making development possible.

Frog spawn is a mass of clear round balls of jelly, which can be seen floating in the pond.

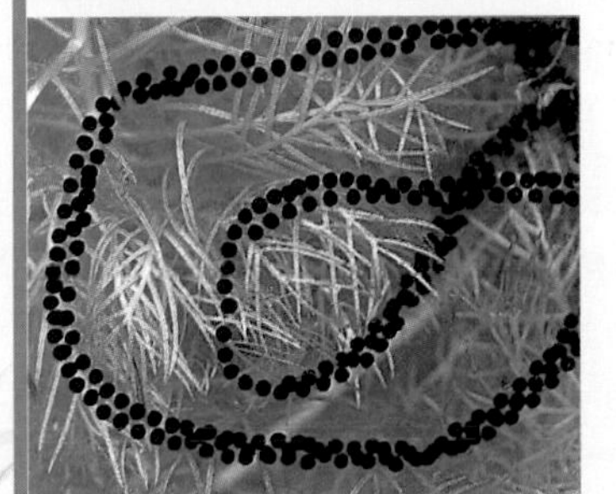

Toad spawn is laid in strings 1-2m (3-6ft) long, often twisted around waterweed to anchor it.

Newt eggs are difficult to see. They are laid singly, in a gelatinous covering, on the leaf of a water plant which is then folded over and stuck down to hold the egg safe (see page 51).

FROM TINY TADPOLES...

Wriggling tadpoles hatch from spawn in about 10-14 days. You can tell the difference between frog and toad tadpoles quite easily: frog tadpoles are brown with gold speckling (inset right), while toad tadpoles are black.

Both types of tadpole remain in the water for about 12 weeks. During the fifth week the hind legs begin to develop and at eight weeks they make the final transformation from tadpole to frog. Initially, tadpoles are vegetarian, but at eight weeks they start to add meat to their diet, eating other weak or dead tadpoles and dead fish. Meanwhile, other creatures are eating them. If you watch the pond you will see the tadpoles being picked off by beetle and dragonfly larvae in the water, and by birds wading in the shallows.

When the froglets and toadlets have all four legs and are able to breathe air, they leave the pond. You will find them clustered near the bank at first, seeking protection from predators, in the damp conditions that prevent dehydration.

On the hop *You may come across hundreds of tiny frogs or toads on the move at the same time. This is because they wait until conditions are right, usually after a spell of heavy rain, before leaving the shelter of the pond to find a home. Sightings of this mass exodus led to the belief that it can 'rain frogs'.*

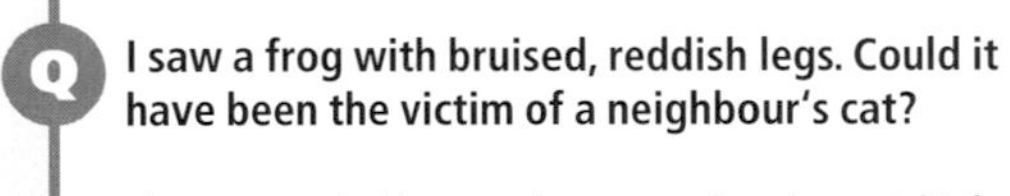

Q **I saw a frog with bruised, reddish legs. Could it have been the victim of a neighbour's cat?**

A The most probable cause is a contagious bacterial infection known as red-leg. It is thought to be most prevalent where frogs are stressed due to overcrowded conditions.

WHERE DO THEY GO? After mating, the spawn is left to take its chances as the parents move on.

Toad in a hole Toads leave the water after mating. You will find them in rockeries, greenhouses and even in drainage pipes (right). If you see one, go back and look again another day because they often return to a favourite resting place, after a night spent hunting for insects. Toads overwinter under heaps of stones or in holes in the ground. You may find several together.

Pond life After mating, frogs disperse, but they never stray far from water. Quite often you will find them sunbathing on the edge of a pond (right), ready to leap back in if threatened. In winter, females and immature frogs hibernate under logs or in compost heaps, but the males retreat under the mud at the bottom of ponds – ready to compete for the females when they return to the water at breeding time.

When the buzz, flutter and scurry never stops

Midsummer sees wildlife populations peak in field and hedge

As the days grow longer and warmer, life in Britain's fields and pastures reaches its annual high point. Flowers, now in full, vibrant bloom, are attracting bees, butterflies and other insects, and birds and mammals are busy searching out food for their young. In some parts of the country, mostly in the west, small fields are still enclosed by neat hedges and walls, creating a patchwork of vivid colours where meadows and pastures supporting cattle and sheep are interspersed with fields of ripening arable crops. This variety contrasts sharply with the monotonous landscapes of areas such as East Anglia, where the hedges have been removed to allow the easy passage of juggernaut machinery across the land.

Variety through tradition

The traditional rural scenery of farmhouses set among small, irregular fields remains in areas such as around Lyme Regis in Dorset (above). The rotation of crops, fallow land and pastures, creates a variety of grassland and open habitats. Look at the way thick, winding hedges and wide tracks divide up the landscape – these often represent old parish boundaries and may have survived for a thousand years or longer.

If you find a hedgerow of mature hawthorn in such a setting, it was probably planted between 150 and 300 years ago. At that time, a revolution in agriculture saw open fields and commons being enclosed to increase the yield of food for an expanding population. The planting of thousands of miles of such hedges provided a wide variety of new habitats, which in

Herb Robert grows mainly in the shade, but if you do see it in exposed areas, its leaves and stems may be red, because sunshine causes a pigment, anthocyanin, to build up in the plant.

their turn have attracted a large number of different plants and animals. More recent times, however, have seen the increasing mechanisation of farming. One result has been the disappearance of many of the old hedges and areas of woodland, another the cultivation of land which could not be ploughed previously. Where these events have occurred, wildlife is in retreat.

Hedgerow sanctuaries

The country lanes, like the one in Wiltshire (above), that weave their way across Britain act as linear nature reserves. Small mammals, such as voles and shrews, use the cover of overgrown verges to search for food in relative safety. You should also look among the masses of blossoming hawthorn and swathes of cow parsley for smaller wild flowers, birds, butterflies and other insects.

The reason many country lanes weave about so much comes from the way they were formed. The oldest ones follow the paths once taken by herds of sheep and cattle as they picked their way along the easiest routes through the open country. Land enclosure forced changes, and you tend to see straighter roads running between the more regular-shaped fields it created. A sudden sharp corner, apparently for no reason, may mark a place where such a road was built around farm boundaries that have long since disappeared.

Many extra-wide drove roads, built between hedges or walls to contain herds going to market, are now reduced to a hard, narrow strip, with wide verges that offer sanctuary to plants such as hemlock, hogweed and hoary ragwort, driven from the fields by modern farming practices.

High-pitched squeaks in the verge near the base of a hedge, may be produced by a common shrew (right), foraging for food in the leaf litter that collects there.

Flowers in the fields

You can tell a lot about a field from the plants you find there. Many will grow only in particular soil conditions. Some prefer acid soil, others alkaline; plants may be tolerant of drought or prefer damp soil. The types of plants you see are also governed by the way the land is managed. Today, many fields and open grasslands are described as 'improved grass' because they have been treated with fertilisers and weedkillers to produce the best crop for grazing or silage (see pages 28-29). Grasslands not altered in this way are described as semi-natural or unimproved. These are where you are most likely to discover a diversity of wild flowers.

Semi-natural grasslands that have not been ploughed for centuries, if ever, are those most renowned for their wild-flower displays. They now exist mainly as nature reserves, although you may find remnants of them in churchyards, village greens and the borders of ancient paths.

If you suspect that you are in semi-natural grassland, check by looking for traditional grasses, such as sweet vernal and false oat grass. You may also see the blood-red flowerheads of great burnet, which grows in hay meadows, the feathery leaves and lacy white flowers of pignut and yarrow or the pinkish purple flowers of knapweed.

Plants preferring particular soils are known as indicator plants and if you find one of these soil-specific types you can expect to find others with the same soil preference. For instance, on the acid soil of the Welsh hills, you will see purple moor-grass and mat-grass, along with patches of sheep's sorrel, and heath and lady's bedstraw.

Don't rely on a single plant – species occasionally grow in the 'wrong' soil. Wild clematis, for example, is a good indicator of chalky soil, but can also be seen in more acid areas, so always look for several indicators as confirmation of soil type.

Search, too, for the more delicate grassland plants that have difficulty establishing themselves in the dense turf. Look where animals graze: their hoofprints create small, sheltered hollows in which such plants may thrive. A glance into a sheep's hoofprint could reveal tiny, white flowers of fairy flax.

Chalk lover *The lilac flower heads of field scabious can be seen scattered across grasslands throughout Britain in summer. Each head contains up to 50 individual florets.*

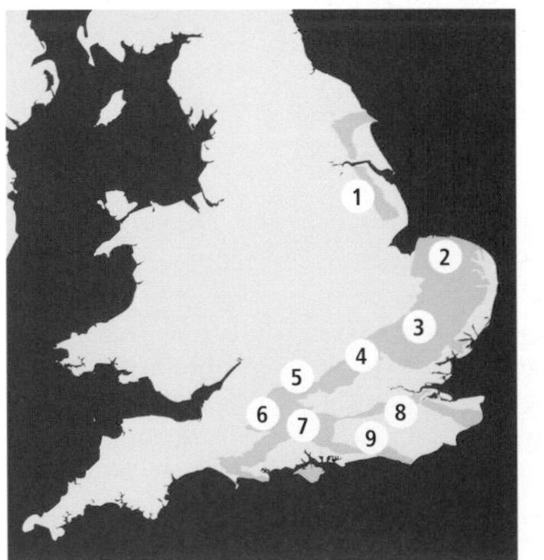

Chalk outcrops Look in these areas for typical chalk grasslands, except in Breckland, which is covered by sandy heath.

1 Wolds
2 Breckland
3 East Anglian chalk
4 Chilterns
5 Berkshire Downs
6 Salisbury Plain
7 Hampshire Downs
8 North Downs
9 South Downs

Chalk-loving plants On walks through wild-flower meadows at this time of year, use the plants that are in bloom all around you to identify the type of soil you are crossing. You are highly likely to come across patches of tor grass **[1]**, slender bedstraw **[2]** and dark mullein **[3]** – all telling you that you are on chalky land. Having found these, look around for other chalk-lovers, such as upright brome, quaking grass, salad burnet, hoary plantain and, in damp places, dropwort.

SEEDS IN YOUR SOCKS

After a walk along an overgrown path you may notice that your socks are speckled with seeds. Look at the seeds through a magnifying glass: some, such as those of agrimony, have hooks, some, like forget-me-not seeds, barbed spines, and others, like those of upright brome, are pointed. The seeds have evolved to cling to the fur or feathers of passing creatures, so that they are carried away from the parent plant before falling to the ground and germinating.

A hazard to dogs *If you see wall barley (right) in a field, keep your dog away from it. The spiky bristles, or awns, can become embedded in the soft flesh between your pet's toes. The bristles can work their way into the animal's foot and require removal by a vet.*

Nature's Velcro *Tiny hooked spines on the surface of common cleavers seeds (right) attach themselves to the fur of passing animals.*

IDENTITY PARADE – ORCHIDS

Despite their reputation for rarity, you can see several British wild orchids – if you know where to find them. Look for their flowering spikes on old, semi-natural grassland and country roadsides. Don't worry if a patch you discover vanishes the following year: some species flower only once a decade. Also, there may be several years between germination and flowering, so you may overlook young plants until they flower.

Common spotted The most abundant British orchid, you will find it in damp meadows and marshes. Its leaves have dark spots. Watch bees on the flowers. The pollinia (modified stamens) stick to their heads, and so are carried off by them to pollinate other flowers.

Heath spotted This looks similar to the common spotted orchid, but the dark spots on its leaves tend to be fewer and rounder. It dislikes chalky soil, so is absent from large areas of Britain. You will find it mainly in the north on the acid soils of heaths and bogs.

Bee orchid The flowers resemble female bumblebees, so are thought to attract male bees that then transfer pollen. Look for them on chalk and limestone grassland, except in Scotland, but note that a site with huge numbers one year, often has none the next.

Green-winged Short, damp, undisturbed grassland is a good place to seek the less common green-winged orchid, which often grows among cowslips. Don't confuse it with the larger early purple orchid, which has distinctive purple spots on its leaves.

Along the boundaries

Hedges and the land that runs alongside them combine features of both grassland and woodland, so are home to a wide variety of plants and animals. Because they were planted to mark boundaries, and as fences to keep farm animals from straying, most hedges were designed to become dense, and often prickly too. This thick woody growth offers support to a host of summer climbers and gives shelter to adjoining verges, making them good places to look for wild flowers.

If you look at a hedgerow and the land beside it, you will start to see distinct zones, each one an ideal niche for a different range of plants.

In summer the edges of many country lanes are trimmed back. These short grass verges are a good place to look for low-growing flowers, ranging from familiar daisies and dandelions to rarer orchids.

Behind this strip, you will see taller plants, such as mallow and teasel, and further back still, cow parsley and its relatives (see page 24) often dominate. Some hedges also have a ditch bordering them and here damp-loving species, such as meadowsweet, water dropwort and various rushes, can flourish.

Salt lovers

You may notice bare patches along the verge of a main road. These could have been caused by saltburn, which can occur when salt is spread on roads in winter to de-ice them. Few plants like salt, so if it drifts on to the roadside, many die back.

Salt-tolerant plants, however, which you normally see only in coastal areas, love conditions like this and their seeds have been steadily spreading inland, carried on the wheels of motor vehicles (see page 201). The next time you are stuck in a traffic jam, try to spot sea plantain, sea spurrey or sand spurrey, which are appearing increasingly beside motorways and other roads running inland from the coast.

Climbers and scramblers

When you examine the flowers in the hedgerow, you will discover that some have long, thin stems that weave their way through the dense, woody canopy. These are climbers, which rely on their neighbours for support. If you spot the white-trumpet flowers of bindweed, look how the stems spiral tightly around adjacent shrubs. Other climbers are black bryony, honeysuckle and hops.

Some hedgerow plants are scramblers rather than true climbers: they start by growing upright, then bend under their own weight until they meet a suitable prop. Wild clematis, cleavers and brambles are common scramblers.

Also search below hedges for the white flowers of greater stitchwort or the purple and yellow of bittersweet: note how their weak stems are supported by surrounding undergrowth.

GAINING SUPPORT Yellow-green flowers of **white bryony** (below left) creep through the hedgerows of England and Wales from May to September. Look closely to see the spring-like tendrils that it uses to hold onto the shrubs it climbs on. Another common hedge brightener at this time of year is **wild clematis** or traveller's joy (below right). You will see sprays of its white or greenish flowers rampaging through hedges in chalky areas of southern England. It also climbs, this time by twisting its thin, woody stems around supporting plants.

STANDING TALL From June to September, creamy white clusters of **meadowsweet's** feathery flowers (above left) are a common sight above the ditches and damp ground often found bordering hedges. Their sugary, heady scent might alert you to their presence, although meadowsweet is fairly conspicuous, growing to a height of 60-120cm (2-4ft). **Teasel** (above right) can grow even taller – up to 2m (6ft), so you should have no trouble spotting its prickly, purple-pink, flowerheads, which you are likely to find in bloom nearby.

SNIFF IT OUT Don't forget to use your sense of smell while exploring a hedgerow. Abundant patches of red and **white dead nettles** (far left) throw out a delicate, sweet aroma and you can't miss the cloying scent of elder blossom. The sweet fragrance of honeysuckle is best appreciated at dusk, when it releases its perfume to attract night-flying moths.

Try to catch the scent of leaves, too. Crush them between your fingers to release their aroma. In this way you can sniff out wild thyme, basil and marjoram and occasional garden escapes such as lemon balm, rosemary and lavender.

An unpleasant musty smell could mean you have discovered hedge woundwort or another wild mint, **black horehound** (near left). Unusual scents include the distinctive, camphor-like odour of feverfew, vanilla, which indicates valerian, and the scent of pineapples that wafts from the pineapple weed. After rain you might catch the appley scent of sweet-briar's foliage.

IDENTITY PARADE – Dog roses

Wild roses are the most sweetly scented flowers of the midsummer hedgerows. Like brambles, their thorny stems help them to scramble through hedges.

The dog rose is the most common species of wild rose in Britain, with white or pink flowers that brighten hedges all over England and Wales, although it is rare in Scotland. It can scramble to a height of 3m (10ft).

The downy rose can be distinguished from the dog rose by its hairy leaves. Gall wasps often deposit their eggs in the stem of this species: look for bright red, tufted growths, known as galls, which appear as the larvae develop.

The burnet rose has the sweetest perfume of all native British wild roses. In early summer, especially near the sea, look for its creamy white flowers densely covering bushes no more than 20cm (8in) high. The stems are thick with prickles.

SLEEPY SNAILS In the thick herbage at the base of a hedge, you may find 'sleeping' snails. They are conserving moisture by staying in their shells during the heat of the day – look for the papery, waterproof membrane over the entrance. The large garden snail is the easiest to see, but pull open the grass and you may uncover the **dark-lipped banded snail** (inset top) or its white-lipped 'cousin'. They can be hard to spot as their shell colour, which their surroundings tend to match, ranges from white through yellow to dark brown. The shell also acts as protection, although it does not deter the song thrush. If you see a stone surrounded by fragments of snail shell, this is a **'thrush's anvil'** (inset bottom). Song thrushes hold a snail in their beaks and smash the shell against a stone to get at the soft flesh.

Summer babies

The birth of many mammals and birds coincides with the long days and short nights of summer. For diurnal creatures, having plenty of daylight is an advantage both for newly weaned and independent young and any parents that have to spend many hours finding food for their offspring. Nocturnal species have to compensate for the short nights by emerging earlier in the evening and staying out later in the morning. Both activities offer the countryside detective more opportunities to see adults and young.

On a quiet stroll along a thick hedgerow near woodland, you may be lucky enough to see badgers. Although badgers are nocturnal, in summer they often emerge before dusk and even before sunset, when it is still very bright. Look out for cubs and adults playing near the sett.

Foxes are also out by day and the place to keep watch is near their likely hunting ground, such as a rabbit warren.

Moulting their fur

You may see a fox carrying prey back to its cubs, and you might be able to track it to its den. You should find it fairly easy to tell the larger dog fox from the vixen, and to also notice how tatty both sexes now look as they moult, especially the vixen. Patches of short, summer coat appear among the long, winter one, while the tail loses much of its bushiness.

Early morning or evening are good times to spot fox cubs playing around the entrance of their earth. Tell-tale signs of fox-cub activity are patches where the vegetation has been flattened and the ground trampled bare. As well as the distinctive, strong foxy smell, you could find the remains of prey scattered about. If the cubs spot you, they may bolt down the earth, then if you hear the bark of an adult, you know they won't reappear for some time.

Mother's care *Fox cubs emerge from the earth at four to five weeks old, but the family remains close until autumn, when the young males begin to establish territories.*

QUICK AS A FLASH

Wait by a rabbit warren and you may catch a glimpse of a female stoat or weasel out hunting with her young. Small, slim and fast, they are not easy to distinguish except by size: a female stoat is about 25cm (10in) long without her tail, while a weasel is around 18cm (7in) long. Stoats also have a black-tipped tail. Both can be seen at any time of day, but you usually see no more than a flash of movement as one rushes by or stops to put her head up and look around. The best sighting is of a family, perhaps crossing a road in a tight group of parents plus six or more young, which, at a glance, can be mistaken for an old sack blown by the wind.

BIRDS AND THEIR BROODS
The number of clutches a bird lays in a season depends on species and breeding conditions.

Bird	Clutches/year
Collared dove	3-6
Blackbird	3-5
Song thrush	2-4
House sparrow	1-4
Swallow	2-3
Pied wagtail	2-3
Robin	2-3
Starling	1-2
Blue tit, jackdaw, jay, magpie, tawny owl	1

Taken for a ride *If disturbed, a mother stoat will carry her young to a new den. The young become independent at about ten weeks.*

Home alone *Young deer (above) and hares (right) are often left alone, so well hidden in long grass that you may trip over one. If you do, don't handle it. The mother will return with food, and may reject any offspring with human scent on it.*

FLEDGLING BIRDS

The nest is a dangerous place for young birds because a single predator can easily devour a whole family, so fledglings leave as soon as they can and disperse. For birds nesting in exposed places, such as grassland, this means before their feathers are fully grown. (Birds, such as tits, which nest in the greater safety of holes, spend longer in the nest.)

You can recognise these youngsters by their short tails and clumsy, whirring flight, which betrays the fact that their wings are still too small to fully support them. Keep watching and see how they land: they often find it difficult.

Most birds continue to be fed by their parents after they leave the nest, sometimes for several weeks. Listen for piping calls along hedgerows or up in the trees as fledglings keep in touch with their parents. A sudden burst of piping tells you that a parent has arrived with food and a youngster is begging to be fed.

Squeaks and whistles *Young starlings make a great deal of noise as they clamour for the food their parents bring.*

Who's in charge?

Some birds, such as house martins and swallows, pass food to their young on the wing.

If you can identify a parent bird's sex by its plumage, you will be able to tell whether or not both parents are feeding their young. Sometimes a family splits up, leaving the fledglings in the care of one or other parent. For instance, you may find a male blackbird in sole charge of his offspring. This is almost certainly because the female is sitting on another clutch of eggs.

It can be difficult to identify some young birds in summer, as their plumage often differs from that of their parents. Immature starlings, for example, have plain brown feathers, and young male robins lack a red breast.

Some birds, such as starlings, gather into flocks when they leave their parents. The reason is that many pairs of eyes make it easier to find food or spot danger. You may also see mixed flocks of young tits and goldcrests in hedges.

Close-up on Butterflies

During its lifetime a butterfly exists in two very different forms. It begins life as a caterpillar – an eating machine which spends its time chewing leaves and growing. Then it pupates, during which time it changes into the winged adult, designed for breeding and travelling. You will see numerous butterflies flitting through wild-flower meadows and flowering hedgerows in summer, and they are also frequent visitors to railway embankments (see page 200), attracted by the buddleja and other flowers that grow along them.

Visitors from the south

Many favourite British butterflies are not full-time residents but summer immigrants from Europe. No painted ladies or clouded yellows, and few red admirals, can survive the British winter. Each year a new influx arrives from the Continent. The numbers of resident species, such as the small tortoiseshell, are also boosted by immigrants. In some years you can see clouds of butterflies flying north in spring, but few ever return south: as summer turns to autumn, they die. Some of our resident butterflies seldom move far from their birthplace – silver-studded blues rarely travel more than 50m (165ft) – but small whites and small tortoiseshells are nomadic and you can often see them fluttering across the fields in search of somewhere to settle.

Mating games If you come across a meadow brown, speckled wood or tortoiseshell butterfly and are unsure what sex it is, try very gently lobbing a small pebble over it and see how it responds. If it is male, it will fly upwards, thinking that the stone is a mate; a female will not react. But if you see two of these butterflies spiralling around together, each one trying to get into a position higher than the other, you are looking at two males in competition. When a male is on its own territory it usually wins the fight, although neither is ever fatally injured.

You may notice a number of butterflies patrolling along a length of hedgerow or wall, or a fallen tree. These are very likely to be small tortoiseshell or peacock males that have established territories there, hoping to find a mate. As a female flies past she will meet the waiting males – often conveniently stationed near a patch of stinging nettles on which she must lay her eggs to provide food for the caterpillars when they hatch.

Sometimes, if you wait quietly and patiently, you will see a male fanning its wings, then flying off for a short distance, landing and fanning its wings again. The butterfly will perform this action repeatedly, and you may wonder what it is doing. It is, in fact, wafting the scent of its pheromones – tiny amounts of chemical that it secretes – through the air. This scent can travel great distances and is extremely attractive to the females, which respond by seeking out its source.

Battle scars *A butterfly with nicks in its wings, like the gatekeeper (right) is probably the lucky survivor of a bird attack. If you find two pairs of disconnected wings – with no sign of the body to which they were attached – you have found the remains of a less fortunate individual.*

A **red admiral** butterfly (top) feeds on nectar, but its caterpillar (bottom) eats only nettle leaves.

KNOW THE HOST PLANTS Unlike its parents, a caterpillar often feeds on one plant only. Knowing what plant this is tells you where to look for the butterfly, or for eggs about to hatch, though both will be camouflaged.

Grasslands

Butterfly	Host plant
Dark green fritillary	Violets
Grayling	Sheep's fescue
Meadow brown	Meadow grass, bent grass, rye grass
Ringlet	Cocksfoot
Small copper	Common and sheep's sorrel
Small heath	Meadow grasses, fescues
Small skipper	Yorkshire fog

Hedgerows

Butterfly	Host plant
Brimstone	Alder and purging buckthorns
Peacock	Stinging nettles
Red admiral	Stinging nettles
Small tortoiseshell	Stinging nettles
Small white	Cabbage and relatives, garlic mustard
Speckled wood	Cocksfoot, Yorkshire fog

The **meadow brown** caterpillar (left) is well camouflaged on the grasses it eats, while the adult (below) is hard to miss.

SPOT THE DIFFERENCE

BUTTERFLY OR MOTH? In general, you will see butterflies flying around by day, especially when it is bright, and moths by night. But a more reliable and easier way to tell them apart is to look carefully at their wings when they are resting.

A **butterfly** (top left) rests with its wings pressed together vertically over its back and the camouflage markings showing on the underside. Notice also the terminal knob on each antenna.

A **moth** (bottom left) folds its wings flat over each other, the forewings overlapping the hindwings. Its camouflage pattern is nearly always on the upper side of the wings. The antennae, which are sometimes feathery, have no terminal knobs.

Don't be fooled by skipper butterflies – some hold their wings like a moth when resting.

SUN WORSHIPPERS

In the early morning and late afternoon, you are likely to notice butterflies basking in the sun. They do this because they are cold-blooded animals and cannot fly until their body temperature is raised to over 30°C (86°F). They achieve this by sunbathing. The Scotch argus is so dependent on sunshine to keep warm that it will usually stop flying if a cloud passes in front of the sun.

Most butterflies bask by spreading their wings at right angles to the sun's rays and turning their heads away, so presenting the maximum area to absorb heat. If you gently rotate the leaf or stone on which a butterfly is sitting, you can see how it will turn to maintain its position relative to the sun. When they have warmed up, butterflies rest with their wings closed and held upright.

A butterfly that appears to be leaning to one side, such as the grayling, is using a different method of basking. It keeps its wings closed but gains maximum warmth by turning its body sideways to the sun.

Basking beauties Early morning is a good time to identify butterflies, especially those that look similar like the chalk-hill blue (top) and common blue (above). It is easier to see their wing markings at that time of day, as they will probably be basking in the warm sun with wings outstretched.

Outstaring the enemy A peacock butterfly rests, like most butterflies, with its closed wings held upright, so that it is generally well camouflaged. But if you disturb one, its wings will open out to reveal the eyespots on each forewing. To an approaching predator, such as a bird, this will look as if a large animal has suddenly opened its eyes, and, with the menacing hissing noise the butterfly makes at the same time, this should warn off any creature intending to eat it.

You will notice that many butterflies have eyespots. The meadow brown has them on the underside of its forewings, along with small dots on its hindwings, which deflect the aim of a predator away from its body to the edge of its wings. Most eyespots, in fact, have probably evolved for deflecting a predator's aim rather than scaring it away.

A riot of colour

Early summer brings a huge change to the appearance of the fields, as cereal crops start to grow tall and turn from green to pale yellow and then to gold in the warm sun. The familiar patchwork quilt of green fields and muted gold is brightened in places with splashes of colour from patches of wild flowers, and broad bold strokes of stronger, more vibrant hues make their appearance as a variety of commercial crops bursts into flower. There is a buzz of activity, too, from the insects, birds and other animals, large and small, that are drawn to the meal that the farmer's crops offer them. The whole of the landscape vibrates with a sense of abundance.

Green or golden cereals, hazy blue flax and vivid yellow drifts of oilseed rape are now a familiar part of the summer landscape. You may also spot splashes of bright yellow, or nodding heads of barley, dotting roadside verges where the seeds have spilled from trailers or been carried by the wind or birds.

You will also come across many fields of green stippled with white: this tells you that grass and white clover have been sown together to make a grazing pasture. Look, too, for the pink-and-black flowers of broad beans, usually grown for animal feed. Their strong scent is a great attraction for bees in early June. A close inspection may reveal small holes at the base of the flowers, where visiting bees have cheated the plant by drinking its nectar without picking up and transferring its pollen.

Blue stripes A patch of hazy blue indicates flax, cultivated mostly for its seeds, which yield linseed oil, and for the fibre in its stems, which is used to make linen.

Yellow dazzle Fields of oilseed rape are now commonplace. It is mainly grown for its oil, which is extracted from the seeds and used in the manufacture of food.

IDENTITY PARADE

Cereals are members of the grass family which have been bred over the years for their seed, or grain. Wheat, barley and oats are the main ones: here's how to tell them apart.

Wheat is Britain's most important crop. Look closely at an ear of wheat and you will see that the grains are arranged in fours.

Oat grains hang on slender, bowing stalks. Wild oats, a common weed in cereal crops, are distinguished by hairs around the base of its seeds.

Barley is easily recognised by the long bristles growing from the tip of each grain. (Rye is similar, but with shorter bristles.)

LEFT TO GO WILD

Between the well-ordered fields of crops, you may notice some arable fields that appear to be full of weeds, like the one in Cambridgeshire shown below. This is probably 'set-aside', the result of a scheme for avoiding the overproduction of grain. After harvesting, the stubble is left and the farmers are paid to allow the fields to run wild.

Some set-aside is rotational. Here the land is cultivated again after just one year. In such places, wild plants and animals do not usually get a proper chance to re-establish themselves. They do better in non-rotational set-aside, as this is left in a natural state for a number of years.

In the areas of set-aside where wild plants do take hold, they attract insects and many, sometimes rare, farmland birds, such as skylarks, corn buntings and lapwings. In other areas the farmer may plant crops of kale, mustard, rye or flax, not as crops but as food for pheasants and partridges. The vegetation is cut or sprayed later before any weeds can set seed.

What is a weed?

Remember that the plants you see on set-aside cannot strictly be called weeds. A weed is simply any plant growing in the wrong place, and the wild plants on set-aside have been allowed to invade.

However, a wild plant in the middle of a crop is competing with it for space and nutrients. Farmers control these weeds by spraying with herbicides, but where spraying has missed a patch, look out for plants whose seeds have survived in the soil, waiting for the right conditions to grow. Scarlet poppies are a typical sight among cereal crops. Others to seek in arable land include bindweed, field forget-me-not and redshank, which produces pink flowers at the tips of its stems.

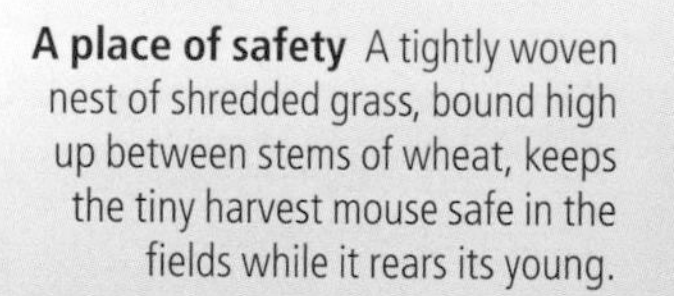

A place of safety A tightly woven nest of shredded grass, bound high up between stems of wheat, keeps the tiny harvest mouse safe in the fields while it rears its young.

WHAT HAS BEEN EATING THE CROPS?

Although spraying with pesticides will control most insects on crops, they are also targeted by larger animals. In recent years, the number of geese in some parts of the country has increased dramatically, making them a major pest: a flock of geese can destroy newly sprouting cereal crops. Slugs can also cause widespread damage by tearing at leafy crops such as oilseed rape **[1]**.

Rabbits sometimes dig their burrows in arable fields **[2]**. If you find one, you'll see that the real harm comes not from the rabbits digging but from when they start to crop the surrounding seedlings. And rabbits living in the hedges will come 10-15m (12-18yd) into a field of cereals to feed. The clue to their presence is a crop pruned along the edge so that, while the rest is lengthening and ripening, the edge strip remains short and green.

Hares also feed on arable crops, but do less harm because there are fewer of them, and they move across the field so their activity is not concentrated in one place. This also makes their depredations harder to detect.

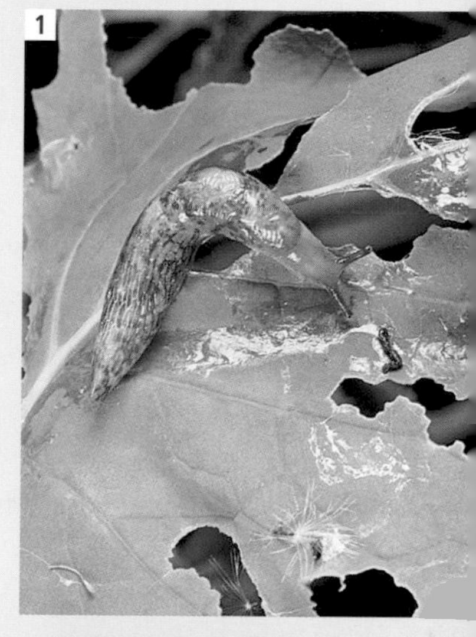

Nibbled giveaways

You may come across a crop of wheat that has been torn and nibbled **[3]**. A flock of geese could have done this, but here it is probably the work of deer or rabbits. Look where the stems have been bitten: the frayed ends tell you that **deer** have been tearing at the crop as they grip it between their lower front teeth and horny upper palate. Rabbits cut more cleanly, and lower down, using their front teeth like secateurs.

Root crops such as sugar beet are attacked by various animals, from rooks to deer and rabbits. One sign of deer is churned up ground where they have pawed it to expose the crop. The size of the toothmarks **[4]** is another clue: rabbits leave marks 6-10mm (¼-½in) across, so this is rabbit damage; the toothmarks of deer are wider.

Danger in the grass

The way grassland looks in summer depends largely on how it is managed. If pasture is constantly grazed, it remains short: grassy turf will be scattered with low-growing flowers, such as the bright purple heads of self-heal and golden-yellow of creeping buttercup. Where the grazers are choosy feeders – horses, for example – you will also see 'islands' of taller growth. But tall plants feature more in meadows where the grass is left to grow until cut for hay or silage in early summer. Here early flowers like brome grasses, ragged robin and yellow rattle have time to set seed.

Since it is not in the interests of a plant to have its leaves eaten, many species produce chemicals that make them poisonous or give them an unpleasant taste. Grazing animals will select the plants they find the most palatable, leaving the rest to thrive. So next time you see pasture, check which plants have been left to grow tall – they are likely to be distasteful to the animals that graze there. High patches of ragwort, for instance, can often be seen in fields of short grass, especially those grazed by horses, because these animals find the ragwort is rich in poisonous alkaloids. Sheep, however, are unharmed by these alkaloids, and so are cinnabar moth caterpillars.

Other plants that produce poisons to avoid being eaten include bird's-foot trefoil: it contains cyanide. But if you come across a clump of it, you may find that parts have been nibbled at while others have not. This is because it is not necessary for all the plants in a clump to produce the poison, as long as enough do for grazers to learn to avoid it.

Another, particularly interesting, example is perforate St John's wort. Hold a leaf of it up to the light and it will appear to be dotted with tiny holes – hence 'perforate' (if you don't see any 'holes' you have found a leaf of the imperforate type). These 'holes' are translucent glands which secrete a rather unpleasant smelling chemical to warn off grazers. You may, however, find small, bright green leaf beetles feeding on it. Again, these creatures are immune to the plant's poisons.

Some plants bear spines, prickles and hairs that make them difficult to consume, but these may only serve as a partial defence, because even prickly holly and gorse get eaten by horses and cattle. But they are a sufficient deterrent to stop such plants being seriously damaged.

Shaped for survival

In an area of short grass, notice how the leaf rosettes of daisies, thistles, dandelions and plantains are pressed against the ground. By 'growing low' they avoid being cropped by grazing

Keeping a low profile The daisy has evolved a rosette of ground-hugging leaves – an arrangement of foliage which survives being trampled on by animals, and proves too low for many grazers to eat.

Warning stripes Cinnabar moth caterpillars signal to birds to steer clear – their striped bodies are full of deadly poisons from the ragwort they are able to feast on with immunity.

animals. They can produce short-stemmed flowers and set seed quickly when the animals are moved off. In long grass, where they are partially shaded, you will see the same plants growing quite tall.

Try to examine the structure of a rosette from above. You will see that the leaves grow as a spiral on a very short stem, so they do not overlap and shade each other from the light needed for photosynthesis. New, short leaves cover only the leaf stalks of older leaves. On plantain leaves, you may also spot holes and ragged edges – the damage caused by feeding slugs and snails.

Q Why are those birds standing on the back of that cow?

A Starlings often ride on the backs of cattle – and sheep – using them as mobile observation posts from which to spot insects among the grass or gathering on cow pats. They can then swoop down onto their prey.

You may also see yellow wagtails following grazing animals to catch the insects that they disturb, and sometimes they too will fly onto a cow's back, this time to feed on the blood-sucking parasites that live on the animal's skin. You can often see jackdaws doing this too.

Who made these? *The mounds shown on the left look smooth and would feel hard if you touched them – they are ant hills, made of solid, compacted earth; the molehills (right), made of freshly dug earth, would feel soft and loose.*

Buttercups These bright yellow flowers blaze across meadows and pastures in summer. Farmers hate them because they are unpalatable to cattle and compete for space with plants that cows will eat.

Of the three common species, the one farmers most dread is the creeping buttercup. It grows from runners which spread out rapidly in all directions. In this way it can completely take over and destoy good pasture.

More common, however, is the tall meadow buttercup, which you will see everywhere on damp, chalky ground. Also look on drier soil for the bulbous buttercup, identifiable by a bulb-like swelling at the base of its ribbed stem.

ANT HILLS

If you see solid-looking mounds, about 20cm (8in) high and 60cm (2ft) across, in old grassland, you are probably looking at the nests of the yellow meadow ant. These ant hills can last many years, because the ants continually add to their structure, packing the earth firmly down.

Plants grow easily in the warm, well-aerated and enriched soil of ant hills, but notice how those growing there are different from those in the surrounding field. You will often see the tiny, white flowers of whitlow-grass or bright blue ones of wall speedwell on the ant hills. These are completely absent from the land around them, where they are shaded out by taller, more aggressive perennials. Other plants, such as dwarf thistle and ribwort plantain, will grow near an ant hill but not on it. This is because they cannot survive being buried as the ants continue their building work. Scrape a little soil from the ant hill mound and you may find the remains of buried plants.

Ant hills are also good places to look for grasshoppers, which like resting on the warm, dry surface and find the loose soil on top a good place to lay their eggs. And you will often find rabbit droppings on or near ant hills, because they use them as lookouts: standing on their haunches on top of an ant hill to see over the surroundings.

Staying below *Yellow meadow ants emerge on the surface only occasionally, even feeding underground.*

Busy summer evenings

Long summer evenings are a perfect time to walk in the countryside. Once the sounds of traffic and other human activities have died down, you may see animals that normally stay out of sight. Some will be crepuscular species, such as the nightjar, which prefer dim light and are most active at dusk and dawn. But you may also spot nocturnal species such as badgers, deer, foxes, or hedgehogs emerging from their daytime resting places. If you keep still and they do not catch your scent, they may come very close.

Sentry post *If you are on a country road at night, check the fenceposts. If one appears taller than the others it may have an owl, such as the short-eared owl (right), perched on it. The ghostly barn owl hunts over fields with a slow buoyant flight (far right), hovering at times to inspect a potential meal.*

Most owls are woodland birds, but they hunt over grassland in summer when the undergrowth makes it hard to catch prey in the woods. Even tawny owls, a truly nocturnal species, may be seen over grassland on summer evenings when they have young to feed. Listen for the wheezing *ke-sip* calls made by the owlets, which have left the nest and are waiting in trees for their parents to bring food, and their squeaks when sustenance arrives.

Other owls are more likely to be seen in daylight, often over open ground. Try to distinguish their calls: a hissing, eerie screech is likely to come from a barn owl; a sharp, shrill *kee-ew* warning cry is a little owl and a soft, deep repeated hoot is the song of the short-eared owl.

The *to-whit to-whoo* cry is made by two tawny owls, not one. The *to-whit* part is the call one owl uses to keep in contact with other tawnies or, more fiercely, to warn of danger. The quavering *to-whoo* is actually the male tawny owl's song. He sings it in response to a female's *to-whit*, but because he answers her so swiftly, the two calls seem to come from the same bird.

Decipher bird sounds

While you are waiting to see what might emerge in the dusk, you can listen to the birds' evening chorus. It mirrors, though less intensively, the dawn chorus.

A regular ***chink-chink-chink*** will be coming from blackbirds preparing to roost and, as the birds fall silent one by one, the robin is usually the last to be left singing.

As you walk home, you may hear the rather eerie ***pee-wit*** of lapwings out in the fields: they remain active all night.

In the wetter, wilder fields of northern England, Wales and Scotland in summer, listen for the monotonous ***chip-chip-chip*** call of snipe, or a faint, hollow bleating sound, known as drumming. This is made by a snipe diving from a height and spreading its two outermost tail feathers so that they vibrate in the slipstream.

MULTITUDES OF INSECTS

Many insects are on the wing on warm, humid evenings. Biting midges and mosquitoes can make life uncomfortable, but the clouds of them that you see illuminated by the setting sun are made up solely of males, which don't bite. Look in the tree tops for huge numbers, swirling like smoke. Females visit these congregations of males to mate.

Summer evenings are also the time when cockchafers, commonly called May bugs, emerge from the soil where they have spent their larval life eating the roots of plants.

These beetles sometimes appear in hundreds and climb grass stems in order to take-off. As adults they eat the foliage of deciduous trees growing in woods and hedges. You are likeliest to see one, however, when it flies against a window at night, having been attracted by an electric light.

Carrying a light for him

In rough grassland, look for tiny pinpricks of light. These are the tell-tale signals made by the glow-worm, a kind of beetle found in a few parts of southern England, especially on chalk downs. The glow is made by the wingless female when she climbs out on to the vegetation to attract the winged male. During the day she hides away to avoid predators

THE CRICKET CHORUS The stillness of a summer's evening amplifies the chirruping of crickets. Though field crickets are rare in Britain, bush crickets, and in particular the **great green bush cricket** (left), the dark bush cricket and the speckled bush cricket, can be heard singing from hedgerows, nettle-beds and bramble thickets in the south.

It is the males that 'sing' to attract the females. It is possible to locate them by their singing and catch them in the light of a torch, when you can see the wings vibrating – their song is made by 'stridulating', in which they rub one wing against the other. Grasshoppers sing by rubbing a hind leg against one of their stiff forewings, but are only active during the daytime.

As with many birds, identification of crickets is best made by song. The loud song of the great green bush cricket sounds like the ticking of a free-wheeling bicycle. The dark bush cricket emits a single metallic chirp at intervals and the speckled bush cricket manages only a weak chirp.

Night life *A cockchafer beats its wings (below) to warm up for its night flight. The glow-worm's shine (bottom) is greeny yellow in the evening, bright yellow after dark.*

Tracking a bat Calm humid evenings are best for bat-watching, since rain and wind keep them in the roost. Any place where you find lots of flying insects is a likely spot to see bats.

Several bats often work the same beat, but a stream of bats flying in one direction indicates the whereabouts of a roost. If you track them over a number of evenings, you should be able to locate it.

The nursery roost is usually in a warm place, suitable for birth and rearing. Once the young can fend for themselves, around late July, the bats leave for cooler quarters, but you may find them back at the same nursery roost if you return to check next year.

The noctule, one of Britain's largest bats, emerges shortly after sunset: watch for a bat flying high, swooping occasionally. The little pipistrelle flies more erratically, while the long-eared bat, round-winged for manoeuvrability, hovers around trees in the hedgerow, plucking insects off the leaves.

Close-up on

The cow pat

They are unpleasant to tread in, but cow pats are a rich source of interest for naturalists. Every cow pat is important as an overlooked but significant ecosystem of the countryside. From the moment that a cow pat is dropped, it makes a well-stocked larder for many insects and these, in turn, provide a meal for other insects and animals. Furthermore, the demolition of cow pats by dung-eaters prevents the pasture from being smothered and allows the grass to keep on growing. This is essential, since the droppings of five cows would cover an acre of ground in just one year.

Observing cow pats from the time they are deposited in a near-liquid state, through the formation of a crust to solidification and eventual break-up, reveals a succession of animal activity. Some creatures, such as slugs and wood lice, use cow pats only as a shelter; others, including spiders and centipedes, visit to prey on other creatures. You may see butterflies and worker wasps sipping fluid from the cow pat surface, while earthworms can be found between the cow pat and the soil.

The consistency of the cow pat depends on what the animal has eaten. Cattle grazing on semi-natural grassland produce rich cow pats with plenty of fibre, but cattle that have been fed on silage produce sloppy dung which offers little to the cow pat community. When drugs called avermectins are used to control worms living in the guts of cattle, the drugs pass into their droppings and kill the beetles and flies that live in them. This, in turn, results in a serious food shortage for the animals that rely on dung-feeding insects.

FRESHLY MADE INCUBATOR

Watch how flies find the cow pat within minutes of its appearance: the horn fly has been seen to lay her eggs before the dung even hits the ground. A black, bluebottle-sized fly with orange patches, the horn fly is one of many that lay their eggs on fresh cow pats, where the warmth of the new dung acts as an incubator They home in on the cow pat's smell, mate on it then lay their eggs. The ***Sepsis* fly** (right) is laying her eggs through an ovipositor; the **common yellow dung fly** (below right) is guarded by her mate as she lays hers.

Dung flies feed at two levels in the food chain: the larvae consume the dung, while the adults are predators. Look for adults perched on nearby vegetation, waiting to pounce on other insects and suck their body fluids for food. If you get close you might see flesh flies, identifiable by their red eyes, large feet and chequered abdomen. They lay live larvae, not eggs, on the cow pat. And the maggots of the autumn fly (a relative of the housefly which, despite its name, can be seen from spring to autumn) wriggle through the dung in search of other maggots, which they kill and eat. Because its victims can include large numbers of the maggots of the noonday fly, which spreads cattle diseases, the autumn fly is considered the farmer's friend.

Feeding time *The thriving community of insects that breed on healthy cow pats, and the offspring they produce, provide vital food for jackdaws, which rely on a mainly insect diet. Birds arrive when the cow pat has started to break up, exposing its tiny inhabitants to their beady eyes.*

THE NEXT LINK

The insects and small animals that live and breed on the cow pats provide food in turn for larger animals. You can see this best at dusk or dawn when you may find hedgehogs and shrews exploring cow pats for food, especially when hot dry spells make the ground hard, so that it is difficult to dig up food elsewhere. If you find a dry cow pat torn up or turned over, it may be the work of a hungry badger. Look for pits beside the cow pat where it has dug for beetles or worms, attracted to the rich soil under the decaying dung.

Dung beetles and flies are particularly important food items for many bats. Large serotine and horseshoe bats hunt over the fields at dusk for dung and dorbeetles. Small bats, such as pipistrelles, patrol along the hedges where flies from cow pats rest.

Birds share the feast by day. Jackdaws, lapwings, rooks and starlings all prod the cow pat with their bills, helping to break it up. And you may see a yellow wagtail picking up insects from the ground around a cow pat.

THE CRUST FORMS

If you look at the surface of a cow pat when it is a few hours old, you will notice it has crusted over. When it reaches this state, you can usually find several small holes in the crust. These are made by dung beetles, which burrow into the cow pat to lay their eggs.

The most complex burrows (near right) are dug by the ***Onthophagus*** beetle. The female digs with the forelegs, piles the loose earth into a heap behind with her other legs, then turns round and butts the spoil to the surface at the side of the cow pat with her head. If the male helps, she can work faster and make more shafts. She then lays an egg in each chamber and fills it with dung from the cow pat.

The **dorbeetle** (left) excavates burrows up to 60cm (2ft) deep under the cow pat (far right). Each egg is buried with a ball of dung for the larva to feed on when it hatches out, then the chamber is filled in with excavated soil.

Prime time for animals in the greenwood

Something new is stirring among the shade and silence

By midsummer woodland trees are in full leaf. The sun filters between them, forming shafts and pools of light in the sea of dark green. Beneath, the ground may be surprisingly damp, and the air inside the wood is relatively cool, humid and still, even when the upper branches rustle in a light wind. But where the wood opens into a glade, it feels warmer, and you may find broad fronds of bracken, flowering bramble and foxgloves with their tiers of magenta bells. Here there is a sense of intense hidden activity: the hum of insects feasting on the flowers and the high cheeping of hungry fledglings, maybe wrens or long-tailed tits. Yet for the most part, the summer wood has an almost cathedral-like timelessness and peace.

Penetrating the oakwood

The New Forest's Bratley Inclosure (above) is the popular image of a deciduous wood in high summer. In the middle of the day, the trunks of oak trees throw little shadow and rise like dark columns. These trees are standards: that is, they have grown up largely uninterrupted from seedlings to their mature forms, although the low branches show that some may have been lopped in their youth. Splayed branches bear thick bunches of leaves, casting a deep shade. Few flowers grow in this half-light, although hummocks of moss and tussocks of grass relieve the monotony of the woodland floor.

In shady woods like this, finding wildlife, or even signs of it, is difficult. But these trees are rich in invertebrates – a huge group that includes worms, wood lice, centipedes, millipedes, slugs, snails, harvestmen, spiders

The speckled wood butterfly is fiercely territorial. It likes to perch in a shaft of sunlight, and if a rival invades, it will fight it off with an audible clash of wings.

and mites, as well as springtails, insects and their larvae. Because many of these are hard to see, the more rewarding places to look for animals are in open spaces, where the sunlight can penetrate and more shrubs and flowers can grow, attracting bees and butterflies. In the surrounding thickets you may spot a flycatcher or warbler, busy seeing to the needs of its brood, and hear the angry chatter of a disturbed squirrel.

Coppice variations

The deer's eye view of Church Wood at Blean, Kent (above) is typical of a chestnut coppice. The ground is bare but for mosses, and thick with fallen leaves. There are few large trees. Instead, a thicket of young growth rises from stumps, some of which are half-buried in leaves and rotting in the centre. The shade is heavy, even though the growth is only a few metres high.

Until the Second World War, huge areas of Britain were clothed in coppices like this. Cutting the trees back to ground level every 10 years or so rejuvenates them, producing new fast-growing shoots from the sap wood at the edge of the stumps. These grow straight, and in handy sizes to be used for fencing and tool handles and for firewood. This coppice is nearing the end of its cycle and is ready for cutting.

This kind of management opens up the wood, producing a mosaic of glades and young copses as well as the older growth seen here. If you walk round a managed coppice wood, try to trace the different phases of regeneration in different parts of the wood, with wild flowers carpeting the new clearings where the trees have been newly cut, to older areas of dense thickets where birds such as the nightingale nest.

The willow warbler is a classic coppice bird: it prefers woodland with a fairly open canopy because this provides it with plenty of small insects and their larvae to eat.

Old or new? *In general, a wood with a curved edge, like the one in the Lake District (above), is old. The straight boundary of the conifer plantation in the Yorkshire Dales (left) shows it is fairly new.*

Discover the wood's secrets

Every wood has a story to tell. Using your detective skills, you can pick out clues that reveal its secrets. Some clues can be discerned from a vantage point such as a hill, where you can see how the wood fits into the landscape; others can be found by looking at the map. Both avenues of inquiry enable you to work out whether a wood is newly planted or ancient, what sort of trees it might contain, and what features you should look out for. And, since old woods are usually much richer in wildlife than new ones, you can direct your steps to the most promising areas.

The best place to start studying a wood is from a distance. Is the wood on a hilltop? If so, it probably lies on clay, in which case, the ground will be wet and sticky after rain. Many old woods have survived because they occupy such ground – land too poorly drained to be worth clearing for farming.

In the hilly west and north you'll see that valleys too steep for agriculture are often covered with woods. Some, such as those on the edges of Snowdonia and around Loch Lomond, are surprisingly large. The reason is that iron and steel were produced there at the start of the Industrial Revolution and great quantities of wood and charcoal were needed for smelting, so the woods were conserved. Other ancient woods survive because of their former privileged status as royal forests.

But most of Britain's very largest woods, have been extended by planting, such as

Historic marker *A bank of earth perhaps a few metres into the wood and sometimes with a ditch alongside, or a double bank with a lane down the middle, is typical of a medieval wood and is often rich in wildlife.*

the vast conifer plantations in Northumberland and central Wales. Even the large beech woods of the Chilterns, which seem natural, were in part planted to provide timber for the local furniture industry. The clue to this is that most of the big beeches are the same size, indicating they are the same age.

How to find the best woods

With the help of a map (the 1:25,000 series is best), study the wood's shape. A circular, or jigsaw-shaped, wood is almost certainly ancient, with parts cleared away over the centuries for farming, while a straight-edged one is probably planted.

As you walk through a wood, consider its structure. Is it open, with glades and broad rides, or is it uniformly dense? The structure suggests what wildlife you can expect to find. Many plants and animals prefer woods with plenty of open spaces, while others need rotting timber cloaked in partial shade.

Are there large mature trees or do they all look fairly young and of a similar size? Old woods tend to have more variety of trees than young ones, so they support more plants, animals and insects and make the most rewarding hunting ground.

Before you enter a wood, pause at the edge. Here shrubs like blackthorn, bramble, dogwood and privet grow and flower. They make a good place to start your investigations as they provide nectar for insects and shelter for small mammals, and for nesting birds such as dunnocks.

WHAT THE TREES TELL YOU

Which trees you find in a wood provide other important clues to its age. Some species are rare outside ancient woodland, so if you identify sessile oak, small-leaved lime, wild service tree and midland hawthorn, for example, you can be fairly sure you are in an ancient wood – and therefore in a good place to look for wildlife.

Particular associations of trees offer more pointers to the age of a wood. In the lowlands, if you find ash together with field maple and hazel, you are likely to be in ancient woodland on lime-rich clay. On the sides of limestone valleys in the west, old woods are often dominated by a combination of ash and wych elm. Both types are rich in wild flowers, so if you identify an ancient wood, be sure to return in spring when they will be out.

When woodlands are clear-felled, birch quickly dominates the area. Its delicate leaves cast a light shadow, forming a good habitat with plenty of food in the form of insects and seed, so stands of birch are good places to look for bird and insect life.

Try visiting old woods in different parts of the country and comparing them. Almost every one has some special feature there for the finding.

WHERE TO SEE WOODS AND PARKS WITH FINE OLD TREES: PAGE 340

SHAPED BY CIRCUMSTANCES Study the shape of the trees and try to work out what has made them that way. Woods on the sides of valleys often become progressively more stunted towards the hilltop: the effect of wind pruning. And you may find **clifftop trees** such as these in Cornwall (right), bent in the direction of the prevailing wind because salt spray kills the windward buds.

In woods like the New Forest, try to locate a browse line made by animals such as deer. All the branches up to about 2m (6ft) from the ground will have been nibbled off, leaving a forest of bare trunks.

In old woods, every tree has its individual characteristics – a different shape or bark texture – since each is the product of different parents and has grown up naturally. In plantations, all the trees may come from a similar basic gene stock and look very alike.

The most interesting places in woodland often lie in the glades between the trees – in clearings made by felling and in broad woodland paths or 'rides'. Here, where shafts of sunlight can penetrate, you will find more types of plants than in the shady places. They include grassland flowers and even waterside ones if there is a ditch or wet hollow, and bushes such as bramble and bilberry. Where flowers go, insects follow, and glades are alive with the buzz of bees and the flash of butterflies.

Windows in the wood

Newly felled areas afford a fascinating insight into the battle between plants to colonise bare ground in woodland. The seeds of some, such as the foxglove, lie dormant in the soil for many years until conditions are right; then they germinate. Look for large rosettes of leaves; these mark the foxglove's first year of growth, when the plant puts all its energy into growing deep roots – it does not flower until its second year.

The lush new vegetation of woodland glades becomes a magnet for rabbits, deer and other herbivores with young to feed. But notice how pristine the leaves of the foxgloves are. They are untouched because they are deadly poisonous. This is common in short-lived plants – perhaps because they flower only once they must succeed first time. Two other plants, mullein and hemlock, use the same strategy and also contain poisons that deter most grazers.

While the seeds of foxglove bide their time in the soil, other plants depend for their survival on the help of animals. Bramble seeds, for example, arrive at a possible site in bird droppings, but soon after germination they put out long trailing runners which spread across clearings. Try detaching one from the ground and you will see how it grows new roots as it travels. Other contestants in the rush to fill a clearing, such as wood avens, burdock and enchanter's nightshade, hitch a ride to the spot by having seeds that cling to the fur of animals.

Hooking on *Some plants such as wood avens* **[1]** *and lesser burdock* **[2]** *produce dense heads of hooked seeds as the flowers die. These become detached from the plant when an animal* **[3]** *or passer-by brushes past, and so get transported to clearings in a wood.*

Grip and go Bramble stems rapidly anchor and establish themselves in open ground with numerous root shoots or suckers.

Monopolising space *Foxgloves (below left) and great mullein (right) have densely packed rosettes of leaves, which allow no space for other plants to get a foothold.*

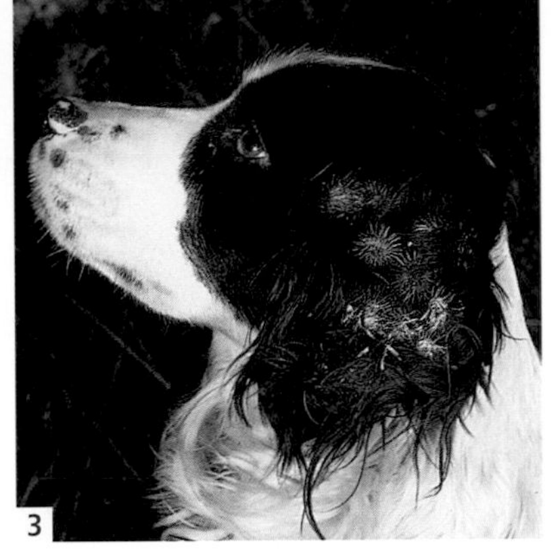

MAGNETS FOR INSECTS

With so much nectar available in the flowering glades and rides, many insects head straight for them. Bumblebees and solitary wasps have a twofold interest in rides: as a source of food and also of nest sites on warm, well-drained soil and even in deep dry ruts. Solitary bees and wasps often make nest burrows in the soil plate clinging to the roots of fallen trees.

Sunny woodland glades are often marvellous places to watch butterflies. They attract large numbers of browns, blues and whites that you usually see in grassland and heaths, but glades are also the places to spot true woodland butterflies such as the white admiral and silver-washed fritillary (both limited to southern Britain), which depend on the woodland habitat for their food plants and lifestyles.

Butterflies don't always settle on plants for long enough to allow identification, but luckily the arboreal specialists have distinctive ways of flying. To get the most out of these airshows, carry a pair of binoculars (see page 15).

Pairs of silver-washed fritillaries may catch the eye as they perform a distinctive aerial courtship dance, in which the golden-brown male repeatedly swoops under and over the darker female. All this happens at low level – just 2m (6ft) above the ground – so it is easy to observe.

You will need luck to see the rare purple emperor butterfly but there are ways of increasing your chances. If you drive to a wood known to contain them, such as Bernwood Forest near Oxford, don't rush away from the car: purple emperors sometimes fly down to settle on roofs and windscreens. Wear something white, too – it's known to attract them. Minerals in the moisture produced by carrion and fresh animal droppings, and sugary sap 'bleeding' from bark also attract purple emperors, so if you come across any of these, try watching from nearby. Goat willows are also worth observing because the female lays her eggs on the foliage.

Look out for the combination of bellflowers and old beetle holes in nearby dead wood. The small black campanula bee exploits both, collecting pollen from the flowers and laying its eggs in the beetle holes, sealing the entrance with dark resin.

Persistent fern Bracken is an exception among plants that grow in glades as it often creates semi-permanent conditions for itself. If you part the underlayer of dead bracken, you can see why this happens: the ground beneath is so dry and shaded that young trees cannot get established.

The few plants that do share the ground with bracken, such as bluebells and creeping soft-grass, can do so because they flower early, before the bracken unfurls its leaves and shuts out the light and rain. They also have shallower roots, so do not compete for the same layer of soil nutrients.

Flights of butterflies The summer flowering of woodland glades makes them a great place to spot butterflies. The purple emperor [1] spends most of its July flight season high up in the treetops, but the silver-washed fritillary [2] and the white admiral [3] are easier to see as they swoop down from treetop to shrub layer in a few powerful wing beats.

The amount of light that reaches a woodland floor in summer varies considerably. Young trees, growing vigorously and competing for space, cast a heavy shade. So do mature trees like beech and oak with tiers of spreading branches and foliage. Other species, such as ash, birch and rowan, cast a lighter shade, while woods on the thin soils of rocky slopes are usually more open than those on level ground with deeper soil. For the woodland flowers that bloom in spring before the leaves open, shade is not a problem, but the summer plants that replace them have to adapt to a strict ration of sun and rain.

Deep in the shadows

With broad flat fronds, ferns are well adapted to garnering what little sunlight reaches the woodland floor (right). But how do the fronds develop without getting trapped by leaf litter and vegetation?

Fern fronds can push through to reach the light because they expand by unrolling outwards. The shape of the young frond, known as a crozier because it is curled over at the top like a bishop's staff, enables it to punch through the debris on the woodland floor. The leaf only unfurls once it is in the clear.

Two-stage life cycle

What really limits most ferns to shady habitats is their dependence on water for reproduction. Examine the underside of a fern frond and you will find small, blister-like containers packed with spores.

After dispersal, the spores grow into a small, fleshy structure which looks like a liverwort, called a prothallus. From this new fronds finally emerge, but only if conditions are wet enough, which is why the best places to look for ferns are where it is cool and damp.

One genus of small, dark green ferns, which you may spot on open ground and on rocks and walls, are the polypodies. They are also epiphytes (able to grow on other plants) and can be found on trees, where their branching roots and numerous root fibres enable them to grip the branches and so grow closer to the light. The roots can also penetrate crevices in the bark to obtain rainwater and nutrients.

Thin layer of soil

Even with these aids, however, polypody ferns are more commonly found in the wetter woods of the far west of Britain, where moss on trunks and branches often produces a thin layer of soil.

Just add water Spores lie in neat rows on the underside of the fronds of a male fern. When they disperse, they will grow into an intermediate stage, the prothallus, but only where the landing site is moist enough. This is why they flourish in shade, where the soil is damp.

High life The oak, with its fissured bark, where moisture and organic matter collect, provides a better support for this polypody fern than smooth-barked birch or beech.

SURVIVING IN SHADE Look at summer woodland-floor plants, such as dog's mercury, herb Paris and twayblade, and you will notice that they have broad spreading leaves which can absorb the maximum amount of sunlight filtering down through the canopy for photosynthesis. But there are exceptions. The leafless **bird's nest orchid** (below left), whose yellow-brown flowering spikes actually look dead, is able to grow in deep shade although it contains no chlorophyll to make photosynthesis possible. It can manage without because its roots are heavily impregnated with special fungal partners, which provide it with nutrients from the rotting humus. **Cow wheat** (below) can grow in shade despite having small narrow leaves. It survives as a semi-parasite, attaching itself to the roots of grasses and taking some food from them, while its green leaves photosynthesise to help supply additional energy.

WOODLAND GRASSES

There are a number of features which distinguish grasses that grow in woods from those found in open country. First, you will see that they tend to grow quite tall, and secondly, they bear large, loose panicles (flowering heads) which are at their best between June and August – later than pasture grasses. The large panicles are useful in the relatively windless environment of a wood because the slightest movement of air can set the flower stalks moving. Look for the hanging purple or yellow stamens and watch how the pollen wafts into the air like smoke, especially when the weather is warm.

If you touch the leaves of woodland grasses, you will discover that many are covered in fine hairs. These trap a film of moist air, which prevents them from drying out and, incidentally, deters herbivores.

An observant walker might notice that woods growing on poor acid mountain and moorland soils contain a higher proportion of grasses and woodrushes than those growing on richer soils – woodrushes are distinguished by the long silky hairs on the margins of their leaves, especially towards the base.

The reason why there are so many is that grasses like wood melick and greater woodrush can trap water flowing downhill in their tangle of roots. This allows them to flourish on the nutrient-poor steep slopes of woods in the north and west.

Root trap Wood melick can grow on the slopes of steep woods because it has numerous fibrous roots. After a shower, the grass is irrigated by water flowing downhill and dissolved nutrients are trapped in the thicket of its roots.

Release *The flower head of pendulous sedge is so delicate that it can be shaken even by the faint breeze that penetrates a wood and releases its pollen in a little cloud.*

Close-up on Squirrels

Few animals are more attractive than squirrels, whether sitting on their haunches or leaping from branch to branch, fluffy tails extended. Their life in the trees demands agility and keen eyesight, which explains why squirrels prefer to move about by day than in the dark, making them easier to observe than most mammals. Even in winter, squirrels can be seen out and about. There are two species of squirrel in Britain, the rare native red and the grey, which has spread to almost every part of Britain since its introduction from North America in the mid 19th century. Though normally easy to tell apart, red squirrels are tinged with grey in winter and the grey squirrel sometimes has a reddish tinge, especially in late summer.

DETECTING A SQUIRREL

If you are walking quietly through a wood, squirrels often betray their presence by their alarm calls. A squirrel that is disturbed while feeding shows its displeasure by a scolding chatter, accompanied by tail-flicking, and sometimes by stamping its feet. You may be able to work out which species you have alarmed: the grey squirrel makes a distinct ***chuck chuck cheree*** and a low chattering ***tuk-tuk*** with its teeth. The red squirrel makes a shrill rasping sound.

In late summer, a noisy jostling from inside a hazel bush is probably a grey squirrel at work, but the first clue to the presence of a grey squirrel in woodland is often the rustle of dry leaves as the animal runs for the nearest tree.

If you are quick, you can catch sight of the squirrel before it moves around to the far side of the trunk. If not wait: once it thinks it is safe, it often pops round again to take another look at you.

NURSERY QUARTERS

Squirrels sleep and rear their young in spherical nests known as **dreys** (below left). A pair will build several in their home range, 10 to100 yards apart, and move from one to the next. A typical drey is slightly larger than a football, constructed of twigs and lined with moss and grass.

Young squirrels are born in large dreys, up to 60cm (2ft) in diameter, which are usually well hidden, often in a hollow tree. Squirrels breed early, between January and April, although when food is plentiful the grey squirrel may have a second litter in summer.

The young remain with their parents for about six weeks until well grown. In a spring wood, listen for their shrill piping calls, and the protective scolding of the parent squirrels when they spot you.

A **magpie's nest** (below right) is similar in size to a drey and it is not unknown for a squirrel to take over their tenancy! So how do you tell the difference? One sign is that most dreys are built close to the trunk of the tree, often in the angle of a branch, whereas magpies normally build their nests out on a branch. Another clue is that dreys incorporate twigs with the leaves still attached, while the birds use only bare dead sticks for nest building.

Squirrel styles The grey squirrel (below) is always more grey than brown, its tail is less bushy than that of the red squirrel, with a white fringe. The red squirrel (far right) is smaller, has a bushier tail that is all one colour and, unlike the grey, has long tufts on its ears in winter.

CONE CLUES

Squirrels leave plenty of signs of their activity for the nature detective to watch out for. In conifer woods, a clue that red or grey squirrels are feeding high in the trees is the patter of cone cores hitting the ground. Pine seeds are the major item in the red squirrel's diet, though grey squirrels eat them too. Squirrels feeding up in the canopy scatter bits of cone over a wide area. If you find a neat pile of cones and scales, the squirrel was feeding on the ground.

Examine the fallen cones: squirrels bite off the scales to get at the nutritious seeds on the tip of each scale, leaving the stripped core with a tuft of scales at the end (inset). Although mice and voles also eat cone seeds, these smaller animals have to gnaw at the scales – they lack the strength to tear them off – so the discarded cone has a smooth round base. Moreover, they seldom leave the evidence lying in the open, and never in large quantities.

Tooth and paw

In autumn, another clue to the presence of squirrels is a scattering of hazelnut shells cracked in half, with clear signs of gnawing at one end. To get at the kernel, squirrels hold the shell between their paws (right) and gnaw a groove across the top. When the hole is large enough, they insert their lower incisors and lever the shell open, leaving the tell-tale evidence. You can often find the shells on a stump, or some other raised place: the height enables the animal to keep a wary lookout as it feeds. If the shells are copiously gnawed but imperfectly cracked, they are probably the work of young squirrels, still practising their technique.

Bare **pale patches** on a slender young tree or branch, where strips of bark have been gnawed off, is another sign of squirrels feeding (inset left). They choose smooth-barked trees like beech or a young common lime – look for clear tooth marks in the exposed wood. The bark itself is seldom eaten and if you look around you may find it lying on the ground near the tree. The squirrels strip it off to get at the nutritious sappy tissue underneath, especially in early summer.

RED ALERT

Why is the grey squirrel so much more numerous than the **red squirrel** (above)? There seem to be a number of reasons. One key factor is that the red squirrel feeds mainly in the tree tops, leaping from tree to tree. This means it needs a continuous canopy of mixed woodland, which is growing increasingly scarce.

The grey squirrel, however, feeds on the ground as well as in the trees, so it is better adapted to a countryside consisting of small woods and open fields, as well as to parks and gardens. Moreover, the grey has a more catholic diet than the red; for example, it can eat acorns that the red squirrel seems unable to digest.

Survival of the fattest

While the red squirrel needs a constant and sufficient supply of food, the grey squirrel has fat deposits within its body, which enable it to survive better in lean periods. The grey squirrel is also larger than the red, and lives at a higher population density. Both factors mean that it tends to find and grab the lion's share of limited food such as hazelnuts. There is little evidence that grey squirrels attack red squirrels. However, the reds are more prone to epidemics, and the grey squirrel is well placed to move into the vacancy left by their deaths.

One place the red squirrel can hold its own is in pinewoods: being lighter and more nimble than the grey, it can more easily reach cones at the tips of branches. But the red has benefited little from the surge in conifer plantations because most trees are felled before peak cone production.

WHERE TO SEE RED SQUIRRELS: PAGE 340

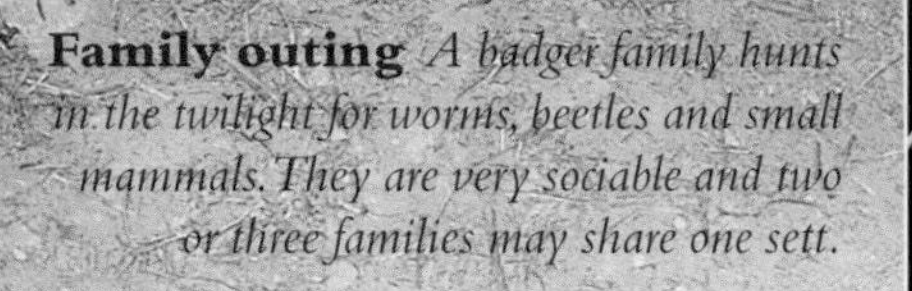

Family outing *A badger family hunts in the twilight for worms, beetles and small mammals. They are very sociable and two or three families may share one sett.*

Hissing for mother *Three-week old little owls in their nest hole in a hollow tree reveal their youth by their downy feathers. Even if you can't see them, you might hear the hissing sound they make when they are hungry.*

Time to see busy parents

By midsummer, the wood has become a quieter place. The vibrant birdsong of spring has slackened, though you will still hear occasional lively outbursts from chaffinches, robins, song thrushes and wrens, and the plaintive calls of chiffchaffs and willow warblers. At dusk or in the early morning in July you may detect the gruff bark of roe deer bucks as they enter their rutting season and compete for does, and by August some birds, such as chiffchaffs and robins, start to sing subdued autumn songs. Most of the migratory birds will leave the woods silently, in contrast to their noisy arrival a few months earlier.

Despite the relative quiet, the summer woods teem with activity. Birds are busy feeding their young at this time of peak insect availability and small mammals are also raising broods.

The short midsummer nights force mammals that are normally nocturnal to emerge in daylight, and this improves your chances of seeing them. If you are lucky, you may see a family of young badgers or stoats at play, or a hedgehog snuffling out to look for food at dusk followed by several small replicas, their spines still soft.

To observe parents and their young you must be very patient, because mammals and birds are extra wary when they are raising their offspring. The best strategy is to lie low and hope that they will come to you. Choose a spot that has plenty of tempting food, such as the edge of a glade or pond, where berries, nectar-rich flowers, young shoots and insects will be plentiful.

How to identify youngsters

If a family of birds comes into view, you can usually tell the young from their parents by their more subdued plumage and their different calls. Young robins, for example, have a speckled breast not a red one and make a strange squeaky buzz. Young blue tits make an incessant hissing murmur as they follow their parents in search of caterpillars. By mid July, most youngsters have flown the nest.

You will need to mount a dusk vigil if you want to see young owls, but there are two clues to look out for in daylight that could lead you to the right place to find a family of long-eared owls. First, these birds prefer large predominantly coniferous woods and secondly, they appropriate old crow and magpie nests.

At dusk, a family of long-eared owls can seem relatively tame, lined up along a branch. Listen for the fledglings' distinctive hunger call, like the squeaking of an unoiled hinge – quite different from the deep *oo-oo-oo* song of the adult birds.

If you visit a broadleaved wood, you are more likely to hear a continuous wheezy two-note hiss, which reveals tawny owl youngsters – again, a sound quite unlike the hoots and ***kewick*** calls of the parents.

RUSTLES IN THE DARK

If the silence of your dusk vigil is broken by little rustling sounds in the undergrowth, watch out for wood mice or bank voles. They emerge from their lairs underneath stumps and in thickets at night to feed on seeds, berries, shoots, insects and larvae.

There are plenty of these small mammals. It has been estimated that a wood covering 65 hectares (160 acres) can support more than 5000 mice and voles – so a hidden rustling animal is quite likely to be one or the other.

If you make a sudden noise, you may even disturb a mother mouse with her brood still grimly hanging onto her teats! If you come to close quarters with a mouse, or find a freshly dead one, look at the markings on the lower neck. If it is a large mouse with a prominent yellow band across the chest, it will be the uncommon yellow-necked mouse, restricted to woods in southern Britain.

Shrews are also active at night, but are very hard to see as they stay in cover on woodland banks and in the long grass at the edges of tracks. If you listen hard, you may be able to hear them give themselves away by their high-pitched twitters.

On the trail of dormice

Dormice still live in woods in England and Wales, especially those with a thick understorey containing berried shrubs and hazel. They are nocturnal and very hard to find, partly because they are good climbers and are often in the branches overhead, but a few clues can lead you to the right locations.

Look for a honeysuckle with some of its bark stripped off: dormice shred the material and use it to weave their summer nests, usually in a tree hole or a disused bird's nest or nest box.

Honeysuckle home *The dormouse makes its nest out of shredded honeysuckle bark (above), emerging at night to forage in the dark for hazelnuts (right).*

Another clue in late summer is hazelnuts scattered on the ground with a round, finely chiselled hole in the side. This shows where a dormouse has turned the nut round in its paws, gnawing on the side to extract the kernel. Wood mice and voles make similar holes, but leave a coarser gnawed edge.

Non-stop nurture *The wood mouse, with her distinctive big ears, hides her nest away, usually underground. But she raises up to five litters a year and so you might glimpse her out foraging for food to support them.*

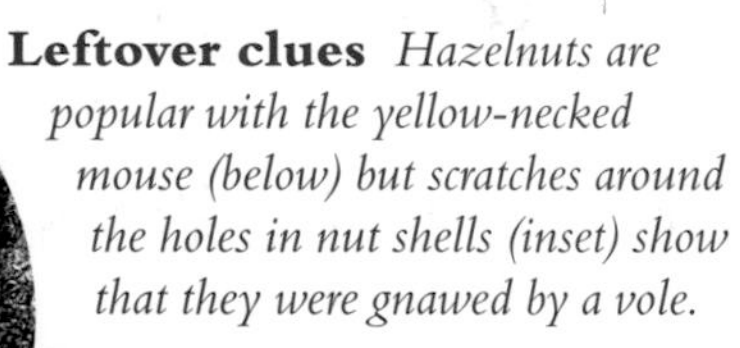

Leftover clues *Hazelnuts are popular with the yellow-necked mouse (below) but scratches around the holes in nut shells (inset) show that they were gnawed by a vole.*

The heart of the tree

Between a third and a half of all woodland invertebrates live on dead and rotting wood. This includes the twiggy debris you find underfoot, large logs and stumps lying on the woodland floor and, most importantly for wildlife, old decaying trees. Fungi, insects, bats and birds also find a niche on rotting wood or in hollow trees. Visiting a park or wood that has some fine old trees will give you the opportunity to study this busy world in action.

Signal flight A hornet flying out of a tree trunk is a clear sign that the tree is hollow enough for it to nest in.

Old trees are rewarding places for a countryside detective because they produce a variety of micro-habitats, such as loose bark, rot holes where rainwater and fallen leaves collect, dead branches and hollow interiors filled with a moist, organically rich pulp of sawdust, leaf mould, fungi, droppings and other decaying matter.

How do you recognise a hollow tree? Some are easy to spot: they have gaping holes that you can peer into. But by this time the tree is like an empty shell and much of the wildlife attracted by its rotting phase has departed. It is more worthwhile to investigate a tree that is still undergoing the process of decay.

One sign of an ageing tree, which has probably started to rot, is dead boughs protruding through the canopy. Wasps, bees or bats entering a hole in the trunk also indicate a hollow.

The clinching evidence is finding bracket fungi on a tree. They are often prominent, but some can be hidden among the grass at ground level so look there too. As a tree increases in girth, more and more of the interior is heartwood, which no longer conducts water and sap and so is not needed to keep the tree alive. It is this that is rotted by bracket fungi. Once the

Rotting core *Bracket fungi (left) enter the tree through damaged bark, and feed on the heartwood. The birch polypore (above) attacks only birch trees.*

Nursery branch *The presence of some insects specifically indicates a hollow tree because their larvae depend on it for food. The long-horned beetle (below), with its stout antennae, is typical of the many beetles that lay their eggs in rotting wood, which the larvae consume after they hatch.*

heartwood has been reduced to fragments, invertebrates get to work on it. Some beetles and moth larvae eat wood with the help of bacteria in their gut, others eat the fungi, or decaying matter trapped in the hollow.

Tree watch

To see something of this rich life, sit and watch an old tree in a sunny position to see which insects visit it. And look for supporting evidence round about you: many of the insects associated with dead wood are easier to find on nearby flower heads, especially on brambles or hogweed. If you spot them, you can search for a hollow tree somewhere nearby.

See if you can find insect larvae, millipedes or wood lice, and look for spiders and snails. A good indicator of a hollow tree is the lesser stag beetle, a large black beetle with short 'antlers', which are in fact, its jaws. Its larvae feed on the rotten wood of broad-leaved trees, leaving holes as wide as a pencil.

NO HARM DONE

Does hollowing kill the tree? No, it is a natural event in the life of any long-lived tree, and probably helps to prolong the tree's life by lightening the load on its roots and recycling nutrients into the soil beneath. Hollow trunks also stand up quite well to winter gales.

Many hollow trees were pollarded in the past and these old pollard trees can assume extraordinary shapes, with gnarled, embossed trunks and sometimes corkscrew branches. They should not be thought of as being 'sick' as their hollowness and stunted shape are not caused by disease, but by ageing.

If you make a note of the hollow trees you find and revisit them, you'll discover that trees rot at different rates. Those with the hardest wood, like oak, hornbeam and yew, take longest to decay. Beech trees have softer wood, so rot faster and beech woods are particularly likely places to look for hollow trees.

AT HOME IN THE TRUNK

Hollow trees offer valuable nest sites. Walk through a wood with a large proportion of old broad-leaved trees and you have far more chance of seeing hole-nesting birds like redstarts, marsh tits or woodpeckers than in a wood, or plantation, where all the trees are the same age.

Bats, too, are dependent on hollow trees for their summer roosts and nurseries, and the scarcity of ancient woodland is one reason for their decline. Foresters remove old or hollow trees from commercial woodlands, so the place to look for bats is in mature woods, with water nearby where they can feed on mosquitoes and other aquatic insects. Dusk is the best time to search for bats, when they emerge, one at a time, from exit holes high up on the trunk.

Flight patterns

Try to recognise the shape and characteristic flight patterns of bats. Noctules emerge early, are noticeably large with narrow wings, and fly very high and fast. Pipistrelles are much smaller, with a fluttering flight at about rooftop height, which gave them the alternative name of 'flittermice'. You can also see the extraordinary ears of long-eared bats in flight, extended like horns.

If you stand in a glade in the woods on a still warm evening with a big torch, bats will often come to investigate. You can then watch them catching moths attracted to the light.

WHERE TO SEE WOODS AND PARKS WITH FINE OLD TREES: PAGE 340

Safe inside *By making their homes in hollow trees, animals such as the long-eared bat (above) and the pied flycatcher (below) are protected from their predators.*

Watching ants work

Mounds of debris, up to a metre high and several metres in diameter, can sometimes be found in woodland clearings. These are ant hills built by wood ants, and on a warm day you may spot large numbers of these insects scurrying over the surface of their home and the ground around. Some will be working alone, carrying small objects back to the ant hill. Others will be in teams, taking large items, such as a dead caterpillar, back to their nest in the ant hill.

Construction techniques Wood ants often build a nest around an old stump: the roots of the dead tree create a ready-made system of underground passages to house the eggs, larvae and adult insects. Look closely and you will see that the ant hill is composed of thousands of fragments of woodland floor debris (inset below), restricted to the size a single ant can carry. In conifer forests, pine needles predominate, but in broad-leaved woodland, the mound will contain small dead twigs, leaf stalks and fragments of dry grass and leaves.

The shape of the ant hill and where it is suggest which of the three species of wood ants you're dealing with. In England or Wales, the red ant (*Formica rufa*), which builds tall, dome-shaped hills, predominates. In Scotland, however, *Formica lugubris*, which constructs broader, flatter ant hills, and *Formica aquilonia*, a builder of small, pyramidal hills, replace their English cousin.

Why do wood ants build such large and prominent nests? Probably the main reason is that they need a big nest in the sun to create warm, humid interior conditions in the nest. Some of the warmth comes from the sun, but most is generated from decay, because the ant hill is like a compost heap. You can gauge how efficiently a hill generates heat by holding your hand over it and feeling the warmth.

The nests are also very waterproof, with the outer layer acting like a thatched roof; even in a downpour, only the top inch or so gets wet.

Wood ants' nests are larger than they look: the ants excavate galleries deep in the underlying soil to house their stores of food and developing eggs and larvae. An average colony contains around 100,000 individuals, and a large one up to three times that number.

They have few natural predators except the green woodpecker, which slurps up ants with its long tongue (see page 43). Humans, however, do pose a threat – by depleting the woodland habitat on which wood ants depend, or destroying nests, which take months to build and can last for decades.

Pollination pals *Rosebay willowherb provides a high-energy snack of nectar for a wood ant, which will carry off its pollen.*

Q I disturbed a jay lying on top of a wood ants' mound with its wings stretched out. What was it doing?

A Jays and other birds are pestered by parasites, such as feather lice, which live on their skin and plumage.

By spread-eagling itself over the ants' mound, the jay was encouraging the insects to rush to the surface and squirt formic acid – an effective de-louser – over its feathers. The behaviour is known as 'anting'.

Protecting the nest Hold your hand close to the surface of an ant nest – the one pictured belongs to the Scottish species *Formica lugubris* – and the ants will probably treat you as an enemy and take defensive action. Smell your hand and you should detect a sharp, vinegary smell: the ants protect their home by squirting jets of formic acid from glands in their hind-quarters. Watch carefully and you may see them doing this, curling their bodies between their legs and aiming carefully. You can see it with the naked eye but don't get too close in case you get a dose of stinging liquid in your face.

If you don't want to be a guinea pig, test the strength of the ants' defences by dropping a blue flower like a speedwell or forget-me-not onto the nest, then waving your hand over it. The blue petals should quickly turn pink and shrivel from blasts of acid. If you drop a tiny bit of debris onto the nest, you will see it being quickly removed or covered up by the ants.

TRAILS Look at the ground around the nest and you will spot columns of ants on the move – marching out into the surrounding woodland or returning to the nest. Try following a few individuals to see how far they range. The 'streets' are usually fairly straight, kept meticulously clear and can extend 100m (110yd) up to the main hunting grounds for their insect prey in the tree canopy: watch for columns of ants marching up and down the trunk.

Search tree trunks and low branches along the trail and you will almost certainly find **hunting parties** (above). They work in teams and paralyse creatures such as caterpillars with formic acid. Then they either cart them intact to the nest working in teams, or butcher them on the spot with their jaws into pieces small enough to be managed by one ant. Once back at the nest, adult ants eat the food before regurgitating it in a form digestible to the larvae.

UNWELCOME VISITORS

Wood ants' nests are used by some 300 other species of insects, including many specialist beetles such as *Cetonia aurata*, a shiny, coppery green rose chafer. Some of these visitors are harmless, or even useful scavengers. Other lodgers, however, feed on the defenceless larvae of the ants.

Where a wood meets a heath, keep an eye open for a little dark, hairy hover fly, *Microdon eggeri*. It lays its eggs in the ant nest and, when the larvae hatch out, they feed on the ants' faeces, helping to keep the nest clean. If you are in a wood in the Scottish Highlands in summer, you may find little beige moths emerging from the nest. These are the offspring of *Myrmecozela ochraceella*, whose caterpillars perform a similar role.

Ready to mate *Male wood ants swarm from the nest in summer, each trying to mate with one of the nest's virgin queens.*

Starting a new colony

On a very warm still day in June or July you may, with luck, come across winged male ants emerging from the nest.

Mating takes place on the ground, either on the nest or on nearby plants. You may, however, notice many males with deformed wings, which are unable to fly. The cause is unknown, but it may be due to a widespread viral disease.

Wood ants' nests contain a large number of virgin queens and you may see one of them flying off after mating to establish a new colony. She sheds her wings soon after the mating flight, then burrows into the ground to found a new colony.

Close-up on
The oak

Look at the fruit *The acorns of the English oak (far left) are long, and they are carried on long stalks. Those of the sessile oak (near left) are dumpier, with short stalks or none at all.*

The mightiest of Britain's native forest trees is the oak, and its spreading boughs, furrowed trunk and bunches of lobed leaves, make it among the most easily recognised. There are two species of native oak: to tell them apart, examine the leaves. Those of the English, or common oak (also called the pedunculate) have very short stalks and they turn up at the base to form two small lobes like ears; the sessile, or durmast oak has long leaf stalks and no 'ears'.

If you can get a view of the whole tree, the shape offers you another clue. The English oak normally has a short trunk with broad twisting branches. The sessile oak has a longer trunk and narrower, straighter branches, which give it a more rectangular shape. But you will often find that many trees share features of both shapes, probably because they are hybrids of the two species.

The oak is an excellent place for countryside detecting because it supports more wildlife than any other British tree. If you know of a big oak, try looking for the opportunities it might present. Are there holes where rainwater and detritus might collect? Look for places where the bark has sloughed off, perhaps after a lightning strike, which leaves a characteristic long scar. Oak is vulnerable to lightning because its furrowed bark holds water and so conducts electricity. Are there wounds from which sap is leaking? This sugary substance will attract many butterflies, such as the comma and red admiral. If the tree has started to hollow out, there will be a teeming world of insects hidden inside, feeding on fungi and detritus. Such trees also provide valuable roosting sites for bats, and nesting opportunities for owls and stock doves.

1

HOW OLD IS THIS OAK?

By comparing an oak with the following descriptions, you can guess its age, although a tree which is growing in rich soil will be bigger than one of the same age in poor soil.

1-10 years A first-year oak seedling **[1]** consists of a stalk topped by a single bunch of leaves. By its second year it has developed branches.

10-80 years A young oak is tall and slender and does not reach full size until about 80 years of age. Then the trunk starts to increase in girth instead of height, and the canopy widens as the branches spread out.

100-200 years The oak reaches maturity sometime between 100-200 years **[2]**. Now the bark is deeply furrowed, some of the lower branches will have been shed and the trunk may have started to hollow out. The now decaying roots cannot support the weight of the canopy and the crown starts to die back, producing a 'stag's head' look as dead branches protrude like antlers from the leafy crown.

300 years At this stage the oak's trunk will be massive – 6m (20ft) or more in girth while its crown consists mostly of a few thick branches.

400 years Now there will be more dead wood than living, **[3]** with holes where branches have fallen, and dying limbs, without bark, exposed to the weather.

500 years Britain's oldest oaks are well over 500 years old and often have names, like Major Oak and Parliament Oak of Sherwood Forest. They look hollow and decrepit, yet still produce leaves and even acorns from their stumps and remaining branches.

By the time it reaches this age, the tree will have been host to innumerable invertebrates, fungi, nesting birds and foraging mammals, and will have fathered five generations of mature oaks.

2

3

THE OAK TEEMS WITH MINIATURE LIFE

A large oak tree is the larder for astronomical numbers of insects and their larvae – more than 1000 different species. On a still day in early summer you can sometimes hear the patter of their droppings, or frass, as it falls onto dry leaves beneath the crown. Common caterpillars include those of the buff-tip moth, which you can recognise from their gregarious habit **[1]**. Later they retreat alone under loose bark, or burrow in the soil and pupate. Another group to search for on the oak are the moth caterpillars called 'loopers', from the way they walk by looping their backs.

However, you won't find so many caterpillars as summer progresses. The reason is that oak leaves become tougher with age and accumulate bitter-tasting tannins, so many insects complete their life-cycle while the leaves are still tender.

The curved projection, or rostrum, of the acorn weevil **[2]** has jaws at the end for eating leaves. The female also uses it to drill into an acorn, where she lays a single egg. When it hatches, the larva feeds on the acorn fruit within the protective shell.

Sometimes it is easier to see the damage than the insect. A transparent tube around the edge of leaves is the work of leaf-mining caterpillars; leaves in tatters have been eaten by the sawfly larva, an important source of food for redstarts and warblers.

The time is right By timing their breeding to coincide with the period when the greatest number of caterpillars are feasting on the oak leaves in early summer, birds like the blue tit can feed up to 12 hungry youngsters at once.

OAK GALLS When you examine an oak tree, you will often come across strange growths and swellings, some of which look like miniature fruits. These are galls, distorted plant tissues produced by the tree as a reaction to an invading insect, fungus or other organism.

Oak trees have a greater variety of galls than any other plant, most of them associated with tiny, rarely seen wasps, which lay their eggs in the leaves or leaf stalks. The tree responds by forming a gall around them, which provides soft nutritious food for the developing larva and keeps it safe from predators and hard weather. Galls seem to do the tree no harm, although knopper galls may severely reduce an acorn crop.

Perhaps the best known of the galls common to oak trees is the **oak apple** (above left), a round pinkish brown growth, about the size of a 10p piece, which you find attached to oak twigs. If you cut one open in early summer, you will discover about 30 tiny wasp larvae inside – you will find it easier to see them if you use a magnifying glass. Sometimes you may also spot a large plump grub preying on the larvae – this is the caterpillar of a small moth, which lays its eggs in the oak apple gall. For more about galls, see page 238.

Long, warm days make banksides green

Natural and man-made waterways burst with life in summer

By early June the freshwater world is at its busiest. With warm weather and up to 16 hours of sunlight a day – twice as much as in midwinter – waterside plants grow at a breakneck pace, smothering the banks in deep drifts of greenery.

This tangle of vegetation can make it difficult to get close to the water's edge, but it also brings many waterside animals right up to eye-level. Dragonflies and damselflies bask on leaves in the sunshine, darting away to chase their prey, while pollinating insects throng around the waterside flowers.

Below the surface of the water, too, life is reaching its annual crescendo, as more and more plants and animals join in the race to reproduce.

Man-made routes

Britain has more than 2000 miles of canals and other man-made waterways. Most, such as this one in Lancashire (above), are more than two centuries old, with well-established communities of plants and animals.

Canals were originally lined with clay soil, pounded flat to form a waterproof layer that stretched from bank to bank. Although clay is difficult to dig, and therefore not easy to cultivate, it is very fertile, which is why canalside plants often grow well. Where the clay is still intact on the canal bed, yellow flags, bur reeds and bulrushes sprout from below the waterline, while willowherbs and purple loosestrife flourish on the banks. Together, they provide food for many kinds of insects, and just the sort of cover that swans and other water birds need to nest in seclusion and safety.

The sides of canals provide swans with good nesting sites, while the waters contain plentiful supplies of aquatic plants and insects for their cygnets.

Canal banks crumble over time, and modern repairs are often carried out using steel and concrete in place of the original clay. If the edge of a canal is concrete then the canal bed usually is, too, but if you see steel used to repair minor bankside problems, the original clay bed is probably still in place. For the widest range of canalside wildlife, search out places where there is nothing man-made between the water and the bank.

Still waters

Rivers carve deeper and wider channels with time, whereas lakes only diminish, filling up with silt and the remains of dead plants, and turning into marshes and eventually dry land. But it is a slow process. Many of Britain's lakes, including Llyn Dinas in Snowdonia (above) were formed when glaciers retreated at the end of the last Ice Age, more than 12,000 years ago. They have been filling in ever since but it will still be many millennia before they disappear.

In summer, Llyn Dinas burgeons with plant life and what was open water in spring becomes a floating jigsaw of weed. You can expect to find this kind of lush growth in any shallow lake in a valley or on low-lying ground. Where there are cattle and cultivated farmland nearby, lakes will be even greener. Water draining into the lake brings nutrients from cow dung and crop fertilisers, encouraging blooms of microscopic algae, which block out the light essential for rooted plants to thrive.

This lakeland idyll is a world away from the deep, dark waters of mountain lakes and lochs. There, summer brings fleeting warmth to the water near the surface, but the depths stay dark and cold, so that most plant and animal life is concentrated in the shallows.

Lily pads on a lake act as mid water resting spots for frogs, landing platforms for damselflies and other insects, and as nurseries for newly hatched water snails.

How plants live in water

For plants, living in water has many advantages. They will not dry out and are not exposed to buffeting winds. To spread they simply creep through the mud, or scatter their seeds or parts of their bodies to drift downstream. But there is a disadvantage: plants need to get oxygen to their roots, and this is not easy in water. Only a small number of plants have developed ways of doing this and they grow with little competition for space or nutrients in their watery world.

If you look at any pond or small lake in summer, you will see there are two obvious kinds of water plants: those that have floating leaves and others that grow clear of the water's surface. But these are just the visible ones. If you trawl a net beneath the surface, you will come up with a variety of smaller plants that are not anchored to the bottom but spend their lives adrift. These three different lifestyles – afloat, aloft and adrift – allow water plants to grow in a range of depths and situations.

A spread of glossy, dark green leaves floating on the surface will probably belong to either water lilies or pondweed. If you can reach a leaf, try giving it and its stalk a squeeze and you will find that in both plants they feel slightly spongy. This is because they contain air-filled spaces to make the plant buoyant. These spaces also help oxygen in the air diffuse down from a plant's leaves to its roots.

In early summer you might see a clump of leaves, like a pineapple top, floating on the water. This is the water soldier, one of Britain's strangest water plants. It lives in ponds and lakes – now mainly in East Anglia – and spends most of the year on the bottom, but it rises to the surface in summer to flower.

Some normally submerged plants, such as the spiked water milfoil, reproduce by producing flowers that stick up above the water's surface for pollination. However, truly submerged plants like Canadian pondweed mainly spread by pieces breaking off and developing as independent plants.

Feeding in water *Long stalks allow* ***water lilies*** *(above) to float on the surface while taking up nutrients through roots anchored in the bottom. The small up-standing white flowers of* ***bogbean*** *(above right), fringed with cottony hairs, are found only in shallow, slow-moving water as the leaves and flowers are held up by hollow, floating stems, which would bend and break in a fast current.* ***Bladderwort*** *(right) floats freely without roots. Among its feathery leaves are hollow swellings (inset) which trap water fleas and other tiny animals. These provide the bladderwort with extra nitrogen-rich nourishment.*

A SHADE TOO GREEN Few scenes are more peaceful than cows drinking at the water's edge, but for plants the comings and goings of these heavy-footed herbivores is a mixed blessing. Where muddy water is stirred up by cattle hoofs flote grass thrives, but their trampling flattens and damages most other riverbank plants, opening up bare ground where plantains, docks and thistles can take over.

Cow dung and urine make potent fertilisers and leach into the water where they encourage the growth of algae. If the water is still or slow-flowing, these multiply into a **slimy green mass** that floats to the surface. This is harmful to other kinds of aquatic life because it cuts off light to the lower layers and, when it dies and decays, soaks up oxygen that water animals need. For this reason, careful farmers keep slurry and running water a safe distance apart where possible.

SPOT THE INTRUDER Many plants have been introduced – some accidentally, others deliberately – from other parts of the world. A mass of tangled greenery below the surface, with tiny pink flowers floating on thread-like stalks, is the curly water thyme from South Africa. It is popular with aquarium owners and, like many introduced species, was originally brought to Britain for this market.

Found first in the New Forest and now throughout Britain, the New Zealand swamp stonecrop is taking hold so fast it is driving out native water plants. Most stonecrops live in dry rocky places, but this antipodean species thrives in ponds.

A particular success is the unsinkable **water fern** (below) from North America. Try splashing one and see how the water rolls off the silvery, water-repellent hairs on its upper surface. It grows so fast it can push other plants right out of the water, stifling life in shallow ditches and ponds in places like the Somerset Levels.

COPING WITH THE CURRENT

Lean over a bridge spanning a shallow river or stream and look for the stems of plants snaking in the current. Only plants with flexible stems can survive in this fluid environment without being snapped off.

Stems trailing like dark green locks of hair from a practically smooth surface, such as a rock or a tree root, will probably belong to willow moss. Like all mosses, it can get a hold where other plants cannot because it does not have true roots and therefore does not need to be bedded in soil. Instead, willow moss anchors itself with hair-like rootlets called rhizoids.

Water crowfoot, like many water plants, has two types of leaves. Those above water are broad and flat in order to float; the underwater ones are divided and feathery so they are not torn to shreds by the current. Try lifting a strand out of the water with a stick to see the difference.

Scattering seeds *Many freshwater plants grow creeping stems but some, such as yellow flag (above), alder and branched bur-reed, spread by releasing their seeds into the current which carries them off to new sites.*

The tip of the tale *A mass of water crowfoot covers the River Avon in Hampshire. The white flowers float at the end of stems up to 1.2m (4ft) long, which are almost entirely submerged.*

Quiet life in slow waters

Slow-moving canals, river-fed lakes and quiet backwaters make perfect watery habitats because there is plenty of light, food and oxygen, and sheltered places to hide. Open, sunlit water is the best place to see damselflies and dragonflies and the birds that hawk over the water feeding on them. But where the water is overshadowed by trees plants do not get enough light and fallen leaves alter the water's acidity, creating an environment unsuitable for many animals.

Some fish prefer to lurk among roots or weeds, safe from the eyes of predatory birds. These are usually the fish with sluggish lifestyles, such as bream and tench, which root for food in the muddy bottom.

In summer, still or slow water may be low in oxygen but that doesn't trouble these slow-movers, who have equally low oxygen requirements. Even the carnivores, such as perch, are energy efficient, darting out from weedy lairs only to ambush passing roach or younger perch.

Many of the large fish in canals, such as perch, were introduced for angling. Smaller fish such as gudgeon and stickleback have probably spread naturally, and feed on invertebrates, including damselfly and dragonfly larvae.

Damselflies and dragonflies

If you are walking by or boating on a lake or quiet backwater in early summer, look out for damselflies and dragonflies. This is when the nymphs emerge from the water to take up life as adults in the air. Damselflies are smaller than dragonflies but their behaviour can also help you to tell them apart.

Damselflies snatch small insects from plants. Their flight is weaker and more fluttery than the purposeful flight of dragonflies as they patrol the waterside and they often stay close to the ground or to the water's surface.

Dragonflies attack prey in midair, and have two feeding techniques, both visible from the bank. 'Hawkers', such as the emperor, mount an airborne patrol of their feeding territory, ready to attack anything edible flying within range. 'Darters', such as the broad-bodied libellula, perch on plants and rush out to snatch passing prey.

If you see one damselfly or dragonfly clasping another by the neck they are probably not fighting but have just mated (see above). The pair flies together over the water as the female prepares to lay her eggs. In some species she simply drops them, but in most she carefully fastens each one to a plant, often under water. Sometimes both insects dive and stay under for up to an hour.

Mating wheel Damselflies and dragonflies mate in a unique way, with the male and female linking back-to-front in a heart or wheel shape. Here, the blue male damselfly grips the female behind the head while she bends her abdomen forwards, underneath her.

Q Do dragonflies sting?

A Dragonflies can look menacing, and, as aerial predators, they take a keen interest in any kind of movement. This is why they may fly close by if you walk through their feeding territory. But despite appearances they do not have stings, and are completely harmless to us, though not to other insects.

SPOT THE DIFFERENCE

DRAGONFLY OR DAMSELFLY? The first clue to distinguishing dragonflies from damselflies is the way they hold their wings. Most **dragonflies** (above left) hold their wings outwards when they rest, but **damselflies** (above right) fold them lengthways along their backs. Body size is another good indicator: if the body is thicker than a matchstick, it's a dragonfly.

IDENTITY PARADE – Damselflies & Dragonflies

During summer, nearly 40 species of damselflies and dragonflies are on the wing around Britain. Most of them are native species, but a few are migrants from the Continent. The ones shown here are all commonly seen over slow-flowing streams, ponds and lakes. All the descriptions below refer to males; the females are often duller in colour.

Common blue damselfly This very widespread insect is one of several British damselflies with black-and-blue bodies. It can be seen flying along roadsides and hedgerows, as well as over rivers and ponds that contain plenty of water plants, between May and September.

Banded agrion One of Britain's most beautiful waterside insects, the banded agrion damselfly can be easily identified by its wings, which have a large sooty coloured patch. The best place to look for it is over slow-flowing rivers and streams, between May and August.

Broad-bodied libellula The libellula is a 'darter' dragonfly with a fat, bright blue abdomen (in females the abdomen is brown). You may come across a broad-bodied libellula on your garden pond: it is on the wing between May and August.

Emperor dragonfly Britain's largest 'hawker' dragonfly, the emperor, is distinguished by its enormous eyes and a wingspan of about 10cm (4in). It patrols over ponds and lakes from June to September, and often preys on other dragonflies.

SHELL SPOTTING The two water snails that you are most likely to see in Britain are the great pond snail and the great ramshorn snail.

The **ramshorn snail** (right) is the smaller of the two. It has a flat coiled shell without a spire, which does look just like a ram's horn. It can be found in both ponds and ditches and also in large lakes.

The **great pond snail** (below) has a shell with a sharply pointed spire. Look for it in drainage ditches and weed-choked ponds.

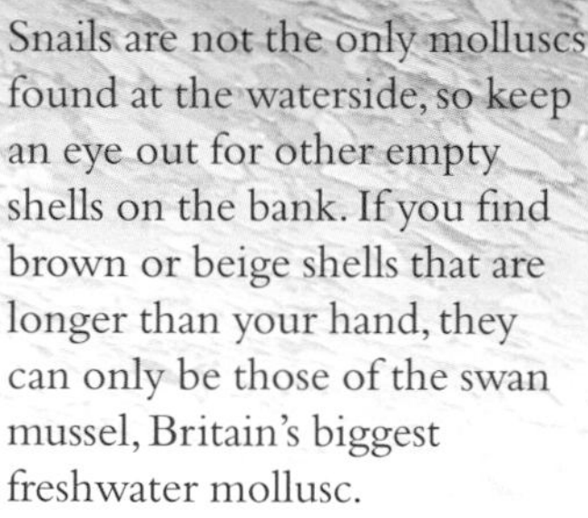

SNAIL TRAIL

Of all Britain's freshwater animals, the snails are among the easiest to find, usually crawling about on underwater plants. In summer they can often be spotted at the surface. Look for them particularly where the water is covered by duckweed.

The great pond snail and ramshorn snail (see above) and their relatives breathe using a single lung, like snails on land, and so come to the surface to breathe. Other water snails have gills, just as fish do, which enable them to take their oxygen from the water. You can recognise a gilled snail because it has a trap door (operculum), that it can use to shut itself inside its shell. To see the operculum at work, pick a snail out of the water and watch it close itself in.

Snails are not the only molluscs found at the waterside, so keep an eye out for other empty shells on the bank. If you find brown or beige shells that are longer than your hand, they can only be those of the swan mussel, Britain's biggest freshwater mollusc.

Swan mussels live half-buried in the beds of rivers, canals and lakes, and feed by filtering food from the water. Live mussels are rarely seen, but their empty shells are sometimes thrown up on muddy riverbanks after flooding or they may be brought to the surface when canals and ditches are dredged.

Close-up on
The food web

Every animal or plant features on something else's menu, even if only after it has died. By noting what eats what, you can trace the chains that link one element of the natural world to the next, which depends on it for its existence, and see how the chains link up to make the food web. The water's edge is a good place for doing this, because you can see each link in the chain in this habitat from a spot on the bank. And spring and summer are the best times to carry out these observations, because with the onset of the breeding season the food needs of animals grow and activity in every part of the food web becomes increasingly brisk.

Eaters and eaten

At the beginning of all food chains are living things which harness the energy in sunlight and use it to make food. On land, these are almost always leafy plants, but in fresh water they include floating and rooted plants, and microscopic algae. Beyond this, the levels that animals occupy in the chain are not always easy to work out. As underwater larvae, midges feed on microscopic animals, which in turn live on algae, but as adults midges may feed on the blood of mammals (including humans) or the nectar of waterside flowers. As a result, they take up different levels in the food chain at different stages of their lives. Many animals also eat a varied diet.

The hobby has no natural enemies in Britain, putting it at the end of the food chain. It snatches dragonflies and other insects in midair, and also preys on sand martins and swallows.

The dragonfly preys on midges and mosquitoes, putting it on a level with the swallow and sand martin in the waterside food chain. But it also eats other dragonflies, raising it to the level of the hobby.

The midge is near the beginning of the waterside food chain and is eaten by dragonflies, other insects, and birds such as swallows and sand martins. Swarming male midges are easy prey for birds, but being in a large group increases their chances of attracting and mating with females.

You might see a hobby catching dragonflies, but it also hunts small birds, which themselves eat dragonflies. This puts the hobby simultaneously one level and two levels above the dragonfly.

The most successful creatures are often those with wide-ranging eating habits since they can cope best with fluctuations in their food supply. But because many creatures have very precise dietary requirements, the slightest change in a habitat can lead to the decline of a string of creatures. The causes may range from a farmer spraying his crops with insecticide, thus ridding the fields of leatherjackets, which provide sustenance for rooks, to a natural loss of a habitat when a pond silts up or a tree dies. Once one link in the chain is broken, everything above is affected. This is why every plant and animal matters, as does their great diversity.

THE FOOD WEB UNDER WATER Even in the artificial environment of a garden pond dozens of food chains exist; in a river or lake things are many times more complex. The example of a six-link chain described below concentrates on life under water.

The first link in this underwater food chain is vegetation. Water plants and algae create the food that fuels most freshwater food chains. In this one **frog tadpoles [1]** graze on algae from the leaves of underwater plants and, as they begin to metamorphose, on tiny insects. Next in the chain come dragonfly nymphs: (larvae) using a 'mask' – a set of stabbing mouthparts that shoot forwards at lightning speed – they make short work of the tadpoles. Roach then search out the dragonfly nymphs among the water plants and crush them with serrated teeth at the backs of their mouths. Roach are often preyed on by mature pike, which can swallow a young roach whole.

All food chains end with a top predator – an animal with no natural enemies of its own once it becomes an adult – and in many ponds and lakes, the pike's only enemy is man, so the food chain stops with this fish. But other areas of fresh water may contain the **otter [2]**, an animal which will sometimes catch and eat a pike – particularly a small one – making it the top predator in an underwater food chain.

The swallow occupies the same level on the food chain as the dragonfly, since it feeds on midges and mosquitoes. But because it eats dragonflies too, it is also at a level above.

Daubenton's bat enters the waterside food chain at dusk and occupies an equivalent level to the swallow. It flies over water, hunting late-flying dragonflies and other insects. Like other bats, it eats only the bodyparts of its prey, biting off and discarding the wings.

LINKS ON LAND Many food chains begin with grass. Its leaves capture energy in sunlight to provide food for grazers, such as rabbits. The rabbits then convert the grass into muscles and fat: food for meat-eaters, such as foxes.

A fox is a top predator, but the chain carries on after its death, when the scavengers move in. The **burying beetle [1]** eats the flesh of dead animals, and uses it to provide food for its grubs. Beetle and larva both become food for the **carrion crow [2]**, which also feeds on the corpse. As the dead animal decays it returns nutrients to the soil, which are taken up by the grass and the cycle begins again.

The deepest water in canals is always in the middle and the shallowest by the banks, which usually have the same plants growing on either side, but rivers follow a snaking path, with the deepest and fastest water on the outside of bends, and gentle shallows on the inside. This lopsidedness influences plant and animal life, and means that if you explore a stretch of river you will find a variety of habitats, including new ground ready for plants to grow on, hideaways for predatory fish, and welcome refuges for their prey.

A river panorama

IN THE SHALLOWS Stand in clean shallow water at the edge of a river or stream and gently stir up the bottom with a stick – within just a few seconds, a flurry of inquisitive tiddlers will be darting around your ankles. If you want to get a closer look, try scooping some up in a net or trapping them in a jar baited with bread or a piece of red wool, which looks enticingly like a worm. You might pull out **minnows**, which live in shallow water, or small fry, the young of other river fish such as dace and perch, which lay their eggs in these nursery waters in the shelter of weeds.

When a river is in its middle reaches it meanders through the landscape in ever-widening loops. As it twists and turns the current gouges soil and gravel from the outside edge of bends, and drops it on the insides of other bends, where the water slows as it rounds the corner.

This makes the inside edges interesting places to explore, because the ground is constantly being built up, creating vacant lots for 'pioneer' plants, which are adept at spreading into new areas. Among them you will find hemp agrimony, willowherbs and young willows, all of which have seeds that spread to new sites on the wind.

Some plants arrive on bare ground in a different way. If you scramble down onto a spit or gravel bank in summer, it's likely that you will be carrying hooked seeds on your clothes as animals carry them on their coats when they come to drink. These come from burdocks – large, soft-leaved plants that look similar to thistles – and if they drop on to suitable ground, they will germinate and take root.

The quiet water downstream from these gravelly banks is a good place to search for water parsnip, a plant with white umbrella-shaped flower heads that grow up to shoulder height. The soft mud at the water's edge often also suits clumps of horsetails and reeds. Horsetails have brush-like stems full of silica, which makes them stiff and hard. Rub a stem between your hands and you will feel why they were once used for scouring dishes.

Taking a short cut

As the current chisels away at the outside of a bend and builds up the inside it can create a loop so tight that the river eventually breaks through, and the loop is pinched off. This cut-off loop is known as an ox-bow lake. You are most likely to find one on a wide, flat flood plain, where a river has had space to wander. Starved of flowing water, the ox-bow lake is no more than a crescent-shaped pool, showing the remains of the riverside vegetation. Like all lakes, ox-bow lakes eventually fill up with decaying vegetation – often they develop into swamps and willow carrs.

You may be able to trace the original meandering path of the river by looking for the raised lines of the old banks, cradling the dry, overgrown riverbed in between.

SHADY WATER Study the anglers along a meandering riverbank and you will see that many of them choose to sit by the shady water at the outside of a river bend. This is where large **brown trout** are most likely to lie up during the day, hiding in holes gouged out by the current. They are very hard to spot as they are well camouflaged against the muddy riverbed and completely hidden in their lairs, but look out for them at dusk when they leave their holes and rise to the surface to catch insects and smaller fish.

HIDDEN IN THE WEEDS One of Britain's largest freshwater predatory fish is the **pike**. This 'monster of the deep' can grow to 1m (3ft) or more and has few predators except for anglers. It skulks in weeds in slow water, ready to pounce. Swimming in shoals offers fish protection against pike, which find it hard to pick out a single target from a large number of fish. Its size also restricts the pike to deep water, where vulnerable young fish seldom venture.

OUT IN THE STREAM Some fish live only in a particular situation, in shallow or fast-moving water or among vegetation, but others are much less fussy. **Rudd** thrive in slow-flowing rivers where there is plenty of plant growth but they also feed on insects at the surface and swim in deep water in the middle of the stream. With its bright red fins, the rudd can be mistaken for the orange-finned roach, which is found in the same waters and is often more numerous. Both fish grow to around 30cm (12in) long. The chub also swims here, particularly in rivers with strong currents, but is about twice the size.

FAST-FLOWING RIVERS

Rocks give shelter from the current and are often fringed by bright green algae which cling on tight in the swift waters. The algae provide food for **mayfly nymphs** (inset right), found beneath the water's surface, either clinging to rocks with their sharp claws or burrowing into the mud and weed. These are the immature forms of the adult mayfly and look rather like miniature crayfish, with three pointed and often feathery tails.

In clean rocky rivers lift up some large stones and look for the chunky outline of a **bullhead** (right) – a brown, spiny fish, about 10cm (4in) long, common in England and Wales. Its alternative name is miller's thumb because millers were said to develop broad thumbs, like the fish's broad head, from rubbing grain between their fingers. In spring, the female bullhead lays clusters of sticky eggs in a rocky nest chosen by the male. He guards the eggs for about a month, until they hatch, fanning them with his fins to keep them well oxygenated. Bullheads zigzag away at the first sign of danger but a male guarding eggs will be quick to return to his post.

Holes in the riverbank

For small animals, few places are more secure than a burrow – particularly on a steep bank above water, where intruders find it hard to get in. In a boat or on the bank, you are ideally placed to spot these desirable homes. Some insects dig nests but birds and mammals are the main burrowers and the shape and size of a hole and its height above the water, will often tell you what made it. If you spot a potential inhabitant try to keep it in view: it might show you the way to its home.

If you see the blue flash of a kingfisher, just a little simple detective work can pinpoint its nest. First, search for a stretch of river with steep banks and some bare earth. Try on the outside of bends. Here, earth is exposed where the water undercuts the bank, removing vegetation and causing soil to fall into the water. Next, scan the bank an arm's length down from the top. If you see a single round hole, slightly larger than a golf ball, it is probably a kingfisher burrow.

The entrance to the burrow has to be high enough to escape most springtime floods but low enough to be out of the reach of predators on top of the bank. Kingfisher burrows can be up to 1m (3ft) long and keep out floodwater by sloping upwards.

It takes patience and luck to see kingfishers arriving at their burrow with food. But even if you don't witness any comings or goings, one piece of evidence will confirm that the hole is a kingfisher residence: white splashes outside. These are the dried remains of droppings, which the adults and young squirt out of the nest – close up, you'll notice their fishy smell.

Kingfishers breed from late April onwards, and usually raise two broods, so most burrows are still in use in midsummer and beyond. The male and female share the tunnelling, pecking at the earth then shovelling it backwards with their feet. They do not use any nesting material and, once the young are being fed, the interior of the nest soon becomes smelly and soiled with the regurgitated remains of fish, including many bones.

Communal living

Unlike kingfishers, sand martins live communally and need large areas to burrow in. Suitable riverbanks are often scarce and you are as likely to come across their burrows in abandoned sand and gravel pits, where the ground is soft.

Sand martins also dig up to a metre deep into the bank, and raise two broods a year. They are close relatives of swallows, and have the same insect-eating lifestyle. By early summer, their breeding colonies are bustling with activity, as the males and females fly back and forth with beakfuls of insects to feed the young in their nests.

ABOVE WATER As they burrow in exposed ground **brown rats** leave a pile of excavated soil in front of their **hole**. But this is soon flattened by passing feet. Look for rat runs leading from the nest and for **prints** at the water's edge, where they feed.

Bird burrows *Kingfisher's holes (left) are round and always found singly whereas sand martins (right) breed in groups. They dig clusters of burrows in large vertical banks (below). Each entrance is about the size of a golf ball, but flattened at the top and bottom.*

BURROWING RODENTS

Water voles and brown rats both burrow in riverbanks. Rats dig holes the size of a cricket ball, always above the water level. Radiating from each entrance you will see rat runs, well worn trails that keep close to cover.

Brown rats are mainly nocturnal. They eat a wide range of food, including waterside plants, snails and small frogs. You are probably more likely to see a water vole because they are

SECRET ENTRANCE **Water voles** usually come and go unobserved from their **underwater holes**, but in summer water levels fall and these concealed entrances can be left high and dry, surrounded by bare mud. These are the holes you are most likely to see from the river. **Tracks** (inset) left by a vole show their widely splayed toes, thinner than the toes of the common rat. Where the vole has sat up to feed by the water, look for marks left by the tail and back legs – these stabilise the vole as it sits.

SNAKE IN THE SHALLOWS Despite its name, you are as likely to see a **grass snake** in water as in grass. Frogs are its staple food, and it will swim through plants at the water's edge to find them. Look out for one if you are very near the bank, or mooring or pushing out a boat. Grass snakes have lustrous grey-green skin, small black markings and a yellow collar behind the head. Their bite is harmless to humans but they rarely attack.

Playing dead If a grass snake feels threatened it displays some unusual defence tactics. First it hisses and emits a foul-smelling fluid that will put off most attackers but if this fails, it pretends to be dead, turning belly-up and hanging its tongue out of its mouth (below). This strategy might seem a desperate gamble but it often works. Many predators will only attack live animals, and leave the 'dead' snake alone.

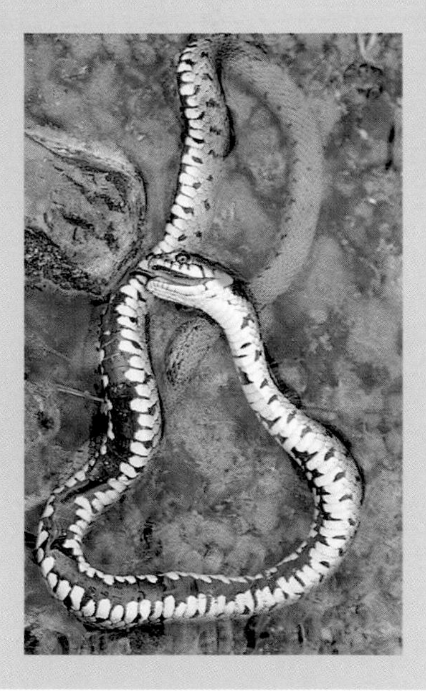

active by day and night. Look for them as they sit up on their haunches to chew grasses and other waterside plants.

Water voles are sometimes mistakenly called water rats – this is the creature made famous as 'Ratty' in *The Wind in the Willows*. They build a system of burrows with entrances above and below the water (see above), about the same size as rat holes.

High on the bank you might spot their above-ground holes by the 'lawn' nibbled in the vegetation around them, but when it leads to a nesting chamber a hole may be plugged with grass. Some distance away you may come across a latrine, containing piles of greenish black cylindrical droppings.

Marauding mink

Since the 1950s, Britain's water vole population has been in steep decline. One reason is that the quiet, overgrown watersides they prefer are becoming rare. Another is the presence of a new and efficient predator: the American mink. Mink entered the wild in Britain after escaping or being released from fur farms and have been widespread since the 1970s, living on riverbanks.

Evidence of mink includes scattered feathers from bird kills, fish remains and foul, strongly smelling twisted droppings up to 8cm (3¼in) long, with pointed ends. If you find a cage trap on the water's edge, it could well have been put there to control this unwanted animal.

Fishing at the waterside

Fishing can keep freshwater birds busy all day long in early summer. With hungry chicks in the nest, birds such as cormorants, grebes, herons and kingfishers that feed on fish have to increase the amount they catch, as a large proportion has to be given away. The best time to witness their fishing techniques is now, when they are at their busiest. Freshwater birds have two main strategies: some lie in wait for the fish to come their way, others track them down. While both methods have their merits, the active hunters are usually the easiest birds to detect on the riverbank.

The grey heron is an unrivalled expert at the waiting technique and can be found in most freshwater habitats, estuaries and sheltered coasts. If you spot one before it spots you (not as easy as it sounds) watch it stand statue-like as it waits for fish to come within range. Camouflaged colours help to hide it, but for a heron, keeping still is far more important because fish react to movement and do not regard the heron's stationary, hunched silhouette as a threat.

This fishing method requires solitude and concentration, and herons don't like being disturbed. If you walk nearby, a heron will usually fly off with an irritated, harsh ***fraaank*** call. But they are less solitary when nesting. Herons breed in groups, usually in the tops of trees, and can fly 10 miles or more from these heronries for a day's fishing. The young often stay in their nests until the end of July, so heronries are busy for much of the summer.

Strong swimmer *Compared with other water birds, cormorants swim very deep in the water. They dive from the surface and hunt by sight, pushing themselves forward with their feet, and steering with partly opened wings.*

Hunters for fish

Active fishers are less troubled by humans, and less likely to fly off as you approach. Kingfishers and terns attack fish by diving from the air into the surface water, while cormorants and grebes dive from the surface and pursue their prey under water.

These underwater specialists can hold their breath for a remarkably long time – if you see one dive, time its immersion. Grebes and cormorants both normally dive for up to a minute but cormorants can stay under for longer. They rarely eat under water, so wait and see whether the diver surfaces with a fish.

If, at dusk, you see a bird grabbing fish with its feet you can be fairly sure that it is a tawny owl: they eat all kinds of small creatures, including insects, bats and frogs. Even in town owls sometimes fish over park lakes and garden ponds.

Spring loaded *If a fish swims by, a heron curves its neck like an 's' then suddenly straightens it, stabbing its victim with its beak. With a flick, the fish is thrown into the air to drop headfirst down the heron's throat.*

EVIDENCE IN PELLETS

Birds usually swallow their food whole and any indigestible parts – such as the scales and bones of fish – are regurgitated later as a pellet. If you find pellets near the water's edge, you can often tell what the local water birds have been eating.

Kingfisher pellets can be almost as long as a match – a substantial size for such a small bird. They contain fish bones and scales, and are often dropped inside the bird's nesting burrow, although some are also scattered along the water's edge.

Although fish are a large part of their diet, herons can digest scales and bones, so that they do not need to regurgitate them. Feathers and fur do turn up in pellets, though, revealing that the herons have been eating small birds or mammals. Look for them under nests, and at favourite fishing sites.

Fish scales, seedpods and beetle wings reflect the black-headed gull's varied diet. Unlike many other bird pellets, these are loose and crumbly, and they fall apart easily if handled.

Indigestible *A mass of silvery fish scales is clearly visible in this kingfisher's food pellet.*

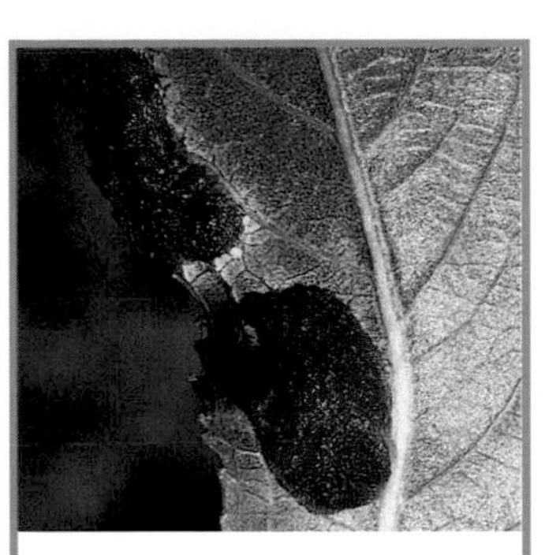

ALIEN GROWTHS If you are birdwatching on a riverbank in summer you may notice that some of the willows have bright red swellings on their leaves. They look like a kind of fruit but are actually **willow bean galls** – fleshy growths caused by the willow bean sawfly. They start to form in late spring, when the sawfly lays its eggs on the tree. By the time the grubs hatch in summer, a shiny bean gall has swollen up around each one to provide a store of food. A small hole allows droppings to be discharged. When the grub is fully grown, it leaves the gall and drops to the ground, where it develops into the adult sawfly.

A FLURRY OF FLIES

A cloud of flies hovering ahead as you walk along a riverside path is a familiar and irritating experience in summer. Most people imagine that, given the chance, all of them will bite but, in daylight at least, those that bite humans are in the minority – they are much more interested in one another. **Dance flies** (right) gather in swarms over water (below), where males and females pair up to mate.

BRIGHT ARMOUR Some flies are surprisingly colourful. Brilliant, metallic blue or green flies with blunt-ended abdomens, large eyes and flattened bodies are **soldier flies** (right). They are weak fliers, and despite their military name, most feed on nectar rather than by hunting. You might see one perching on the waterside vegetation.

UNSTEADY ON ITS FEET Look for the **stilt-legged fly** (below) feeding on small insects on waterside plants. You will recognise it by its slender black body and spherical head, and its characteristic wavering, halting gait. It has very long legs – when they are stretched out, the fly measures about 1.5cm (½in) long – and moves slowly and clumsily when it walks.

Close-up on

Pond life

Until the early 20th century almost every village in Britain had a pond, providing drinking water for horses and other livestock that grazed on the green. But since ponds do not, like rivers, have a current to sweep away debris, they need dredging out regularly to stop them from filling up with decaying plant matter and silt. Left to nature, a pond will gradually become overgrown and may eventually turn into an area of wet woodland.

When you stop by a pond, try to spot whether its origins are artificial or natural. This is easy if it has been made recently – bare earth banks and waterproof liners are clear evidence – but harder when it blends into its setting. Site and shape will usually help.

Natural ponds always form in depressions in the landscape, whereas artificial ponds are often created by blocking a stream and might be contained by raised banks. If you find the remains of sluice gates on opposite banks, used to regulate the water level, it is evidence that the pond was created to stock fish; sometimes all that remains are the metal guide rails for the gates, concealed in the undergrowth. Ponds on chalk are also frequently artificial – dug by sheep farmers for their flocks, and lined with clay to make them waterproof and to prevent the water seeping into the porous rock. Although such ponds are known as dew ponds, they are fed by rain.

TESTING THE WATER With a leg span the length of a little finger, the **raft spider** is Britain's largest spider. Look for it on floating leaves, such as lily pads, where it sits with its front legs touching the surface of the water. If prey, such as a mosquito larva or water beetle, swims nearby the spider senses the vibrations and attacks.

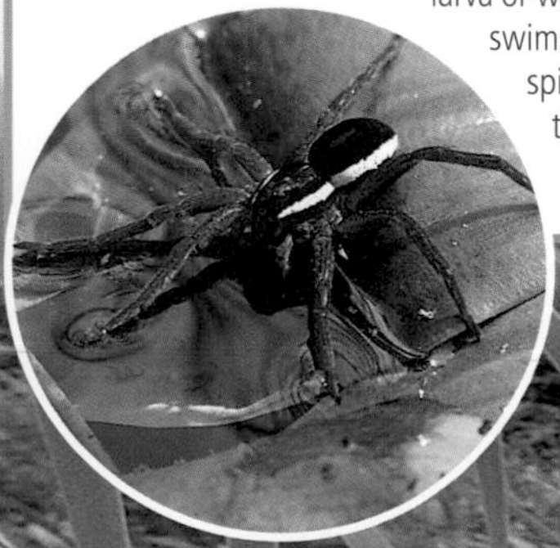

RESTING SPOT For freshwater animals, floating leaves provide platforms for hunting and cover from prying eyes. From the bank, you might see damselflies touching down to bask in the sun, but small beetles, such as the **water lily leaf beetle**, and hover flies also land on the pads as they shuttle to and from the bank, to reach the lily flowers.

NURSERY PADS If you can reach a lily pad, turn it over: you may find sausage-shaped blobs of jelly on the underside. These are **great pond snail eggs**. Look at them closely: if the contents are well developed, you will see hundreds of baby snails with transparent shells waiting to hatch. You might also see these on pondweed.

HOW TO GUESS THE DEPTH

In summer, pond water is often murky with weeds and algae, which makes it difficult to estimate how deep it is. But you don't need a measuring stick to find out, just make a note of the pond plants that are growing: each kind of plant lives in water of a particular depth.

AT THE EDGE Around the edges of a pond you will often find **bulrushes** (*Typha latifolia*). They will also extend in solid-looking platforms into waist-depth water – take care not to venture onto these in the belief that you are on dry land.

A 'LAWN' OF WEED In summer, small ponds and ditches often seem to turn completely green. This is caused by a layer of **duckweed** – a mass of tiny floating plants coating the surface. Duckweeds are Britain's smallest flowering plants, but they rarely bloom. Instead, they reproduce at a phenomenal rate by growing buds that break off and develop into new plants. There are five different kinds of duckweed – fish some out of the water with a stick and see what you can find. Two of the most widespread are common duckweed and fat duckweed. Common duckweed has a flat disc and a single trailing root; fat duckweed has a tiny raft of bubble cells beneath each disc, giving them a spongy texture. It often turns reddish brown in late summer, which makes it easy to recognise.

SURVIVAL AND DISPERSAL Small ponds often dry up in hot summers, but this isn't necessarily the end for the pond life. Some animals lie dormant for the dry spell: **water fleas** (inset) might deposit eggs – visible here in the adult's abdomen – in the damp mud at the bottom of the pond, where they won't hatch until the pond refills. Other insects fly in: diving beetles and water boatmen are not only excellent swimmers, but can also take to the wing. Fish eggs, particularly strings of perch eggs, can arrive tangled around birds' legs, and floating plants also sometimes hitch a ride: duckweed can spread to new sites on the back of a creature, such as the **toad** (below). Once there are plants and animals to eat in the pond, other creatures soon begin to move in.

OVER YOUR HEAD The water where **white water lilies** float is normally around 2m (6½ft) deep but could be more than 3m (10ft) – equivalent to one adult standing on another's shoulders. Yellow water lilies can grow in a depth of 5m (16ft).

WAIST DEEP Where the bulrush zone peters out the **broad-leaved pondweed** spreads over the surface of waist-depth water, although you can also find it growing in shallower depths.

Dressing down
Male mallards (left) shed their fine feathers from June to September and wear their eclipse plumage (far left). In mid moult the ducks are very vulnerable to attack as they have no flight feathers and cannot fly, so they tend to stay out on the water until their new feathers have grown.

Duck-spotting in summer

By midsummer, the frenetic business of courtship is over for freshwater wildfowl, and the surviving young are nearly independent. Unlike coots or moorhens, ducks rear only one brood a year so once their young are fledged family life is over. Suddenly all the brightly coloured male ducks, so evident in spring, disappear and wildfowl activity seems to come to a standstill. But although things are quiet, the birds are going through an essential period of transition and near the water's edge you will find the evidence to tell you what's really going on.

If you see a duck flapping its wings in summer you will soon realise why most ducks try to stay inconspicuous at this time of year. Like all birds, they need to keep their plumage in good condition to survive, and this means replacing feathers when they get worn out.

Most birds renew their wing feathers a few at a time but waterfowl shed them all in quick succession, leaving them with very gappy wings. Moulted feathers on the bank can help you to identify which ducks are around. But until their new feathers grow, it is best to remain unobtrusive.

In spring, when they were vying for a partner, the males sported colourful plumage. In summer they no longer need to compete and they can lose their bright feathers. Now they look much more like their dowdier mates. This subdued colouring is called their eclipse plumage.

TELL-TALE TRAILS Where waterside plants are growing high, you might spot trails leading through the vegetation to the water's edge. The size and shape of these trails is a good indicator of the creature that made them.

Duck trails (right) are narrow and run directly to the water's edge. Ducks flatten the plants with their broad webbed feet but in summer, when the plants have grown taller than the height of the ducks, these narrow trails turn into tunnels that disappear into the greenery.

At dusk, deer make their way to the water's edge to drink. **Deer trails** (right) are also narrow as deer are slender animals, but deer are taller than most waterside grasses so even the tall summer vegetation is parted to either side, making the trail easier than a duck's to spot.

If you see a trail more than 25cm (10in) wide heading to the water, it will almost certainly have been made by an angler. **Human trails** (right) are unmistakable as we have bigger feet than any of Britain's native wild animals and trample the widest paths of all through the vegetation. The bags and bulky equipment of anglers and picnickers can also bend or break vegetation higher off the ground.

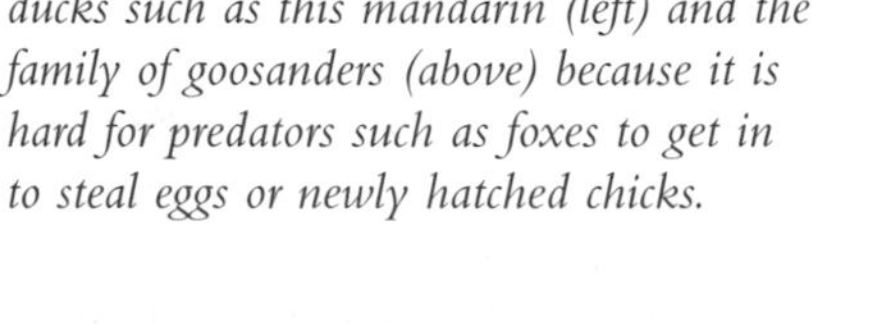

A place of safety *The inside of trees make very good nesting places for ducks such as this mandarin (left) and the family of goosanders (above) because it is hard for predators such as foxes to get in to steal eggs or newly hatched chicks.*

AVIAN OUTLAW On lakes and reservoirs in southern England and the West Midlands a duck originally from North and Central America is causing a stir. The **ruddy duck** has become naturalised but its success in Britain has made it a threat to another, rare species – the white-headed duck, a closely related species that lives in southern Europe. There have been calls for England's ruddy ducks to be culled without delay.

The male ruddy duck's bright blue bill makes him instantly recognisable at close quarters but from farther away, a dumpy shape, thick neck and stiff pointed tail are three features to look out for. However during his courtship display he is unmistakable. He inflates an air sac in his chest, and beats it with his bill. This makes a distinct drumming noise and expels the air from his chest, which then bubbles up around him in the water. Female white-headed ducks in parts of Europe where British ruddy ducks migrate to in winter find this display impressive and the two species have already interbred. Conservationists fear that pure white-headed ducks could be lost to ruddy duck hybrids – offspring born from one parent of each species. Culling is a drastic step but they believe the only way to preserve the white-headed duck is to rid Britain of all its ruddy ducks.

DUCKS UP TREES?

Don't be surprised if you see a bird that looks like a duck up a tree. The 'duck' is probably a goosander or a mandarin as, unusually for waterfowl, these species nest in holes in trees. In parts of Scotland you might see a goldeneye, nesting up to 15m (50ft) high in lake or riverside trees. Moorhens sometimes climb trees to look for fruit and may also nest on lower branches.

The best place to look for goosanders is by watersides in the Scottish Highlands, but they also breed in the Borders, Lake District, and parts of Mid Wales. Mandarins are not native to Britain, but were introduced from the Far East over a century ago. During the 1930s they started to breed in the wild on wood-fringed lakes in scattered parts of southern England.

Taking the plunge *Ducks do not feed their young, so the flightless chicks must leave the nest after just one day to find food. For this young mandarin chick, there is only one way to do this: jump. Ducklings almost always survive the leap from their elevated nest as their fluffy down cushions the impact when they land.*

On warm summer days, the inland waterways of East Anglia shimmer beneath wide-open skies. This landscape of rivers and reed beds – one of the richest wildlife habitats in Britain – is at its most welcoming at this time of year and whether you are aboard a boat or on two feet, animals and plants will be all around. Many are species that live in other parts of Britain too, but some – such as the marsh harrier and the swallowtail butterfly – rarely breed anywhere else.

Fens alive with activity

An immediately obvious feature of a reed bed is that, unlike other habitats, it is dominated by just one kind of plant: the common reed. This is Britain's tallest native grass, reaching 2.5m (8ft), and one of the most widespread plants in the world. Reeds grow in almost any wet, low-lying ground – even drainage ditches between fields and along roads.

In reed beds the ground is flat, fertile and waterlogged, and the common reed grows so well here that it smothers almost everything else. The plants are quick to colonise open water and, as they grow, take up large quantities of nutrients so they are often planted in sewage treatment works, where they help to cleanse the water.

Although they grow quickly compared with most grasses, common reed does not begin growing until late in the year. Even in June, most reed beds are only just starting to sprout green shoots and you won't see the purplish flowers until the end of August. If you do see flowers

IDENTITY PARADE – Fenland grasses and sedges

If you are trying to moor a boat during the height of summer, you may well find that extra-large grasses and sedges line the bank, where they help to stop erosion. It pays to be able to recognise these waterside plants, because some of them are floating grasses, and will quickly sink if you try to walk on them.

Flote grass Also known as floating sweet-grass, flote grass has pale green, soft, succulent leaves that float on the water. It can grow up to 1m (3ft) high, although it often sprawls across the surface: don't step on it. Narrow green flower heads appear between May and August and cattle find it delicious – they often wade into the water to eat it.

Reed canary grass This widespread waterside grass grows on solid land to about 1.2m (4ft) in height, and is often mistaken for common reed. An easy way to tell the difference is by looking at the flower heads: they appear from June onwards on reed canary grass – much earlier than those of the common reed – and are in dense clusters, not open.

Greater tussock sedge True to its name, greater tussock sedge grows in large tussocks more than 1m (3ft) in height and spread. Its flower heads appear in May and June only. The grassy clumps look solid and sturdy but they may be rooted in deep water rather than on dry land, so don't tread on them and remember that the water between them can be treacherous.

RARE SIGHTING If you are in a reed bed and hear a loud, repeated, echoing ***ping ping*** call, use your binoculars, follow the noise and look for a **bearded tit**. This is one of Britain's scarcest birds with only 300 breeding pairs, living in coastal reed beds from the Humber estuary to as far west as Devon. It feeds on insects during the summer, but relies on reed seeds to get it through the winter.

TRIANGULAR TRAIT Grasses and sedges often grow side by side so to tell which is which, examine the stems. The stems of a **sedge** (right), have three distinct sides, whereas grass stems are round. Remember: sedges have edges.

earlier than this, they are almost certainly left over from the previous year.

Strength and shelter

Look at the stem of a reed that has been cut and you will see that the stem is hollow. Just like the frame of a tubular chair, this attribute gives reeds strength and the flexibility to grow tall and remain standing even when their green tissues die.

The stems carry oxygen to the roots but also provide a home for insects such as solitary wasps and bees, which nest inside. Below the waterline, the larvae of some specialised leaf beetles puncture the stem with two spikes on their abdomen to breathe the air.

You may find plenty of cut stems to investigate as some reed beds are regularly harvested for thatching. Harvesting takes place in winter, when the leaves have withered, but the dead stems which bore flowers at their tips are still standing. Left uncut, the reeds provide birds with nesting sites and small mammals with welcome cover in an otherwise open and often windy landscape.

In summer, the shallow water teems with life. Shoals of young roach and rudd thread their way through the reeds, while perch lurk among the underwater stems, waiting to pounce on smaller fish swimming past.

In a reed bed which is fully grown you might notice that all the leaves seem to point in the same direction. This is because they can swivel around the stem in a stiff breeze and all line up on the opposite side of the plant. Traditionally they have shown sailors which direction the wind is blowing from.

Reeds are also affected by the wind and, as a result of trying to grow upright against the prevailing wind, often develop a curve in the opposite direction.

HUNTERS OVER THE REEDS

If you see a large, long-winged bird of prey flying slowly across the reeds, it is likely to be a marsh harrier hunting for food. This migrant arrives from April onwards and is among Britain's rarest birds of prey, with only around 130 breeding pairs.

Nearly all of these birds are found in the East Anglian coastal reed beds. Wetlands are their natural habitat and these reed beds are among the few places in the country where the wetlands have not been drained.

Even from a distance you will see that the marsh harrier alternates between flapping and gliding flight as it hunts, holding its wings in a shallow 'v' when gliding. It looks for water voles, moorhens, coots and ducks, and grabs them with its talons.

Honed hunter *Marsh harriers have strikingly owl-like faces. This arrangement of feathers may help to funnel sound to the bird's ears – a great advantage to a predator which hunts over dense reeds.*

IN SEARCH OF THE SWALLOWTAIL The Norfolk Broads are the only home of Britain's biggest and most impressive butterfly – the **swallowtail** (inset below right), which has a wingspan of about 7cm (2¾in) – nearly as long as an adult's index finger. Its bright yellow-and-black colours make it easy to recognise as it speeds powerfully over the rivers and reeds, and at close quarters, its black 'tail' extensions are unmistakable. The butterflies are confined to the Norfolk Broads because their **caterpillars** (below left) feed almost exclusively on one plant – milk parsley – which is found only in that area. Newly hatched caterpillars look like bird droppings, but they develop bright colours as they grow, which help to deter predatory birds. They also have a pair of orange inflatable 'horns' on their head which give off a repellent smell.

At one time, swallowtails bred all over the East Anglian fens, but after two centuries of drainage, the Broads are now their final stronghold. Thanks to a determined conservation effort, this spectacular butterfly is making a comeback and may start to spread back into other parts of the fens. Swallowtails are also found in continental Europe, but the ones that breed in Britain are very distinctive. Their markings are darker in colour, and, unlike their continental counterparts, they rarely breed more than once a year, in early summer.

See how the wild places soften in the warmth

Summer sights and sounds on open heaths and exposed moors

Mountains, heaths and moors are at their most welcoming in summer. Now is the time to explore, safe from the threat of harsh weather, to smell the honeyed heather and hear the calls of birds, from the ringing cries of buzzards to sweet skylark melodies. In the grass, small rodents are breeding, providing food for the birds of prey circling overhead.

Heaths form at low altitudes or by the coast, mostly in southern England. They are warm and dry and their sandy soils have a thin layer of peaty humus which adds to their acidity and infertile nature. On the upland moors plants grow close to the peaty ground for protection from buffeting winds. Alpines flower on scree slopes and lichens spread over the rocks.

Dry, sandy heath

In southern England's broad shallow basins filled with sand and gravel, heather and gorse grow on extensive heaths. Britain's largest remaining heaths are in the New Forest (above) and Dorset, with remnants to the east in Surrey and East Anglia.

The New Forest heath, with its stony ridges rising between wet, peaty valleys, is characterised by green 'lawns' cropped short by half-wild ponies. Woodlarks, scarce relatives of the skylark, sing as they glide in wide, circling song flights; and around the mixture of heather and gorse you may spot the tiny body and long, slim tail of the secretive Dartford warbler, a bird found only locally on the heaths of southern England.

The New Forest woodlands are home to buzzards and rare honey buzzards, best seen circling over the trees from the open heath.

Fallow deer often move out of woods on the edge of a heath on to open ground to feed, especially near dusk. In summer, adults may be accompanied by their young.

By day on the dry, open heathland, a suite of elusive reptiles emerges to bask in the sun. Adders curl up in the grass near rocks and smooth snakes can most easily be discovered under a discarded piece of metal. Common lizards rest by tussocks of heather, into which they dash if disturbed: listen for the rustle. Sand lizards – less common but bigger and with more conspicuous spots – soak up the sun on south-facing sandy banks.

Rugged moor

Windswept Dartmoor (above) is south-west England's largest area of exposed moorland. In some places its 300 million-year-old granite rocks stand out in jagged tors; elsewhere are gentle hills clothed in swathes of bracken, heather and grassy bog.

Butterflies and emperor moths flutter around the heather, and clumps of yellow, coconut-scented gorse complement the greens and golds of lichens on rocks and stone walls. The trunks of twisted oaks on streamside slopes, dwarfed by exposure and poor soil, are wreathed in thick moss and shining liverworts while rowans and hollies mingle with banks of bilberry.

The brown hare crouches on its form, or resting place, in the grass until disturbed, when it dashes away with zigzagging springs. On sheltered slopes, or in the shadow of a tor, breeding herds of tough Dartmoor ponies crop the summer grass. The summer warmth brings birds to sing in the winding valleys, but when they are alarmed wheatears dive into their nests in hollows beneath small stones and stonechats complain from the tops of gorse bushes. Meanwhile, cuckoos sing monotonously, and search for meadow pipit nests where they can lay their eggs.

Meadow pipits flutter across the moor in shuttlecock flights, catching the insects that throng around the fragrant gorse. Listen for their trilling song.

ROCKY CLUE The colour of the stones in walls and lying in fields is a clue to the underlying soil. **Dark stones** (left) indicate acid soil; pale stones are probably limestone.

ACID YELLOW The bright flowers of **tormentil** are an indication of acid soil. You will spot the plant as you walk, since it is most obvious beside footpaths and where sheep graze.

Harsh ground and acid soil

Many of Britain's wildest places are areas of acid soil, where farming has always been difficult and where only specialists such as mat-grass and purple moor-grass will grow. Areas of chalk, mainly in the south-east, have their own distinctive plants and animals, while the flora and fauna of harder limestones are different again. While walking in wild places the best clues to acid soils are the dark stones of the boundary walls. Once you know the soil is acid you can deduce what else you are likely to find.

Ground cover *Red grouse chicks are well camouflaged in the heather on northern acid moors. They can fly when they are still young and, in the air, can look confusing – like adult birds but of an unidentifiable species.*

The Dark Peak (above) in the Peak District is an area of acid millstone grit – a coarse, dark brown rock quite unlike the limestone of the White Peak.

If you visit the Dark Peak in midsummer, you may see the rough vegetation softened by a haze of delicate pink flowers. This is wavy-hair grass and it is a sure indicator of acid soil. It grows well on bleak moors as the wiry leaves minimise water loss by offering little surface area to the drying wind or sun.

As you walk on, you may find your way dotted by tormentil (inset above), a plant with four-petalled yellow flowers and five-fingered leaves. It uses the grass around it as a support, growing to the same height but no higher. So where the turf is short, tormentil can devote its energy to producing a bright display of flowers rather than tall stems and deep roots.

Another low-growing plant is heath bedstraw. Its white flowers with four petals grow in clusters and its short, narrow oval 'leaves' (many of which are actually bracts, not leaves) in whorls of five or six. Get down close, or brush past and you will smell the sweet sickly scent which attracts flies to pollinate the flowers.

Heath bedstraw is weak and spindly and, like tormentil, grows among grass for support. It relies on moderate grazing – too much and the supports are destroyed, too little and it is swamped by bigger plants.

INHOSPITABLE MOUNTAINS

Flowering, setting seed and germination are a gamble in the most exposed, mountainous areas. But one variation on the common fescues (grasses) of moorland areas – viviparous fescue – has evolved a tactic that helps to avoid the problems.

Slender green shoots sprout in place of flowers and then detach and drop to the ground. There they take root as already part-established plants, which are less vulnerable than seedlings in the harsh environment.

If you are in these remote places in summer, be wary of birds such as buzzards, kestrels and peregrines. They might have young in the nest and may suffer from being disturbed. Peregrines in particular will leave you in no doubt if you are too close: they flap around, announcing their displeasure with loud, nasal, ***haak-haak-haak*** warning calls.

Seedless signifier *Viviparous fescue (above) grows only in acid soils. Its similar-looking relative, sheep's fescue, is more widespread because it also lives on lime.*

SPOT THE DIFFERENCE

WHICH TYPE OF HEATHER? Heathers thrive in the acid soils on heaths and moors. **Ling [1]**, also called just 'heather', is the most common and is distinguished by its tiny, stiff leaves, growing in two opposite rows along a woody stem. The flowers are pale pinky purple, or sometimes white, and form long, branched, tapering spikes. **Bell heather [2]** grows on dry heaths and moors. It is a thin, woody shrub with short, bronzy green leaves arranged in threes and tiny leaflets at the base of each cluster. Bright purplish red egg or bell-shaped flowers bloom along the stems. **Cross-leaved heath [3]**, a short, pale greyish, downy plant, is found on bogs and wet heaths. Look for its leaves, arranged in whorls of four, and its drooping, bell-shaped rose-pink flowers in broad clusters at the tip of each stem.

FINDING FOOD ON HEATHS

Heathers (see above) grow in abundance on heaths. Among their flowers you will sometimes find clusters of different blooms: a pale pinky white but almost transparent. These belong to dodder (above right), a parasite plant which taps in to the heather's food supply.

On heathland that is not heavily grazed, such as Cannock Chase in Staffordshire, you will see banks of low bushes. They may be cowberry, with thick, fleshy, dark evergreen leaves or deciduous bilberry, which has paler yellow-green leaves and dark pink bellflowers. In late summer their berries provide food for a variety of birds, including grey partridges and mistle thrushes.

In grassy areas look out for short-tailed voles. They need good-sized tussocks of thick grass in which to build spherical nests. Look for their tunnel-like runs crisscrossing through grass that has not been grazed short.

Summer is the peak breeding time for short-tailed voles, when four to six young are cared for by one female. These furry 'sausages' are the staple diet of short-eared owls, kestrels and other birds of prey, as well as weasels and foxes, so wherever voles are plentiful you are also likely to find their predators.

Clues that both prey and predators are in an area include owl pellets – indigestible matter regurgitated after a meal. Look out for ones containing small bones and tiny skulls embedded in the vole's grey, matted fur.

Tapping in *A mass of thin red stems tangled up in heather or gorse is dodder. These parasitic plants have no green chlorophyll to turn sunlight into food, and no roots to absorb soil nutrients. Instead they curl anti-clockwise around the stems of the host and penetrate them to take sustenance.*

SOGGY TERRAIN On wet ground **purple moor-grass** (inset), with its long branched flower heads of purple 'spikelets', grows in dense tussocks which can withstand the force of flood water. Look for sphagnum moss and shiny wet peat nearby – these are the places where **dunlins** (below) nest. Listen out for the males, singing in flight in descending trills like an old-fashioned policeman's whistle.

In summer, dunlins and golden plovers both have a black rectangle on their underside. You might see a dunlin standing behind a flock of feeding plovers like a page boy – in Scotland the dunlin is nicknamed 'the plover's page'. In fact the bird is taking advantage of the plover's nervous nature, feeding in safety, sure that the plovers will call out at any sign of danger.

Soaking up the sun on heaths

The grassy pastures of southern heaths may be cropped short by grazing cattle or sheep or by groups of half-wild ponies, helping to maintain the heathland vegetation. In places the ground is stripped bare by rabbits, revealing the light sandy soil. This is the realm of the woodlark, with its broad round wings, very short tail and distinctive floppy swooping flight, and other birds, drawn by the insects that feed on the heather.

At dusk in summer, stand on a quiet roadside or track by a large expanse of heath, particularly in the Brecklands of East Anglia, and listen for an odd mechanical churring, like the sound of a distant motorbike. It may go on for several minutes, unvaried except for sudden slight changes in pitch. This is a nightjar. Close up, the song is a fast, 'wooden' rattle and as it 'runs down' you may hear two or three claps as the bird takes flight, striking its wingtips together.

Stand still and the nightjar might come to investigate you, whirling around like a maniacal, long-winged moth. Nightjars feed on moths after dark: flap a white handkerchief and you might bring one closer, thinking the flash of white promises a good meal. Many moths thrive on the short vegetation of heaths but they are hard to spot as most fly at dusk, when they are most difficult to distinguish.

Insects in disguise

A slow-moving bundle of twigs and bark moving across the sandy soil is the protective case of a bagworm moth larva. The larva makes a cocoon of twiggy material, held together by silky threads, and moves about feeding on lichens and grasses.

Adult female bagworm moths also live in these cocoons for safety because they cannot fly. In summer you may see a small brown moth with a lazy flight investigating this shuffling case. This is a male, in search of a mate within her cocoon.

A medium-sized butterfly might flit up from fescue grasses just ahead of you in summer as you walk on a heath, dunes or a coastal clifftop. In flight you will see that it is grey-brown with a hint of orange, but as soon as it settles on the ground, the butterfly disappears from view.

This is the grayling butterfly: watch it carefully until you spot where it lands. A patch of pale orange and a beady black 'eye' will be momentarily visible on the wingtip before it performs its disappearing trick by tilting its closed wings over so that it casts no shadow, making it nearly impossible to spot.

Disappearing act *The undersides of a grayling butterfly's wings are marked like a piece of bark to add to its effective camouflage when at rest.*

SHAM SNAKES They may look like snakes basking in the early morning sun on sandy heaths, but **slow-worms** are actually lizards with no legs. They can move quite fast when disturbed but are sometimes preyed upon by pheasants, which peck them to pieces.

Woodlarks are well camouflaged against the sandy soil on heaths, where they hunt for beetles and spiders.

ROAMING WILD

Ponies descended from ancient stock roam freely on southern moors and heaths. They are well known on Dartmoor and Exmoor and in the New Forest, with its wide open pastures and shrub-free 'lawns'. Horses differ from ponies only in size: an animal whose back is more than 1.5m (5ft) high is a horse; one smaller than that, a pony.

The ponies that live on Britain's common ground are not really wild but they live in family groups, unconfined and without care or attention, for most of the year. You can usually tell them from domesticated animals by their dirty coats and unkempt manes and tails.

They are owned mainly by local farmers, and most are rounded up only once a year so don't assume they will be tame – they might bite or kick. It is also important not to feed them. If the ponies begin to rely on scrounging for food they may become unable to fend for themselves when the tourists have gone home.

There is some cross breeding as different types of pony are released on to the heaths but it is still possible to see the distinct characteristics of the Dartmoor, Exmoor, New Forest and Welsh Mountain ponies.

Controlled grazing helps to keep trees at bay so many nature reserves manage small herds of ponies, or cattle or sheep, to prevent heaths from becoming scrubby woodland with less specialised wildlife.

IN THE FOOTHILLS Despite their name, the predominantly grey, bay or brown **Welsh Mountain ponies** (right) roam mainly on lowland heaths, salt marsh grazings and open, rushy hillsides, not on the bleak mountain tops. Look for them on the lower slopes of the Brecon Beacons and Black Mountains, on Tregaron bog and on estuaries along the south Wales coast.

NIMBLE GRAZER On rough slopes look for sure-footed **Exmoor ponies**. These hardy animals graze on new grass after a winter diet of wiry grasses and leaves and there are two types. The 'anchor' ponies are small and light, with a concave face while the 'withypools' are larger and darker with a Roman profile. Exmoor ponies typically have black nostrils in a pale muzzle and pale areas around the eyes and inside the legs. Their predominant colour is dark brown.

ELEGANTLY AGILE The bay or brown **New Forest ponies** are full-bodied and large-headed with short but slender legs – features that betray the introduction of some Arab horse blood in the 19th century by owners attempting to improve the breed. Their long necks and strong teeth mean that they can reach and browse on holly, ivy, gorse and other woody shrubs, but they are very agile and can pick their way through the New Forest mires to graze on purple moor grass in the acid valley bottoms.

ON THE OPEN MOOR Small and tough, **Dartmoor ponies** are stockier than those of the New Forest but very similar in colour – bay, black or brown. You might see them sheltering around granite tors in bad weather but in the summer they bask in the sun. This foal, stretched out prostrate on the springy turf, is taking full advantage of the seasonal warmth. The ponies are handled only for branding to show ownership and you may be able to pick out the different marks used.

Living at high altitude

Mountain survival is a challenge for plants and animals. Summer is short and the nights cold and often frosty. Strong winds dry out plants and frequent gales batter tall woody stems until they break. In the far north, Scottish hilltops are little different from Arctic tundra, with sparse vegetation on grits, gravels and solid granite. To survive in such harsh conditions demands specialisation.

As you near a mountain peak you'll notice there are few trees – just one or two low-growing species – and no tall plants at all. Instead, mountain plants grow in low clumps with small or hairy leaves to combat the drying winds. In very exposed places even usually tall shrubs, such as broom and juniper, may grow in a flattened form. Dwarf willow lines shallow, snowy hollows where few other plants can survive.

Where water seeps through rocks and crevices to wet ledges it delivers nutrients to the thin soil and you will find more plants flourishing than in similar soils in dry places. In damp shade, look for a low, creeping, mossy plant with bluntly lobed leaves and tiny yellowish flowers. This is opposite-leaved golden saxifrage; its hairy leaves trap a layer of air, helping to prevent water from blocking the pores on the surface.

Taking hold in awkward places

Steep scree slopes of loose rock are particularly difficult places for flowering plants to take root, but you will find lichens in even the driest and most exposed areas. On high heathery moors and mountains look for Iceland moss, a lichen with wavy reddish fronds edged with stiff spines. Snowy Scottish peaks display the cream frond, with crisp, wavy edges of *Cetraria nivalis*: the second part of its scientific name means 'of the snow'.

Some ferns live alongside the lichens on scree, but you might need to poke about in the loose rock to find them. Look in sheltered spots beneath cliffs or under a constant drip of water. If you are walking over acid slates in north Wales, watch out

Sure-footed *Stout but nimble, feral goats graze on mountain flowers on even the most perilous slopes. Despite their 'Billy goat gruff' image they are not fierce and will make themselves scarce long before you get near.*

Out of reach Many cliffs, such as this one at Ben Lawes in Tayside (above), have ledges which are inaccessible to sheep. Here, flowers such as alpine forget-me-not, purple saxifrage, the white mossy saxifrage and purple and white alpine mouse-ear flourish, safe from grazing.

The high life *Some plants have adapted to mountain living by evolving a miniature variety: dwarf willow (below) grows in a broad but low mat. Lichens such as* Rhizocarpon geographicum *(bottom) can survive higher up than most, even where there is no soil.*

for parsley fern; on shady acid screes in northern England oak fern grows; and on limestone rocks you might find holly fern.

Spreading seeds

Limestone areas are particularly rich in mountain flora. The Knockan area and Ben Lawes, both in the Scottish Highlands, are worth visiting in summer for their displays of flowers alone.

A rare limestone speciality is mountain avens, which grows in a mat of scalloped evergreen leaves and eight-petalled flowers like white buttercups. During the day, the flowers follow the path of the sun, turning to focus what warmth they can onto their reproductive organs to ripen the fruits, which then drift off in the wind. A huge number of seeds is produced as only a few are likely to fall on a suitable limestone ledge.

On thin acid soils you may come across sheep's sorrel. You are most likely to spot it as autumn approaches, when it turns bright red all over, but in late summer greenish flowers and fruits are spaced out on the upright stem. Look closely and you will see that some plants have male flowers with extended anthers, which release their pollen to the wind and others have feathery female flowers with hairy stigmas to 'catch' the pollen.

At this altitude species of mountain flowers can become isolated and confined to a small geographical area. Yellow mountain saxifrage, for example, is common in the Lake District but does not grow at all in nearby north Wales. And alpine lady's mantle, though common in Scotland, is not found in Upper Teesdale.

Citrus scent *By mountain streams, footpaths and on the edges of woodland on acid slopes you can often detect the lemony smell of a mountain fern.*

HIGH FLYER Beside a rushing mountain stream in summer you might be surprised to see dragonflies. Some species are happy at this altitude because they roost in heather. The **powder-blue keeled skimmer** (above) patrols a regular beat and often disputes territory with the golden-ringed dragonfly, easily identified by its distinctive black and yellow stripes.

INLAND CLIFFS Some coastal plants grow far from the sea, where mountainous conditions mimic the harsh habitat of cliffs. In summer you might find **thrift**, often called sea pink after its brush-like tufts of pink flowers, in Snowdonia. And roseroot, which has rosettes of fleshy grey-green leaves and heads of greeny yellow flowers, grows in the Pennines and central Scotland.

Searching for prey *A buzzard (right) will soar on thermals, scouring the ground for food, then swoop down on its prey.*

Close-up on
Birds of prey

When you visit any moor in summer you may well hear and will probably spot at least one bird of prey – a predatory meat-eating bird with powerful claws and a strong beak. They can be difficult to identify as they are usually seen briefly and flying at a distance, but it is possible with practice to recognise the key features of each one.

To distinguish between these magnificent birds you need to appreciate at a glance the relative proportions of head, neck, wings and tail, and the individual shapes of wings and tails. Flight styles also vary: some are fast and dashing, others fly slowly and smoothly. And when they glide or soar, some hold their wings horizontally, others raise them in a 'V'.

On the ground you may come across the remains of recent kills. Birds of prey use their sharp beaks to pluck out feathers before eating their catch, and leave each quill broken or with a hole in it. By contrast, foxes and other predatory mammals untidily bite through or pull out large mouthfuls of feathers.

GOLDEN EAGLE

Occasionally utters **feeble yelping or whistling calls** at the nest.

The majestic **golden eagle** is almost entirely restricted to Scotland in the British Isles. Eagles approach their prey in a fast, slanting glide on long wings – 1.9-2.3m (6ft 3in-7ft 6in) from tip-to-tip – which appear pinched-in at the body. They never perch on poles and seldom come near humans.

If you think you see a golden eagle it is more likely to be a **buzzard** (above left) – nicknamed 'the tourist's eagle' in Scotland. They can appear deceptively large from a distance but, with a wingspan of 1-1.3m (3ft 3in-4ft 3in), are only half the size of the eagle. Buzzards usually nest in trees and you will often see them above wooded ground or perching on fenceposts, poles and trees. They drop on prey such as rabbits, voles and mice, although they can catch birds as big as crows.

SPARROWHAWK

Rapid, shrill ***kek-kek-kek*** calls when breeding, and plaintive ***whee-oo*** in display flight.

Although they breed in woods, **sparrowhawks** (especially the females) sometimes hunt over more open country. Good places to look are where a moor borders woodland or in valleys with clumps of trees, shrubs or hedges. The short, blunt-tipped wings are a vital clue to distinguishing a sparrowhawk from the similar-sized kestrel, though the latter's wingtips can look less pointed when it is soaring. Sparrowhawks often soar with spread wings and tail, especially on fine, breezy days.

A sparrowhawk never hovers as a kestrel does but hunts fast and low. It zips along behind a hedge or other cover, suddenly flicking over to pull a small bird from its hiding place.

HEN HARRIER
Male gives chattering calls and high-pitched ***pee-yoo*** in display flight.

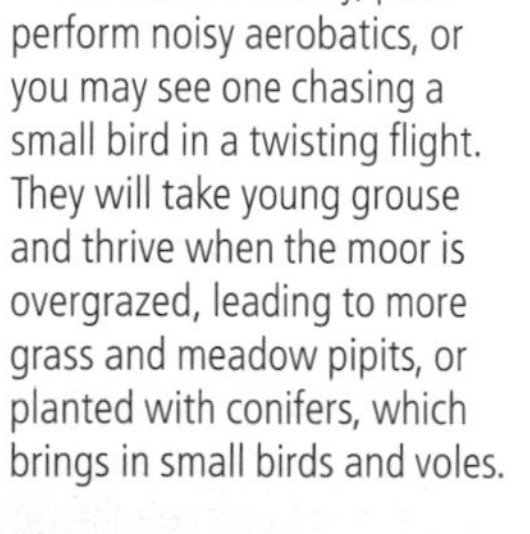

Look for a **hen harrier** sailing low over the ground with its wings raised in a 'V', then suddenly dropping on prey. The hen harrier has a wingspan of 1-1.2m (3ft 3in-4ft), a long tail and a head like an owl's.

Over their territory, pairs perform noisy aerobatics, or you may see one chasing a small bird in a twisting flight. They will take young grouse and thrive when the moor is overgrazed, leading to more grass and meadow pipits, or planted with conifers, which brings in small birds and voles.

PEREGRINE
Raucous, screaming ***kee-arrk, kee-arrk, kee-arrk*** and a high-pitched ***kek-kek-kek*** alarm.

The powerfully built **peregrine** soars high, making a distinctive anchor silhouette with its flat or slightly drooping wings, spanning about 1m (3ft 3in). The peregrine spots prey from the air or by perching, hunched, on a favourite rock-ledge, then makes a 'stoop', a breathtaking, steep, high-speed power dive on closed wings to strike prey – mostly birds of pigeon size – in midair with its talons.

KESTREL
Shrill, rasping, repeated ***kee-kee-kee-kee***, rising in pitch, notably at nests.

Kestrels are a common sight over grassy moorlands. They are medium in size, with a distinctive two-tone plumage and long, tapering wings spanning some 65-80cm (2ft 2in-2ft 6in). Kestrels often hover for long periods when searching for prey, as if suspended on a piece of string, so if you spot a hovering bird it is probably a kestrel.

CUCKOO
Cuc-koo is the male's song; the female has a loud bubbling, liquid trill.

Although everyone knows the song of the male **cuckoo**, its appearance is less familiar and the adult can be mistaken for a sparrowhawk or the young for a female kestrel. But in flight, the cuckoo has none of the soaring majesty of a bird of prey. It flies low, with shallow fast wing beats and the wings are not raised above the level of the body. The cuckoo holds its head up as it flies, as though uncertain of where it is going.

MERLIN
High-pitched, chattering ***quik-ik-ik-ik*** around a breeding site.

The **merlin** is Britain's smallest bird of prey: the male is only the size of a blackbird and the female a little larger. In flight, with its similar plumage and low-level twisting and turning, the merlin may be confused with a sparrowhawk but sparrowhawks have barred, not streaked, underparts and are usually seen only near wooded areas. Look for the merlin in open spaces, perching on rocks or in pursuit of the small birds such as skylarks and meadow pipits it catches on the wing.

Descent to a kill *The kestrel often drops to the ground in stages, hovering in between each one, before seizing its prey.*

A REGULAR PERCH Birds of prey often use the same tree stumps, rocks, mounds of earth, fenceposts or even grouse shooting butts repeatedly to rest or to eat their prey. Splashes of white droppings are clues to a frequently used spot and these are good places to look for the birds.

Hunt around the perches for pellets of undigested bones, feathers and fur coughed back up after a meal. They are good evidence of the kind of prey the bird has been eating, such as skylarks and meadow pipits.

You might find a **plucking post** (right) where a bird of prey takes its prey to pluck and perhaps dismember before eating it or carrying it to its chicks. Feathers under the post are also good clues to the bird's prey. Small, dull brown ones and wisps of pale buff feathers with dark streaks will usually have come from a meadow pipit like the one held in the talons of this male **merlin**.

Magnificent plateaus of limestone break out of the grassy landscape of West Yorkshire in places like Malham and Ingleborough, and in the old Westmorland Pennines, north Wales and western Ireland. Rock fractured by the weight of Ice Age ice sheets has been weathered over thousands of years to leave raised blocks (clints) separated by deep clefts (grykes) where plants and creatures can find shelter, soil and moisture.

Survival on a rocky platform

Soil on limestone is thin but rich in calcium from the rock, calcium carbonate. Limestone is soluble, especially in slightly acid water, such as rain, and this erosion also leaves calcium – a mineral many plants need to survive – in the limey soil.

Where sheep graze freely, as at Gait Barrows in Silverdale, Lancashire (right) or at Malham, the pavements are bare. The rocks rapidly dry out in hot sun and bitter wind but there is refuge to be found for animals and plants in the grykes.

Flowers of the pavement

In the barest pavements, these fissures are the only places where soil is found. Plants must germinate in deep shade and grow up into the light but their roots remain cool and moist.

On limestone rocks of the north-west Pennines and north Wales you may find holly fern. Its thick, almost fleshy, blue-green leaves retain water and help it to withstand the drying conditions. Other plants to watch for include ramsons, with their oniony stench and herb Robert (see right).

The baneberry grows knee-high on limestone in the Pennines. It has broad leaves split into several deeply toothed leaflets and wispy white early summer flowers. These produce green berries which turn black in late summer, providing food for birds, but all parts of the plant are poisonous to humans.

A rare orchid found on a few northern and western limestone pavements is the dark red helleborine. The tall stems bear several neat two-lipped blooms of deep maroon in June and July.

Where sheep are fenced out, such as at Ingleborough, a thick turf grows over the rocks. There is much more soil here and taller ash and sycamores can grow. You might also find bird cherry, guelder rose and elegant rowans, whose copious coral-red fruits are food for ring ouzels and mistle thrushes.

Under overhanging limestone cliffs, house martins build their mud-pellet cup nests, revealing how they lived before they discovered the merits of the suburbs. Look out for them as they fly to and from the nest after they return from Africa in April until their last broods fledge in September.

Hidden feature

You might not know that you were on a limestone pavement if it is overgrown, but the plants can help you to recognise one. There are areas of limestone in the Gower peninsula and on headlands near Torquay and Weston-super-Mare.

Look for broad rock ledges with a little soil where you might see small flowers with narrow, deep yellow petals: the hoary rock-rose. Near wet 'flushes', where standing or slow-flowing water keeps the grass and moss bright green, you may find bird's-eye primroses. In May or June its cluster of lilac-pink, yellow-eyed flowers stands on a short, fleshy stem rising from a rosette of pale thin leaves.

CRAMPED CONDITIONS
A young spindly **ash** (below) has taken root in one of the deeper grykes on this pavement. Where there are trees nearby saplings often germinate in crevices, but few reach maturity in the thin soil and restricted space. Even old trees are rarely more than 5m (16ft) high.

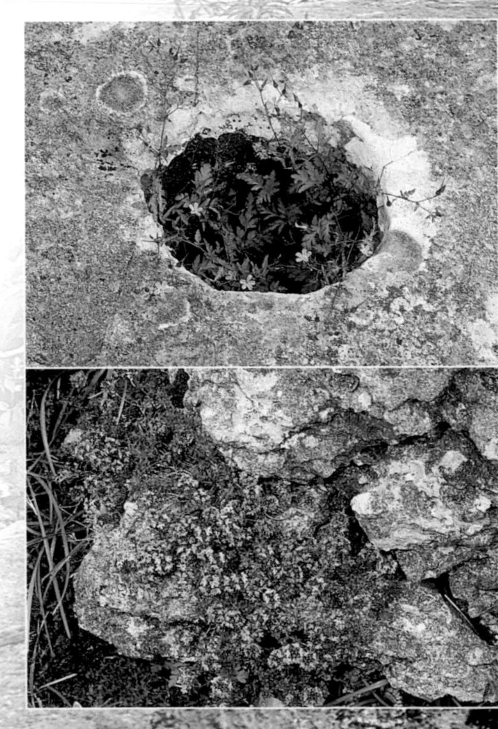

Herb garden *Herb Robert (above right) is often found on walls, a similar environment to limestone pavements. In dry, exposed places its leaves and stems turn a fiery red. Wild thyme (right) grows well in dry sites, sprawling low to avoid harsh winds.*

FLUTTERING AND SLIDING OVER THE ROCKS

The butterflies you may see on limestone pavements all look confusingly similar – small and brownish. They could be pearl-bordered fritillaries, meadow browns, small coppers, small heaths, wall browns or, if you are on a northern limestone pavement, the mountain argus (also known as the northern brown argus). Only a close examination aided by a detailed field guide will enable you to be sure. Look for them settling on the carpets of low flowers or rising up in a cloud before you as you approach.

Limestone pavements are the only moorland habitat where you will see snails. Slugs are found more or less everywhere but most moors do not provide enough calcium for snails to make their shells.

On limestone pavements the plentiful calcium means that snails can survive but you are still unlikely to see them out on the rocks at midday. The sun and wind would soon dry them out, with fatal results. Follow their tell-tale trails of slime in the early morning and look for the snails where they end, in dank, shady spots within the crevices.

Two to search for are the glass, or lapidary snail and the rock snail. The glass snail looks much like a common garden snail in shape but has more flattened, broader whorls and a sharp raised rim around the edge of the shell. The rock snail's shell is a broad, flattened spiral, perfectly suited to squeezing into the narrow crevices between the rocks.

In hiding *The large wall brown's wings are grey underneath so that when they are closed they blend in with the limestone. It also basks on rocks in the summer sun, showing the eyespots on its orangey wings.*

OUT OF PLACE Even woodland species, such as the **hart's tongue fern**, can grow in the damp crevices between the grykes on limestone pavements.

SCENT OF SPICE The tall pink **fragrant orchid** (right) has a fungus growing on its roots which helps it to extract the minerals it needs from the limestone. As its name suggests, you will probably detect this plant by its smell before you see it – the scent of cloves wafts from the flowers, attracting butterflies and moths.

Wet and wild

BOG BASICS The most common plants on bogs are the many **sphagnum mosses** and they form the main constituent of peat. Some are 98 per cent water – try squeezing a handful and see.

The squelchy terrain of blanket bog country can appear monotonous from afar, but a closer look reveals a rich and unusual way of life. For the best bogs, head north-west. In Wales bogs develop only above 425m (1400ft), but they occur almost down to sea level in Scotland, with the very best in the flow country of Caithness. There, they are found not only in remote areas but bordering the roads and railway track. At Forsinard a nature trail shows you all the clues to this acid soggy way of life.

The key to a blanket bog is rain. Combined with a year-round damp atmosphere and a lack of minerals this prevents trees growing. Without trees to suck up the water, any slope that rises less than 15 degrees from the horizontal will fail to drain and will become waterlogged.

The sodden soil contains so little oxygen that the worms, insects, fungi and bacteria that would normally break down the dead remains of plants cannot thrive. Instead, the remains accumulate, layer upon layer, compressing the dead matter and turning it into peat. This process takes thousands of years, which is why the large-scale commercial extraction of peat for gardens is so destructive to the bog.

Peat bogs cover large areas of the wettest parts of Britain, even where there was once forest. If you are lucky you may see the boles of ancient trees, chopped down by prehistoric farmers, perfectly preserved at the base of the peat, and made visible where it has been eroded or extracted.

In areas such as Tregaron in mid Wales, or Fox Tor Mires on Dartmoor, you may find raised bogs. Here the peat grows in a broad dome, above the level of the surrounding ground and the wettest parts wobble like jelly.

Occasionally you will see big dead trees, particularly pines, in quaking bogs, which are bogs that develop over water. As they grow, the trees sink under their own weight and break through the surface peat to the water below, where they drown.

On all bogs it is important for walkers to keep to the boarded paths which are provided along nature trails. Bogs can be treacherous to tread on and are also very special and easily damaged endangered habitats.

AROMATIC SHRUB A rich scent of resin wafts from **bog myrtle**, a knee-high shrub with reddish twigs that gives off its scent when a walker brushes past. Look for it in wet places on southern heaths, such as New Forest valley bogs, and upland moors. Scratch one of the grey-green leaves to release the perfume.

A splash of colour *Bog asphodel brightens the landscape, each upright stem topped with a cluster of yellow star-like flowers.*

BRIGHT FLOWERS

Few woody plants grow on bogs but some heathers live in the best-drained areas. The most common type is the cross-leaved heath (see page 155), whose hairy leaves reduce water loss, a curious trait in this wet place, but winter winds can dry plants out, especially when their water supply is frozen. Minimising water loss may also help to control the unwanted uptake of iron, which is found in high concentration in the acid water.

BLOODSUCKING INSECTS Does your face smart? Feel those sharp nips? Bogs are the perfect places for midges: their larvae live in the peaty mud and are well adapted to survive in acid conditions and where oxygen is in short supply. The combination of bogs and mild summers in western Scotland is ideal for the tiny biting midges that belong to the family *Ceratopogonidae* to thrive. The most common people-biter is the species *Culicoides obsoletus*. Clouds of these bloodsuckers can attack and make your skin burn. They are so abundant and voracious in summer that they can make it unbearable to walk in parts of the Scottish Highlands.

Biting midges usually obtain their sustenance from the blood of mammals or birds, unlike most other midges which feed on other insects. There are 400 different species of chironomid midges (small, hump-backed flies) in Britain which are not bloodsuckers. In fact many of these midges don't feed at all during their adult life – they just hatch, breed and die.

Remains of the dead *Butterwort and other insectivorous plants, such as the sundews, absorb and digest juices from their insect prey. When the plant's leaves are open, you might see little black dots on them – remains of recent captures.*

Bog cottons are abundant in these wet regions. Varieties with many flowers are found in the wettest areas and those that grow in tussocks with only a single flower indicate drier land.

In north-west Scotland deer sedge grows widely. Though it is poor food for browsing red deer, by necessity it forms a large part of their diet. The plant's nutritional shortcomings might explain why red deer in the Highlands don't grow as big as their continental cousins.

Within the bogs you may find especially wet flushes, bright green with vivid moss. On steep slopes excess water seeps down through the spongy soil and sodden vegetation in shallow crystal-clear streams stained with peat, where rushes and purple moor-grass grow.

Bog asphodel (above left) is rare in southern Britain but more frequent in the north. In the 16th century, Lancashire women used it in place of saffron and to dye their hair. Its scientific name, *Narthecium ossifragum*, means 'bone-breaker' and sheep that graze where it lives are prone to develop brittle bones. This may be because bog asphodel can tolerate a lack of calcium in the soil, so animals that eat it will not get enough of the calcium crucial for healthy bones. In these exposed places, wind is the main seed-dispersal agent and the eyecatching orange seeds have a tail at each end to make them buoyant.

MURDEROUS PLANTS

While sphagnum mosses and other bog plants take their nutrients from the meagre supplies in the acid water, some specialists catch prey. Look for a plant with red leaves covered with short spiky red hairs, each topped with a glistening sticky droplet. This is the sundew. Common sundew has a rosette of round leaves but if you are in Scotland, look for the great sundew, whose leaves are broader, tapering and more upright than its common cousin. All the sundews have small white flowers, which are self-fertilising, so they do not need the services of the insects which risk their lives in among the leaves.

If you see a limp, pale green 'starfish' growing on the peat, this is butterwort. The flat, broad leaves also catch flies and curl around the prey to keep out ants which will try to steal the plant's meal. The purple flowers of butterworts attract quite different insects from the leaves – it would not make sense for the plant to kill its pollinators.

A sticky end *Passing flies and the midges that swarm over bogs are attracted to the sticky drops on the sundew's leaves (right). When they investigate more closely they are caught on the gluey secretion (inset above), which helps to digest them to make food for the plant.*

Close-up on

Little holes in the ground

Take a closer look if you see a bank of sandy soil perforated with hundreds of tiny holes. These are not the effects of erosion or of a pecking bird but are the openings to the nests of burrowing insects. Ants and many species of bees and wasps dig where the soil is light and easily worked and you might not need to venture far to find evidence of them as they often nest in the disturbed ground around the edges of car parks in moorland beauty spots.

Hot spots for holes

South-facing banks of exposed clay, sandy soil or friable chalk are favourite locations for nests because they are warmed by the sun. Sand dunes, the sides of sand and clay pits where earth has been excavated or the soil plate attached to the roots of a fallen tree are also ideal. On moors, look out for bare patches of earth cleared by a burrowing rabbit or badger, or by a sheep scraping out earth to create a low cliff for shelter, and scan the bends in silty riverbanks, which have been scoured by winter torrents.

You might see large numbers of small holes in such places, each one the work of a solitary mining bee. Although they do not build a single, large communal nest, these bees are sociable and as many as a thousand individual nest holes could be found grouped together in one area. In summer you might see the males of this neatly banded, short-haired bee cruising in their hundreds above a nest site, apparently fighting with one another. In fact they are seeking mates and jostling for position as they wait to pounce on a new-generation female, emerging from her nest for the first time.

Dug out Badgers often dig into a sandy bank to get at the grubs which are maturing in the nests inside (above). If you come across evidence of digging look in the loose soil or exposed bank for small sacs (right). Each of these is filled with a yellow mixture of pollen and honey to feed the single grub developing inside.

PREPARING FOR A NEW GENERATION

Ground-nesting bees and wasps seal their eggs in their burrows. But before they do this they stock the nest with a source of nourishment ready for the larva when it hatches.

The bee wolf wasp **[1]** catches a live bee for its larva, paralysing the victim so that it can carry it back to the nest. Hairy-legged mining bees **[2]** collect nectar and pollen to make a nutritious mixture, which they store in dark brown sacs – one for each egg.

You might see a bee fly go out on a foraging trip but be unable to find a hole, because it seals its nest temporarily while it flies off in search of a caterpillar.

These food stores sustain the insects' young until they are mature enough to dig their way out of the nest. Summer is a good time to watch the adults out collecting the supplies.

Erupted earth A heap of earth (left) like a miniature volcanic crater marks the entrance to the vertical nest of a tawny mining bee. You may find many nest holes close together – they are most visible in the short grass of garden lawns.

SQUATTING IN NESTS

Some insects nest in existing holes – bumblebees and social wasps often take over vacant mouse holes – so to identify the owner of any small hole in the ground you have to wait to see what goes in or comes out.

Others are more aggressive and don't wait until the holes are empty before moving in. Look for bee flies (below) hovering low over the ground, above the crater-like nest of a mining bee. The bee fly is probably scattering its eggs in the nest, where its larvae will develop as parasites and eat the mining bee larvae.

The female cuckoo bee also lays her eggs inside the nest of the mining bee, but she does it before the nest is sealed over the egg. She waits for a chance to enter the nest while the mining bee is foraging for food for her larva. The cuckoo bee larva hatches before the mining bee and eats both the host egg and the nectar supply stored in the nest by the host female.

You may be able to spot cuckoo bees as adults in a group of mining bees. They are yellow-striped and waspy-looking and stand out among the slim, brown male tawny bees with their tufts of pale hairs on their heads.

Fly disguise *As their name suggests, bee flies (left) are flies that look like hairy bees. One way to tell them from real bees is that bee flies have two wings but bees have four. Bee flies can appear to be hovering over a flower as they probe for nectar with a long proboscis but are actually steadied by their long and almost invisibly slender legs.*

BEETLES BELOW

Many beetles bore into dead wood, making holes which may later be inhabited by bees or wasps, but some species burrow in the ground.

On southern heaths look for the glossy, long-legged green tiger beetle with its pale spots, or the purple-black wood tiger beetle. Both dig in loose light soils or humus to make nests where their larvae will develop. The adult beetles of both species live above ground.

Dung gatherer

If you see a group of holes made in sand and surrounded by rabbit droppings (below) look around for a minotaur beetle. Each hole on the surface may lead to several brood chambers underground and the shiny black beetle packs one ball of rabbit, or sometimes sheep, dung into each chamber. The female then lays an egg on each ball of dung and leaves the nest.

This unappetising dung diet is sufficient to support the developing minotaur beetle larva for around three months after it hatches.

Burrowing beetles *The green tiger beetle [1] does not stock its nest with food: the larvae hunt for themselves, seizing ants and other insects that pass the opening. The male minotaur beetle [2] collects dung for his larvae while his mate digs the nest.*

Golden sands

Undisturbed coves, such as Porthcew, near Rinsey Head in Cornwall (above), are always rich in signs of wildlife. What looks like bare sand may be full of shells – the former mobile homes of bivalves such as carpet shells, or coiled top shells and periwinkles, torn from their homes on the rocks. Paddle or swim in the shallows and you might see shoals of young fish, or coloured seaweeds swaying in the tide, forming a marine forest for small animals to cling to or hide in.

Cornwall is famous for its coves, perfect half-moons of golden sand enclosed by rocky headlands. As the tide goes out, you can pick out the zones of lichen and seaweed on the exposed rocks, and peer into weedy pools for signs of life. The rock pools richest in life are found at low tide and will

Long summer days for exploring the coast

Discovering signs of life in sand, shingle, rocks and water

Sun warms the beach on a summer's day. The tide is on its way out, exposing stretches of clean-washed sands and rocky outcrops dotted with tide pools and festooned with slippery seaweeds.

The scene could be almost anywhere on the coast, but the detail changes from place to place. The beach you're on might face the breakers of the Atlantic, with sand piled into steep dunes. You may be in a wide bay where low tide reveals mile upon mile of flat sand, or a cove enclosed by headlands displaying the structure of the rocks: banded slate, massive granite, reddish sandstone or pale chalk.

Wherever you are, a day at the coast will provide hours of exploration, from the pools and shallows to the windy clifftops.

The shells of burrowing bivalves such as tellins often litter the beach at low tide. You might find the two halves of the shell still joined together by their strong hinge.

be fringed with green, brown and red seaweeds. In the water you might catch a glimpse of a well-camouflaged fish such as a blenny or rock goby.

On the upper shore, life is harsher. Here, plants and animals are exposed to the sun and air for most of the day. Some, such as mussels and limpets, are safe within their shells. Others, like the shore crab, hide in pools or under rocks.

On the rocks

In early summer many rocky offshore islands and cliffs, such as Handa Island off the north-west coast of Scotland (above), are inhabited by colonies of sea birds. Large numbers of guillemots cluster together and launch themselves from their rocky perches towards the sea. There, they catch sand eels and other small fish for their chicks, which huddle in recesses and crannies. At the edge of the colonies look for green and white mats of sea campion, a salt-tolerant plant that thrives on the birds' waste.

Most sea bird colonies contain more than one species. Here the guillemots share their space with a few razorbills, with their broad bills and darker upperparts. There may also be fulmars, with their strange tubular beaks and soft grey wings, and visiting waders, such as oystercatchers.

Sea bird cities are dirty, noisy and smelly, but they are wonderful places for the nature detective to discover how these specialised birds attract a mate, look after their young, hunt for food, or just pass their time. Many colony sites are now protected in nature reserves, where there may be facilities for birdwatchers. Use the hides or find yourself a safe perch, and look in on the teeming sea bird world through binoculars.

Guillemots do not build nests. Instead, the male and female take it in turns to incubate their single egg by balancing it on their feet and covering it with their belly plumage.

Beachcombing on the sand

Years of pounding by the sea breaks empty shells into tiny pieces and eats away at the coast, chipping off fragments of rock and reducing them to pebbles and, eventually, to particles fine enough to run through your fingers. See how the colour of the nearby rocks compares with the colour of the sand. They may not match, since beach sand is not necessarily made only from local rocks but also from particles carried many miles by currents.

Worm hole *The familiar ribbons of sand on beaches (above) are made by the lugworm (inset right). A hole marks the other end of its burrow.*

Looking up *The sand goby sits at the bottom of sandy pools. It has eyes near the top of its head to look out for danger from above, so to watch it unobserved try to avoid casting a shadow on the water.*

Sand varies widely in colour and texture. Cornish coves are often golden yellow, while some of the beaches in western Scotland are almost white, with a very high proportion of shell in them. Where there are hard rocks, like granite, sand can be coarse and crystalline – even uncomfortable to walk on barefoot. In western England beaches are often made up of tiny grey fragments of slate, which stick to your feet like fish scales, while in East Anglia shores may be fine and silty.

At first sight a sandy beach appears lifeless – all you can see are broken and empty shells, egg cases, decaying seaweed and other debris from the sea. What life there is on the beach is hidden but the birds will give you a clue to the whereabouts of living creatures. Waders, such as oystercatchers or sanderlings, probe the wet sand with their long bills to pluck out worms and other burrowing creatures.

These animals can stay hidden in the sand because every tide brings a fresh helping of nutritious marine detritus. Lugworms feed on the sand, extracting anything edible from it then ejecting the remains in spaghetti-like casts of more or less pure fine sand. They live in 'U'-shaped burrows, so search about a hand's width from a cast, and you will find a shallow conical depression which marks the other end of the 'U'.

To see a lugworm, dig down between these two openings. You should find a fat, reddish or yellowish worm about as long as your hand. Anglers like the man pictured digging in the sands of a Norfolk beach (top) often use lugworms as bait when they go fishing.

Mop top *In shallow water at low tide look out for a mop-like tassel projecting above the sand. This is the top of the vertical tube where the sand mason worm lives. The worm stays well down the tube when the tide is out but once its entrance is covered with water you may see it extend its many long thin pink or red tentacles. These are supported by the tassel and are used to search for food.*

IN THE SHALLOWS

Young open-sea fish feed in shallower waters in summer – you may even see shoals of tiny silver fish stranded in pools at low tide. To watch fish without scaring them away, try wearing polaroid sunglasses (which are not as reflective as normal sunglasses) and avoid standing between the sun and the water, so that you don't cast a shadow.

The shoal fishes, particularly young saithe or pollack, which remain close inshore during the summer, are most easily seen by wading or snorkelling. You may also spot sand eels, which occur in huge shoals and form an important part of the diet of terns and other sea birds.

Sand eels are very thin, with pointed heads and shovel-shaped jaws. You may see no more than a flash of silver in the water as they move, or a puff of sand as they disappear in the blink of an eye by burrowing into the sandy bottom.

Hunting in the sand

On sheltered beaches and flats, large numbers of common shrimps live in sandy pools. You will need to be patient to see them because their speckled camouflage makes shrimps almost invisible until they move.

Unlike a prawn, a shrimp has a broad flattened body with a pair of pincers at the front end – a sign that it is a predator. Shrimps probe the sand with long fine antennae, and catch morsels with their pincers. But if you want to see a lot of them, visit the beach after dark with a torch, because shrimps hunt mainly by night.

BEACH CLEANER The rotting seaweed and dead castaways found along the strandline offer rich pickings for gulls and crows. But some small invertebrates, such as the **sand hopper**, also scavenge on the rotting debris and without their services the beach would be a much more untidy and less pleasant place. You might notice these reddish brown louse-like animals, about 2cm (¾in) long, because they jump out like fleas as you pass, but when they leap they are merely getting out of your way, not trying to attach themselves to you. In summer, the weed often swarms with kelp flies, which lay their eggs there. Their larvae develop very rapidly, feeding on the rotting material, and several generations will mature each summer.

STRANDED BY THE TIDE

A little beachcombing may uncover animals that have been stranded on the beach. The most common victims are free-floating animals, such as jellyfish, which are at the mercy of the currents. Out of water, the **common jellyfish [1]** looks like an inverted saucer of transparent jelly 10cm (4in) across. It has four horseshoe-shaped purplish marks on the top side, which are its reproductive organs. To see the tentacles and purplish 'mouth arms' beneath, put a freshly stranded one back in some water.

Be careful: all jellyfish sting. The common jellyfish has a weak sting, which most people will not even feel but others, such as the brownish compass jellyfish can sting like nettles.

The first sign of a **sea potato**, or heart urchin, may be the shell of a dead one **[2]**. If you come across a shell, look for a live sea potato near the water's edge. The creature can bury itself up to 20cm (8in) deep in the sand using specially flattened spines, so a good clue to look for is a shallow conical depression on the beach with a small hole at the bottom. The spines fall off after death so if you find a live sea potato, compare it with a cast shell: it is hard to recognise them as the same animal.

Also on the strandline you may come across a strange sea creature known as the **by-the-wind-sailor** – a jellyfish relative. When alive it is a translucent blue oval disc with a diagonal upright 'sail' and floats on the surface of the sea, being carried along by the wind. It shrivels quickly after death and often all you find is the desiccated brownish remains of its float and sail **[3]**.

Another creature to keep an eye out for, particularly in south-west England, is the sea gooseberry, or combjelly, which looks like a glistening transparent marble. Put it in a jam jar of sea water and it reveals a pair of long tentacles and rows of comb-like hairs on its body. As the animal moves these hairs show up as irridescent flashes of light.

2

3

Close-up on
Sea shells

Pick up a few shells as you walk along a beach and you will soon realise that most are empty. The shells are the outward evidence of molluscs, soft-bodied creatures often protected by a shell, living beneath your feet, where the sand is still wet. Burrowing into the sand ensures safety from predators, and food is delivered twice a day on the incoming tide, but one disadvantage of this lifestyle is that at low tide these creatures are exposed to the sun and air.

You will see that many of the shells on the beach are bivalves: two shells connected by a hinge. Even if you find just one half you can usually identify the hinged edge. Bivalves open up to feed and breathe, and close when the tide goes out and they are stranded. On an average beach you can find 20 species or more of bivalves, although there will be a greater variety on southern and western coasts than on the more uniform soft shores of eastern England. Molluscs that live inside a single shell, such as periwinkles and whelks, are classified as gastropods.

Backwards motion *The scallop escapes predators, such as starfish, by jet propelling itself backwards. It does this by opening and closing the two halves of its shell like a clacking pair of false teeth and squirting out a jet of water. Two 'fins' where the shell hinges help it to change direction.*

CUTTLEBONE

Most shells are the outer casing of the creature they once belonged to but a **cuttlebone** comes from the inside. In life, it was filled with gas and liquid and acted as a float in a **cuttlefish**. When the cuttlefish – not a fish, but a mollusc related to squid – has decayed, the cuttlebone remains and may be found washed up on the strandline.

WHELK

Whelks are unusual gastropods because they do not graze on seaweed, but prey on a wide variety of slow-moving animals and scavenge carrion, which they can **'smell'** as they siphon the sea water. In summer females gather in groups to lay a spongy mass of eggs, whose empty cases are often washed ashore and look a little like bubble wrap.

PAINTED TOP SHELL

As its name suggests, the **painted top shell** is beautifully marked, with pink splotches and streaks, and is shaped like an old-fashioned spinning top. The snails grow up to 3cm (1¼in) high and live mainly low down on the shore and in deeper water among the forests of kelp seaweeds. They are sensitive to extremes of temperature and so cannot survive high up on the shore.

An expert climber, the painted top shell can crawl up the stalks of kelp just as a snail crawls up a cabbage stalk, moving on a flat slimy foot. Tentacles on the head and along the sides of its foot, help it to feel its way around, since it has only **small eyes** set low down at the base of the long head tentacles.

PERIWINKLE

While most bivalves live in sand, gastropods, such as **periwinkles**, choose rocky places. Black and white **tentacles** help them to find food by touch, and 'smell' by detecting chemicals in the water. They graze on seaweed or algae, leaving pale patches on lower shore seaweeds. When the tide goes out, periwinkles are exposed, but survive by sealing themselves inside their shells. A hard disc, or operculum, acts as a trap door and if you examine a periwinkle you should see this covering the opening. When the winkle emerges it carries the operculum at the end of its foot. Winkles are often swept off the rocks in rough seas – you may find large numbers in gullies on the shore.

PREDATORY SNAIL Wedge shells are often found on the beach. They are similar to tellins, but more elongated in shape and are more likely to have come apart. The most common is the **banded wedge shell** (inset left), whose inner surface is purple, yellow or orange. A neat bevelled hole in the shell tells you that its owner came to a sticky end. The hole has been made by the **necklace shell snail** (left), which drills through shells to suck out the nutritious contents. You are unlikely to see this snail, but may see its **spawn**, which looks like a coiled snake of jelly and sand on the shore (right), and which gives the snail its name.

TELLIN

Thin flattened shells with rounded sides in pink, orange or with rays like a sunset, are likely to be **tellin** shells. A good clue to identifying tellins is that the shells stay paired for a long time, thanks to a particularly tough hinge, and are often found open, like butterfly wings. When a tellin burrows in sand or mud, pulled down by its muscular 'foot', its thin shell offers little resistance. The tellin feeds and breathes through two long flexible tubes, or **siphons**, one sucking in oxygenated water and debris from the sediment and the other expelling waste. Keep watch and you may see the tips of these siphons protruding from the surface. Or drop a live tellin in a jar of seawater and watch the siphons extend.

MUSSEL

Since they live in beds attached to rocks, not buried in the sand, **mussels** are easy to find. They are easily identified by their blue-black colour and mother-of-pearl interior. How do they feed? At high tide **the shells open** and the animal filters food out of the water using its gills. For this reason, mussels usually grow in places where there is plenty of water movement. They withstand the force of the necessary current by anchoring themselves with threads, stuck together like a cable rope. Try pulling a mussel off a rock – the threads are incredibly strong, but they are also flexible enough to let the mussel twist round in the current so that it always presents the least resistance to the tide.

COCKLE

The thick ribbing of a **cockle** shell looks clumsy, but cockles live in fine sand in shallow water, where plenty of plankton is brought by the tide, and so have no need to move about. They often occur in vast numbers and on eastern shores, such as at Shell Beach on the Isle of Sheppey in Kent, you can find banks of cockle shells washed up by storms. You can encourage cockles to the surface by treading with your feet. Gulls know this trick, too, and can be seen 'puddling' on the sand. Clever gulls crack the cockle's shell by dropping it from a height, then swoop down for the **edible contents**. Oystercatchers, on the other hand, prise open the shells with their powerful beaks or hammer their way in.

RAZORSHELL

Their blade-like shape enables **razorshells** to burrow quickly in wet sand when the tide goes out. To track down a live razorshell scour the lower shore for a keyhole-shaped depression in the sand. This forms the entrance to a burrow. The razorshell has a **powerful foot** which anchors it deep inside its burrow and holds it firm against the wash of the tide. But you can entice a razorshell to the surface by sprinkling salt on the 'keyhole', a practice often used by people who gather the creatures for food. You have to be quick to catch the shell as it surfaces, but if you succeed, let it go again and watch how it upends through 90 degrees and plunges back into the wet sand.

Signs of shore birds

Few birds live on busy beaches, but in less frequented places – on shingle bars, dunes and cliff ledges – look out for gulls, terns and waders. Many of the best shore bird colonies are now in nature reserves and are roped off during nesting time in May and June. But some reserves provide hides, where you can watch parties of young birds learning to find food; spy on intimate moments, such as the piping, head-nodding territorial display of the oystercatcher; and study the birds' different feeding habits.

Slippery prey *Terns pluck fish from the water with long, sharply pointed bills, which have serrated inner edges to keep a firm hold on a struggling catch.*

Shore birds' bills vary widely in shape and size, allowing them to feed in different ways and probe to different depths in sand or silt for molluscs, worms and other invertebrates. This means that several species of birds can live together, side by side on the shoreline, without competing for the same food supply.

If you see an elegant streaky brown bird with a long, downward curved bill probing deeply into the mud, it is likely to be Britain's largest wader: the curlew. The curlew uses its long beak to search for large worms, such as lugworms or ragworms, which normally lie buried too deep in the sediment for waders with shorter bills, such as dunlins and knots, to reach.

Dunlins and knots prospect for food nearer the surface of the sand but the ringed plover – a plump little bird with a black breast band and eyepatch, and a stubby beak – hunts only by sight. Watch one repeatedly run-stop-pause-peck-run across the beach. You may also see a ringed plover 'foot trembling' on soft mud. This encourages any worms and molluscs near the surface to move, making them easier to locate.

1

Feeding techniques *The avocet* **[1]** *feeds in shallow water, sweeping its bill from side to side to sieve out mosquito larvae and small crustaceans. Its prints (inset) are distinctive, since it is rare for a wader to have partially webbed feet. Ringed plovers* **[2]** *pick food from the surface with their stubby beaks whereas godwits* **[3]** *have long legs, which allow them to wade into the water and long bills, able to penetrate several centimetres into the sand. Gulls, such as the great black-backed gull* **[4]**, *don't forage on the beach but use their strong bills to tear apart the fish they catch.*

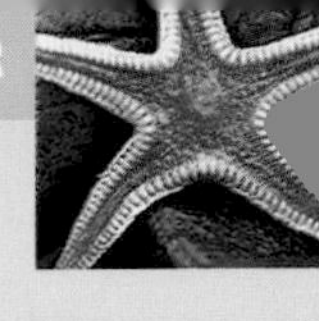

If you see a bird that seems to be almost squatting on the sand it could be a tern. Because terns catch their food in flight, they do not need to walk much, and have extremely short legs, which are almost invisible when the bird is not in flight.

Versatile wader

On RSPB reserves on the East Anglian coast you can observe avocets close up. Listen for their simple but far-carrying fluting call, ***kluit***, and look out for their striking black-and-white striped plumage. You might see one standing in shallow water on a single, slender leg.

The avocet's method of sieving water through its up-turned beak allows it to feed in muddy pools where food may be invisible. But in clear water the avocet also hunts by sight, pecking at choice items such as ragworms or prawns.

Its partially webbed feet enable the avocet to swim in the coastal lagoons where it is most at home. It sometimes up-ends like a duck to feed in these shallow waters.

INTERPRETING THE EVIDENCE

A sandy beach or muddy estuary can also hold more clues that birds have been feeding. 'Stitch' marks made in an erratic line are a sign of dunlins. These little birds begin to arrive at the coast in late summer and scuttle along the shore, probing as they go. Curlews leave large holes often in a wide semicircle, not a line, where they have made test probes from a stationary point.

Oystercatchers leave smaller, more slender tracks than the heavier curlews and similar semicircular or oval marks, but usually within a smaller radius, as they are smaller birds. More obvious signs of their feeding activity are the broken remains of mussels, cockles and limpets, or discarded whole mussel shells with bill marks at the edge.

The oystercatcher has a powerful bill, which it uses to lever apart or smash open these bivalves to reach the nutritious flesh inside. Despite their name, oystercatchers in Britain and Europe hardly ever eat oysters. Shelducks, which prefer muddy estuaries to beaches, leave semicircular troughs where they have sifted mud through their bills with a side-to-side action.

A shallow excavation where a bird has tried to dig for a worm, or peck marks on a cuttlefish bone or dead animal remains, are probably the work of gulls. They are more opportunistic feeders, as their food pellets will show you. These often contain non-marine items such as cereal husks, small mammal bones and even bits of bin liner ,which the birds pick up when scavenging on rubbish tips.

LOST FEATHERS As you walk on a beach look for cast feathers. The colour, pattern and shape will give you clues to the bird a feather belonged to, particularly the most robust and distinctive ones: the tail feathers and flight feathers from the wing. A feather resembling a classic quill pen might have come from a large gull whereas those of jackdaws and crows, which scavenge on beaches, are blunt ended, and dark. Tern feathers are long and slender for sustained or acrobatic flight when fishing at sea and waders have long slim primaries – the feathers at the tip of the wing – which enable them to achieve their long migrations. Heavy-duty stiff feathers with thick quills suggest a heavy bird, such as a duck or large gull, which puts a great strain on its feathers during flight. The feathers of cormorants or gannets are very stiff and strong in order to cope with the strains of 'flying' under water when the birds dive for food.

Making a collection If you plan to keep the feathers you collect, clean them in warm washing-up water and leave them to dry. Then preen them – as the bird would have done – by brushing them in the direction of the barbs with a stiff paintbrush or toothbrush or by smoothing them with your fingers. As long as they are kept dry, feathers will retain their colours well.

Primary The white tip and strong, thick quill tell you that this feather is one of the primary flight feathers of a large gull.

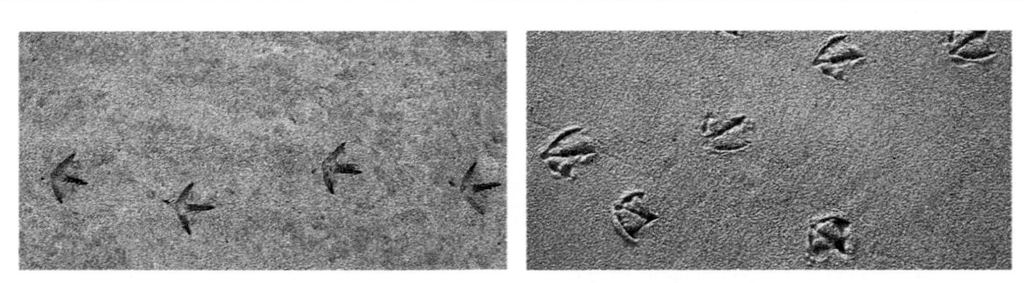

TRACKS IN THE SAND Gulls, plovers and waders feed mainly on the ground and soft sand is ideal for recording their activity. Bird prints are not always easy to identify but as a general rule, prints running in a **straight line**, with feet facing forwards (above) indicate a wader, such as a curlew. The tracks of terns, ducks and gulls (above right) show that they have turned-in feet, or are **pigeon-toed**, and seldom walk in a straight line for long.

Determining the type of foot can help when identifying the bird which made a print. Most waders, apart from a few such as the avocet and godwit, have unwebbed feet with three toes, whereas ducks, gulls and terns have broadly webbed feet. Other clues are the stride length. A stride as long as your hand betrays a long-legged bird, such as a curlew; smaller waders, like dunlin, knot and ringed plovers, take short steps and run, rather than walk.

Leftovers *Pellets, the regurgitated remains of indigestible food, reveal what the local shore birds have been eating. The fish bones, shell fragments and marine worms in these gull pellets (above) indicate a purely marine diet, unusual for a gull.*

Close-up on
Kelp forests

Forests of giant olive-brown seaweeds called kelps grow all around the British coast except in places with no rocks, such as off East Anglia. Kelps are strap or spade-shaped and can grow several metres long, supported by strong stalks called stipes. If you find kelp washed up on the shore you will see that it has three main parts. The frond, like the foliage on a tree, presents a large surface area to sunlight and is often split to prevent it being torn by waves. The stipe represents the trunk, while the structure called the holdfast – in one species as big as a dinner plate – anchors kelp, like a root.

In shallow waters you will find tangle kelp, whose stipes bend when buffeted by breaking waves. Rough kelp has longer, more rigid stipes and grows in deeper water, while sugar kelp can attach itself to loose boulders and pebbles, not just solid rocks, although its short stipes and undivided fronds mean it cannot cope with strong waves and it is usually found in more sheltered areas.

Kelps need sunlight to survive. The depth of a forest depends on how clear the water is – and therefore how far the light can penetrate – and can vary from a few metres up to 30m (100ft) in the exceptionally clean waters of western Scotland. Because kelps grow in clear water the best way to see a kelp forest is by snorkelling over it – this way you do not damage the kelp and won't risk slipping on the rocks. You can join a guided snorkel trail in the Lundy marine nature reserve off the Devon coast and Purbeck marine wildlife reserve in Dorset, but if you don't want to get wet, visit the virtual reality dive at the Purbeck reserve.

A rich underwater habitat

At first glance kelp forests appear brown but look closely and you will see that they are full of colour. Because the forests are seldom exposed by the tide, they support a greater diversity of life than the seaweed beds higher up the shore – a single kelp plant can be home to more than 300 other species such as crabs, sea snails and worms. The stipes, particularly of rough kelp, may be covered with red seaweeds, their colouring adapted to living in the shade of the kelp: one of the most common is dulse, whose flat divided fronds grow from a sucker-like disc. Around the bases, sponges and sea mats grazed on by spiky **sea urchins** (below) add an exotic touch.

FOREST LIFE

A rummage in the kelp may reveal the beautiful, if bizarre, sea slugs. They come in many bright colours and one, the **sea hare [1]**, is so-called because it has flattened tentacles, which look like a hare's ears.

In summer look for the sea hare's strings of orange or pink spawn, draped around the kelp or washed up on the shore. If you see the creature itself, tap it and it may eject a purple dye, intended to confuse a hungry fish while the sea hare escapes.

Predatory **starfish [2]**, such as the seven-armed *Luidia ciliaris*, lurk in the weed preying on other creatures, such as oysters and sea urchins. But to see the **scorpion spider crab [3]** you will need to explore the niches in the holdfasts of the kelp.

Fish are easier to see here than in rock pools. Some, such as the striped tompot blenny or spotted ballan wrasse – which is a spectacular emerald green when young – may be as curious as you are and come quite close to investigate as you snorkel above them.

CLINGING TO THE KELP Examine a frond of kelp and you may find a wide variety of other living things attached to it (below), many of which look like plants but are actually sedentary animals. Waving its tentacles amid the kelp you might see the **snakelocks anemone [1]**. Anemones are common in rock pools but this variety can only grow where it is permanently submerged. In appearance anemones look like plants but they are primitive animals which use the kelp as a base; some of the other creatures found here actually graze on the kelp. These include the grey topshell, which feeds on the bacterial and algal film on the fronds, and the attractive **blue-rayed limpet [2]** which prefers to eat their stalks or holdfasts. The limpet will chew its way into the plant until it is almost concealed from view and can weaken the kelp's stipe so that it snaps in rough seas.

The tips of the kelp fronds may seem to be covered by a delicate lacework of pale threads. These are hydroids, relatives of corals, which catch plankton and other food from near the surface of the water. Run your fingers along the broader surface of a kelp frond and if you feel a chalky or slimy film, it is a **sea mat [3]**. These mats are made up of hundreds of tiny animals, each living in its own cell about 2mm (⅛in) across. Through a hand lens you will see that each cell has a halo of tiny tentacles – feelers put out by the animal inside to catch food in the water.

Farther down the stipe you may find a colony of jelly-like **sea squirts [4]**. They have openings which inhale and eject sea water, filtering out any food in the process. If you find one out of water, try gently squeezing it – the resultant squirt of water explains their common name. **Sponges**, which encrust the stipes of kelp as well as rocks, are often confused with sea squirts but belong to a different group. One of the most common is the orange ***Hymeniacidon perleve*** **[5]**, which forms knobbly crusts on the kelp.

Unlike the gradual slopes of sandy beaches, shingle forms steep banks parallel with the shore. Pebbles are heavier than sand and are mostly dumped ashore in strips during storms, rather than being evenly distributed by the wash of the tide. Moreover, while the wind will sculpt sand into dunes, it merely rattles the shingle. Long-established beaches display a succession of ridges, where new shingle has been deposited in front of older banks, each ridge marking a former shoreline.

Shifting shingle shorelines

Pick up a handful of shingle and you will feel that the pebbles are smooth and rounded, worn by the force of the water and years of being jostled together. You might identify a wide variety of rock types – grey slate or granite mixed with white marble or orange-brown sandstone – indicating that the pebbles have come from many different places.

Shingle produces dramatic scenery. Where the coastline turns a corner, the waves often continue to dump shingle in a straight line, matching the direction of the current. This forms a hook-shaped spit such as the one at Hurst Castle by the Solent in Hampshire. In other cases, such as on The Fleet in Dorset, a shingle bar may cut off part of the coastline, leaving an enclosed lagoon behind it.

Where shingle is driven high up the shore in ridges by storms an apposition beach forms. The finest example in Britain is Dungeness in Kent (below) but there are several smaller ones along the south coast.

PLANTS AMONG THE PEBBLES

Shingle is a hostile habitat: dry, sunbaked, short of organic matter and mobile: the pebbles nearest the sea shift with the tide. Few plants can survive among loose stones but move a little way inland and you will start to find specialist plants, adapted to living on the shingle.

It is rare to see wilted shingle plants, even in very hot weather, because they have waxy leaves, which repel saltwater and help to prevent water loss.

Study the plants growing in shingle and you will see that they employ two very different survival strategies. The first is to have big, broad or cabbage-like leaves in large, tight clumps, which make the plants robust. Sea kale, one of Britain's most striking shingle plants with its white blooms like cauliflowers, can withstand bruising by loose stones kicked up by the water.

The other strategy is to spread out in a low carpet of leaves and flowers. This avoids a battering by salt-laden winds and also provides a large spread for the roots. 'Carpet plants' also help to fix the shingle and sea campion, identified by its white flowers and waxy blue-green leaves, grows prolifically enough to make it an important stabiliser. You can easily uncover the surface roots to see their spread, but remember to replace any shingle you move.

But sea campion's roots are not all at the surface. Like sea kale and most other shingle

Taking in water *Sea kale (below), which puts down long roots in search of moisture, and sea campion (bottom), whose shallow spreading roots absorb dew, are typical of shingle beaches such as Dungeness.*

plants it also has deep roots. These anchor it in place and reach down for moisture into what little soil has formed from decomposed strandline debris and previous shingle vegetation.

Seaside relations

You'll often see the large leaves of curled dock growing in shingle and may wonder how this common roadside plant can live among the stones. In fact, the particular challenges of these environments are very similar: both have dry soils, are low in humus, and are prone to frequent disturbance.

The dock takes advantage of colonising a difficult habitat where competition is low, and produces masses of seeds as an assurance of persistence.

You might also come across sea beet, another common large-leaved shingle plant. The dull green flowers are wind-pollinated and, since sea beet is the wild ancestor of cultivated sugarbeet, the two plants can interbreed if the pollen is carried inland to sugarbeet fields. Even without digging you will be able to see the upper part of the massive taproot, which is edible in the cultivated variety.

Wild ancestor *In places where some soil has accumulated you may see wild carrot, an umbellifer with a flat head of white flowers with finely divided bracts (flower leaves). This is the predecessor of garden carrots; crush any part of the plant and smell the juice – it is definitely carrot-like. The fleshy, nutritious roots and leaves which make the edible cultivated relatives of sea beet, carrot and cabbage so tasty are perfect adaptations for the dry and nutrient-poor coastal environment.*

KEEPING COOL IN THE SUN Many successful coastal plants, such as the **yellow-horned poppy** (below) and sea holly, have blue-green leaves. This is because this colour reflects sunlight better than green and so lessens the risk of overheating where there is no shade.

Plants such as **biting stonecrop** (bottom) combat the drying conditions by storing water in succulent leaves. Biting stonecrop forms carpets on the leeward side of shingle banks, and in summer its masses of yellow flowers attract bees and other nectar seeking pollinating insects. The stonecrop has another trick designed to put off grazers – a hot taste. Try it, and you will quickly discover the reason for the name 'biting'.

NESTING ON THE SHINGLE

The birds you are most likely to see nesting in shingle are the **oystercatcher** (right), ringed plover and Britain's four species of terns – the Arctic, common, little and sandwich. All these birds lay their eggs in shallow depressions on the beach, relying mainly on the similarity of their eggs to pebbles to escape detection – in this stony environment a well-made nest would be dangerously obvious.

There is safety in numbers for birds that nest in colonies but solitary nesters, such as ringed plovers or oystercatchers, must develop strategies for fooling predators. You may see an adult ringed plover feigning injury to draw a predator from its nest. Like oystercatchers, they sometimes pretend to brood on decoy nests of stones, with the same purpose.

Terns, often called sea-swallows, are distinguished from gulls by their narrow pointed wings, tail streamers and graceful buoyant flight. They need to be exceptionally good fliers to complete their long migrations over the oceans. The **little tern**, the species of tern most typically seen on shingle beaches, does most of its fishing close to the shore. You can observe the birds with binoculars as they plunge into the sea or dip down to catch small fish near the surface. They give these to their mate (right) in a formal presentation accompanied by a courtly dance. Watch the display from a distance, but never disturb birds near their nests.

Hard times Both sexes of oystercatchers (above) and little terns (below) share the incubation of their eggs on their shingle nests. Little terns bring food for their sitting mates to break their vigil.

Sea bird cities

The first impressions of a sea bird city are a pervading smell of fish and the deafening noise of the inhabitants. Look up and you will see the citizenry coming and going: guillemots and razorbills swooping in and out, and fulmars passing by like toy gliders. There can be few better opportunities for a close study of birds than in this noisy, smelly environment but keep a wary eye out for terns, which will dive unnervingly close if you get near their nests.

Cheek-by-jowl living *Gannets nest in dense concentrations, only just over a beak's reach apart. But this high density helps each bird to guard against predators such as large gulls and skuas.*

Why do sea birds choose to nest in such uncomfortable spots on cliffs and offshore islands? Many species of sea birds are not very agile on land, having short legs positioned well back on the body for swimming or paddling in water. This makes them vulnerable to predators such as foxes and rats.

Sites that are inaccessible to these predators – as well as to curious naturalists – offer protection while the birds lay their eggs and rear their young. The sites are also conveniently close to the birds' food supply.

However, eggs and chicks could easily fall off the narrow rocky shelves and sea birds have developed ways of safeguarding their young.

Guillemots do not build nests, but the young chicks huddle together for warmth and never wander far. You may also see birds, like razorbills, tucking their eggs into crevices in the rocks, where they will be safe.

Island birds

Gannets are too large to nest on steep cliffs and breed mainly on small offshore islands. Their closely packed nests are made of seaweed and turf torn from the clifftops and whitewashed with droppings, called guano.

Young gannets take most of the summer to fledge. During this time, you can watch the parents as they fish for herring, mackerel and sand eels. Their great, black-tipped, white wings scythe over the waves and arrow into a dive when the gannet spots a shoal of fish.

The gannet is superbly adapted for diving: its forward-looking eyes are situated close above its massive beak and a well-padded breast cushions the impact as it hits the water. The

Perilous perch *The shape of the guillemot's egg (inset) means it will roll in a circle on its bare rocky ledge if disturbed, but not fall off. The kittiwake (below) nests in the most precarious places.*

Rag-and-bone bird *For the shag, rope, bones, lobster pots and even plastic beach toys are all potential nest-building materials, along with the conventional twigs and seaweed. This bird nests at the bottoms of cliffs.*

BURROWING BIRDS A flock of **puffins** offshore in June or July is a sure sign that the birds are nesting nearby. The largest puffin colonies are in the north, on remote Scottish islands, but there are some on Bempton Cliffs in Yorkshire and Portland Bill in Dorset. The nests themselves are hidden in burrows and, although puffins can dig, they often take the easier option of adopting abandoned rabbit burrows so look for them on sloping grassy banks above the cliffs, rather than on the cliffs themselves.

The puffin's main food is sand eels. Its huge beak conceals backward-pointing spines on the roof of its mouth which enable it to hold onto a row of fish while it catches yet another until the bird has a **beak full of fishes**, all neatly arranged in a row and usually all hanging the same way (below). As it alights at the nest, you might hear a strange groaning from beneath the ground – this is the female greeting its mate. Clashing beaks, as if fighting, is another common couples' greeting.

The Manx shearwater also nests in burrows but is less often seen on land than the puffin since it alights only at night to avoid large gulls and other predators. If you are near a shearwater colony, such as on Skomer or Skokholm, in June, wait until midnight and you will see birds begin to land with sardines caught far out at sea. Listen for a greeting cackle from the depths of the burrows – a sound which soon rises to a crescendo of excited squawking as returning birds crash land and struggle to their burrows. If you scan the grass with a torch, there will be stunned-looking shearwaters everywhere but return to the spot at daybreak, and there will be no sign of them. By then, the new shift of birds will be fishing at sea, their mates waiting out of sight in their burrows.

long wings are relatively narrow and pointed, enabling the bird to glide on air currents but also to swim under water, using its feet to change direction.

Guillemots, like penguins, can 'fly' under water but as their wings are short they have to whirr fast to fly in air. This burns up a lot of energy and so guillemots tend to nest close to a good food supply.

Precarious nests

The most gravity-defying nests are built by kittiwakes, birds which are named after their call: you will hear the cacophony of nasal ***kitti-waaaks*** from a colony of kittiwakes long before you reach it. Their untidy grass and seaweed nests cling to the sheer cliff face because, like martins and swallows, kittiwakes stick them to the rocks with mud, which dries like cement and can withstand the harsh sea breezes.

These ocean-going gulls have a graceful flight, rising and falling in long bounds even in winter gales. Unlike auks and gannets, they normally feed at or near the surface of the sea, though they can dive after fish or crustaceans. If you watch patiently you may see a parent at the nest allowing its young to forage inside its open mouth for what food they can find.

The fulmar also lives on cliffs, but it prefers broad ledges with some soil, where it can scratch out a hollow for its rudimentary nest. Where a fulmar cannot find a cliff it will nest on coastal banks, and occasionally even on coastal buildings. Listen for the sudden loud cackle of greeting as one parent joins the other at the nest.

WHERE TO SEE SEA BIRD CITIES: PAGE 340.

Winged pirates If you see an incoming sea bird being harried by another, you may be witnessing an avian mugging. The worst culprits are great skuas, which steal much of their food from other birds. They are about the same size as herring gulls, strongly built and with a mainly dark body and dark pointed wings but are best recognised by their laboured flight, which suddenly becomes faster and more hawk-like when the birds are in pursuit of food.

You may see these bandits attacking terns, gulls and even gannets in midair, buffeting them with their wings and feet or grabbing at a wingtip or tail feather with their beak. Watch how the skua persists until its victim releases or disgorges its food. The robber then dives to catch the fallen food and flies off. Skuas are equally aggressive towards humans and if you stray too close to a nest in their remote breeding colonies (in northern Scotland and its islands) you may be repeatedly swooped upon.

Clue on the bill *Fulmars are often mistaken for gulls but their tubular nostrils distinguish them.*

On cliffs and offshore islands in midsummer you will often come across vast natural rock gardens blooming with wild flowers. The coast is a challenging habitat: as well as being hot and dry, the salt-laden winds make life difficult for the flying insects many plants rely on for pollination and can also be fatal to foliage. But as you walk along a clifftop path you can find clues that reveal how the plants survive.

Bringing colour to the coast

Low growers *For plants, such as the pink thrift and blue sheep's-bit, which can survive on the arid, salty cliffside, there is an abundance of light – any taller plants are soon battered down by the force of the wind.*

In the teeth of the wind *Rock samphire* **[1]** *has fleshy leaves and sea spleenwort* **[2]** *a thick waxy cuticle to combat the moisture-stripping coastal wind, whereas sea plantain* **[3]** *relies on the winds for pollination.*

Many common inland plants have specially adapted coastal forms. On windy south-western cliffs, for example, you may spot broom growing horizontally in mats rather than in the bush form seen on the moors. By creating a low mat the broom avoids the full force of the on-shore wind. Even if it were moved inland, its growth would continue in this way, because it is a genetic trait.

Sea mayweed has a thicker, more waxy cuticle than its landward counterparts, to keep in moisture. Coastal kidney vetch is covered in hairs, which hold moist air around the plant, reducing water loss from its leaves.

Other cliff plants, such as rock samphire, tolerate the dry conditions by storing water in their succulent foliage. To survive the intense sun, sea wormwood has pale foliage, which reflects the strong light and keeps it cool. Crush a leaf and you'll discover another survival tactic – a strong aroma, which warns trampling grazers of its intensely bitter taste.

Breezy tactics

Inland flowers, such as thistles and ragwort, flourish by the coast because their huge numbers of wind-borne seeds are well served by the strong sea breezes. The success of wind pollination by the sea explains why plants such as sea plantain have dull flowers. They have no need to attract insects: a useful attribute on exposed beaches and headlands, where insects fly at their peril.

The most successful grasses on exposed coasts are fescues: their wiry in-rolled leaves enable them to cope with drought. You may find the leaves are covered in a white bloom, which repels water and aids survival in the salty winds. If they are not grazed, these grasses can form a dense mattress as bouncy as a trampoline.

On the landward side of south coast dunes, look for heather or broom. You may think this an unlikely place for these plants of heath and moor, but sand grains form a similar nutrient-poor environment. You will not find heather on all sand dunes, though. Some, especially along the Atlantic coast and around the North Sea, contain a lot of shell fragments. These give the sand a high lime content, making it unsuitable for heather.

Bird's-foot trefoil and clovers have a special attribute which allows them to survive in the thin soils of dune slacks and cliff edges. They contain micro-organisms in their roots which enable them to 'fix' nitrogen – an element vital to growth – from the air.

Invader *The succulent, South African hottentot fig can be found on mild southern shores. It spreads by growing lateral shoots, which put down roots, to make an expanding mat with which few other plants can compete. You may also see pink blooms: as the yellow flowers mature, they change colour.*

INSECTS IN THE DUNES

Some moths, such as the sand dart or shore wainscot, can live on open dunes and even on the strand line. Their caterpillars survive the hot summer by burying themselves in the sand by day, and coming out to feed at night when it is cooler.

You can track down the larvae by looking for their droppings (frass) – dull brown pellets not much larger than a pinhead. If you find some, sift the surrounding sand and you might uncover some caterpillars. Adult moths – of all kinds – are more easily detected by treacling (see box).

The **burnet moth** (far right) is easy to spot because it flies by day. Both the adult and its **caterpillar** (right) are easily recognised because of their conspicuous colouring – a result of the caterpillar's diet. The caterpillars graze on bird's-foot trefoil and absorb the cyanide which is produced by the plant. The poison persists in the adult, and the red-spotted wings are a vivid warning to potential predators that the moth is not good to eat.

WELL-STOCKED SHELLS Where there are yellow-horned poppies, look out for the golden-red **dune snail nesting bee** – it is particularly fond of their nectar. The female bee fills empty snail shells with eggs, each one in a cell stocked with a pollen-honey mixture and sealed with a mastic of chewed leaves. The easiest way to find one of these snail shells is by watching out for a female bee hovering over the sand.

Treacling for moths You can make up an alcoholic treacle to attract moths. Experiment by boiling up black treacle, soft cane sugar, jam and beer, adding a spoonful of dark rum as the mixture cools, to find the recipe your local moths prefer.

Store the treacle in a tin then on a still, warm moonless night, paint it onto palings or bunches of marram grass that you have tied together.

The moths are attracted by the sweet scent and gather to feed (the mixture does them no harm). Watch the moths at their feast using a torch with a red filter, which won't disturb them.

Urban oases overflowing with opportunities

Parks, gardens and wasteland are magnets for wildlife

For urban wildlife, summer is a time of opportunity. Flowers bloom in every available patch of soil, providing food for a host of insects that thrive in the warmth of towns and cities. Alongside those that feed on the flowers, there are others dining on leaves and sap – a vast array of flying food that is exploited by swifts and bats. Squirrels find plenty to eat among the tree tops, while hedgehogs patrol green spaces for earthworms, insects and slugs. This is a good time for scavengers such as the fox, because our open-air lunches mean more leftovers. But for most nocturnal animals, midsummer has its drawbacks: fewer hours of darkness means having to venture out in daylight to find food for their young.

Nature stakes first claim

Even in the busiest city centre, nature is always close at hand, waiting for a chance to move in. Wherever there is a patch of waste ground like this one in Birmingham (above), nature's green pioneers are quick to claim it as their own. And once plants take root animal life quickly follows.

Small mammals are common in this kind of habitat because it provides the kind of cover they need. During summer, you may spot shrews and mice dashing across stretches of bare concrete or asphalt, but you are more likely to detect their whereabouts by the quivering of plants on a calm day, or the high-pitched squeaks, which shrews especially make as they hunt for food.

Up above, watch out for goldfinches descending on the first seed heads of thistles. Their sudden, whirring arrivals

can put insects to flight, among them two day-flying moths that turn up from the Continent. The hummingbird hawk moth rarely gets farther than southern England, but the silver Y moth can be found across all of Britain by the end of summer. Both these nectar feeders visit flowers in hanging baskets and window boxes as well as those growing on wasteland, so you may spot them without leaving home.

The goldfinch's scarlet-and-yellow plumage makes it unmistakable. The birds feed on seed heads in small flocks or 'charms', making short flights between plants until disturbed.

The wildlife garden

On summer weekends, towns up and down the country reverberate to the sound of lawns being mown. But if you are one of Britain's growing band of wildlife gardeners, mowing is a task you'll undertake with care. Leaving part of the lawn uncut until late July, as in this West Midlands garden (above) allows flowers to grow and seed. This gives butterflies such as meadow browns and skippers, whose traditional hay meadow habitats are growing scarce, an alternative place to lay their eggs.

At this time of year, such a garden teems with insects, particularly if it contains a pond. Even quite small patches of water can attract damselflies and dragonflies. If they stay and use it as a breeding ground, you will be rewarded with the sight of new adults each summer. Some of these spectacular predators fly far afield on hunting trips, but others remain around the pond, darting out from waterside plants to catch prey that flies past.

By midsummer, blue tits that took up residence in nest boxes in spring can be seen attending their noisy brood in the wider space of the garden. While many small birds raise several families, blue tits rely on just one very large clutch of up to 12 eggs.

Damselflies like this common blue are highly adapted predators: their legs are so specialised for snatching prey that they cannot walk on a horizontal surface. Instead they perch or cling on vegetation.

Plant pioneers and settlers

Step into many town parks today and you will find corners from which the mower and hoe have been banished: areas where the wild plants on which so many wild creatures depend for cover and food are allowed to grow unrestricted. Waist-high stands of grass provide a home for creatures such as the meadow grasshopper – an insect that is hardly ever found on mown ground. Dead trees, once quickly tidied away, may now be left for animals as diverse as the great spotted woodpecker and stag beetle, both species that need decaying wood to survive.

Green deserts Wide expanses of mown grass like this offer few opportunities for wildlife. Robins and thrushes appreciate neat lawns because worms are easier to detect through the short grass. But for most creatures the lack of cover and the dominance of one sort of vegetation are disadvantages.

Cow parsley, ragwort and thistles are among the wild plants to be seen in this picture of Peartree Park, in Southampton. Such species are typical of nature-friendly park management and of patches of waste ground at a certain stage in the natural succession of vegetation. By identifying the plants growing on derelict land, you can tell how recently it was cleared.

The plants with a head start are those whose seeds can lie dormant in the ground for years until conditions suddenly encourage them to germinate. One of the best known of these is the common poppy. Its scarlet, tissue-like blooms spring from tiny black seeds to cover newly cleared sites in a matter of a few weeks. But the plant is an annual, dying once it has flowered and produced seeds.

Arriving by parachute

Other plants arrive by different methods. Dandelions and thistles parachute in on downy seeds. The hooked seeds of burdock and cleavers hitch a lift on animals and clothing, while bramble patches spring from blackberry seeds deposited by birds, ready-coated in fertiliser.

Many of these plants are perennials – unlike the poppy they establish deep roots before they flower, but can then live for many years. It will take bushes and trees, which need 20 years or longer to cover the site, to squeeze them out.

THREAT IS ALL BLUFF A patch of rosebay willowherb growing on waste ground is a good place to look for caterpillars of the **elephant hawk moth**. Although a dull, brownish grey, they are the length of a finger, so not too difficult to spot. If you find one, observe its spectacular but harmless reaction when it feels threatened by tapping it lightly with a blade of grass. The caterpillar will withdraw its head, causing the front of its body to swell and magnify a pair of markings that resemble large eyes. Next, the caterpillar rears and lunges from side to side – a performance which is enough to disconcert a hungry bird. If you don't find any caterpillars, examine the plant carefully for the eggs, laid one to a leaf.

Q **What is cuckoo spit – the saliva-like blobs often seen on grass and other plants in early summer?**

A Cuckoo spit is sap or honeydew, exuded by the larva of the common froghopper bug. The larva, which sucks up plant sap through its hypodermic-like mouthparts, uses its breathing tubes to aerate the excess while voiding it from its rear end. If you tease out the foam with a stalk of grass, you will soon spot the yellowish grub lying in it. The main function of the foam is probably to prevent the grub from drying up, but it may have other uses, including concealing the exact location of the grub and being distasteful to hungry birds.

CONQUERING CONCRETE

Some plants find a niche in the least promising environments – pushing up between paving slabs and poking through asphalt.

For pavement plants like mosses and the mossy pearlwort, survival is a miniature version of trench warfare: as long as they keep their heads below the top of the cracks, they won't get trampled. But in other ways these plants have different strategies. Mosses don't have roots, but can survive with little water and few nutrients – in hot, dry spells they become brown, but soon turn green after rain. The pearlwort, however, puts down roots and anchors itself in the soil below the slabs.

When temperatures rise and the tar starts melting, look for egg-cup size bulges on the softened surface. These are the first signs that creeping thistles will soon break through.

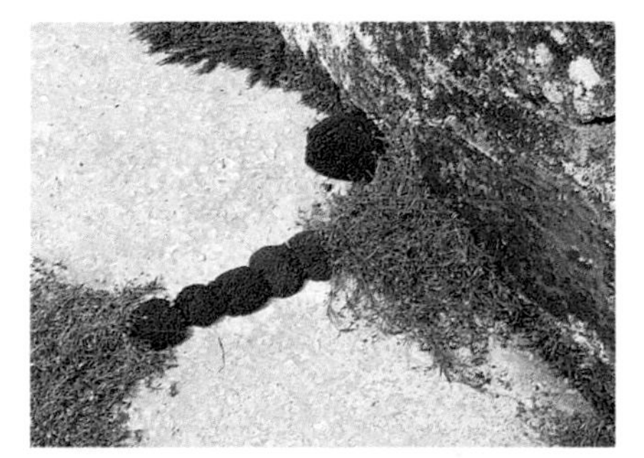

Streetwise *Clumps of bright green moss and mossy pearlwort grow strongest at the foot of walls, where they are least likely to be trampled (top). Plantain (above) has tough, leathery leaves and can thrive in gutters, even when driven over.*

Landing strips

For flying insects, town and country are often only a few minutes apart, with no traffic jams blocking their way – one reason why built-up areas are good places for a summer 'bug hunt'. Gardens and allotments abound with insects that are hidden or absent during the rest of the year. There is also a good chance of seeing some species that may only be making a refuelling stop while on a long-haul journey from mainland Europe.

Aphid predator *The aphids that feed on vegetables on allotments provide the main diet for the ladybird – both as an adult beetle (above left) and as a larva (above right). If you cannot find either life form, try looking under the leaves of infested plants: you may discover clusters of yellow ladybird eggs, laid close to the food source needed by the emerging larvae.*

If you have ever wondered how so many hungry insects find their way to your neat, weed-free garden or allotment in summer, try looking over the fence or at the next plot; the chances are your neighbour is not so diligent. Allotments in particular tend to be patchworks of care and neglect, with overgrown plots harbouring huge numbers of insects.

Fox dens

The combination of cover and ready food supplies also attract birds and other small animals. Finches gathering seeds, blackbirds raiding fruit bushes and wrens catching insects are among the birds to be seen around allotments. Toads and frogs can often be found in the cool damp shade of rhubarb leaves or in dense clumps of grass. Foxes, too, often set up home on allotments, digging their dens in inaccessible corners where brambles and nettles have sprung up.

There are ways to encourage your natural allies in the kitchen garden or allotment. Honeybees are drawn by raspberry canes because they are particularly attracted to the flowers, and a clump of flowering mint encourages bumblebees to call.

Aphid defender *Ants collect the excess sap, or honeydew, that aphids exude, and protect them from predators such as ladybirds.*

Larger than life

Blackfly, greenfly and other aphids do an enormous amount of damage to vegetables and flowers, but before using a spray to kill them, make sure you won't also be targeting their natural enemies, ladybirds and hover flies.

It is also worth using a magnifying glass to study aphid reproduction before declaring war on them. This is fascinating because the females do not have to mate, and produce live young. These are born singly, but as the event happens several times a day there is a good chance of seeing it occur.

What are flying ants and where do they go?

They are black ants – the species which generally lives under garden paths and patios. When a colony reaches a certain size, new queens are produced and the colony swarms. By looking closely at the ants boiling up from below ground, you can distinguish three types, two with wings, the third without. The smaller, more numerous of the winged ones are males, the larger ones virgin queens. Milling around on the ground are the third, wingless, type. These are sterile females, which make up the colony's most numerous group, the workers. The virgin queens crawl up walls and objects like garden furniture – anything that gives them height – before launching themselves clumsily into the air, pursued by their suitors, and frequently by birds eager for an easy meal. New queens that survive and mate jettison their wings before moving under ground and laying the first eggs of a new colony. The males die.

Next generation *If you wonder where all the garden spiders that decorate the shrubbery with their late summer webs come from, look through the foliage early in the season. Then you'll find clusters of hundreds of spiderlings.*

TRAPPER OR HUNTER?

Web-spinning spiders depend on sensing vibrations to locate prey and recognise danger, while those that don't make webs rely on keen eyesight for the same purposes. Here's the way to prove that this is so.

Look for newly hatched garden spiders in early summer. These can be found in clusters on nursery webs strung between the branches of shrubs. If you touch the web, the spiderlings will scatter to the edge for cover.

Eyes of the hunter

Next look on sunny walls and wooden fences for a grey-and-white zebra spider, a small hunter which locates prey using its eyes – all eight of them. If you find a zebra spider, dangle a fingertip in front of it, then move it around the spider, which will turn to keep your finger in view.

KEEP A WATCH ON THE LIKELY HAUNTS

Street trees and many of the plants that grow in gardens and on waste ground attract butterflies and day-flying moths, so keeping an eye on the host plants is a good way to see these winged callers. Holly trees and ivy-clad walls, for example, attract the holly blue, a dainty butterfly about the size of a standard postage stamp.

MAJOR ATTRACTION

Buddleja is the best plant to watch for butterflies; it attracts so many, it is known as the butterfly bush. As well as **peacock butterflies** (right), which overwinter in Britain, you are likely to see red admirals – which migrate from Europe – and small tortoiseshells.

IDENTITY MARKS The **silver Y moth** – named after the shape of its prominent, white wing flashes – visits many garden flowers. Although very common right across Britain as far north as the Shetlands, this moth is a migrant from across the Channel and none of the adults survive winter.

FOLLOW THE MALE The fast-flying, chestnut-coloured male **vapourer moth** has a distinctive white spot on each wing. If you can follow him, he may lead you to the female – a flightless well-camouflaged insect (pictured left, with male), usually found on a rose or fruit bush. She lays her eggs on the outside of her empty cocoon, where they remain until the next spring. You can recognise one of the **caterpillars** (below) by its tufts of yellow hair. These are a warning sign to birds and other predators that they produce an irritant. Humans are also sensitive to it, so don't pick up one of these caterpillars.

Close-up on
Pollination

Flowers are the fast-food outlets of the plant world. They advertise their presence to insects using colour, shape and scent, and serve them a quick and easy meal of nectar, a sugary liquid packed with energy. In return, the insects involuntarily carry away a dusting of pollen and deposit it on the next flower they feed at. Pollination is mating by proxy: the plant cannot move and so uses insects to transport its pollen to a flower of the same species nearby. And it is a juggling act: the flower must secrete enough nectar to attract the insect, but not so much that the visitor goes away satiated and does not need to visit another bloom.

The first thing to notice if you watch insects on flowers is that some blooms attract many species and others far fewer. For example, the plate-like flower heads of hogweed (below), one of the commonest large plants of roadside verges, are covered with all sorts of visitors because the shallow shape of each tiny flower allows the many insects with short tongues, such as hover flies, to reach the nectar. You might assume from this that hogweed stands a good chance of being pollinated, but if you track insects from one flower to the next, a different story emerges. Because diners on hogweed can take their next meal at many similarly shaped flowers, the pollen they carry may be dusted off on a different plant species and wasted. Other kinds of flowers don't go in for this sort of mass catering, restricting their nectar supply to a smaller clientele.

Shallow dish The nectar of the dog rose, which brightens summer hedges with its pale pink blooms, can be reached by a wide variety of insects with tongues measuring only 8mm (3/8in) or less, including this spotted longhorn beetle.

Goblet shape The tubular flower of the foxglove reserves its nectar for bees, the tongues of which range in length from the honeybee's 6mm (1/4in) to this bumblebee's 15mm (5/8in).

APPEALING WAYS

Many flowers increase the likelihood that their pollen will be carried to other blooms of the same species by secreting their nectar where only certain insects can obtain it – at the bottom of long, tubular blooms. In this way they encourage insects with long tongues, such as bees and butterflies, to concentrate their custom on them. The longer the throat of the flower is, the fewer the types of insects that can sup at it. Among those with the deepest throats are the flowers of buddleja, scabious and teasel. Only butterflies and bumblebees have tongues long enough to extract the nectar, although two species of solitary bees with short tongues can also reach it by thrusting their entire heads into the flower.

Flowers often combine smell with shape in a further attempt to attract insects guaranteed to help them with pollination. If you smell the tubular-shaped flowers pollinated

Food of love Soldier beetles are a common sight on hogweed, often using the blooms as places to mate, as well as feeding on them.

Sipping deep Butterflies like this clouded yellow have very long tongues, measuring 15mm (⅝in) and longer, for drawing up the nectar in scabious flowers.

After dark The pale colour of the honeysuckle attracts night-flyers like this elephant hawk moth – a family of insects that contains one member, the privet hawk moth, with a tongue measuring 42mm (1⅝in) in length.

by bees, you will find many have the sort of heady scents that people like too. However, flowering laurels, bird cherry, ivy and hogweed produce a slightly cloying, almond-like smell which seems to be far more attractive to flies than bees.

Colour coded

Flowers also use colour to attract insects. And it's not just a case of drawing attention to themselves with a bright yellow or red: some flowers use colour to indicate to the pollinator exactly when to call. For instance, the flowers of viper's bugloss are pink when they are immature, but become blue when they are ready for pollinators and purple after they have been pollinated and started to wither.

The same is true of honeysuckle flowers. They are white when they are ready to exchange pollen, which makes them easily visible to moths, but the flowers quickly turn yellow and wither once they have been pollinated by insects.

Extra signposting

The way colour is arranged on many flowers also aids pollinators. Some, like the foxglove, have centres with contrasting patches or spots that act like runway lights to guide insects to the nectar. Ultraviolet light reveals that many flowers that look plain to the human eye have additional strips or spots of colour in the part of the ultraviolet spectrum visible to many insects.

Signposting with a physical accent can be seen in the case of the antirrhinum, toadflax and some other flowers. These have grooves, called pollen guides, running down their petals which channel a bee's tongue towards the nectar. Although difficult or even impossible to detect with the naked eye, these grooves can be seen with a magnifying glass.

ADDED INCENTIVES

Many flowers offer passing insects an extra bonus for stopping. The dish-shaped blooms of the common poppy form a parabolic reflector which focuses warmth from the sun at the centre of the bloom. This gives the flower extra appeal for insects – all cold-blooded creatures unable to regulate their body temperature.

Look at poppy blooms when it's cloudy, or early in the day while the air is still cool, and you will find insects like the buff-tailed bumblebee (inset) basking in them. Once their energy levels are recharged they fly off, warmed and carrying a cargo of pollen – much as a sunbather might leave a beach with a coating of sand.

Timing device

Flowers like the rosebay willowherb and foxglove, with blooms made up of many individual flowers, need to avoid self-pollination and ensure the seeds contain genetic input from another plant. You can see how they achieve this if you watch the buds open – not all at once, but in a fixed sequence starting with the lowest ones. In this way, insects are forced to fly to another plant to continue feeding.

Sun traps Poppies produce a long succession of blooms, continually attracting insects to the warmth-trapping flowers.

Colourful cargoes Many insect visitors to plants gather pollen as well as nectar. Honeybees, like this worker on fleablane, are particularly efficient at this. If you watch them, you will see them combing the grains off their bodies and pressing them into special areas called pollen baskets on their hind legs. The pollen is often easy to see because its bright colour stands out against the black legs of bees. Back at the nest, the pollen, which is rich in protein, is fed to the developing larvae.

As you walk down any street in summer, birds are the most conspicuous wild creatures you are likely to see. Many find parks and gardens the urban equivalent of copses and fields, but a few, like the city pigeon and house sparrow, are such townies that they seem inseparable from the human population's hustle and bustle. There are also more unlikely incomers, such as birds which have found a substitute for sea cliffs and mountain rock faces in the high concrete-and-glass buildings of the modern city centre.

Denizens of concrete cliffs

Q **Why are there so many pigeons in the city?**

A The availability of food at every season, together with the warmth and light of buildings, enables city pigeons to breed all year round. So while courtship displays are most usually seen in spring, you can see male birds strutting around females, bowing and puffing out their chests to emphasise the metallic lustre of their neck feathers, at any time of the year.

Looking down from the top of a tall building is very much like looking over the edge of a cliff: it's a sheer drop to the bottom, interrupted only by windowsills – the equivalent of the narrow ledges on a real cliff. For birds that naturally nest on rock faces, such urban cliffs feel familiar and secure.

On top of the block

As on real cliffs, many of these birds look for specific locations for their roosting and nesting places, so if you know their preferences you stand a better chance of seeing them. For instance, herring gulls like to be on the tops of high buildings. If you live in a town or city on or near the coast, such as Bristol, try to find a vantage point that overlooks the flat roof of an office block, factory or block of flats. You may find herring gulls have nested there and are raising their young. The chicks' mottled plumage is good camouflage against the greys and blacks of roofing felt and chippings.

The adult birds are fiercely aggressive in defence of their young, so if you hear the birds calling even more stridently than usual, it may be a sign that there are people working on the roof, or one nearby. The young will scuttle for cover behind parapets, chimney stacks and air conditioning vents, while the adults swoop on and mob the human intruders.

Parapet patrol
Gulls which nest in the city defend their chicks (inset) just as vigilantly, aggressively and noisily as their cousins living on the coast, although rooftop homes are safer from natural predators than sea cliffs.

Overhang required

City pigeons, the most numerous by far of the urban cliff-dwellers, seem to favour the protection of a roof between themselves and the sky – an echo of the rocky overhangs and clefts favoured by rock doves, from which they are descended.

City pigeons like to nest in places such as rail and bus stations, under bridges and in derelict buildings. Run your eye along the edges of girders and parapets, and you can frequently see their flimsy nests. These often incorporate items like plastic drinking straws and lengths of wire – the city-centre equivalent of twigs.

The huge numbers of city pigeons has encouraged the arrival of a spectacular predator in town – the peregrine falcon. Although it is still a very rare

sight on the urban scene, there is a chance of spotting this raptor. Look for the pale colouring of its breast plumage – a giveaway among the shadows of its high-rise perches and nesting places. There are audible clues too: the peregrine's shrill ***kek-kek-kek*** will carry above traffic noise.

If the pigeons sense an attacking peregrine, they will take off in a sudden explosion of wings, but you're very unlikely to see the event because the peregrine hurtles in at a silent 180mph. Instead you may find evidence of the kill: a pigeon with its breast – the peregrine's favourite portion – torn out.

Eye in the sky *The kestrel is Britain's most widespread bird of prey. Many, like this one in Wolverhampton, nest on high buildings and hunt over parks.*

WILDFOWL SPLASH DOWN

For ducks, geese and swans, living in built-up places is an easy way of obtaining food. With lots of bread and other scraps on offer, it is not surprising that they often touch down in towns, and sometimes stay to breed.

If you hear a noisy chorus of honks coming from the air when you're near an ornamental lake or stretch of river running through town, look out for a flock of Canada geese arriving in V formation.

These handsome birds, with distinctive white cravats, long black necks, and pale feather-edgings that give their breasts, flanks and wings a subtle barred pattern, fly at little more than tree-top height, so usually you hear them before seeing them.

As well as wild birds, parks often contain ornamental waterfowl. It is often easy to distinguish which category a bird belongs to by watching it when it flaps its wings – if these are short and stumpy, the bird is an ornamental one which has had its flight feathers clipped to prevent it from flying away.

Get out of town!

There are three species of swan in Britain – the mute, whooper and Bewick's – but the only one you will see in towns and cities is the mute, which has a bright orange and black bill.

If a pair of mute swans has raised a brood on your local pond, remind yourself to watch them at the end of winter when the cygnets start to develop their white adult plumage. This change triggers a reaction in the adult male: he regards them as rivals and interlopers, and drives them off the adults' territory.

Soured ground *Look at the banks of park lakes and you will see that they are often bare and muddy – the result of overgrazing and trampling by water fowl such as the Canada goose. If the birds' droppings are present in large volumes, they can also sour the ground and deter regrowth.*

Hollow threat *The bony knob half-way along a swan's wing is an effective weapon against another bird and it can also inflict a painful bruise on a person. However, the chances of a swan doing more serious injury with it are unlikely. Because, like all birds that fly, it has hollow bones, there is more chance of the swan sustaining a fracture than anyone it strikes.*

Time to watch family fortunes

During June and July, garden birds are busy with their growing families. For blue tits and great tits, the hard work is nearing its end, because these birds usually raise just one brood a year. By contrast house sparrows regularly raise three lots of young, and robins and blackbirds up to four if the weather stays warm and food plentiful. Then, you can watch the parent birds collecting food for the successive young into August.

As young birds grow up, their nests become increasingly dangerous places. The constant comings and goings of the parents, and the chicks' own restlessness and noisy chirrups, increase the risk that the nest will be discovered by a marauding cat, magpie or other predator. For this reason the parents encourage the fledglings to leave the nest as soon as possible – even though they may not fully be able to fly.

Once the young are out of the nest they become scattered in different parts of the garden. This forces the parents into a busy round of feeding trips, but offers the spectator a golden opportunity to watch bird behaviour because the fledglings increasingly come into the open to pester their parents for food.

Size and shape *Young birds are soon as big as their parents, although until fully fledged they have a stubby outline like the young robin (inset). Once the wing and tail feathers develop juveniles, like this young blackbird, resemble adults in shape as well as size. But the plumage remains dull, making them inconspicuous to predators and recognisable to the parent birds, which might otherwise attack them.*

SUMMING-UP OF EVIDENCE

Because it was thought to bring bad luck and because it eats eggs and nestlings, including those of game birds, the **magpie** was persecuted in the past. Since the 1940s, however, numbers of the bird have increased and its range has widened so that it is now a common sight in town as well as the country. Some of this success is due to the magpie's appetite for carrion and scraps, but its ability as a predator – taking small mammals like the mouse in the picture, and the eggs and young of other birds – still makes it a controversial species.

Recent research shows that in some areas where magpie numbers are increasing, those of songbirds are also on the rise. This suggests that the quality of habitat is the crucial factor, with cover as a vital element. If small birds have thick vegetation in which to nest and conceal themselves, whether in town or country, they're less likely to fall prey to magpies.

For concerned gardeners the best advice seems to be, keep nature in balance by not overthinning hedges and creepers.

Although the young are often as big as the adults, their behaviour sets them apart: if you see a bird open its beak and flutter its wings at another, it is almost certainly a fledgling begging a meal from a parent.

Juvenile plumage

Among the boldest, and most visible fledglings are those of robins and blackbirds. Young robins look completely different from the parents, with yellow-speckled brown plumage and no red breasts. They tend to stay around shrubberies rather than venturing into the middle of lawns. Young blackbirds, which are brown like the mother bird but with more mottled breasts, often follow the parent birds across lawns, rushing up to them whenever a worm is pulled up.

As well as providing their young with an endless supply of food, blackbirds assiduously, and noisily, defend them from predators. That persistent, metallic ***chink-chink-chink*** that breaks the silence before daybreak on summer mornings is the alarm call of a blackbird. If you look out of the window, you can often see the bird on a neighbour's roof or the top of a wall, and the target of its attention – usually a cat. The bird will continue calling until the animal moves off.

Q What should you do if you find a stranded fledgling?

A Nothing, apart from taking the cat indoors. The parent birds will probably be close by, squawking and waiting for you to go so that they can feed the chick or lead it out of harm's way. If the bird is very young, without feathers, it has probably fallen out of its nest. Then, its chances of survival are poor, but never try to return it to the nest – the disturbance you would cause might make the parents abandon the rest of the brood.

FEATHERED SQUATTERS

Several kinds of birds nest in houses and buildings if they get the chance. If they can find a way in, sparrows and starlings will nest in roof spaces and jackdaws in chimneys. But the real specialists in household nesting are those summer visitors, swallows, house martins and swifts. Of the three, swifts are the most keen urbanites, but if you live on the edge of the city, close to open countryside, swallows and house martins may build on your property.

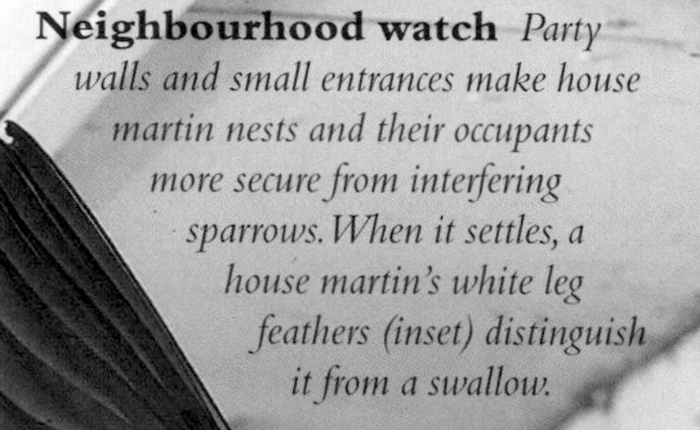

Neighbourhood watch *Party walls and small entrances make house martin nests and their occupants more secure from interfering sparrows. When it settles, a house martin's white leg feathers (inset) distinguish it from a swallow.*

Under the eaves

Swifts and martins are group-nesters, but a pair of swallows will often build an isolated nest. This is usually sited on the top of the beam or joist, and if you look up you can often make out feathers and bits of grass – the materials used for the untidy nest lining.

House martins' nests are much neater, stronger mud structures, usually built against a wall, and sometimes attached to the underside of the eaves as well. These are very sociable birds, and a colony's nests will often be crowded together along a wall or inside a garage, so that they touch one another. Neither bird likes to fly far for a supply of mud, so you are most likely to play host to them if your house is within a couple of hundred yards of wet ground or a stream. The nests of house martins and swallows often stay up for years, and may be repaired and re-occupied by the same pair of birds in successive seasons. The white splashings of fresh droppings on the wall or ground under an old nest are a sure sign that the birds have taken up residence.

Survival aid *An insulated loft is a typical nest site for a swift. One brood, of two or three chicks, is raised, their survival aided by an ability to go without food for days when wet, cool weather grounds insects.*

Collected on the wing

Swifts like to nest in roof spaces, so look for them coming and going through holes at the eaves. Because their short legs, which are feathered to the toes, are useless for walking, swifts cannot collect mud as nesting material. Instead, they catch pieces of dry grass, feathers and even scraps of paper in the air, then cement them together with a salivary secretion.

Whose turn to eat? *Young swallows, noticeably duller than the parent, clamour for food. Soon they may be forced to leave the nest, allowing the female to lay a further clutch of eggs: a pair of swallows will raise two or even three broods in a summer.*

Custodians of the night

Ask someone to name half a dozen wild mammals, and the chances are that bats would not feature on the list, despite being found all over Britain, in town as well as country. The fact that they have wings is one reason for this: mammals are not generally associated with an ability to fly. Bats also have little mass appeal. But their lack of popularity is undeserved: they are harmless, and far too agile to get tangled up in people's hair. Instead, bats on night patrol make a fascinating subject for study.

Dusk on still, warm summer evenings is the best time to look for bats – after they've come out to hunt and while there is still some light in the sky – but bat detection is something you can do at almost any time of day. Start by looking at places where they are likely to set up home.

Old barns and church towers are the places associated with bats, but if they can squeeze between the roof tiles, or get through a crevice at the eaves, they will set up home in the attics of ordinary houses too.

Spaces behind weatherboards and slate or tile cladding on walls also provide homes for bats, especially pipistrelles, small creatures that prefer cramped quarters to airy lofts.

It is not a good idea to poke into such recesses in a search for bats in case unintentional injury is caused. In fact, all dozen or so species are protected by law, so if you find bats in your home you

Rafter residents *Look up if you see droppings like these (inset left) on the loft floor – you may be greeted by the sight of long-eared bats (above) on the rafters. Insect wings (inset top) under an outside light are also a sign of resident bats.*

Fashioned for flight *Caught against the light, this pipistrelle shows how a bat's wing membranes are supported on long, slender bones – the equivalent of our fingers.*

In-flight refuelling *When the waterfowl retire for the night, bats visit ornamental ponds and pools to hunt for insects or simply, like this long-eared bat, to skim above the surface and take a drink.*

must seek advice from your local authority if you want them removed or intend to carry out any building work that may disturb or harm them.

Instead, look for their droppings below possible roost sites. These resemble those of mice, but are jet black rather than brown and consist entirely of beetle wing-cases and other hard body parts from insects. If you find droppings, keep watch at dusk, when you should be rewarded with the sight of the colony streaming into the evening sky.

Illuminating evidence

If you also switch on an outside light in advance, it will attract insects, encouraging the bats to hunt near the light. In the morning there will be little piles of beetle wing-cases and moth wings under the fitment, pulled off and discarded by the bats before eating their prey.

Bats fly on silent wings but they are constantly squeaking, and sometimes it is this sound that first draws them to your attention. However, younger people generally have the advantage in this: anyone over the age of 50 is less likely to be able to detect these high-pitched sounds.

Keys to identification

Distinguishing different species of bat is not easy, but you can make informed guesses, based on size and where you see them.

The bat you are most likely to see in towns and cities is the pipistrelle, which starts hunting about 20 minutes after sunset, and often flies just above head height as it searches for insects. Its fluttery, erratic flight contains frequent twists and dives.

Trees with blossoms that attract moths make good places for spotting long-eared bats. You are unlikely to get close enough to see the size of their ears, but these bats are the only ones able to hover below the canopy.

Waterside watch

If you live in the south of Britain and see an unusually large bat with a wingspan about the length of an average person's forearm, it could be one of four bat species – a serotine, noctule, Leisler's or greater horseshoe.

A good place to watch for bats is by a pond on a common. You may see them dip their mouths into the water to drink. Look out for one flying to and fro, possibly a Daubenton's bat, which feeds on aquatic insects.

ROADSIDE HAZARDS Many dangers face small mammals scurrying through the grass and bindweed beside this Devon street – metal cans, plastic containers and glass bottles like the one that has become the last resting place of this **shrew** (inset).

ANIMAL TOMBS AMONG THE RUBBISH

Wherever they are dropped as litter, from pavements and roadside lay-bys to the deepest countryside, empty bottles and ring-pull cans make deadly traps for small mammals such as shrews, voles and mice. These creatures are small enough to crawl through the neck of the bottle or the hole in the can, but then find that the slippery sides prevent escape. Even the plastic rings holding packs of drink cans together spell danger: dead hedgehogs have been found with their heads trapped in them.

If you find discarded bottles, cans and plastic packaging, put them in a litter bin. If this is impractical, crush cans and stick empty bottles neck-down in the soil.

Mass grave If you make it a practice to tip up old containers, you will soon exhume remains like these 27 skulls – sorted from the sludge in a single milk bottle. There may even be times when your action saves a small creature's life.

Exploring your garden after dark

As dusk falls over the garden, nature's nightshift emerges to feed. If you go out about half an hour after sunset with a torch, preferably one throwing a red beam because it disturbs wildlife less, you will be able to see many creatures, such as insects, hedgehogs and toads. Foxes and badgers are much more wary: take a folding chair, choose a likely spot, and then settle down to wait. It is worth using binoculars: as well as magnifying the view, they collect more light than your eyes alone, making it easier to watch twilight wildlife.

Family outing *For hedgehogs, gardens can be well-stocked larders, full of worms, slugs, beetles and other invertebrates. In summer, you may even see a female leading her hoglets across your lawn on a foraging expedition.*

Food cache *If you find scraps or the remains of a small animal buried in your lawn, leave them there: they could be a fox's food cache, to which it is likely to return.*

Night vigils demand a keen sense of hearing, but one garden visitor, the hedgehog, gives itself away even if you're not listening hard. It will snuffle and snort as it forages down borders or in a compost heap, and squeal noisily if alarmed. A hedgehog is also very regular in its wanderings: if your garden is on its rounds, you can expect to hear it and see its dumpy outline every night at the same time.

Humid summer nights bring earthworms to the surface to mate. Keeping their tails in their burrows, mating couples lie side by side. Earthworms are hermaphrodites (each has male and female sex organs) so pairs

Food or shelter *As light fades, a silent army invades the garden. Some like the colourful netted slug (inset) come to feed on plants and flowers – the lush leaves of hostas (left) being a special favourite. Others, including many insects, come seeking lodgings in flowers like the common daisy (below) before they close up for the night.*

Night-time nuptials Worms can burrow as deep as 1.8m (6ft) into the soil, but they have to come to the surface to mate. With many thousands of them in an average lawn it is not unusual to see their night-time nuptials.

fertilise each other, and both partners eventually produce eggs. Although mating can last several hours, witnessing it requires light footwork. The worms do not completely emerge from their burrows, allowing them to rapidly withdraw into the ground if they sense vibrations. Waiting for night visitors gives you the opportunity to discover where some insects spend the hours of darkness. Tease open flowers that close up at night, such as mesembryanthemums, and you are likely to uncover shiny black pollen beetles and other species taking advantage of the shelter and safety within.

When foxes visit a garden, they leave a number of calling cards. The most obvious is an acrid, persistent smell of urine – powerful enough for even the relatively insensitive human nose to detect – where dog foxes and vixens have marked their territories. Look out too for their droppings; these are shaped like a dog's, but contain such things as rabbit fur – the indigestible parts of their prey.

If the clues add up, try watching for a fox from an unlit, closed window inside the house. That way the animal is less likely to see you or detect you with its keen sense of smell. In mid-summer, you might even be rewarded by the sight of a vixen taking her cubs on one of their first hunting excursions.

Hunting urge

A pair of yellowish green eyes caught in the beam of a torch will almost certainly turn out to belong to a cat. Domestication has not dampened the hunting urge of these pets, and with excellent night vision they specialise in stalking prey after dark. It's not just mice they catch. Cats kill great numbers of garden birds because the birds' poor night vision makes them reluctant to abandon their roosting places.

Toad in a hole *Cats prey on many creatures, including frogs and newts in garden ponds. This toad has inflated itself to look threatening, but it is the poison glands in its skin that will fend off the cat.*

Close-up on

Man-made corridors

Railways, roads and canals feature in more than just the movement of people and goods. In the 1790s, a plant introduced to Britain from southern Europe escaped from Oxford University Botanic Garden and began spreading along the city's stone walls. Sixty years later, it took root on the crushed stone beneath Oxford's new railway tracks and from there passing trains blew its feathery seeds along the line to London and other destinations. Today the bright yellow flowers of Oxford ragwort can be seen from Exeter to Edinburgh – and it is still on the move.

Oxford ragwort is just one of many plants that has spread along the thousands of miles of man-made corridors crisscrossing Britain. Many of them have airborne seeds that get swept along in the slipstream of passing trains and traffic, but others have seeds that stick to shoes or tyres, and still others seeds that float. Where these germinate and grow, animals follow, helping to spread them along embankments, verges and towpaths.

RIDING THE RAILS

Railways provide two very different habitats for plants. The ballast under the tracks suits those that thrive in dry rocky places – like Oxford ragwort – while cuttings and embankments are perfect for plants that thrive in shelter and warmth.

The buddleja or butterfly bush was introduced to Britain from central China in the late 19th century and soon showed it was purpose-made for life along urban railways. The seeds easily get blown into cracks and crevices, and the plants cope well with dry conditions and lack of soil, even growing out of walls, high above the tracks.

Ticket to ride This single Oxford ragwort may produce 10,000 seeds in its long flowering season, all set to catch a passing train.

Another rail plant, Canadian golden rod, resembles Oxford ragwort, but prefers the soil of embankments round its roots to the stones of the ballast.

Ideal for basking

Hot stones and warm embankments provide ideal basking places for the common lizard, a reptile found in London's southern suburbs, thanks to the railways. Where you find common lizards, there are often slow-worms too, although they tend to spend more time hidden from view under old sheets of corrugated iron and similar items.

Hands off A slow-worm will shed its tail to avoid capture, so be content to watch one.

Nibbled turf

Next time you find yourself aboard a train at a standstill in a cutting, try some wildlife investigation from your seat. If the grass on the banks looks mown, you will probably be able to spot rabbit burrows, particularly on warm, south-facing sides of the track. Where rabbits go, predators follow. Foxes often build their dens on railway banks, although these are usually concealed. Stoats and weasels also frequent rail lines, preying on rabbits and small rodents.

Where access is allowed to disused lines, it is possible to walk and spot wildlife rail travellers without breaking the law or risking life. Then, if an old railway is left to become a strip of woodland, you can observe how the creatures using it change: rabbits abandon it and species such as the muntjac deer and grey squirrel spread along it from the country to the town.

Stuck to the wall Zebra mussels grow to only 4cm (1½in) long but their striped shells makes them easy to spot in a Cheshire canal lock (left).

TAKING TO THE WATERWAYS

August is a good month to discover how the **Himalayan balsam** (left) has a flying start in its spread along canals. Find a clump with full seed capsules (empty ones have rolled-up sides) and brush the plants with your hand: the ripe capsules will spring open, sending a broadside of seeds into the water, where they float until cast up on the bank. This feature also accounts for the plant's alternative name of impatience – *Impatiens* in the Latin.

Look at the bows of passing canal boats and it won't be long before you see one with strands of Canadian pondweed wrapped against it. Although common on waterways, this aquatic plant depends on passing vessels for its spread. This is because only female plants grow in the wild in Britain, so fertilised seeds are not an option for successful reproduction.

Watch as the level falls

An emptying lock is a good place to spot the striped shells of zebra mussels. These high-speed commuters – they have spread from their Asian home right across the Northern Hemisphere in the past 150 years – attach themselves to hard surfaces and sometimes clog lock gates and sluices.

Verge invaders Oxeye daisies, poppies and charlock spring up on new motorway verges.

Travelling north The hoary cress originates from southern Europe but in the 200 years since its introduction it has spread right across Britain.

ON THE ROAD

Plants have been travelling by road ever since the first trackways were established. Yellow corydalis seeds may have arrived in Britain on the sandals of Roman soldiers, and it is possible that those of some kinds of poppies did too.

The seeds of hoary cress first arrived inside straw mattresses used to bear wounded from the Napoleonic Wars to Channel ports. When the straw was spread on local fields, the seeds germinated and the plant soon started spreading, helped by the fact that its hot-tasting seeds were collected as a cheap substitute for pepper, earning it the alternative name of pepperwort.

Scent of pineapple

If you ever walk on a roadside and catch a faint but distinct scent of pineapples, look down: you will almost certainly have trodden on a patch of pineapple weed. This low-growing, bright green plant, which might get its name from its smell or its greenish yellow flowers (they resemble miniature pineapples) is thought to have been introduced to Britain from the American state of Oregon in the 1870s, since when its seeds have been spread all over the country by cartwheels, car tyres and human feet.

Seashore plants are the last thing you would expect to see on roadsides far inland, but since the 1980s Danish scurvy grass, whose natural habitat is cliffs, shores and salt marshes, has been recorded spreading along verges made slightly saline by the spreading of road salt in winter. It even grows far from the sea in the Midlands.

Another seaside plant, the spear-leaved orache, is so salt-tolerant that you can find it around the edges of piles of salt stored in laybys, where nothing else will grow.

Resident of the margins Field voles thrive among the rough vegetation of motorway and railway embankments.

Discovering the secrets of field and hedgerow

Combine harvesters and dying foliage leave wildlife exposed

A glance across the fields in early autumn will reveal evidence of the harvest. The remaining stubble can be seen for just a few weeks before it is ploughed in and the fields prepared for the next crop. Sowings of winter wheat, oats and barley take place throughout autumn,quickly turning the fields green as they germinate. As the weather grows cold and wet, cattle are often moved into sheds for the winter and fed on silage. The structure of hedges is revealed as summer growth begins to die back and leaves are shed. Most hedges are kept in shape with an annual trim from a flail mower at this time of year. However, in autumn you still stand a good chance of seeing one being laid in the traditional manner.

Fewer places to hide

Fields like these in a Lancashire valley (above) give you a chance to pick out a variety of creatures. With cereals and other crops cut and gathered in, rabbits and hares can be spotted more easily in the fields. In the evenings, you may also catch sight of deer emerging from the shadows of surrounding woodland to graze.

Birds start adjusting to the approach of winter. Many combine into flocks, with parties of finches, sparrows and buntings searching the fields for seeds. They are joined by rooks, gulls, lapwings and starlings – all of which prey on small creatures, although you might notice that the large numbers of ladybirds searching out places to hibernate in clumps of vegetation are unaffected. This is because the birds recognise the bright colours of these little beetles as a warning

Rabbits tend to stay around the edges of fields, where there is more cover. But new crops of winter wheat will tempt them out into the open in autumn.

that they secrete a poison – the yellow fluid a ladybird will sometimes exude on your hand if picked up.

Migrant birds, arriving and departing, mingle with permanent residents. The visitors include flocks of fieldfares and redwings, and passing wheatears, stonechats and whinchats. In wilder places, you might also see geese and swans from colder northerly latitudes grazing in the fields.

Hedge history at a glance

While many hedges have been removed to create bigger fields, new ones like this five-year-old example from Yorkshire (above) are also being planted – ensuring a supply of autumn fruit for wildlife. Traditional hedge management practices are still followed, too. The hedge pictured has been reinforced with stakes and roughly woven to encourage bulk and thickness. When the branches grow thicker, they will be split and laid sideways.

There are two main types of hedge for the nature detective to search for: enclosure hedges and woodland relics. Enclosure hedges are the more numerous and include new ones. First look for lots of hawthorn, the tree most often used now and in the past when planting hedges, then for blackthorn, ash, elder and wild rose – plants that are quick to seed and grow in a hedge.

By contrast, woodland relics are not planted. These are the woody strips left when fields were created by clearing old forest. They are generally the oldest and, in terms of the number of woody species they contain, the richest type of hedge. Look for hazel, spindle and field maple – good indicator species of a woodland relic – but remember that climate and soil also have a bearing on the type of plants growing in a hedge.

Although this hawthorn hedge is only five years old, it has already been colonised by wild rose – a plant whose autumn fruit, or hips, are devoured by birds.

Look in the hedges and you will see the ripe fruit that forms such a vital food source for many insects, birds and small mammals at this season. On chalky soils, hedges are swathed in old man's beard – the fluffy, grey seeds of wild clematis – and on bare branches everywhere, you can already see next year's buds forming. But it isn't all seed and dormant bud: a few verge plants, such as wild parsley, are bearing a flower here and there, and the ivy is in bloom, providing a late nectar supply for butterflies, hover flies and the last wasps.

Autumn bounty of the hedgerow

Fruit has evolved to be eaten. It is a plant's way of distributing its seeds: the flesh of the fruit is digested, but the seeds are not and pass through the body of the animal. Sometimes, too, birds regurgitate indigestible seeds, possibly as a way of allowing them to consume more berry flesh over a shorter time. Either way, the result is that seeds are usually deposited some distance from the parent plant.

Why red and black?

By having evolved nutritious, fleshy coverings for their seeds, plants encourage birds and other animals, such as mice and even foxes, to help in their dispersal.

The fruits are also eye-catching. You may notice that many – the hips of the wild rose, for example – are red, a colour to which birds are particularly attracted. Others, such as blackberries, are bluish black, another colour easily picked out by birds because it reflects ultraviolet light, which is visible to them.

One of the showiest shrubs in autumn is the spindle. Its leaves turn a rich dark red and it bears bright pinkish red berries, which split open to reveal orange seeds. Sometimes you find spindle berries where the seeds have been extracted. This is because some birds – tits, greenfinches and bullfinches, especially – prefer the seeds to the flesh and peck them out, leaving the pulp behind.

How birds take the fruit

Some birds, such as tits, warblers, and woodpeckers, turn fruit-eater in the autumn because insects, their usual diet, are becoming scarce. If you watch them, you will see they have different ways of obtaining it.

A robin has long slim legs, well suited to hopping over the ground but not for supporting it while reaching out from a branch. So the robin snatches fruit while in flight. Some other birds, including the blackbird, mistle thrush and song thrush, have a heavy body weight to wing area ratio and tend to reach for fruit from a perch.

Now that they are no longer busy collecting insects to feed their larvae, wasps also turn to fruit. They favour those that have been pecked into, or which are overripe and turning soft.

Taking their pick *A male blackbird (top) perches to gather a sloe from a blackthorn bush. Later it will deposit the stone in droppings stained dark by the flesh of the fruit. A greenfinch (above), also a male, hacks into the flesh of a rose hip. The hairy seeds are not one of this bird's favourite foods, and it will probably leave them intact on the stalk.*

IDENTITY PARADE – Autumn fruits

Foraging for wild fruit can be fun, but don't overpick the hedgerows: remember this harvest is essential to many birds and animals. Be sure, too, that berries are safe to eat – many that are consumed by wildlife are poisonous to humans.

Blackberries are one of the most familiar fruits of hedges and banks, but try the berries before picking – some of the 2000 varieties taste better than others.

Sloes are the fruits of the blackthorn. Eaten raw, they taste bitter and astringent, but when left to soak in gin for a month or two they make a Christmas liqueur.

Privet is most familiar as a garden plant, but the wild variety is common in field hedges, especially on chalky ground. The berries are poisonous to humans.

Haws cling to the hedges long into winter, providing valuable food for animals. Although harmless, they taste unappetising and stale to the human palate.

Fruit food *Birds eat the berries of black bryony (right) and pass the seeds in their droppings, but the orange seeds of spindle berries (below) prompt different behaviour. Some birds, including the tits, eat the pink pulp and let the seed fall to the ground. Others, such as the blackbird, swallow the fruit whole then regurgitate the seed.*

IS IT A BERRY?

Although the autumn fruits growing in hedgerows are generally referred to as berries, this term has a distinct scientific definition. Botanically speaking, many berries are defined as drupes. To recognise whether a fruit is a berry or a drupe, you need to examine the seeds.

The feature that determines whether a fruit is a berry or drupe is the nature of the seed coating; the seeds of berries have a hard coating, and usually there are more than two of them. Among the true berries are the fruits of the honeysuckle, ivy and privet.

A drupe is a fruit which contains a hard stone containing a soft seed. True drupes are more common than true berries in the hedges. Common examples include the fruits of the holly, sloe, wild cherry and elder. A segmented fruit such as the blackberry, where each seed is contained in a separate fleshy segment, is really a collection of tiny drupes.

Family feast Although mostly found in and around buildings, many house mice live outdoors for all or part of the year. Hedges are a favourite habitat, and in autumn you might hear their rustlings as they clamber through branches to feast on fruit such as these blackberries.

Shapes in the grass

With the cereal crop harvested and grass growth slowing down, distinctive shapes and patterns on the surface of the ground, which are normally hidden from view, become apparent. These can provide clues to past human activity, to the presence of creatures that live underground, and to fungi. Land that was farmed in a particular way for centuries may still show signs of how it was managed. On the wildlife front, autumn is a good time to look for evidence of moles and the best season for observing how fungi grow.

If you stand on a hill in the evening and look at the fields below, you may see a pattern of broad, gentle corrugations, picked out in the lengthening shadows cast by the setting sun. Called ridge-and-furrow, the pattern results from the same strips of land being ploughed year after year, each strip separated from adjacent ones by a wide furrow. The pattern always runs parallel to the slope to enable water to drain off the land more readily.

Ridge-and-furrow strips, which can date back to the 8th century, were made to a more or less standard size – in traditional units of measurement, around one furlong (one furrow) long and one rod or pole across. If you think you have found one, measure it to see if it equates to this in today's terms: about 200m x 5m (220yd x 5½yd).

Undisturbed pasture

Ridge-and-furrow is erased by modern ploughing methods, so its existence is reliable evidence that a pasture hasn't been disturbed for a hundred years or more – the practice having died out in the 19th century.

ANATOMY OF A MOLEHILL

A freshly dug molehill is always worth investigating, on the chance that construction is still going on. But approach it quietly and softly – moles are sensitive to vibration, and don't stay around if they sense a large animal overhead. The mound of soil is the waste from a mole's network of tunnels. These narrow passages are like miniature pit traps – worms and larvae tumble into them and are seized by the mole before they can burrow back into soil.

As the mole excavates, loose earth accumulates behind it in a shaft leading to the surface. Periodically, the animal turns around, braces itself against the walls of the shaft and pushes this material towards the surface with a forepaw. Then the molehill heaves, as though at the epicentre of a tiny earthquake. But the chances of seeing this are fairly infrequent: once made, the passages need little in the way of maintenance and may be used by the next generation of moles with no need to push waste up to the spoil heap on the surface.

Seeing the creature itself is an even more chance event. Occasionally, you may see a mole on the road – usually one

Sign of lean times *A field containing many molehills indicates a scarcity of earthworms: the moles have extended their tunnel systems, and so created more spoil, in their search for food. Molehill systems are often started at night, but you might see the rapidly disappearing rear end of a mole (below) as it digs the initial burrow. Only when it is safely underground will the mole drive a vertical shaft to the surface to make a molehill.*

Terrace system In some parts of Britain, especially on the chalk downlands of south-east England, the shapes of ancient terraces can be discerned along hillsides. Called lynchets, these terraces date from the Iron Age and were usually made to prevent rain washing the soil downhill. Some, however, may be the result of erosion, with the terrace forming where soil has accumulated behind a feature such as an old rampart.

Flood defence Moles usually build their nests under ground, at the centre of their tunnel systems – around 30cm (12in) below the surface in deep soils. However, where the ground is prone to becoming waterlogged, the animal will build a fortress, raising its nest above the level of the surrounding ground and protecting it with a mound of earth. Its larger size distinguishes a fortress from an ordinary molehill, and if you watch one, you may see signs of mole activity, although by autumn the young will have left.

The nest will be abandoned by the time autumn arrives.

Exit tunnels link the nest chamber to the rest of the mole's passages.

that has been run over. This is because they frequently colonise verges, where water run-off keeps the soil damp, so attracting worms. Field drainage works disrupt the mole's existence and can be worth watching in case a nest is exposed. Look out for a ball of vegetation – the bedding – contained in an enlarged chamber in a deep tunnel.

Detecting a fortress

You could also try looking at areas that become waterlogged after rain, keeping a lookout for an extra large molehill. This could be a mole's fortress – a nest built above ground level to protect it from floods, and covered with an insulating pyramid of soil up to a metre high. Although built in the spring, a fortress might still be recognisable in autumn.

FAIRY RINGS

In closely grazed fields, and on the short turf of garden lawns and playing fields, you often see fairy rings – circles or arcs where the grass looks darker. In autumn the cause of these patterns on the ground becomes apparent – the underground mycelium or 'root system' of the fairy ring champignon, which at this season may sprout a circle of small toadstools.

Where you find a ring, look closely at the grass and you will probably find that it is made up of two zones – an outer one of slightly darker, taller grass and an inner one where growth is sparse and bare ground shows through. This is a clue to how the fungus grows.

As the ring expands, the fungus breaks down organic matter in the soil into simple nutrients, including nitrates, which encourage the grass to grow thicker and faster. Behind this growing, living edge of the ring, however, is a mass of dying or dead fungus threads, which clog the soil and crowd out grass roots – the inner zone of the ring. In some rings, you can find a third zone, where the dead portion of the fungus has broken down in the soil, releasing a second batch of nitrates. This shows up as a dark inner ring of growth.

Rate of growth

Fairy rings spread outwards by up to 20cm (8in) a year, so a very large ring, which can measure several metres across, may be decades old. This shows that the land has not been ploughed in that time, and also that it has not had artificial fertilisers spread on it – a practice which soon causes the fungus to vanish.

Some other common grassland fungi, including the St George's mushroom (see page 25) and waxcaps (see page 248) also grow in rings.

In a circle *The fairy ring champignon is the best known of many fungi that grow in circles, spreading out from the point where the fungus first became established.*

Watch out for wildlife when you are travelling by car or walking along tracks – against the bare background, creatures like stoats and weasels are easier to spot than when they're in vegetation. Autumn is an especially good time to see such animals: as the evenings draw in, many nocturnal creatures are up and about at the same time as us. Wildlife numbers are also high in the wake of the breeding season, and verges are dying back, so that there is less cover. There is animal traffic in the air, too: bats and owls hunting insects drawn by the warmth radiating from the road.

Breaking from cover

You are most likely to catch sight of animals crossing roads and tracks when they are setting out on or returning from night-time foraging expeditions. In autumn, these can include young as well as parents.

Creatures with established territories have regular itineraries, for example, if you see a badger crossing the road one evening, there's a good chance of seeing it in the same place at the same time the next.

Compared for size *Alongside a pet cat, which measures about 80cm (2ft 8in) from nose to tail tip, many wild mammals are surprisingly small. A polecat is about 55cm (22in) long, a stoat about 35cm (14in) and the weasel just 25cm (10in).*

Cat

Polecat

Stoat

Weasel

But don't be surprised if it fails to appear: families are starting to break up by now, and young, especially the males, can travel great distances in search of a territory, rarely retracing their steps. There are records of young dog foxes, for example, travelling hundreds of miles to find a place of their own.

Although most small mammals take only a few seconds to cross the road, you can still pick out visual clues from their speeding form to help you to identify them. Try to judge an animal's size, perhaps by comparing it with the width of the white line in the road: a standard 10cm (4in). Or compare the animal in your imagination with a familiar creature, such as a cat.

Weasel or stoat?

You might even be able to persuade the animal to retrace its steps. Here's how: stand still and make a squeaking noise by sucking the back of your hand. If the creature is curious, it may come back to investigate. A stoat or a weasel, especially, can sometimes be coaxed to within a couple of metres by this ploy. The creature might even stand on its hind legs as it tries to locate the source of the sound.

It is not easy to tell a stoat and weasel apart. Both carnivores are active by day and night, have a slender body and short legs, and bound with an arched back unless they sense danger, when they streak across a space.

The size difference between the animals may help – the length of a stoat from nose to tail equates to the width of three and a half white lines, the weasel to two and a half. But the real distinguishing feature is that the stoat has a black tip to its tail.

Eye-catching *Flashes of white can aid or confuse: the dark mask of the true polecat (below) is sharply accentuated by its pale surround, but the stoat's white bib and belly (bottom) is also found in the weasel.*

Polecat, ferret or mink?

Wales and the adjoining English counties are the likeliest places to see a polecat cross your path. Elsewhere the animal became almost extinct from trapping and poisoning, and is only now returning to former haunts.

Wild ferrets, by contrast, turn up wherever they have escaped from captivity and established themselves in the wild. The longer they have been wild, the more indistinguishable they are from polecats. This is because a captive ferret is a domesticated polecat: succeeding generations of escapees gradually revert to polecat colouring as the two animals interbreed. The resulting creatures, known as polecat-ferrets, are paler than the true polecat and often lack the distictive 'mask' of dark fur around the eyes.

The wild mink is a similar sized animal to the ferret and polecat – as long as five and a half white lines laid side by side – and you usually see it in daylight.

CAUGHT IN THE HEADLIGHTS

The eyes of nocturnal animals have a layer that reflects incoming light back out through the pupil. This explains why they can see in the dark, and why their eyes shine in vehicle headlights. Concentrate on recognising the colour of this eyeshine – although it can differ according to whether the creature is looking straight into the lights or not, it is a clue to what is crossing the road.

Seen head-on, the eyes of a fox glow white or pale blue in headlights, but from the side they are red. **Cats' eyes** glow green, although blue-eyed Siamese have red eyeshine. Eyeshine in otters is dull red and in pine martens blue. You don't have to be in a car to see eyeshine; if you shine a torch into an autumn hedge, the light will be reflected in tiny pinpricks from the eyes of moths and spiders.

CATS ABROAD A cat is probably the animal you are most likely to see running across a road after dark. On city streets, it is likely to be a domestic cat, put out for the night. In the countryside, it could be a feral animal descended from an abandoned pet or farm cat run wild. Like true wild creatures, both these sorts of cats have regular night rounds, often measured in miles. In central and northern Scotland, the cat in the headlights might be a true **wild cat**. The feature that distinguishes it from its domestic and feral cousins is a thick, blunt-ended tail with three or four distinct, black rings.

Bound for the other side

The average territory of a stoat is about 20 hectares (50 acres), which in Britain means that there's a good chance of a road crossing it at some point. When you're walking down country lanes, watch the road about 14m (15yd) ahead, stay by the edge and be as quiet as possible: you might see a stoat on a hunting expedition. It will cross the road in easy bounds if it senses no danger, but otherwise streaks along.

World of wings *A formation of brent geese, winter visitors to Britain, flies over a flock of foraging lapwings, a resident whose numbers are swollen by scores of winter migrants. Both birds will share the same coastal fields, although their diets are different.*

Close-up on Flocks and flocking

Many birds that migrate to a warmer climate for the winter do so in flocks. Throughout autumn, you can see them gathering in the fields in preparation for their journeys. Some birds, however, whether migrants or year-round residents can be seen in flocks at any time of the year. Jackdaws, for example, are usually, though not always, seen in flocks, while chaffinches, greenfinches and skylarks gather together once the breeding season is over.

Flying in flocks brings several advantages. In particular, there's safety in numbers, with many pairs of eyes meaning predators are likely to be spotted sooner than in the case of a solitary bird. Experiments with starlings, for instance, have shown that a flock detects the appearance of a model hawk one second faster than a solitary bird does – enough of an advantage to give every member of the flock a chance of escape. Flocking also allows some birds to feed without interruption, while others stand guard. By contrast, solitary birds must continually be on the lookout.

Finding food can also be easier if birds forage together, especially when supplies are scarce, great tits, for instance, form flocks in late autumn, as insects and larvae become harder to find. When food is found in concentrated 'clumps', flocks – often of more than one species – have a better chance of finding it than individuals, whether it is chaffinches and linnets searching for autumn seeds, or swallows and martins chasing a September swarm of midges.

Combined search *A mixed group of bramblings and tree sparrows are joined by a chaffinch and a yellowhammer as they search a bare autumn field for seeds.*

Close company *Birds that feed on spilt corn, like these wood pigeons, cluster closely so that few grains escape their searches. By contrast, worm and larvae feeders such as rooks spread out to avoid alerting their prey.*

THE BEAT OF WINGS

Flying uses energy, so birds make every flap count. Some, such as gulls, starlings and crows, are good gliders and beat their wings in short bursts to regain height lost in a glide.

Small birds such as tits, finches and sparrows, however, cannot glide effectively. Instead, they close their wings between bouts of flapping, which results in 'bounding' flight. This is best seen when a flock of finches flies into a strong head wind: they make slow progress and look as though they are bouncing up and down on invisible strings.

Formation flying

While all flying birds glide or bound, flocks have another advantage – being able to fly in formation. You're most likely to spot this in gulls, geese, swans and wild ducks, all of which fly in V formation.

Birds grouped in this way have a distinct aerodynamic advantage. A beating wing creates a strong slipstream that is strongest behind the wing and just beyond its tip, so each bird is helped by the birds in front. Compared with a bird flying solo, they can go farther faster for the same output of energy. And if you watch the formation, you will see that the benefit is shared, with birds continually changing places and the leaders dropping towards the back of the line.

Different birds together

That 'birds of a feather flock together' is generally true, but sometimes different species mix together because they forage for the same food and are threatened by the same predators. Mixed flocks on farmland may include chaffinches, bramblings, greenfinches and linnets, and in woodland, blue and great tits may be joined by coal tits, goldcrests, treecreepers and even nuthatches.

If you use binoculars to watch such congregations, you may be lucky enough to spot the odd rarity among them – a migrant blown off course during its autumn journey. Search for an Arctic glaucous gull or Iceland gull among herring gulls, or a rare Pallas' warbler in a flock of tits. Use binoculars to watch the birds when they take to the air, too: they tend to separate into their different species.

As well as watching flocks, try listening for them. Far-carrying ***see-ip*** calls in the night sky reveal a flock of redwings on the move, with the birds staying in contact through simple flight calls. And where vegetation obscures the view, hearing is also more useful than sight, helping you to identify, say, a group of long-tailed tits approaching along a hedge well before you see them.

RIPPLE EFFECT Starlings congregate into the largest **flocks** of any bird seen in Britain, some estimated as containing more than a million members. How do such large flocks come together? Watch starlings from midsummer onwards and you will see the same groups at the same time every day. When they settle, these chattering parties join one another before flying on. In this way, a huge number of birds, perhaps drawn from an area of several hundred square miles, arrives at the flock's nightly roost, which may be in a plantation, reed bed, park or even disused pier. If you live near or pass one of these roosts in the evening, you will see the united flock perform a spectacular aerobatic display, with the birds fanning out, closing up and wheeling before they fall like rain to their roost.

How do starlings maintain their distance from their neighbours and avoid collisions during these apparently simultaneous changes of direction? The answer has been revealed by slow-motion filming. This shows that a change in direction spreads through the flock like a ripple. One bird decides to change direction, its neighbours follow suit, the birds next to them then react, and so the change spreads through the entire flock – but at great speed, because each bird is taking its cue from birds several places ahead.

You will see more birds during the autumn than at any other time of the year. Their population is swollen following the breeding season, then increased still further by immigrants – both birds of passage and those that overwinter in Britain. This makes it an excellent time to observe the behaviour of native birds and rarer visitors. You may hear snatches of song from birds fooled by the similar day length into thinking it is spring. And some species, including the great tit, pair up.

Transit time in the bird world

Lining up to go *Look at overhead wires in late September and early October; you will see martins lined up on them as they gather before flying south to Africa.*

Some migrant birds are merely passing through on their way to warmer countries farther south. But unlike the spring migration, when birds are in a hurry to get to their destination and start breeding, the autumn migration is more leisurely, with birds like the chiffchaff and willow warbler staying in one place for several days. Some of the birds arriving from northern Europe and Asia are the same species as many of the natives. The home populations of chaffinches, blue tits, starlings and lapwings, for instance, are supplemented in this way. Sometimes you can spot the newcomers. For example, the chaffinches you now see in flocks in open fields are likely to be immigrants, because the natives tend to remain near their nesting sites in woods and hedges.

Swallows and martins massing on overhead lines just before their autumn migration are a familiar sight, but there are other places to look for them.

A month earlier, in late August, at the end of their long breeding season, swallows like to gather in reed beds and willow scrub. If you visit such an area towards dusk, you may see them massing overhead before dropping down to roost. You may also see smaller flocks of swallows and martins in autumn. These are mainly young birds, that are visiting to familiarise themselves with a landscape they will return to.

Flocking to a feast *By the time of the autumn ploughing, adult black-headed gulls are losing their dark hood (a feature of the breeding season), while young birds have brown barring on their wings.*

SPOT THE DIFFERENCE

FIELDFARE OR REDWING?

Arriving flocks of fieldfares and redwings in the fields are a sure sign that autumn has arrived. These two thrushes often fly together, and can be confused. The **fieldfare** (above) is the larger and is recognised mainly by its pale grey rump, which contrasts with the dark tail and wings. The **redwing** (below) has a rust-red patch on each flank and bold white stripes on its face. Listen for the calls – the fieldfare has a chattering ***chak-chak***, the redwing makes a harsh ***chittuk*** and abrupt ***kewk*** when perched.

Red patch *A young male great spotted woodpecker begs food from his father. The generations can be told apart by their red head patch – the young bird's is much bigger.*

BADGES OF YOUTH

The younger generation or 'birds of the year' are growing up by autumn, but you can still distinguish many of them by their plumage. The juveniles of many species, including the blackbird, nightingale, pied flycatcher and robin have speckled plumage, possibly because it makes them less conspicuous to predators. In the case of young blackbirds, it sometimes leads people to think that they are thrushes or crosses between a blackbird and thrush.

A grey head may be a mark of human maturity, but for a starling a cap of greyish feathers is the only thing distinguishing it from older birds once the month of September comes. Young male wood pigeons lack the white neck patches of their parents, but they gradually appear from autumn onwards.

GAME BIRDS ON THE GROUND

Autumn is the shooting season and the best time to keep a lookout for both partridges and pheasants. Listen for an explosive whirring of wings and cries of alarm – often the first signs of their presence. These birds are heavily built and are good runners, but they also have powerful breast muscles and short, rounded wings – ideal for a rapid take-off and fast, straight-line flight.

You can recognise a pheasant by its large size and long tail. The cocks have magnificent plumage compared with the dull brown camouflaging feathers of the hens. Outside the breeding season, pheasants live in flocks, often of separate sexes, and roost in trees.

The grey partridge is a secretive native bird that has become much scarcer in recent years. Its plumage provides it with excellent camouflage: if you see what you think are clods of earth in a ploughed field, scan them with binoculars – they could be grey partridges. A family party is called a covey and they often roost in a circle, each bird facing outward so predators cannot approach unobserved.

The red-legged partridge, an introduced game bird, is usually seen in eastern England. Its call sounds like the puffing of a miniature steam engine, and it prefers running away to flying, so keep watching the ground.

Lying low *Scan recently ploughed and planted autumn fields for grey partridges. Invisible to the careless eye, they blend in perfectly with the bare earth, and instinct makes them lie low unless in danger of being stepped on.*

Family bath time *A few loose feathers often mark the spots where birds such as this family of red-legged partridges have made a dustbath.*

AT THE DRY-CLEANERS

If you come across a bare saucer-shaped depression with loose soil in it, it could be a birds' dustbath. Instead of bathing in water, some birds work fine particles of earth into their feathers to clean off surplus oil that remains after preening, and to remove fragments of dry skin and other debris. Once a dustbath is formed, many birds use it, so if you conceal yourself nearby you may see several taking a dry-clean.

Cloud of dust

The bird loosens soil with its claws and bill, and then squats, shaking its plumage and flicking its wings to encourage a cloud of dust to rise into its feathers.

The size of a dust-bath is a good indication of the size of the bird that made it. One made by a pheasant or partridge is usually about the size of a dinner plate; a saucer-sized one could have been made by a lark.

Three black birds – all members of the crow family – serve as nature's dustbin and knacker men. They are the carrion crow, rook and jackdaw, and all three will eat almost anything, including carrion. In this way, they rid the countryside of much unwanted debris. But they can also be destructive. They prey on the eggs and chicks of other birds, and although they eat many insects that farmers consider pests, they also feed on crops. Flocks of them can be seen in the autumn fields, pecking through animal dung for insects. You will also see jackdaws searching for ticks or other parasites as they perch on the backs of cattle and sheep.

Black trio clean up

STUDY THE BILL Flocks of rooks can often be seen following tractors in the autumn, eating leatherjackets (the grubs of daddy longlegs) and other insect larvae turned up by the plough. By this season, adolescent birds compete in foraging with the adults, but, although comparable in size, the generations are easy to tell apart. An **adult rook** (below right) has rough, grey-white skin, free of feathers, extending around the base of its bill and its chin. The **young rook** (below left) has a dark bill and its nostrils and chin are feathered.

It can be difficult to distinguish carrion crows and rooks from one another, especially when they are on the ground in a mixed flock containing youngsters (see panel, right). Once they fly, it's easier to tell the two apart: the crow's tail has a rounded end, while a rook's is wedge-shaped.

The remaining member of the trio, the jackdaw, is more distinctive. It is noticeably smaller than its cousins, and has a contrasting grey nape and dark grey breast feathers, which become especially prominent after the autumn moult.

Rooks are the most sociable of the three, and flocks of these birds are usually the main component in mixed groups containing crows, more solitary birds, and jackdaws, which tend to form smaller bands.

Flight display

If you hear a sudden chorus of *caw-caw* on a warm autumn day, look out for a flock of rooks joining in an aerial display. The birds spiral upwards on outstretched wings, a sure sign that they have found a thermal of warm air on which they can rise effortlessly for perhaps several hundred feet.

Listen for any shriller *jack* calls coming from the column of birds. These will tell you that there are jackdaws flying with the rooks. When the birds reach the top of the thermal, they dive headlong, zigzagging towards the ground – many of the rooks with a partner, as the birds are already pairing up in autumn.

If the rooks are performing this aerial display above their rookery, you can see additional evidence of males and females bonding up. Pairs will perch by nests, usually the ones they used throughout summer if both partners have survived.

Identify the thieves

Look for birds carrying twigs in their beaks, a sign that nest maintenance and repair is under way. And look too for the frequent squabbles that arise when one bird steals material from another's nest.

Home territory *Colonies of rooks continue to stay around their communal nesting site, or rookery, long after the young have left the nest and autumn has stripped the leaves from the trees.*

WEBS TO INTRIGUE

Among the sights of autumn are fields and hedges glistening with spiders' webs. You see this phenomenon on fine mornings after cold nights because the change in temperature causes water vapour in the air to condense as dew on the webs.

The drops of moisture are highlighted by the low rays of the rising sun, making the webs stand out. It is an indication of just how many spiders there are – perhaps over a million to an acre of grassland. Most are too small to be noticed, just 2-3mm (⅛in or less) in length, but there a few bigger species, and with one of these you can carry out a simple test in animal observation.

Try to spot a flat web with a tunnel of silk running down from it into a bush or tussock. This is the home of a sheet-web spider, a relative of the familiar house spider. The spider lives in the tube, and if you imitate a trapped insect by twiddling a grass stem against the web, it will rush out and attack it.

In her lair *This European labyrinth spider, visible inside the tunnel, uses her web as a nursery as well as a trap: laying her eggs in it, then guarding them.*

Mate and meal

The money spider is tiny, but its web is surprisingly big. It consists of a horizontal, domed, loosely woven sheet of silk up to 30cm (12in) across. It is slung like a hammock across grass and hedges, and over freshly turned soil. Look carefully underneath the web and you may see the female spider hanging there, upside down, waiting for insects to blunder into her trap.

The male may also be around: a smaller spider, sitting at the edge of the web. If you have good sight or a magnifying glass, it is possible to carry out a positive identification. The male has what look like tiny boxing gloves on the tips of his short, front appendages, or palps. These are his sperm packets, with which he has to impregnate the female while avoiding being eaten by her.

Hanging around *A female money spider (above) clings onto the bottom of her sheet web waiting for a small insect to settle.*

The abundance of these tiny spiders becomes apparent on dewy autumn mornings, when you will see millions of their moisture-laden webs covering the fields like a wrapping of fine gauze (below).

Bare branches reveal an autumn wood's secrets

As leaves fall, woods offer scant shelter for birds and animals

The soft golden light of a beech wood in autumn produces one of the most serene woodland scenes. The sun is low in the sky, and its slanting rays penetrate farther into the wood than in the summer, making the bronzing leaves glisten like gilt. Already a thick carpet of leaves has fallen, collecting between roots or being piled up in hollows and against banks. There is little living vegetation on the woodland floor. Beech bears dense foliage which lets only thin shafts of sunlight through, but autumn beech woods are rich in colourful toadstools which feed on the leaf litter and have no need for light. They, in turn, become food for insect larvae, slugs and snails, and for animals such as deer, rabbits, squirrels and voles.

Bronzed beeches

Ripe beechnuts, partly concealed in their prickly brown husks, are starting to fall from the trees in this beech wood in Arbroath, in Scotland (above). Soon the floor is strewn with the empty cases of beechnuts feasted on by birds, wood mice and squirrels: by spring, when the time comes for the nuts to germinate, most will have been eaten. However this bounty is not annually reliable. In cool, wet summers, there may be few nuts and only one year in three or four is a prolific 'mast' year, when every nut contains one or two sweet kernels.

Where there is food there is activity. Flocks of tits and finches call as they forage in the canopy or on the ground and the rasping *dzwee* of the brambling, a close relative of the chaffinch, indicates that the first winter visitors are moving in.

Where there are autumn fungi growing on the woodland floor, such as this amethyst deceiver fungus, you might also see clouds of fungus gnats on mild evenings.

Towards dusk you may hear aggressive barking – not of a dog, but of a male deer in the rut. Signs of the deers' presence are also in evidence, such as young trees whose bark has been frayed by the males' splendid antlers, or well-trodden paths through the wood. As you walk on, the drying leaves may rustle as a squirrel rushes to add another nut to its store, while another, disturbed in its feeding, chitters angrily from overhead.

Ancient woodland

The tints of autumn are seldom more glorious than in a mixed wood, such as this one near Symond's Yat in the Wye Valley in Herefordshire (above). On the upper slopes, where the wind is strongest, trees begin to lose their leaves early, but in sheltered places, yellowing leaves cling to the twigs late into the year, even all winter.

Each of Britain's main woodland trees turns a characteristic colour in autumn. When several different species occur together, the result is a muted tapestry of coppers and yellows, with patches of contrasting deep green from an evergreen yew, holly or planted conifer, with its typical pyramid shape. Close up, scarlet berries on yews, rowans and whitebeams further enrich the scene and provide food for migrating birds.

Most trees grow well on limey soils, where the best mixed woods are found. A wide variety of trees is a sign of old woodland: in the Wye Valley there are places that have carried woods since prehistoric times. If you come across the distinctive pink leaves of the rare wild service tree, you can be sure you are in an ancient wood. Younger woods or managed plantations may be dominated by just one or two trees, such as oak or beech.

From a vantage point over a mixed wood such as this, try to pick out the delicate yellow crowns of birch and the heavier copper gilt mass of beech trees.

Turning and falling leaves

Leaves feed trees, so why do deciduous trees drop theirs in autumn? Leaves damaged by frost open up a tree to infection by disease. What is more, precious water is lost by evaporation at a time when the tree's roots may be unable to replenish the supply from cold or frozen ground, so shedding leaves helps to conserve water. Broad leaves also act as traps for snow, which can weigh down and break even stout branches. Finally, leaves resist the wind, making a tree vulnerable to gales, especially if it is standing in sodden ground.

Leaves use sunlight to make food for their tree, but during the short days of winter they cannot produce enough to keep pace with the energy they use. As winter approaches, the tree seals each leaf with a protective layer of cork at the base of the stalk. This is brittle, and when the branch is ruffled by the wind, the leaves break off and flutter to the ground. The upper branches are usually first to lose their leaves, but in sheltered places, yellow leaves may cling to a tree throughout winter.

The colours leaves turn (see opposite page) depend upon which pigments they contain. Oak leaves turn brown almost immediately because they contain large quantities of tannins, while the pinks and reds of the guelder rose or wild

Why do leaves change colour?

Before a tree sheds its leaves it extracts as many of their nutritious contents as it can, starting with the chlorophyll, which gives leaves their green colour, and then other pigments. As this happens, the leaves change from green, through brown to the yellows and oranges made by pigments called carotenoids, which have accumulated during summer.

service tree are produced by pigments called anthocyanins. For the best autumn colour, look for trees growing in full sunlight. The colours are also intensified by an early frost, which stimulates the tree to speed up the leaf-fall process.

WHAT KIND OF FRUIT IS THAT?

As you walk through the woods, you will probably notice that most trees produce their fruits in late summer and autumn. Some are heavy and fall straight to the ground: acorns, beechnuts and conkers, for example. Others are relatively light and are attached to a thin membrane or wing. These two kinds of fruit represent opposite strategies for dispersal and germination. Heavy fruits contain enough food to feed a seedling for long periods, but cannot travel far from the parent tree on their own. Lighter fruits can disperse over a greater distance, but have a smaller chance of survival.

A flying start

Tree fruits have one advantage over the fruit and seeds of other plants: they are dropped from a great height. Fruits from maples and sycamores bear wings, which, like helicopter blades, enable the seed to turn in the air and so fly away from the parent tree, where there is a better chance of germinating.

Ash fruits, called keys, which are held in bunches on the tree, also spin in the air and will travel up to 50m (55yd) in the wind. Elm and birch fruits and pine seeds are set in membranes, to increase their surface area and potential travelling distance. With the help of the wind, a birch fruit can travel 100m (110yd) or more. Heavier fruits need other means of dispersal. Acorns and hazelnuts buried by squirrels or jays might germinate in spring if they are forgotten and left in the ground.

Most woodland trees need plentiful light to grow, and the best place to look for seedling trees next spring is on open ground in clearings or at the edge of the wood.

Considering cones

Most conifers bear seeds within scaly cones. By the time the cones become hard and woody in autumn the seeds are ripe, but they will not be shed until the following spring when the scales open on the first warm days of the year. Some conifers, such as Douglas firs, take two years to ripen their seeds.

Not all conifers have cones and not all cones come from conifers. Yew, though a conifer, has berries, designed to attract birds and flowering magnolia trees drop cone-like structures. In fact, these are not true cones, but scaly fruits.

Autumn shades *See how different trees turn different colours. Ash leaves* **[1]** *drop early, often while they are still green. Field maple* **[2]** *turns a brilliant golden-yellow while beech leaves* **[3]** *turn through yellow to brown. The guelder rose* **[4]** *almost glows in a dramatic pink or red.*

Aiming to travel *Sycamore fruits (below left) have wings, which carry them to open ground, while heavy beechnuts (below) fall to the ground under their parent tree. But beech fruits are unusual, and can germinate there, in the shade. Conifers, such as the Douglas fir (above), release many light seeds from within the scales of their cones.*

Finding life in the leaf litter

Each autumn, more than two kilograms of dead tree material falls on every square metre of woodland. Most of this is fallen leaves – about 25 million a hectare – but you will also find twigs, bark and fruits. Yet somehow each year this debris disappears, a feat carried out by the small invertebrates, such as earthworms and mites, and even smaller micro-organisms, which teem among the litter and in the soil. Although not easy to detect, their work is essential to the natural cycle of the woods.

Leaves from different trees rot at different rates. Ash leaves soon disintegrate, while beech woods retain a thick blanket of leaves throughout autumn and conifer forests are carpeted with fallen needles all year round.

Tasty leaves, such as alder, ash, hawthorn, lime and sycamore are attacked by invertebrates and micro-organisms almost as soon as they hit the ground. But others are less palatable. Beech and oak, for example, contain harmful tannins, and few invertebrates can tackle them until some of these chemicals have been removed by weathering, bacteria, moulds or fungi.

Conifer needles, and leaves protected by wax, such as holly, contain resins, which are even longer-lasting.

How do leaves turn into soil?

If you were to dig down through the litter, you would be able to identify three distinct layers (right). Woodland soil is made up of a mixture of mineral fragments from underlying rocks, and the decayed waste matter of plants and animals, such as earthworms.

The creatures, living in the surface layer of leaves, are the secret of the crumbly texture of woodland soil. Earthworms are the most effective converters of leaves into humus.

Some species of worm live near the surface, but others emerge from deep burrows at night. If you surprise a worm in a torch beam, it may vanish in a flash. Large earthworms anchor their tails in their burrows and can contract their muscles to make a hasty retreat from hungry badgers, foxes, shrews and birds.

Concealed by damp leaves or loose bark you may find large numbers of wood lice, which thrive on a virtually limitless supply of food. Micro-organisms in their gut help them to digest decaying wood, but, like rabbits, wood lice also eat their own droppings, in which bacteria have converted the wood into a more digestible form.

Searching for mini-beasts

Turn over a handful of leaves and you will almost certainly come across some millipedes: there can be up to 600 for every square metre of woodland floor. Watch the way they move, in a

Fallen leaves The top layer of soil consists of decaying leaves and woody debris, such as twigs

Humus The second layer, of rich, dark humus, is the main source of nutrients in the soil

Soil In well-established woods, an annual fall of leaves makes the soil deep, loamy and fertile

Breaking down In damp places, leaves in the top layer of the leaf litter may be stuck together by cotton-like threads. These are the underground parts, or mycelium, of fungi (see page 224), which help to digest the leaves to make the humus.

BARE BONES In damp, sheltered places, search carefully through the leaf litter for partly rotted leaves with only the midrib, edges and veins left in place. These are **leaf skeletons**. The leaves have probably been consumed by micro-organisms, because larger scavengers, such as worms or fly larvae, tend to shred the leaf completely or make holes in its structure. The veins are left because they are made of woody lignin, which can be broken down only by fungi or bacteria, and this is a lengthy process.

You can **make your own leaf skeleton** by simmering a leaf in water for an hour, then leaving it to soak in the same water for several days, until the green parts are soft. Then remove the 'flesh' by rinsing the leaf and gently detaching any stubborn bits with a fine camel's-hair paintbrush.

Frozen with fear *Millipedes do not have the thousand feet their name suggests, but between 36 and 200: one pair for each body segment. When disturbed, some species curl up in tight coils in defence, others simply freeze in the position in which you found them.*

Meat-eater in the leaves
Centipedes hunt by scent and by detecting vibrations, seizing their prey of wood lice and other small creatures with poisoned claws.

rippling motion rather like a Mexican wave as each pair of legs moves in turn.

Search more thoroughly and some small, semi-transparent animals might jump out at you. These are springtails, which jump by releasing their 'sprung' tail, which is coiled beneath them. You will normally find either lots of springtails or none at all, because their eggs are laid in clusters and hatch together. Springtails also communicate by scent, and gather in places where there is plenty to eat.

Even smaller than springtails are eight-legged mites, most of which scavenge on dead plant material and the spores of fungi. The most common kinds are a shiny black or red, or dull brown and shuffle like crabs.

The predators in this jungle are beetles, centipedes and small, slow-moving pseudoscorpions, which brandish huge claws, but lack a sting. They prey on small animals including springtails and if you find one take a closer look: they are quite dramatic under a magnifying glass.

A closer examination You can unearth some of the larger invertebrates in the leaf litter quite easily, but to see the smaller ones, take a sample home for closer study.

One way to separate the animals from the vegetation is to sieve your litter onto a flat white surface, such as an old sheet, or into a flat-bottomed enamel basin. This will enable you to catch the small creatures that fall through the mesh and prevent them from running away. Better still, place some litter in a funnel inserted into a glass jar lined with blotting paper or kitchen paper to soak up any moisture. Place the bulb of a desk lamp or a bright torch above the funnel, and the warmth will send any animals scurrying down through the litter to escape into the jar.

You will probably be able to identify millipedes, mites, money spiders and springtails, but there may also be many more creatures that can be seen only through a lens or under a microscope.

Preparing for winter

There are more animals and birds feeding in woods in autumn than in spring. Most young mammals, like the badgers or roe deer kids born earlier in the year, are moving towards full independence, but must feed up while they can on the autumn crops of berries, nuts and fungi if they are to survive the winter. Parties of tits will include young birds, which – in early autumn – can still be distinguished from their parents by their duller plumage. On the ground, any shrew you see will be from the new generation: the parents of these small, short-lived animals are already dead.

All the activity of feeding birds and animals attracts predators. At night many woods echo to the sound of calling owls, and, without the cover of leaves, foxes, stoats and weasels are also more conspicuous than at other times of the year.

Stoats and weasels sometimes hunt by day but leave few signs, such as tracks or droppings (scats), behind them to help you to track them down.

You may be lucky enough to surprise a stoat at a kill, and it may sit up on its hind legs to sniff the air and get a better look at you. Keep very still and it should stay long enough for you to get a good look.

On warm sunny days, look for grass snakes and, in some areas, adders, basking among the dead leaves or on a tree stump. The last of the butterflies, such as orange tips, peacocks and small tortoiseshells, might also be on the wing.

Take a torch

At night, moths will venture abroad to feast on fallen fruit, over-ripe blackberries or ivy flowers in woodland glades. Particularly common in autumn are the sallow moths, which marvellously mimic the colours of a yellowing leaf – take out a torch at dusk to search for them.

Autumn sights *A fox, already in its thick winter coat (above), can find plenty of well-fed prey in an autumn wood, since other creatures are also stocking up for winter. Adders (right) take advantage of mild days to bask in the weakening sun.*

Tell-tale holes *Dormice gnaw neat holes in the stones of soft fruit (above), as do bank voles and wood mice; hawfinches split them in two.*

WHAT'S EATING THE NUTS?

The food supply for woodland creatures changes in autumn from leaves and shoots to the nuts and berries of shrubs and trees that flowered in spring and summer. Nuts are an excellent food source because they are far richer in protein than leaves. This is because they contain a store of food to launch the shoots and roots of the seedling plant. When food is scarce during winter just a few nuts can be enough to make a nutritious meal.

Where there are beech, hazels and oaks, scavenging woodland creatures are well fed. In a good year, a mature oak or beech will produce around 90,000 large-shelled nuts, although many acorns will be eaten while still green by foraging parties of nuthatches, jays, rooks, tits, wood pigeons and grey squirrels. A single wood pigeon can

Tooth marks *A wood mouse reaches the sweet kernel of a beechnut by gnawing at the sides of the shell until it can be peeled away. A pile of broken husks between a tree's roots shows where a mouse has been feeding.*

consume 120 acorns in a day. Once on the ground, the nuts are scavenged by voles and mice, and huge numbers of acorns are eaten by insect larvae, especially nut weevils. Look for a pinhole in an apparently intact acorn, which tells you the nut has been bored by the long 'beak' of the parent weevil.

Cracking the shell

To get at the nutritious kernel inside a nut an animal must first deal with the hard shell. Acorns have relatively thin shells and are easily cracked by gnawing at one end. The great tit punches a hole in an acorn shell and the greenfinch cracks weak stones such as sloes with their beaks.

Nuts with hard shells, such as hazelnuts, offer the best clues to identifying the feeding animal from its pile of debris. Dormice leave tooth marks around a smooth neat hole whereas wood mice gnaw a rough hole, surrounded by scratches, in the side of the hazelnut.

Bank voles usually gnaw off the narrow end of the shell and squirrels, which often eat the nuts while they are still green, leave irregular holes or remove the narrow end and then split the nut in two.

Birds, particularly great tits, woodpeckers and magpies, bash open hazelnuts with their bills, leaving shattered pieces of shell, often with jagged edges.

Planning ahead *Jays make stores of food for winter, and in autumn you might see one on the woodland floor collecting acorns, which it will bury among the fallen leaves.*

WHAT'S EATING THE SEEDS?

Different trees attract different birds, with different ways of tackling their particular seed capsules. Birch catkins contain lots of small winged seeds, which can only be extracted by a bird such as the redpoll, with its narrow bill and acrobatic prowess.

Pine and spruce trees are more of a challenge, since their seeds remain locked in the cone until spring. Squirrels and mice gnaw open cones by stripping their hard scales, but fallen spruce cones with neatly split scales are a sure sign of crossbills. The crossbill uses its beak to prise open the scales and extracts the seed with its tongue, leaving the rest of the cone almost intact.

Lie down to look

Crossbills feed in groups in autumn: listen for their characteristic ***quip-quip-quip*** call as they fly from one tree to the next. You need to look high up into the canopy to see them: take a waterproof and lie on the ground and you will be rewarded with the colourful sight of the birds feeding. But be prepared for a shower of seed wings and cones landing on you from above.

Thrushes and robins swallow yew berries whole, but digest only the flesh and pass the seeds in droppings, often far from the parent tree. Tits and finches do the opposite, picking off the flesh in order to eat the seed. As you walk through a wood, bright blobs of jelly in the crevices of a tree's bark might catch your eye. This is where a finch, nuthatch or tit has wedged berries to bash them open, leaving the husk and jelly behind.

Delicate operation *The redpoll has mastered the technique of extracting seeds from birch catkins – listen for the patter of discarded husks raining down as a party of the birds feeds.*

Who left this jelly? *Blobs of red jelly on a twig show where a finch, nuthatch or tit has discarded the flesh of a berry and wiped the seed clean before eating it.*

Spore banks *The cep, or penny bun (left), drops its spores from pores under the cap instead of gills. Coral fungus (centre), one of a group of colourful fungi, carries its spores on the tip of its branches. Orange peel fungus (right) shoots out spores from inside its cups.*

Close-up on Fungi

Without fungi, life would choke on its own waste products, and soils lose their fertility. Mushrooms and toadstools – the words are interchangeable, although mushrooms are thought of as edible – are the great rotters of the natural world. They can break down dead leaves, feathers and rotten wood, reducing them to humus and returning nutrients to the soil.

You can find fungi in every natural habitat, even in water, but wherever toadstools appear, they have only one function: to ripen and release spores – the fungal equivalent of seeds. Most spores are probably eaten by mites in the soil: only a very few land in a place where they can germinate, but they are very tough and can survive almost indefinitely until the conditions are right for them to grow.

THE HIDDEN LIFE OF FUNGI For most of the year fungi are invisible. This is because the mushroom we see is only the reproductive part of the fungus, its fruiting body – the equivalent of an apple on a tree. The main part consists of thread-like **hyphae**, which penetrate soil, dead leaves or living plants, absorbing nutrients. The hyphae spread out from each germinating spore, weaving together to form a mass called the **mycelium** (see below).

Warm damp weather and plentiful food provide the right conditions for the rapid growth needed for fungi to produce fruit bodies – and these conditions are most often found in autumn. Then the familiar mushrooms suddenly appear. For a few weeks they flourish, releasing millions of spores, until frosty weather brings the season to a halt. But the mycelium beneath can live for decades.

SO MANY SHAPES

The most reliable way to disperse spores is to release them into the air, and to do that you need either a good drop, or some sort of explosive mechanism.

The need for a dropping zone explains why many toadstools are umbrella shaped. The cap, which has radiating rows of plates called gills, or tiny pores, on the underside, is lifted into the air by a stalk. Ripe spores are released from the gills into the air and borne away. In grassland look for the scaly caps of the parasol mushroom, held up on very tall stalks.

A steady platform is needed for the gills to be held vertically and the spores released freely. This is why many large fungi, such as the penny bun (top left) have stout, firm stalks.

Deliberate decay *The shaggy ink cap, or lawyer's wig, disperses its spores by turning them into black 'ink', to be washed away by rain or carried on passing feet.*

Bracket fungi (see page 226) use the trunk of a tree instead of a stalk to raise themselves upwards, and release their spores directly into the air currents. Look for their white or brownish spores powdering the trunk beneath the bracket.

Cup fungi, such as the orange peel fungus (left), have cups that shoot out spores like bullets from microscopic spore guns sunk inside the tissue. Put your ear to any large species of cup fungi and you may actually hear a faint crackle as they blast off.

New life from old

The extraordinary phallic-looking stinkhorn fungus uses scent to attract insects, just as a flower does. But, rather than being sweetly fragrant, the stinkhorn's scent mimics the smell of a decomposing animal.

The cap produces dark slime containing the spores; blowflies are attracted to it and rewarded with a meal of sweet sticky 'goo' containing the spores. This is carried away on the feet or in the gut of the fly and deposited where it settles.

The shaggy ink cap (see opposite page), often found growing on lawns, also uses decay to spread its spores. Some tiny ink caps last only for a few hours – search for them on your lawn soon after dawn.

MAKING A SPORE PRINT Every fungus produces millions of tiny spores – a 10cm (4in) mushroom can produce 6000 million spores in six days. Spores can be white, yellow, brown, pink or black – they will rub off on your finger if you run it across the gills of a ripe toadstool – and this can help you to identify it.

To obtain attractive **'spore prints'**, a kind of fungal fingerprint, choose a cap with an even rim, cut off the stalk and place the cap gill side down on a piece of clean paper (if you know your fungus has pale spores, choose tinted paper). Cover the cap with a large glass overnight and in the morning you will find a pattern of spores on the paper matching the spokes of the gills. You can fix the print by carefully spraying it with artist's fixative.

HUNTING MUSHROOMS

Before you start searching for fungi, you need to know something of their habits. In woodland, many of the larger toadstools work in partnership with trees. The fungus infects the tree's roots and helps it to obtain nutrients from the soil. In exchange, the fungus receives sugars and other products from the host. So near the roots of a large tree is a good place to start looking.

Oak, beech, birch and Scots pine all have a large number of dependent fungi and so make a rewarding hunting ground. Well-grown trees tend to have more fungi than young ones, but even mature examples of ash and holly have very few.

Some fungi are specific to a particular species of tree. Where there is a birch, for example, look beneath for fly agaric, and near a larch look for larch bolete.

A puff of spores

A drop of rain falling on a ripe round puffball releases a puff of spores, like an Indian smoke signal. Other species of puffball simply crack open as they dry, and rely on the wind to disperse their spores.

Other good places to search for fungi are on bare mossy banks, half-rotten logs and old stumps of felled trees.

In grassland, the most likely place for fungi is in old pasture where artificial fertilisers have never been used. And you will often find horse mushrooms or giant puffballs in pony paddocks where the soil has been enriched by animal droppings. Churchyards are also potentially good sites.

Gathering mushrooms

Never eat any fungus you cannot recognise with confidence. There are several thousand species of large fungi alone in Britain: even experts find many difficult to identify.

There is no reliable way of testing whether or not a fungus is poisonous, so collect only the most easily recognised ones, such as field mushrooms, boletes or chanterelles. Always avoid old or decayed specimens and remember that 'edible' does not necessarily mean 'enjoyable'.

Picking mushrooms does no more harm than picking apples, but you should harvest them in moderation and leave some to ripen then disperse their spores. The code of conduct for mushroom picking suggests a maximum of a small basket, or 1.3kg (3lb), each.

WHAT'S BEEN EATING THE TOADSTOOLS? It is the fate of most toadstools to be eaten. If you find one with grooves or channels in the cap, it has been eaten by a slug or snail, which rasps away at the soft flesh with its rough tongue. In wet weather, they often start on the gills, so look for caps with most of the gills eaten away. **Nibble marks** around the edges indicate the work of small mammals, such as voles, while deer eat fungi whole. Most fungi, however, are consumed from within by small maggots, especially fungus gnat larvae – you can see their holes if you cut or break a mushroom in half.

1

2

3

4

Bracket spotting *The typical bracket fungus shape is displayed by* Ganoderma **[1]**, *which drops piles of rust-brown spores like cocoa powder from its underside onto anything below. The bright yellow sulphur polypore* **[2]** *grows on oak and sweet chestnut but the mazegill* **[3]** *grows only on oak, and is a good clue to identifying otherwise unrecognisable stumps. The antler-shaped candle snuff* **[4]** *is common on all kinds of dead wood.*

Plants that grow on trees

Trees play host to many living things – not just birds and insects, but also other plants. The damp mild weather makes autumn a good time for spotting fungi, which only appear in these conditions. Others, like mosses and lichens, which use the tree as a base on which to grow, are easier to see when the leaves have fallen. Bracket fungi feed on wood, either on dead branches and stumps, or the heartwood of living trees, and are mostly harmless. Parasites, such as the honey fungus, can extract nutrients from living wood, and shorten a tree's life.

Bracket fungi start to appear as a tree grows older and parts begin to die (see page 126). Good places to look for them are on rotting logs and stumps. Some species are soft and fleshy as you might expect, but others, such as the white-rimmed *Ganoderma* found on old beech wood, are hard and woody. This is because they digest the tough lignin from the woody cell walls of the host tree. This lignin makes the bracket fungus waterproof and rot-proof, enabling it to live for months or even years. A large *Ganoderma* bracket expands by growing an extra layer of 'wood' each year, just like the annual rings of a tree.

Most bracket fungi take advantage of the height of a tree to spread their spores. The fungi project from the tree and release their spores into the air from pores on their undersides. In the slanting autumn light on a still day you may see clouds of spores drifting from a bracket as though it were smouldering.

First find the tree

Some brackets can be identified by the tree they are on. On dead branches of beech or willow look for the half-moons of blushing bracket, so called because the white pores turn pink if you press them.

On elder trees, you might find the jelly-like jew's-ear, or, on ash, dark, round cramp balls. Cut open a cramp ball and you will find dark and light bands, representing growth rings.

At the base of a mature beech, look for the leathery brown fan-shapes of the giant polypore, which can be as large as a dinner plate. Its appearance is a sign to foresters that the tree is ready for felling, and you might find this bracket finishing off a cut tree's stump.

A brown stain on oak indicates that a beefsteak fungus or sulphur polypore has been growing there, but a blue-green stain is caused by *Chlorosplenium aeruginascens*: look for its tiny cup-shaped fruit-bodies nearby.

If you find a living beefsteak fungus you will recognise it immediately. It has soft, reddish brown fruit-bodies and, when it is cut open, really does resemble a piece of raw meat.

Fungi that live to kill

Some fungi are outwardly almost invisible, but their effects can be clearly seen. If you come across an elm tree, or the related wych elm with hanging branches whose leaves have turned yellow before the rest of the tree, it is probably infected by Dutch elm disease.

The cause is a wilt fungus, which blocks the water supply to the leaves. The fungus is spread by beetles, which tunnel under the bark – further hastening the tree's demise.

A beech shedding its bark to reveal black patches of fungus has beech bark disease, while black spots on sycamore leaves are a symptom of the aptly named tar spot. Another parasite is the honey fungus, visible as tufts of scaly brown toadstools around living trees and rotting stumps. Look closely and you will discover that the toadstools are connected to black cords, like bootlaces, running through the soil to infect tree after tree by tapping into their roots.

IDENTITY PARADE – Slime moulds

On damp autumn days you often find a slimy substance on a sheltered stump or occasionally on a living trunk. This is a slime mould. Large moulds can look like tinned rice pudding or runny scrambled egg. Others look like pins stuck in the bark, with coloured heads on short stalks. These extraordinary organisms look like fungi, but for much of their lives they can move about in leaf litter or on rotten wood as an inconspicuous 'blob', or plasmodium. Neither animal nor fungus, slime moulds are a unique group of living things.

Fan shaped *Physarum cinereum* spreads as masses of white or yellow slime, and produces pinhead-sized fruit bodies. As the spores ripen, these turn purplish brown. Look for it on fallen leaves on lawns and pastures, especially on chalk or limestone.

Marshmallows Look on the cut end of a fallen log for the slime mould, *Lycogala epidendron*. The balls are pink to grey and 4-7mm (⅛-¼in) across.

Puff ball A single white ball 1cm (⅜in) across could be *Enteridium lycoperdon*. In its early stages it exists as a creamy slime, which looks like buttermilk.

MOSSES AND LICHENS

One of the benefits to mosses and lichens of growing high up on a tree is that it helps them to obtain the light they need to photosynthesise.

Rivulets of rain running through furrowed bark keep the plants moist and provide them with nutrients. Trees such as oak, which have fissured bark, are likely to have more long-lived lichens on them than smooth-barked trees, such as beech or silver birch.

Mosses and lichens do their host trees no harm, because they do not penetrate the bark, although their extra weight sometimes brings down individual twigs in a storm.

In the far west – in Cornwall, Wales or Argyll – where the air is clear, you can find spectacular growths of pollution-sensitive lichens forming beautiful patchworks on trunks, and feathering the upper branches.

Some plants, such as lungwort, with its green lobes shaped like jigsaw pieces, indicate ancient woodland and pure air. In towns, trees may be coated instead by a pollution-tolerant green alga, *Pleurococcus*.

Traditionally, you can tell which direction is north in a wood by looking at the mosses, lichens and algae growing there. They are said to occur most thickly on the side of a tree where driven rain lands most often – usually the north or west. *Pleurococcus* is most conspicuous in winter after the leaves have fallen, and so this is a good time to test the theory.

Particularly around the edges of farm fields, algae can be a sign that chemical fertilisers have been used nearby and drifted against the tree.

Mossy blanket Deep furrows in the bark of this ancient oak on Dartmoor retain moisture and create the perfect environment for mosses to thrive. A thick layer smothers this tree like a duvet, particularly in the forks, where branches meet and water collects.

On the trail of feathers

You can find discarded bird feathers at any time of year, almost anywhere that birds have been active, but woodland is one of the best places to look. Not only do woods shelter many birds, but loose feathers, lost through injury or death, catch in the undergrowth and are less likely to be blown away than in more open habitats. In autumn the number of feathers on the ground increases because at that time birds are in moult, shedding their worn feathers and growing new ones.

THE WELL-GROOMED BIRD Look through a hand lens and you will appreciate how the separate barbs of a feather mesh together with tiny interlocking hooks to make a smooth surface. If you pick up a bedraggled feather you can easily bring the **barbs** into place (inset) with your fingers or by gently brushing the feather with an old toothbrush. Birds preen themselves by running each feather through their bill to 'zip up' the barbs that have become misplaced.

A few feathers, such as the beautiful blue-barred primary coverts of a jay (see below), are easy to recognise, but for less distinctive feathers knowing which birds are common in an area can narrow down the possibilities. However, even if you cannot identify the type of bird a feather belonged to, you can often tell which part of a bird it came from by its size and shape.

The largest feathers on most birds are the long narrow primary feathers from the wing tips, which give the wing its aerodynamic properties. These feathers are the equivalent of an aeroplane's jet engine or propeller and help to create the upward thrust and power of the bird's flight. The primaries also enable a bird to soar, using the aerofoil trim of the narrow leading edge.

Tail feathers are also common finds and, with the exception of long-tailed birds such as the pheasant, are broad and usually blunt-ended.

The secondaries, from the inner 'forearm' of the wing, are shorter than the primaries and more oval. They help to give lift, like the flaps of an aeroplane. You might also find fluffy down: feathers which trap an insulating layer of air next to the bird's body and are not used in flight.

Frequent find *The dark grey primaries of the wood pigeon are the feathers you are most likely to find on the woodland floor, but the bird's blunt-ended, black-tipped tail feathers are also common.*

tail feather

secondary feather

primary coverts

primary feather

downy body feather

Where the feathers fit *The key characteristics of these jay feathers also apply to most other birds. Tail feathers, for steering, are broad and symmetrical. Secondary feathers are wider on one side to create lift. Primary feathers are long and strong for power and are protected at the body end by primary coverts. Delicate downy feathers cloak the body for warmth.*

WHY DO BIRDS MOULT?

Birds moult in autumn when they have finished nesting, and no longer need to look their best to attract a mate and deter a rival. A suit of feathers amounts to 40 per cent of the weight of a small bird – equivalent to both your arms and legs – and to grow a new set demands protein. This is another reason why birds moult in autumn, when protein-rich food is abundant in the form of nuts and seeds.

Wood pigeons roost communally and, during the moult, drop feathers in great drifts. Other birds, especially songbirds, moult in secluded places, and you will have to hunt to find their feathers.

You can tell if a feather has been moulted because it will look worn. The colours may be dull and the end of the shaft dry and cracked. If you find sleek, bright feathers, they have probably come from a dead or injured bird.

Collectables *Attractive feathers, such as this one from a pheasant's tail, can form the basis of a collection (see page 175).*

WHO KILLED THE BIRD?

If you find a dead bird, the condition of the feathers can give you an idea of what killed it. Usually you will not find small birds as they will either have been swallowed whole – feathers, bones and all – by a fox or owl, or carried off by a hawk. But you may come across the body of a larger bird, such as a pigeon, lying in the open.

If a bird has been killed by a hawk or falcon you may find a partly bare carcass and a mass of down and feathers. Birds of prey remove their victims' feathers individually with their beaks, so a feather that is undamaged except for a kink or bend where it has been gripped is a sure sign of a bird of prey.

A murder investigation

A bird lying on its front, looking more or less unharmed, might have been killed by a bird of prey, which will often select only the choicest meat from the breast muscles. The only sign of attack might be a hole in the dead bird's breast, revealed when you turn the victim over. The thin keel of the breastbone may also show tell-tale wedge-shaped beak marks.

Feathers which show marks on the quill where they have been chewed, or soggy clumps of feathers, are signs of a bird killed by a mammal, such as a fox or stoat. Mammals are messier eaters than birds of prey and leave behind scattered bits of wing and tail. They cannot pluck individual feathers but will pull out a mouthful and spit it out, leaving the feathers stuck together with saliva.

Circumstantial evidence *A pile of feathers with their quills bitten off (left) is a sign that a fox has caught a bird – follow a trail of dropped feathers (above) and it could lead you to the fox's earth. A mass of feathers with no body (top) indicates where a bird of prey has plucked a bird before eating it – perhaps while perched in the tree above.*

Residents change places at the waterside

Autumn welcomes new arrivals to British waterways

Once the equinox has passed – in the third week of September – life in and around fresh water undergoes a change of pace. With breeding now accomplished, other priorities take its place.

Winter is now only a few months away – a hard and inescapable fact that spurs animals to feed up while they still can. However, compared with many other habitats, lakes and waterways make a more gentle progress into autumn. After a few frosts, the trees can quickly shed their leaves, but the water itself takes time to lose the last of its summer warmth.

So as swallows and martins stock up with food before leaving, winter visitors fly in from colder parts of Europe and the freshwater world still teems with life.

An autumn harvest

On a late autumn morning the sails of the Turf Fen wind pump (above) turn above a sea of golden reeds. Built in the 18th century, like many others in Norfolk, it is a picturesque reminder that this freshwater landscape owes much of its character to human activity. At one time, reed beds extended over a large swathe of East Anglia, but pumps like this one slowly drained the region's standing water, allowing many square miles of fertile fenland peat to be put under the plough.

In autumn, it is easy to see how the reed beds provide both food and shelter for birds and small animals such as water voles and water shrews. At a time when most plants have already shed their seeds, the reedland crop is still in place and so are the stems. Unless cut for thatch, the reeds will provide

Pochards fly in from central Europe and Scandinavia to dive for food in the warmer waters of Britain. Look out for their chestnut heads and black breasts.

food, cover and roosting sites, and their hollow stems will shelter spiders and insects throughout autumn and winter.

In late autumn, wildfowl shuttle between fens, flooded fields and the coast, picking their habitat to suit the weather. For many of these birds – including wigeon and pintail, ducks that breed mainly in the far north – the British coasts and wetlands are important refuges during the long cold months ahead.

Lochs, lakes and leaves

Loch Garry (above), near Fort William, wears a look of unruffled autumn calm. The still water of this northern loch contains little in the way of calcium and other dissolved minerals. Such soft water is good for raising a lather, but for nurturing the microscopic plant and animal plankton that forms the base of the aquatic food web, it leaves a lot to be desired.

The loch's banks are a more flourishing habitat to explore. The ground is boggy and the soil poor quality, but birches and other hardy trees can survive. A handful of these – including the rowan and Scots pine – are native species, which have existed here for more than 7000 years, but many others have been introduced from abroad. One of them is the larch – an easy tree to recognise in autumn, because it is one of the few conifers that turns yellow and loses its leaves. For freshwater wildlife, bankside trees are a mixed blessing. Fallen leaves and the minerals they contain can provide food for small animals, but too many rotting leaves in a lake will rob the water of its oxygen. This is why you will have better luck searching for wildlife in open lakes and ponds, but much less in water that is shaded by overhanging trees.

The herald moth can survive the cold, even as far north as Lapland, and is most visible between August and October. Its caterpillars feed on waterside willows and poplars.

At the height of summer, few sounds interrupt the swishing of the wind in a reed bed, but visit one on an autumn afternoon and the contrast is startling. This is when starlings and swallows move in to roost among the reeds, swirling over the landscape in flocks that can be tens of thousands strong. Their excited chatter drowns out the calls of permanent residents, such as moorhens and reed buntings, and continues until every latecomer has found a place and the sun has set. Why birds behave in this way is still a mystery, but if you watch a mass roost settling, you can investigate the theories for yourself (see below).

Roosting in reed beds

By September most parent birds have finished raising their families and the young birds are strong enough to take their own place in the flock as the mass roosting season begins. To catch the busiest and noisiest phase of the aerial influx, find a discreet place from which to watch and be sure to get there at least an hour before sunset – once the light starts to wane, things will rapidly quieten down.

If you spot a swallow or two on a daytime visit to a reed bed and want to witness the evening scramble, it's best to plan your dusk birdwatching expedition without delay. Swallows roost in the reed beds as they gather together in flocks before they set off on their migration south, so their stay is only a few weeks long at most.

THEORIES OF WHY BIRDS ROOST

For food Living in large numbers may help young birds to find food. They can follow the more experienced ones when the roost flies out in the morning to forage. But if this is so, why do mature, well-fed birds also gather at roosts?

For protection Watch starlings as they come in to land and you will be able to review another roosting theory. In autumn, the adults are glossy and black and the young birds grey-brown so you can easily tell them apart. Do the dominant adults settle in the centre of the roost leaving the younger ones farther out? It seems that they often do: the older birds use the young ones as a shield against predators, leaving them out on the edges, where they are exposed to attack.

For warmth Roosting in large numbers helps birds to keep warm if they huddle together. But if you watch swallows or starlings settling down in the reeds, you'll see they often space themselves out.

Recognising flight styles

Watch swallows skimming over open patches of water as they feed on midges and other small flies before settling down for the night. As they speed close over the surface, individuals often seem to be in danger of colliding, but their split-second reactions ensure that they keep just out of each other's path.

In some reed beds, the swallows are joined by sand martins. You can soon learn to distinguish the two, because sand martins have a much more flitting, almost bat-like flight, unlike the graceful swallows, a brown band across the chest and short, only barely forked tails.

While swallows and martins fly low down, close to the water, other birds gather higher up in the sky, massing in flocks from all directions. These are probably starlings. As more and more birds join the throng they build up an immense insect-like swarm, which swoops over the reeds like a single living being.

From time to time the birds settle down in a chattering mass, only to burst as one back into the air. Unlike swallows and sand martins, Britain's starlings don't migrate and often roost in reed beds throughout winter.

WATCH OUT FOR HAWKS OVER THE CROWDED REEDS

With so many small birds gathered in one place, a visit to a reed bed in the roosting season gives you a good chance of seeing one of the birds of prey on the lookout for a meal. Often, you can tell which species it is by watching its hunting tactics.

A sparrowhawk usually catches birds close to the reeds or even among them, being able to match every twist and turn of a fleeing quarry, while the

Master of manoeuvre *A flock of sparrows scatters in alarm as a sparrowhawk, its barred wings and tail splayed wide, brakes in midair above their reed-bed roost.*

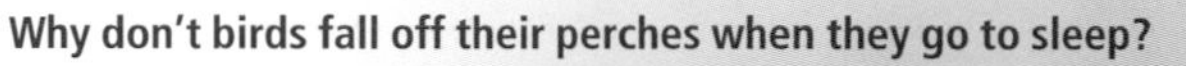

Q Why don't birds fall off their perches when they go to sleep?

A Perching on an almost vertical reed stem may seem like an uncomfortable and perilous way of spending the night. But if you watch the way small birds settle on a perch – you can see this most clearly through binoculars – you'll discover how they manage to stay comfortable until morning. As a bird lands, it flaps its wings and gently lowers itself into place, bending its legs as it rests on the perch. This automatically tightens its toes around the branch or reed stem and, as long as its legs stay bent, the bird will stay in place, even in its sleep, with very little effort.

FOOD FOR HARD TIMES

Reed beds produce their seeds late in the year, when other plant food is scarce. Sparrows often overwinter in reeds taking advantage of the food supply, but look out also for reed buntings, which are among the most common seed eaters.

Reed buntings are about the same size and shape as sparrows and call in a simple ***cheep-cheep-cheep-chizzup***. In summer, the males are easy to recognise because they have a black cap and throat, but by autumn the black has faded to brown.

Like reeds, the bulrush (bottom) also produces its seeds at this time of year. The tightly packed seed heads are brown and sausage-shaped and as the seed head ripens, the seeds swell and burst.

The fluffy bulrush seeds were once used to stuff matresses. The plant was formerly called reedmace, but became known as bulrush from Alma Tadema's painting, *Moses in the Bulrushes*, so the name was changed.

ENTICED BY SEEDS The downy seed heads of **reeds** are held head-high on stalks. This brings small birds, such as this female **reed bunting**, out into the open and makes reed beds rewarding sites for birdwatching.

hobby displays similar flying skills but chases down its prey in midair. Victims of a peregrine often never know what hits them: this fastest of falcons plummets out of the sky, wings tucked back, and kills with a single blow from its talons.

A bigger bird, with long legs dangling, is the marsh harrier. It floats low over the reeds with its wings raised in a narrow V and snatches birds from their perches and small mammals such as water voles from the reeds. This unusual hunting technique means that it is not in direct competition with other birds of prey, so you may see it co-existing with sparrowhawks and kestrels.

If you come across a tree stump or fencepost spattered with droppings, look on the ground for pellets regurgitated by birds of prey, including owls. Use a twig to break open pellets and see if you can identify the prey from the skulls, beaks, teeth or bones that they contain.

Touch and go *When they are ripe, bulrush seed heads burst apart in a ragged mass of down and the feathery seeds drift away on the wind. If you run your thumb down a bulrush seed head you can sometimes trigger this off, particularly if the weather has been dry.*

Where waters run clear

Across south-east England porous chalk soaks up rain like a subterranean sponge. Where this water surfaces in springs, it is crystal clear and pure enough to drink but more importantly to animals, it is rich in calcium from the rock. This is a mineral which many freshwater creatures need for growth, especially those that build hard body cases, such as crayfish and water snails.

In autumn, before their annual recharge from winter rain, chalk streams are often at their lowest level. This is an ideal time to walk along their grassy banks and peer into their clear waters. Most chalk streams emerge in downland valleys, trickling out where the chalk meets a layer of impervious rock or clay. If you find a spring, follow the contour of the land and you are likely to find several more in a line.

An open chalk landscape devoid of trees makes it easy to locate the springs. Look for lush growths of grass or a dark green smudge of wild watercress: both indicate that water is emerging nearby. Watercress and fool's watercress thrive in the clean shallow water of chalk streams. Both plants have white flowers that branch in clusters, but those of true watercress appear from May to October, while fool's watercress blooms in July and August and its flowerheads are umbrella-shaped.

Even if you are certain you have found true watercress, it is best not to eat it. Wild watercress can harbour the larvae of liver flukes. These parasites spend part of their lives in the guts of water snails, which are often found in the same places as watercress and so pass them on. The larvae are dangerous to humans because watercress is eaten raw. Commercial watercress beds are kept free of snails. Chalk streams emerge slowly from the rock, and do not flood after heavy rain on higher ground. As a result, you'll notice that they have a gentle feel, with low banks. Check the stream bed: it is often gravelly because the water is not laden with soil particles, which would muddy the bottom. This gravel provides an anchor for trailing plants such as common water-crowfoot.

Tempting for trout

Gravel also provides the right habitat for trout – both our native brown trout and also, in a few rivers in southern England, the rainbow trout, a fish originally introduced from North America. In early autumn trout are preparing for their breeding season in winter and you may spot them in the clear water as they move upstream to their spawning ground. They

LATE BLOOMER By early autumn, most plants have already gone to seed, and there are few flowers left for bees and butterflies. However, one waterside plant – **purple loosestrife** – is a late flowerer which grows particularly well on chalky ground and often attracts these insect visitors right up until the end of September.

WHAT THRIVES IN HARD WATER?

If you scoop up some gravel from the bottom of a chalk stream you are likely to see and feel some many-legged animals trying to escape by wriggling between your fingers. These are **freshwater shrimps** (below). Despite their name these are not true shrimps – they have 14 pairs of legs while true shrimps have five pairs. They feed on leaves and other debris washed downstream and are sensitive to pollutants, so if you find freshwater shrimps, the water is relatively clean.

Crustaceans such as these shrimps thrive in the calcium-rich waters of chalk streams, but more than any other freshwater animal, the lobster-like **crayfish** (right) requires high levels of this mineral to survive and to form its shell. Soft-water streams, which run over barely soluble rock such as granite, are unsuitable and this is why you may spot crayfish in streams in parts of southern and central England, but will not find them in the peaty and acid water of the Scottish Highlands or on west country moors.

Crayfish feed on a wide variety of vegetable and animal matter, including small animals, which they catch with their powerful pincers. The best time to look for them is at night, when they are active. During the day they lurk in holes in the bank and among debris and litter on the riverbed: if the water is very clear, try to spot their long segmented antennae sticking out of one of these refuges.

In autumn, crayfish are breeding. Females carry their fertilised eggs under their bodies until they hatch. The young crayfish must cling to their mother so they are not washed away. They stay like this for several weeks, until they are big enough to hold their own in the current and have developed the tail fin which they lack at birth.

do this in hollows, or redds, which the female trout scoops out in the gravel with her tail.

Trout are active predatory fish and thrive in chalk streams because the water is clean and well oxygentated and contains many aquatic insects. These insects are mimicked in the traditional flies used in trout fishing. Anglers have learnt to identify the stretches of river where trout are most plentiful, so if you see a line of fly-fishers along the bank, stop and see if you can make out some trout swimming in the water.

The fly-fishing season runs from April to October, but care is taken all year long to keep chalk streams in good condition for the fish. In autumn, you may see weed-cutting in progress to ensure that there is plenty of bare gravel during the winter, when the trout start to spawn.

Fit for trout *Amphibious machinery is regularly used to clear aquatic vegetation from southern England's trout-fishing chalk streams.*

STREAMS THAT DISAPPEAR

You may see all the obvious signs of a stream, such as clumps of watercress, but no water. Many chalk streams dry up in summer and they are called winterbournes. They are easy to recognise by the stretch of bare gravel (above) that is the dry riverbed. In autumn it may be strewn with twiggy debris left when the water dried up.

If you find a winterbourne you'll detect few traces of water life. But the animals have left their eggs behind, ready to hatch when the water starts flowing in the wetter winter months.

If you are near a place with 'winterbourne' or bourne in its name – it is most common in southern England – you can be sure that you are on chalky land. In autumn, look around for evidence of a dried-out stream.

Leap of the salmon

Autumn brings a chance to see the annual run upstream of thousands of wild salmon – the culmination of a migration which begins as far away as Greenland. The adult fish spend most of their lives in the North Atlantic, but after one to four years they return to the fresh waters where they started life. Each fish seeks out the same stretch of river where it hatched out, regardless of any obstacles in its way. Once there it spawns another generation, which will make the same long journey out to sea and back again.

Shin
Shin Falls
Conon
Rogie Falls
Spey
Lui Water
Dee
Falls of Feugh
North Esk
Pitlochry dam & ladder
Tay
Loups of the Burn
Buccanty Spout
Pots of Gartness
Tweed
The Leap, Bushmills
Bush
Dog Leap
Roe
Sion Mills weir
Mourne
Hexham bridge
Tyne
Wylam bridge
Tees
Tees barrage
Lune
Skerton weir
Halton weir
Conwy
Swallow Falls
Teifi
Cenarth Falls
Usk
Llangenny Leap
Taff
Black weir
Exe
Bolham weir
Bickleigh weir
Tavy
Dart
Kilbury weir
Lopwell weir
Totnes weir

Q Why is salmon flesh pink?

A While they are out at sea, salmon eat a wide variety of food including small crustaceans such as shrimp. Shrimp contain pink pigments, which are only revealed when they are cooked, but they pass on this invisible pinkness to the salmon which eat them, and it is clearly reflected in the colour of the fish's flesh. Some flamingoes are pink for the same reason.

WHERE TO WATCH SALMON A wild salmon takes a tremendous leap up a waterfall on its journey back to the place of its birth (above). Some of the best salmon rivers, together with the best places to watch the fish leap are shown on the map. In general, avoid calm downstream sections of salmon rivers and head for higher ground upstream, where steep torrents create bottlenecks that salmon cannot swim past.

Look out, too, for pools where the salmon gather before making the next part of their ascent, and keep watch at man-made barriers such as dams and weirs. You'll find that difficult stretches of water sometimes have **fish-ladders,** such as the one on the River Lui in Scotland, which help the salmon get upstream.

Salmon spawn between late October and January, but the timing of their journey upriver varies. Some fish start as early as April, while others wait until autumn. Even when they arrive offshore, they don't always move upstream at once but may wait until rivers are in full spate. This makes a period of wet autumn weather the best time to look for salmon on the move.

Watch out for the splash

Once they start their journey, salmon do not stop to rest or eat until they have reached their intended goal of shallow water high upstream. By this time they may have lost a third of their body weight.

The breeding season starts around mid October and if you see a commotion of splashing, wriggling bodies in shallow water, you may be witnessing a spawning. Like trout, salmon lay their eggs in hollows, or redds, excavated in gravel riverbeds, but they often do it in water so shallow that the fish can hardly swim, making the activity visible to observers on the bank.

The female turns on her side and uses her tail to dig a hollow. As she lays her eggs the male fertilises them. She then covers the redd with stones. Salmon lay their eggs in batches, and a large female may dig a dozen redds in succession before all her eggs have been shed.

If you wade into a stream outside the breeding season – the eggs usually hatch in March or April – you can sometimes feel these excavations under your feet as dips in the riverbed. Redds can be up to 30cm (12in) deep, and only partially filled in.

The final journey

The young salmon will stay in fresh water for two to five years before setting off out to sea. But the adults turn straight back downstream after spawning to quieter waters to rest.

A few retrace their journey to the sea but most, the males in particular, are too exhausted by their efforts. The female salmon, or kelts, stand a better chance of survival as they do not expend energy fending off rivals as the males do. However, they too are worn out, by the demands of egg-laying and from starvation.

If you see gulls or crows circling over a riverbank, check it out: the birds may be feeding on the bodies of dead salmon that have been washed up on banks and shingle spits. It is rare to catch a glimpse of any surviving fish as they head back downstream: with the current behind them, they are quickly swept along.

Low immunity *Exhausted by their efforts to spawn, many salmon become unable to fight off disease and fall prey to fatal illnesses.*

INSECTS AT THE WATER'S EDGE In autumn, there is still time for insect-hunting. In fast-flowing water and around waterfalls, look for stones or plants covered by grey tufts, about 6mm (¼in) long. These are the larvae of black flies – blood-sucking insects which are on the wing from March until early winter. In some countries black flies plague people and livestock, but British ones are rarely such a problem. Black fly larvae breathe through tiny filamentous gills and can survive only in running water.

On the riverbank, look for patches of watermint, a plant that is still in flower when autumn begins. Try crushing a leaf and smelling it to see if it lives up to its herby name. This is the favourite food of the **mint tortoise beetle**, which reacts rather like a real tortoise when threatened, pulling in its legs and clamping itself against a leaf. The larvae have bristly protective spines, but also camouflage themselves with their own droppings and moulted skins.

TWIGS THAT WALK AWAY

By mid autumn, most of the insects that fluttered over rivers earlier in the year have started to disappear. But the larvae of many waterside insects, such as caddis flies, start life in the water and in autumn are consuming all the food they can get in preparation for surviving winter. Some of them are good swimmers, but most crawl slowly through the shallows in search of plants to eat so that with a net, or even a cupped hand, they are easy to catch.

One larva you stand a good chance of catching is a slender-bodied, caterpillar-like insect about 2cm (¾in) long: a caddis fly larva. At first you might think that you have only scooped up a piece of twig, but put it into a tray of water and wait. Soon the tube, made from twigs, sand, small stones, shells or other materials glued together will get up and walk away!

Caddis fly larvae are eaten by fish and most of them protect themselves by making these cases. The adult insects are also popular food with fish, and anglers often model their artificial flies on them.

Not all caddis fly larvae make cases, but those that do each use particular building materials and designs (although caddis flies kept in an aquarium can be persuaded to create gaudy cases using coloured beads or sand). Try to study the cases through a hand lens. They are often too intricate to be appreciated with the naked eye.

Mobile home *A caddis fly larva in its protective casing, head and legs projecting from one end as it drags the rest behind it.*

Close-up on
Plant galls

By the time summer comes to an end, waterside plants are showing signs of wear and tear. Many have been nibbled by insects, some battered or bent by the wind, and more than a few flattened by passing feet. But some plants bear blemishes of a different kind: strange growths that look like cushions, balloons or even fruit. These are galls. You can find galls in almost any habitat, and on a wide range of plants, so wherever you are it is worth looking for these unusual swellings on trees, bushes and grasses.

Food and shelter for insects

Galls form when a plant's cells are hijacked by an intruder – often an insect grub in need of a home and a supply of food. Insects sometimes lay their eggs inside the cell structure of plants, where their developing grubs exude chemicals, which make the cells divide and mutate, rather like a tumour. Some galls form when a leaf has been pierced by a fly, without it actually laying an egg, and fungi can have the same effect – the rust fungus causes galls on the stems and leaves of groundsel and, in a second stage, on the leaves of Scots and Austrian pines.

Once the gall has reached its maximum size – ranging from the size of a pinhead to a small apple – it stops growing, leaving the grub safely hidden inside. When it has completed its development, the mature insect emerges from the gall to breed and if you look at galls through a magnifying glass you might find some with holes showing where the insect has burrowed out.

The most common gall-making animals are midges and tiny wasps – so small that you will rarely spot them out in the open. Sawflies cause galls on waterside plants, such as willows (see page 145) in spring and again in autumn but gall-formers also include some moths, whose caterpillars trigger the galls. Gall wasps cause galls on the widest variety of trees and shrubs and are responsible for the 'robin's pincushions' (left) found on the stems of roses. These galls look like powderpuffs and change colour from green to pink to bright red in September.

Polka dots *Look closely at a rash of spots on leaves such as these oak leaves (above) and you will see that they are silk button spangle galls (inset above) caused by the gall wasp laying its eggs (inset top). There may be as many as 1200 galls on a single leaf in late August.*

Nursery chambers *Break open a robin's pincushion (far left) and you will find up to 50 gall wasps (inset left) at different stages of development from the grub (on the left) to the adult wasp (on the right).*

GALLS ON OAKS

One of the best places to start if you want to find a gall is a mature oak tree, because more galls form on oaks than on any other species of tree. In autumn, look for a curious fungus-like growth protruding from the side of an acorn (below). This is probably a **knopper gall**. These galls develop in the cups which hold the acorns, giving them a swollen and irregular shape.

Hard, round **marble galls** (bottom) are often mistaken for the more familiar oak apples, which are soft and spongy (see page 131). In autumn, each marble gall has a small hole in it where its owner has crawled out and flown away. The marble gall wasp was deliberately introduced to Devon from the Middle East in around 1830 to produce galls for dying cloth and making ink.

MITE GALLS

The leaves of lime trees, sycamores and **field maples** (above) are often covered with a rash of brilliant orange or red pimples. Within each gall is a mite – a tiny plant-eating relative of the spider. A single leaf can harbour hundreds of these creatures but they are so small that you need a strong hand-lens to see them.

Most galls do not harm the host plant but mites are also responsible for 'big bud' – a troublesome gall which reduces the crop yield of blackcurrant bushes.

SOFT-STEMMED PLANTS

Trees and shrubs are not the only plants that develop galls – soft-stemmed plants are also affected. One of the most conspicuous galls on a soft-stemmed plant is caused by a small fruit fly, which makes its home in **creeping thistles**. The fly lays its eggs on the thistle's stems, and its grubs are soon surrounded by a gall as big as a gooseberry (below). To see the creeping thistle gall's occupants you need to look early in the year, because the adult flies usually leave before the end of May.

One common gall midge lays its eggs on germander speedwell, a sprawling blue-flowered plant of woodlands and hedgerows. If you find this plant and see small growths that look like woolly marbles, it is a sign that the midge's grubs have started to feed.

OPEN SESAME To see some of the strangest galls of all, take a close look at any well-developed Christmas tree or Norway spruce. These trees are sometimes attacked by insects called spruce gall adelgids, which are close relatives of aphids. The adelgids trigger off the formation of **spruce galls [1]** which look like hard wooden pineapples fastened to the end of the tree's branches. Each 'pineapple' has oval portholes that open in autumn **[2]**, allowing the fully grown insects to fly away.

1

2

Fruitful days before the start of hard times

Wildlife's last chance to fill up before the long haul of winter

Autumn days in places like the Highlands, Welsh mountains and expanses of Exmoor and Dartmoor can be among the most dramatic of the year. The purple of the heather and the yellow of dying bracken take on a luminous quality against the backcloth of a stormy sky or dark spruce plantation. The higher you go the greater the sense of impending winter – often its arrival follows so close on the heels of summer that autumn arrives and departs almost without notice. In this brief transition, wild creatures seize on a late glut of food, which enables them to build up their reserves before departing for less harsh surroundings, or simply hunkering down for the winter months.

Shot through with clues

Berwickshire's Lammermuir Hills (above) are a sea of purple in early autumn when the heather is in flower. But take a second look and you can see other colours. Spread across the summits are orange-tinged bilberry bushes loaded with blue-grey berries. Here and there, bracken pokes through, and green strips signpost wet gullies, packed with moss and grass.

Some of the features that you may see on the moor are evidence of its active management. Geometric patches show where old heather has been cut or burnt off to encourage new growth. They indicate that the moor is used for shooting: red grouse nest among the wiry clumps of mature heather and eat the tender new shoots that sprout in cleared areas. You might also stumble across a shooting butt – a low,

The red grouse is reluctant to take to the wing, and its richly coloured plumage provides the bird with excellent camouflage as it crouches in the autumn heather.

camouflaged hide used by the guns. Where moors are used primarily or solely to graze sheep, they look very different. In such places, burning is more indiscriminate and the sheep nibble back the shoots of heather until grass becomes established as the dominant vegetation. Then the red grouse and the merlin disappear along with the heather, but the numbers of meadow pipits, skylarks and hen harriers may increase.

Place of refuge

The scattered trees and rough pasture of upland valleys like the Lake District's Walendlam Tarn (above) are winter home to many wild mammals and birds, some of them evacuees from higher country. Rabbits and voles find cover and food among the grass and bracken, attracting predators such as stoats, buzzards and kestrels. Woods are the territory of black grouse, a bigger bird than its cousin the red, and in the remotest areas of woodland you might see a pine marten.

Ring ouzels and other birds gather in groups to feed on rowan berries, while silver birch seeds draw redpolls, a species of finch. Ripe pine cones, especially those on Scots pine, attract the crossbill, a shy, scarce bird. Listen for a cracking sound as the bird breaks open the cones to get at the seeds, or the thud of a discarded cone falling on the ground. Look out for meadow pipits and skylarks, which rise from the undergrowth, then settle a short distance ahead.

If you are in Scotland, northern England or Northern Ireland and see a squirrel on Scots pine, it is likely to be a red, because the cone seeds are one of this animal's major food sources. But look closely: its colouring and that of the grey are very similar at this season (see pages 122-3).

The lumpy yellow and orange lobes of the lichen Xanthoria aureola *look like bright splashes of paint on the rocky outcrops and stone walls of hill country.*

Short flights fill the bill

The shortening days and falling temperatures of autumn are a signal for many of the birds and wild mammals that spend summer on the mountains and moors to start seeking shelter and warmth elsewhere. Some birds embark on long migratory flights to southerly latitudes, but for many others, and for animals such as deer and otters too, these journeys amount to migration on a small scale – a matter of a few miles downhill to a sheltered valley or the milder climate of the coast.

STAGING POSTS Marshy upland pastures are used by **golden plovers** and curlews as places to feed and congregate into larger flocks while migrating to winter quarters near the coast. It is possible to distinguish these two waders long before they land. The curlew flies with slow wing beats, while the golden plover's are very rapid, and curlews have long curved beaks.

Another species of wader, the common sandpiper, rests and feeds on lake shores. You can tell this small bird – it is the size of a thrush – by the very characteristic movements it makes on the ground and in the air. Look for a distinctive curtseying of the rear of the body when it settles on the ground, and emphatic flicks of the stiffly arched wings when it flies low over water.

As autumn slips towards winter, the high-country larder of insects, berries and seeds soon runs out and the summer population of small birds departs. But this is not a mass exodus: some species hang on much longer than others – journeying only as far as the nearest source of food and shelter. Stonechats, for instance, often move into the nearest gorse patch. There, they give themselves away by bobbing up and down on the tops of bushes and uttering their rasping alarm call – a sound like pebbles being struck together, from

Favoured foods *Gorse and stonechats go together. These birds often nest in gorse bushes, and in autumn can be seen foraging among the spiky thickets for insects and larvae – the black head, white collar and chestnut breast of a male bird (left) making him conspicuous. By contrast, the yellowhammer (right), a bird found on lowland heaths, turns to seeds as autumn sets in and can be seen around farmyards.*

which the bird gets its name. Wheatears favour the short turf beside stone walls – places where they can find small insects to eat and niches to shelter in. Early in the year, wheatears are among the first migrant birds to arrive in Britain, but now they are about to fly back to Africa. Their white rump and contrasting black tail feathers, in the shape of an inverted 'T', make them easy to identify as they swoop and settle a short distance ahead.

Magnets for birds

Where there are cattle and sheep, you will see birds. Crows pick through dung to find small insects, while finches congregate around hayracks.

Fieldfares and redwings, often in mixed flocks, may be spotted on molehills. They are looking through the mounds of soil for worms and larvae. These two types of thrush fly in from colder areas of northern Europe and remain around upland fields until spring, unless bad weather drives them to lower ground.

BELLOWS AND WALLOWS AS STAGS SENSE ONSET OF RUT

Early autumn is the time of the red deer rut – the best time of year on mountain and moor to see Britain's largest native land animal because the usual wariness of the stags is blunted by rivalry and sex.

Most red deer are found in the Highlands and Scottish isles, but there are also herds on Dartmoor and Exmoor, and on heaths such as the New Forest and Thetford Forest.

You are likely to hear stags bellowing before you catch sight of them – a low, eerie, hoarse sound. There are other signs that they are around. A patch of muddy water surrounded by hoofprints marks the wallow where a stag has urinated and rolled, covering his body with a pungent advertisement to hinds and a warning to rivals. Saplings hung with stripped bark show the effects of stags thrashing them with their antlers in displays of prowess.

POPULATION EXPLOSION

If you come across an area of withered grass on an autumn hillside, part the vegetation to discover the cause of the damage. There will be networks of tunnels and runs – the signs of an explosion in field vole numbers, an event that occurs every three to five years.

Short-eared owls are among the creatures that hunt the voles, but the relationship is more than simply that of predator and prey. In years when voles are plentiful, the owls can make plenty of kills for their relatively large broods of up to eight chicks. When voles are scarce, however, there is not enough food to go round and some of the chicks starve.

Which chicks live and which die depends on when they hatched. The short-eared owl starts incubating its eggs, laid at intervals of two days, as soon as the first one is laid. As a result, the chicks' size and strength varies greatly, and when food is short the youngest starve.

Mostly bluster *Like many male animals at mating time, a stag tends to rely on shows of strength to attract and keep a harem of hinds, and to deter potential rivals. These include bellowing matches, when the animal that can bellow loudest and longest wins, and branch-flailing exhibitions of the strength of their antlers. Such displays, coupled with real clashes, chases and frequent mating leave a stag thin and exhausted by the end of the rut.*

Feast or famine *The population strengths of many predators, from owls to stoats, reflect fluctuations in the numbers of the field vole – one of Britain's commonest small mammals.*

The glut of food in the hills in autumn is welcomed by many birds, not just the ones resident there. Species usually found on farmland and by the seashore make an excursion to the mountains and moors to gorge on the bright orange berries of rowan trees, the hawthorn's scarlet haws and the bilberry's purple fruit. Clouds of crane flies and fluttering moths are seized on the wing, and an army of caterpillars, hatched from the eggs of summer-flying moths, are pecked off foliage.

Visitors feed in the uplands

There's efficiency in numbers. A flock of birds hopping through the heather will disturb more insects and locate greater numbers of larvae than one or two individuals searching on their own: there are more beaks looking for a meal, but they uncover more of the food. This is why you will see flocks of rooks commuting from their night-time roosts in the valley to the larder in the heather.

Fellow travellers

If you study these flocks of rooks through binoculars, you will see that they contain hangers-on from their close relatives in the crow family. Look out especially for large numbers of jackdaws, smaller birds with more rapid wing beats and distinctive grey heads. On the ground, rooks stride about deliberately, seeking out beetles, crane flies and their larvae, while jackdaws move more urgently. You might also see carrion crows, or, if you're in Scotland, Northern Ireland or the Isle of Man, hooded crows. Magpies, distinguished by their black-and-white plumage, are also frequent fellow-travellers.

Caterpillar bounty

Flocks of other birds can signal the presence of different insects. For example, black-headed, common and lesser black-backed gulls are attracted by rich pickings of antler moth caterpillars. These striped, glossy brown larvae occur in huge numbers among the coarse grasses and rushes that they eat. Look for a combination of this sort of vegetation with noisy congregations of gulls wheeling above, and you will find the caterpillars. In some years, the numbers of the caterpillar are so great that they block drainage channels if they get washed out of the grass by heavy downpours.

MATTER OF SIZE Although the birds of the grouse family are shy creatures, often crouching in the undergrowth and remaining undetected, their droppings are not an uncommon sight. These look like pale brown cylinders moulded from sawdust. You can tell which bird left them by the length.

Red grouse droppings **[1]** and those of **ptarmigan [2]** are about 2cm (¾in) in length. The calling cards of **black grouse [3]** are about 4cm (1½in) long, and those of a **capercaillie [4]** are the size of an average person's little finger.

A cluster of droppings is usually an indication of where a bird has roosted overnight. Often, such spots also contain a few feathers pulled out during preening, especially in autumn when the birds are moulting. Like the droppings they provide a clue to which members of the grouse family are in the vicinity.

Glossy, blue-black feathers **[3]** belong to a black grouse. The capercaillie sometimes loses a long, square-tipped, brown or black tail feather, flecked with white, while the feathers of red grouse are usually dark brown with wavy bars of buff or red-brown. At higher altitudes, a white feather with a black shaft is sure to have belonged to a ptarmigan.

Starlings often feed on autumn concentrations of leatherjackets, the maggot-like larvae of crane flies (insects sometimes called daddy longlegs). If you watch these birds at work, you will notice how they stop frequently and probe the turf with their beak, then prise the hole wider – a technique known as prying. If there is a grub in the hole, the starling will be able to see it and seize it.

Not all birds gather into flocks to forage. The hobby, a scarce, summer migrant to southern England, makes solo flights over heathland. There it catches large moths and flying beetles in autumn, building up the reserves it needs before flying back to Africa for winter.

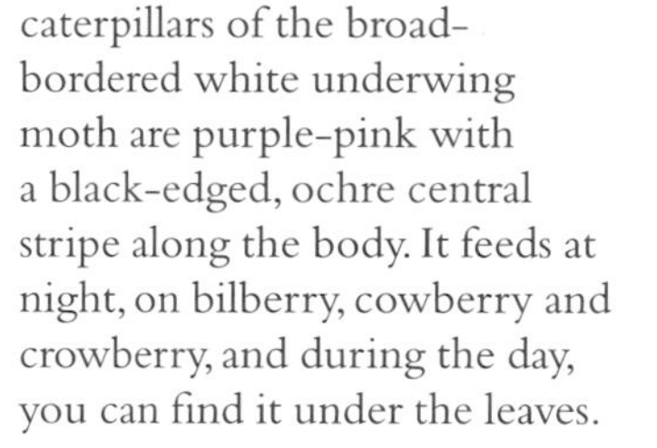

KEYS TO IDENTIFICATION

The caterpillars of the many species of moths that frequent the summer uplands start hatching in August and can still be found in large numbers in October, despite the depredations of hungry birds. Knowing the plant that it is feeding on is the best way of identifying a caterpillar.

Caterpillars of the common heath moth feed on heather. They are green-grey or brown and frequently speckled white. Look on bilberry and heather for caterpillars of the smoky wave moth. They are very slim and wrinkled, and their overall ochre colour is broken up by three pale lines down the back and a dark stripe along each side. The caterpillars of the northern spinach moth are long and thin, mottled brown, and patterned with dark lines and pale triangles, and feed on bilberry and crowberry.

Under the leaves

The caterpillars of the black mountain moth, which feed on heather, have a distinctive white patch half-way along their grey-brown bodies. Black, fish-tail markings distinguish the head end. The colourful caterpillars of the broad-bordered white underwing moth are purple-pink with a black-edged, ochre central stripe along the body. It feeds at night, on bilberry, cowberry and crowberry, and during the day, you can find it under the leaves.

THE HEATHER HONEY FLOW

If you come across beehives among the heather, give them a reasonably wide berth. Honeybees are not aggressive, but if you walk too close to the front of a hive there is a risk of one getting tangled in your hair and stinging you. Beekeepers take hives to the heather because the bees make a delicious, fragrant honey from its nectar. On a warm early autumn day at the height of the nectar 'flow' the bees will be very busy, and a pair of binoculars focused on the front of the hive will reveal the entrance to be smothered with a mass of worker bees clambering over one another as they struggle either to take to the wing or get into the hive.

Blue pollen

If you carefully part the woody stems of the heather you will see honeybees on the flowers. Look for the packed 'baskets' of delicate blue heather pollen on the legs of some bees.

On lowland heaths, you might see small insects foraging in the heather with honeybees. These are likely to be mining bees. If there is a sandy bank nearby, examine it for tiny burrows – the nest tunnels of these solitary insects.

Prime location Hives set in the heather ensure a worker bee (inset) loses little time on the wing. In good years, a colony can make 15kg (33lb) of honey in two weeks.

CATERPILLAR FOOD Bog myrtle and bracken are two food plants of the **broom moth caterpillar** (above), a hairless larva with striking yellow markings.

Heather stems are the place to look for caterpillars of the **northern oak eggar moth** (inset above). These velvety black and tawny creatures hibernate through their first winter and do not turn into chrysalises until their second autumn.

Upland grasses provide succulent chomping for **drinker moth caterpillars** (inset right), strikingly marked larvae with tufts of hairs at each end.

The wild-berry orchard ripens

By September, heath, moorland and mountain contain a vast miniature orchard. Beneath the low vegetation hangs a wild harvest of small purple and red berries. For the plants, these are one means of propagation – the hard seeds inside the soft flesh of the berries are excreted by birds, ready-wrapped in a coating of fertiliser. For the birds and other wildlife that eat them, the berries are rich energy packages.

The open hillside is a tough environment, dried out by summer drought and lashed by winter rain and wind. The berry-bearers of autumn have adapted to their surroundings in different ways. Some have become specialists – you find them growing in sheltered spots, such as boggy pockets; other shrubs tolerate a wide range of conditions – from the shaded edges of woodland marking the lower boundary of the hill to the open, windswept summits.

Waxy coating

Although they grow most densely on the deep peat of high moors, clumps of bilberry are a common sight on thin, gravelly hill soils and on the sandy heaths of southern Britain.

How can the bilberry grow in so many places? Look at the small oval leaves and you can see one reason: they are thick and leathery, with a waxy surface to reduce the amount of moisture lost to the wind. This explains why bilberry can survive on slopes exposed to the prevailing wind, but not why it has taken over from heather in many places. For that you have to find a burned area and look at how plants are growing back. If allowed to, bilberry will re-establish itself more quickly and smother the slower growing heather. For the same reason, it withstands grazing by sheep better than heather.

Vivid red berries

Cowberry grows alongside bilberry in many places. It is common on lower moors, heaths and around clearings in coniferous woods, and is also widespread on the flat uplands of the eastern Highlands. In autumn, it is easy to distinguish from bilberry, even at a distance: just look for the bright green of this evergreen plant among the

Q **I saw a rowan tree growing on a rocky ledge. How did it get to be in such an unlikely place?**

A The tree sprouted from a seed contained in bird droppings. Several birds, including mistle thrushes, redwings and fieldfares, feast on the rowan berries in autumn, then pass the seeds. These germinate and take root if they land in a favourable spot, such as a sheltered, damp crevice on a steep rocky face. You may see hawthorns that started in the same way.

IDENTITY PARADE – Moorland berries

Being able to distinguish the berries you find among the ankle-high vegetation of uplands and heaths is useful, especially if the idea of gathering a few appeals: some have traditional medicinal uses, some produce dyes, a few taste good.

Cowberry bears clusters of jewel-like red berries – luscious looking but bitter on the tongue. The leaves were traditionally used to produce a yellow dye.

Bilberry produces the most delicious of the upland berries. In the past these were picked commercially, to process into a dye as well as to be sold as a foodstuff.

Crowberry may owe its name to the raven-wing blackness of the berries. These taste bitter, and are an emetic, although many moorland birds eat them.

Cloudberry is a member of the raspberry family – as the shape of its leaves and the segmented fruits suggest. The rare fruits are edible, but bland.

orange and yellow of the deciduous bilberry. Up close, the leaves are notched at the tip and the clusters of tart, edible berries a deep plum colour.

Crowberry, which grows on northern moors, has small leaves and looks like heather at first glance, although it belongs to a different family of plants. Look more closely at the leaves and you will see that they curl down and inwards to form a narrow tube, so protecting pores on the undersurface of the foliage from drying winds.

JUNIPER SCALES THE HEIGHTS

A patch of blue-grey vegetation growing high on a mountainside is likely to turn out to be a thicket of juniper. This plant, most common in the Highlands and on north-facing cold, shaded slopes farther south, is slow growing and does not become established where sheep or deer constantly nibble it, or where there is regular burning. Where it does get going, however, the juniper's spiky needles deter browsers, and its dense branches make an impenetrable windbreak.

Lying low *The juniper, which can grow into a conical tree up to 6m (20ft) tall, develops into a low, twisting shrub in upland locations. The berries (inset) are green when they form, and don't ripen and turn black until the following year.*

Raiders of the rowan Mountain ash covered in berries shine like beacons on autumn hillsides. It's then that the mistle thrush (inset) gathers in small flocks to strip the trees of their fruit. Look for the flash of their white underwings and outer tail feathers as they hop among the branches, or listen for the dry ***churr*** of the bird's alarm call. Once most of the berries are eaten and there's no longer an advantage in numbers, the flocks break up. Then, individual mistle thrushes lay claim to single trees and their few remaining fruit.

WATCH YOUR STEP

Keep a look out for cranberry plants when you're walking on moorland – because they grow in boggy spots, you can use them as a warning of areas of ground that are best avoided.

The thin red stems trail over the surface of the ground and have widely spaced leaves, dark above but almost white beneath. The mottled reddish brown berries are round to pear-shaped and the size of a 1p piece. They have a sharp flavour and were a traditional ingredient of sauces, jams and pies until the larger North American variety of the plant was introduced into Britain in the 19th century.

Colour contrast *The scarlet fruits of cranberry are easy to spot among the plants' evergreen leaves.*

Choosy fungi pick their spots

Damper autumn weather and the leaf-fall stimulate the growth of mushrooms and toadstools. Different types occur in all sorts of upland habitats, from burnt patches of heather to hillsides of grazed turf and conifer woods. For the collector, the location of a fungus is a useful aid to identification. But for the countryside detective, the same knowledge can also reveal fascinating information about the habitat itself.

Fungi can be strange, artificial-looking things. Waxcaps, for instance, could be mistaken for pieces of shiny plastic or china until you get close. These hillside toadstools, which come in bright red, green, yellow, orange, lilac, pink and white, owe their shininess to a waxy coating which stops the wind drying them out. Waxcaps are becoming more scarce because they don't tolerate artificial fertilisers, so if you find them, it's a sure sign you're on unimproved hill pasture.

Where there's muck

Grazed hillside is also a good place to look for coprophilous fungi – those that grow on dung. Look out especially for the dung roundhead (*Stropharia semiglobata*), a round-topped toadstool with a slimy yellowish cap, up to 4cm (1½in) across, and a white stem.

White spheres in the grass, varying from golfball-size to as big as a football turn out to be puffballs. On windy days, their attachment to the ground is sometimes broken and you may see one bowling down a slope. Examine a puffball and you will notice that, unlike many mushrooms and toadstools, it doesn't have gills. So how does it release its spores? The answer depends on which of the two types of puffball you happen to be looking at.

With one type, which includes the giant puffball, the top simply breaks open and the airborne spores are carried away. The second type, which are distinguished by their warty or spiny skins, eject their spores through a small pore when they are ripe. You can encourage the fungus to do this by dropping small particles of soil on it: visible clouds of spores will rise from the puffball.

Peat lover *The cinnamon cortinarius is a common toadstool in peaty places such as this area of the Northumberland moors.*

Partial to pasture *Clusters of scarlet hood (left), a waxcap fungus, make a conspicuous splash of colour on a grassy hillside, although they fade and yellow with age. The dung roundhead (below) flourishes on horse droppings and is common where wild ponies roam.*

Fire and water

Scorched ground, whether caused by heather burning or smaller fires, is just the place to find clumps of a smooth, sticky fungus called *Pholiota highlandensis*. It has ochre-brown caps and thick white stalks.

When you're walking near sphagnum bog look out for toadstools with yellow caps growing in dense clusters. This is *Hypholoma elongatum*, one of the few fungi that can thrive in the oxygen-poor environment of waterlogged ground. The massed conical caps flatten with time, revealing more of the densely packed lilac-grey gills.

LEAVING AN IMPRESSION On the uplands, fungi are a food supply for many creatures – from mammals to invertebrates. When you find the nibbled remains of mushrooms and toadstools, it's often possible to tell what ate it by looking at the 'dental impression' left on the cap. **Slugs and snails** leave distinctive grooves as they rasp away with their horny tongues (right). Squirrels take square-ended bites out of fungi, and voles leave narrow, pointed indentations where they have nibbled into the flesh. Crows and other birds peck mushrooms to pieces to get at maggots inside, scattering the fragments across the ground.

AMONG CONIFERS

Because, unlike plants, fungi can live and grow without sunlight, they can thrive in the deep shade of conifer plantations. The lack of vegetation on the forest floor also means they are fairly conspicuous, despite the poor light.

Some, like slippery jack, a dark brown, slimy-topped fungus with a thick stalk and pores, grow among the decomposing needles under many types of conifers, but others only grow under certain types of tree.

Sticky cap

If there are larch trees in a plantation, look for the larch bolete, a fungus with a bright, sticky, honey-coloured cap which grows only under this deciduous conifer. Like all boletes, the underside of the cap is composed of many small tubes, not the radiating gills common in many fungi.

Many species of milkcap fungi – so called because they exude a milky liquid when the cap is broken – also turn up under conifers. These are mostly rather pale, brownish toadstools, all rather similar in appearance, although the red milkcap can be distinguished by its tawny-red cap, which comes to a slight central point, and by the way it often grows in circles or 'troops'.

Contrasting colours

Search around old conifer stumps and fallen cones as these provide food for fungi. One common type on rotting stumps is the plums and custard fungus, named after its contrasting rich brown cap and yellow gills.

Many parasitic fungi will grow on one type of tree only, but *Heterobasidion annosum* – one of the bracket fungi (so called because they form shelf-like projections on the trunks) – has many different conifer hosts. Look near ground level for the flat, semi-circular fungus. It is black-brown with a pale fringe and measures 15cm (6in) across.

Among the needles *The litter of this conifer forest floor suits many fungi, including one of the fairy clubs (growing on the stump, right foreground). The ear-pick fungus, which has a bristly, blackish stalk, often grows on fallen cones (left).*

Close-up on
The weather

The countryside detective taps into a rich vein of folklore when it comes to forecasting the weather: old sayings abound concerning what can be inferred from all sorts of events. Some of these proverbs are fairly reliable, but many of them are based on the way nature has reacted to past weather conditions. For example, a heavy crop of autumn berries in the hedges, like a bumper harvest of apples in the orchard, tells you only that the previous spring was free of frosts and gales, allowing the blossom to bloom and set; it is no sign, as legend has it, that the forthcoming winter will be hard. For the most part, the best clue to approaching weather lies in the broad canvas of the sky and its cloud formations. These can signal quick and dramatic changes, so it's a good idea to be aware of what they mean, especially when you venture into the hills.

Mackerel sky
Layers of small, white cirrocumulus cloud are known as mackerel skies when they appear as ripple-like patterns resembling the scales of a fish. They form high in the atmosphere and are composed of ice crystals.

OMENS IN THE SKY

Britain's climate is characterised by alternating periods of high pressure with fine weather, and depressions, or fronts, with wet weather. Both features are governed by the winds, with westerlies generally bringing temperate, moisture-laden air, and easterlies dry weather – hot in summer, cold in winter. And both are associated with particular types of cloud.

Wispy brush strokes of cirrus, or mare's tail **[1]** high in the sky are the first sign that a front is on the way. Look at which way the tails bend on cirrus clouds: if they sweep upwards, it means the clouds are descending and rain is coming; if they trail downwards, the clouds are rising and the weather will be fine.

When cirrus clouds are followed by altostratus clouds **[2]**, a grey blanket will soon block out the sun, bringing rain followed by showers and a more westerly wind.

The tail of the depression arrives abruptly, often marked by a band of thick, black nimbostratus clouds and heavy rain. North-west winds signal the end of the passage of a depression, with nimbostratus **[3]** and finally cirrostratus clouds appearing.

The clouds that signal dry weather and sunny spells are the white piles of fluffy cumulus clouds **[4]** sailing across a clear blue sky. When the fine spells start to break down, huge cumulonimbus clouds (main picture) can build up. Their anvil heads threaten heavy rain, hail and often thunder and lightning.

How to protect yourself
If you are out in the open and you see thunderclouds coming, take the following precautions. Head for shelter, preferably a car because its metal shell acts as a shield against lightning. If you are caught in the open, put down any metal objects you're carrying, such as a camera tripod, and move well away from them. And don't shelter under a tree.

1

2

3

AT THE WEATHER'S MERCY

Weather forecasts can help you to predict how the annual bird migrations are going, and an unusual weather pattern brings a chance to see migrants blown onto British shores.

If northerly winds gust over the North Sea in autumn, while birds from Scandinavia are flying to southern Europe and Africa, birds like flycatchers, goldcrests and warblers can be blown onto Britain's east coast.

Similarly, the autumn and spring migrations of birds between the eastern coast of the United States and the Caribbean and South America can be hit by westerly gales, blowing American species of cuckoos, sandpipers, wood warblers and other birds all the way to Britain's west coast.

The same winds can blow another North American species, the monarch butterfly, thousands of miles off course to Britain.

Insects caught out

If you find a dead queen wasp or bumblebee on your lawn in the middle of winter, it is because a spell of mild weather has brought them out of hibernation, leaving them vulnerable when temperatures suddenly fall back to normal.

Everyday weather patterns also affect wildlife. For example, you won't see many bats about on rainy, foggy evenings because their echolocation does not work well in these conditions.

Cloudless, moonlit nights, on the other hand, which do suit bats, make many other nocturnal creatures very wary and loathe to venture out. Rain and high winds also limit mammal activity, especially that of squirrels and dormice.

Spot plant responses

Watch wild flowers and you will notice that many, including the daisy, bindweed and scarlet pimpernel, close up when rain threatens. They do this because of the fading light, but as an added bonus it protects their pollen from a drenching.

Traditionally, people have believed that such flowers can predict the weather: the scarlet pimpernel is also known as the poor man's weatherglass. In fact, these flowers are reacting to high levels of moisture in the air – which is often a sign that rain is on the way.

The foliage of some trees also reacts to changes in the weather. For example, when the underside of leaves on poplar, lime and sycamore trees can be seen, it shows that an updraught of warm moist air is causing the leafstalks to bend upwards; hence the old saying, 'if the leaves blow inside out, there's bad weather about'.

Castaways *This north American yellow-billed cuckoo turned up on the Scilly Isles after being swept westwards on an Atlantic depression. Some birds are carried all the way on the wind, but others alight on ships for part of their unintentional voyage.*

4

Q **What causes a heavy dew?**

A A calm, clear night with no cloud cover allows heat to radiate from the ground unhindered. The result is that the surface cools rapidly to the point where water vapour condenses at ground level, covering vegetation with water droplets or dew. If the air is slightly disturbed, morning mists, composed of tiny water droplets, form instead of dew.

SEPARATING TRUTH FROM MYTH

Red sky at night, shepherd's delight Red skies occur when the light is scattered by dry air or dust particles in the atmosphere. Since most weather systems in Britain move from west to east, a red sunset indicates that the weather coming from the west will be dry.

Clicking crickets forecast a heatwave Crickets do click frantically if the temperature at night stays above 12°C (54°F) but that just tells you what you already know – that it is warm.

Swallows flying high mean good weather Swallows fly high when the insects they are pursuing are borne upwards on rising thermals, which is a sign of settled weather. When the air is more humid (and rain is threatening) insects fly low and swallows follow.

A halo around the sun or moon denotes a storm and colder weather Haloes are caused by sunlight or moonlight reflecting off ice crystals in cirrus clouds high in the atmosphere. Often, the formation of these crystals is associated with an approaching depression.

Cows lying down mean it will rain Cows are no more likely to lie down before rain than at any other time, either in the open or under trees.

Secrets of salt marshes

Sheep are fattening up for winter on the luxuriant coastal marshes at Ynys Hir at the mouth of the River Dyfi in west Wales (above). The meat of animals that graze on plants growing in these salt marshes has a delicious salty tang. Some breeds of sheep, such as the Soay and Ronaldsay, even enjoy eating seaweed.

Salt marshes like this – uniformly green from a distance – are found all round the coast in sheltered estuaries where fresh water meets the sea. They are crazed with winding muddy creeks which fill up at high tide, and make wandering there a hazardous activity, which is why salt marshes are among the least explored of all our wild habitats.

However, salt marshes are very special places, full of remarkable plants which can withstand immersion in salty water, and they

Birds and mammals move closer to the coast

New sights to see as autumn brings creatures to the shore

Autumn is the season when birds change shift at the coast. Some summer-nesting birds, such as terns and warblers, are leaving Britain to overwinter in the tropics, while incomers like redwings and fieldfares are arriving from the colder north to spend winter in Britain. This is also a rewarding time for seawatching. Not only will sea birds be passing down the coast, but dolphins and other aquatic mammals are moving inshore in areas such as the Cornish coast or the Inner Hebrides. At the same time, grey seals are preparing to calve on secluded shores. Above all, the estuaries and saltings are coming to life, as waders and wildfowl arrive from the freezing Arctic to feed on the rich life hidden in the mud.

The rich wildlife of salt marshes attracts predators, such as this peregrine, which pursues waders in the creeks, and red kites that soar in search of carrion.

have a strange beauty of their own. Britain has more salt marshes than almost any other European country, and they are important autumn feeding grounds both for seed-eating birds and those that probe the mud for invertebrates. The twite – a small finch similar to a linnet, but darker in colour – congregates in large flocks on salt marshes in autumn to feast on the abundant seeds of glasswort, sea aster and seablite.

Beached seals

Grey seals calve on sheltered shores between August and December. This colony of grey seals (above) is enjoying the late autumn sunshine on Monach Island, in the Outer Hebrides. Their pups are unable to swim or catch food for three or four weeks. Instead each pup is suckled by its mother, and grows fast on her rich fatty milk; these pups are already half-grown and beginning to shed their white fur coats.

Seals are clumsy on land and laboriously haul themselves up the beach by their front flippers. Most of the adults on the beach are cows – fully grown females. The bigger males, or bulls, defend the beach while the pups are being born, and can often be found braving up to one another on the shore, or otherwise loafing in the shallows in bachelor parties.

About 40 per cent of the world's grey seals live in the waters around Britain. They can be distinguished from common seals by their characteristic heavy head and elongated 'Roman' nose. The common seal has a more dog-like head, with a stubbier snout. Seals are easily disturbed when on their breeding grounds so the best way to see them is from a distance, from high cliffs or by boat, on a seal-watching expedition.

Grey seal pups have a coat of white fur to keep them warm. As they grow, they accumulate layers of insulating fat and develop their sleek grey adult coat.

A wet and salty place to live

Salt marshes form on mud between the high and low-water marks. The largest are on the east coast, in Lincolnshire, Norfolk, Essex and the Thames estuary, but there are also good examples around The Solent. Marsh plants stabilise the mud between complex creeks, through which the tides ebb and flow. Exploring can be treacherous, so always keep to firm ground and remember that the tide can come in bewilderingly fast and from unexpected directions.

During spring and summer little disturbs the blanket of green on salt marshes. But as autumn approaches they come to life, bursting into a purple haze of sea lavenders dotted with the reds of glasswort and seablite.

Salt-marsh plants produce many seeds, since the chances of germination are not high. This is why they attract flocks of birds, such as finches and duck. Waders, too, are arriving from their northern breeding grounds to feed, filling the air with their piping calls.

Land plants are unable to take up water from the sea – it is saltier than the contents of their cells and is, in effect, a poison. To them the sea is a desert.

By evolving the attributes described on these pages, salt-marsh plants have found ways of coping with the sunshine, the salt, the flooding around their roots, and the twice-daily tidal scour. This means that they are able to thrive in an environment where they face very little competition from other plants for space and nutrients.

You might expect these tidal areas to be covered in seaweeds, but they are kept out by the flowering plants. However, two have found a niche: *Bostrichia scorpiodes*, whose red curly threads cling to the stems of sea purslane, and *Enteromorpha intestinalis* (below left).

Strategies for survival

Sea purslane is most common along tidal channels, where you should find masses of its broad, silvery leaves. These help the plant to store precious water, and also reflect sunlight and protect it from scorching. Why is it found most commonly along the edges of creeks? Because the sea purslane needs oxygen around its roots, and therefore grows most successfully in the best drained places.

In open muddy places, look for seablite, a bluish green annual with very narrow leaves. Many salt-marsh plants are perennials, with deep woody roots to help them to cling to their patch, but annuals like this one use a different strategy.

Seablite produces masses of seed, enabling it to colonise bare patches where there is no competition from bigger, more established plants.

Floral attractions *Sea lavenders, such as at Burnham Overy Staithe, in Norfolk (below), have no scent, but use their bright colour to attract inland bees and butterflies to pollinate them.*

WHY ARE THEIR STEMS FLESHY?

Most plants in the lower marsh are succulents. On bare mud, look for shiny sprigs of **glasswort** (left), which stores water inside its fleshy jointed stem. Try nibbling a piece and see how salty it tastes. The plant contains dissolved sodium salts which were once used in the making of glass, hence its name. In autumn glasswort turns bright red.

Few seaweeds can survive in salt marshes, because there are no hard surfaces for the them to cling to, but ***Enteromorpha intestinalis*** (inset left) forms inflatable green tubes which can float at high tide.

Blue rinse *Sea asters are often found growing entwined with the grey leaves and stems of sea purslane. They need to be tall, so that the flowers are held above water even at high tide. The flowers are at their best around St Michael's day on September 29, when they give salt marshes a pale blue wash.*

MOVING TOWARDS DRIER LAND

Some salt marshes, such as the one around Poole Harbour in Dorset (above), are dominated by cordgrass, a tall stiff grass whose creeping roots allow it to spread rapidly on bare mud. Cordgrass has the ability to extrude salt, rather as an animal sweats – examine the leaves and lower stem when the tide is out and you may find salt crystals as evidence of this.

Several closely related species of cordgrass are found in Britain and they give a clue to how the plant is evolving. Townsend's cordgrass evolved as a separate species in around 1870 and became the most common type, widely planted by coastal authorities to stabilise the mud. Since 1892 it has been largely replaced by **common cordgrass** (above) – to tell the difference, check the flowers. Townsend's cordgrass is infertile and spreads purely by growing from the roots, so if there is plenty of pollen or ripe seeds, it is probably the newer species.

Meadows with a difference

On the landward side of some salt marshes you may find a low shrubby plant with succulent leaves growing in a narrow band parallel with the coast. This is shrubby seablite. It is so confined because its seeds are dispersed by the sea, and so it does not travel any farther inland than the tide takes it.

The upper parts of salt marshes are often reclaimed for pasture behind a sea wall. This partially drained habitat is called grazing marsh. Though from a distance it looks like ordinary meadow, you can find a very interesting mixture of freshwater and salt-marsh plants along the drainage ditches which divide the fields. If the sea level rises and breaches the sea wall, some of these fields will probably return to being salt marshes.

What's that in the water?

When cliff-walking on rocky coasts in late summer and autumn, keep a lookout for dolphins, seals, basking sharks and even whales. Dolphins surface to breathe and you are most likely to spot them and their relative, the harbour porpoise, when the sea is calm and the air clear. Scan the sea by eye – rocky headlands make ideal vantage points – and if you see a dark shape focus on it with your binoculars. Then follow these clues to identify the shapes in the water.

A rare sight *In waters off the Shetland Isles, look out for the huge ponderous shape of a fin whale, which can reach up to 25m (80ft) long.*

The first question to answer is: how many fins can you see? Dolphins have a prominent, slightly curved fin, which cuts through the water as they swim, whereas basking sharks, which also swim off the coast, have a vertical tail fin which also projects out of the water, so that you see two fins moving along.

Dolphins prefer places where the depth of water varies, and where there are lots of fish, and underwater channels to help them to navigate. They often swim close to boats, and may follow in the wake of the bow wave. If you are very lucky, you might see dolphins leaping out of the water.

To identify the species of a dolphin, note its body markings and the shape of its head. Most dolphins in British waters are either the common dolphin, which has a yellowish patch on its flank, or the bottle-nosed dolphin. In some shallow waters you may spot, near dusk, the smaller harbour porpoise, with its small fin and no 'beak'.

Looking for larger animals

If you want to see a whale you will probably have to take a boat, since these large mammals prefer deeper water – the ferry crossing to Spain offers exciting whale-spotting in the Bay of Biscay. Another area where you are likely to spot minke and fin whales is the north-west coast of Scotland. You may even catch a glimpse of a killer whale there, with its tall triangular fin and distinctive white markings.

Occasionally you may find a dolphin or pilot whale stranded on a beach. These may be sick animals cast up by the tide, but may also show signs of injury, such as snags from fishing nets. Some simply lose their bearings. Mass strandings are thought to occur when a group stays with an individual in distress, but these are rare in Britain. If you find a live stranded dolphin or whale, contact the local branch of the RSPCA as soon as possible, since these animals cannot survive for long out of the water. If the animal is dead,

Shorter by a nose *The bottle-nosed dolphin (below) is paler than the common dolphin (inset below), with a more stubby snout.*

Sharks or dolphins? *Dolphins are often seen in groups, ranging from two or three individuals to pods of up to 50. Unlike sharks, only their prominent dorsal fin is visible as they swim at the surface, and they also lift their snouts and the top of their heads clear of the water to breathe (inset).*

Shark silhouette *If you see a long dark shape with two fins moving slowly near the surface it could be a basking shark, feeding on plankton.*

contact the Natural History Museum in London, which keeps such records.

Is it safe to bathe?

Calm sunny days in summer and early autumn are the best time for seeing the rare but spectacular basking shark. At 2-10m (6½-33ft) long, this is the second largest of all the world's fish, but it is not a threat to humans, since it feeds only on microscopic plankton.

The shark is named from the way it floats and swims slowly at the surface, as though basking in the sun-warmed waters. In fact it is filtering food from the water with sieve-like structures attached to its gills, and it can do this only at low speed.

SEAL SPOTTING

Up for air *The first sign of a seal, such as this grey seal, is often just the head, bobbing like a buoy or fishing float at the surface.*

If you see what look like a few scattered buoys out at sea, scan the shoreline for seals. Two species of seal breed on British coasts: the common seal and the grey seal.

The place where you see a seal can be a good first clue to identifying it. A seal seen on the sands of the Norfolk coast or The Wash is most likely to be a common seal. Grey seals, on the other hand, are more often seen on the west coast, with the exception of a large colony on the Farne Islands, off Northumberland.

Whose pup is that?

The female common seal gives birth to a single pup in summer. The young can swim and dive within a few hours, and are soon hard to distinguish from adults. The white pups of grey seals are born in late autumn, on sheltered beaches backed by cliffs (see page 253) and are dependent on their parents for food for several weeks.

Unlike common seals, grey seals are very vocal. In autumn, listen for the hisses and snarls of the bulls as they challenge one another for territory, the hooting chorus of the cows, and the high-pitched bawl of the hungry pups.

Your best chance of getting a good look at a seal is to find one that has 'hauled out' to bask on a rock, or sandy beach. Seals are easily disturbed by a human profile or shadow, so crouch or lie down as you watch them. Sometimes you can even approach a seal while you are snorkelling – particularly in harbours, where resident seals may be quite tame.

WHERE TO SEE DOLPHINS, PORPOISES, SHARKS, WHALES AND SEALS: PAGE 341

Tracks in the sand *Seals leave characteristic 'train tracks' in the sand (above) as they haul themselves out of the water with their fore flippers (below).*

Fast food for birds *Spire-shell mud snails (inset below) are a key food source for many birds on mud flats, such as shelduck (left). The snails graze on the surface film of algae and bacteria, and are scooped up as the shelduck sifts the mud with its broad bill.*

Don't get stranded Mud flats can be dangerous places. Never explore them unaccompanied, and always seek local advice on the times of tides and which areas are safe to walk on. Visit the mud flats on the ebb tide and be sure to return to dry land well before the tide turns.

The great mud feast

Exposed at low tide, mud flats look almost lifeless, but in fact most teem with life just below the surface. Unlike sand, which is washed ashore by waves, most of the mud in mud flats comes from river silt, transported by the flowing water and dumped when the water slows almost to a halt as it meets the incoming sea. Mud is rich in organic matter, and sustains a complex web of plants and animals, from bacteria through worms to wading birds. The whole habitat is at its busiest in autumn, when large numbers of migratory birds flock in to feed on the invertebrates which are buried in the mud.

Mud flats tend to contain fewer different species than sandy or rocky shores, but those few species are often present in abundance. For instance, a single cubic metre of mud may contain as many as 60,000 spire-shell mud snails (inset above).

Try washing a spadeful of mud through a net or fine sieve and dozens of another resident of the mud flat will be left behind: an amphipod shrimp, about 1cm (⅜in) long. This shrimp, called *Corophium*, lives inside a burrow hidden in the mud at low tide, and feeds on detritus brought to it by the river and incoming waves.

Dig deeper into the mud and you may see pale-coloured burrows running through the dark mud. These are made by ragworms. If you uncover one, pop it into a jar of sea water and the creature will reveal its red and green colours, bristly segments and powerful jaws. Be careful – they bite.

The mud also contains many bivalve shells, some of which feed by sucking up mud or by filtering sea water to extract the edible bits (see pages 172-173). Exactly what you find depends on the grade of the mud, from fine silt to a sandier consistency.

In soft silty mud, look for star-shaped patterns of furrows. These are made by the long feeding tubes, or siphons, of the peppery furrow shell, which extend in all directions across the surface searching for food. Scrape away some of the mud and you will find the narrow shells just below the surface, clamped tightly together. Put one in a jar of sea water, and it should reward you by opening and protruding its siphons and muscular foot as it tries to find some mud to rebury itself.

Putting out feelers *The peppery furrow shell searches for food around its burrow with a tube.*

FISHY MARKS IN THE MUD

At low tide you may find small parallel grooves left on the surface of the mud. These were made by a grey mullet, a sea fish which enters estuaries to graze on microscopic algae growing on the mud surface.

Another fish, the flounder, leaves shallow circular pits behind as it searches for small molluscs. You are unlikely to find the adult fish itself, for it feeds mainly at night. However, you can sometimes catch baby flounders by pushing a net through the shallows.

Like most other estuarine fish, the flounder lays its eggs out at sea, where the salinity of the water is stable, but the young move into the estuaries to feed in the safety of the shallows.

STRANGE MEADOWS

At and just below the low-water mark on mud flats and estuaries, where there is a mixture of sand and mud, look for 'meadows' of a narrow-leaved, grass-like plant (see main picture below). This is eelgrass. You can find meadows of eelgrass on sheltered shores along The Solent, the Thames estuary, the Moray Firth, the Humber and more locally elsewhere.

If you separate the swollen base of the leaves, you should find a row of tiny seeds, which tell you that eelgrass is not a seaweed, but one of the few flowering plants that has been able to colonise the sea. The eelgrass pollen is carried by the sea water that washes over the meadow as the tide turns.

This is a random process and demands a lot of pollen, but at least it doesn't require the plant to produce a big showy flower. In fact, the flowers are grain-like and hidden inside the leaf sheaths, with only the wispy pollen-producing stamens exposed to the water.

Many sea creatures (see below) also take advantage of eelgrass meadows to feed and to lay their eggs. To see some, try running a net through the shallow water covering an eelgrass meadow. Empty it into a pan or wide-mouthed jar of seawater to check your catch.

If you move a stone to look for creatures buried in the mud anywhere in the shallows, always replace it the right way up or the microscopic plants on the top will die in the dark and those sheltering on the underside will be exposed.

Slippery supper *Flocks of brent geese gather at the coast in autumn, where eelgrass forms an important part of their diet.*

Grassy bed *Low tide offers a chance to examine eelgrass, here mixed with japweed in a meadow at Bembridge, on the Isle of Wight.*

IN THE WEEDS Under a stone you might discover a **daisy anemone** (far left), its long body buried in the sediment and only the tentacles exposed. The **sea mouse** (middle left) – not really a mouse but a broad-bodied worm with iridescent protective hairs – also buries all but its back end. The **greater pipefish**, an elongated fish related to sea-horses, feeds on crustaceans among seaweeds, algae and eelgrass.

Birds to seek on sandy shores

By autumn, most sand-dune plants have finished flowering, although the seed heads of carline thistle and sea holly can persist into the winter. Some late-developing plants provide food for birds, but most waders visiting the coast in autumn are seeking the soft mud of estuaries, which they can probe with their sensitive beaks for worms and shrimps. One bird, however – the sanderling – is more typically found on sandy shores. Look for groups of this small, pale wader scurrying to and fro with the waves, as if they are on wheels.

Different strokes

Flocks of sanderlings (below) look like big pebbles being jostled at the water's edge. But the great black-backed gull (above) is unmistakable – watch it in the air and see how it moves its wings in a ponderous flight, like a heron's.

If you come across a party of sanderlings watch them through binoculars, and you'll see how they move their heads from side to side to spot and catch small crustaceans and worms disturbed by the waves. At high tide they also scour the strandline for sandhoppers. The sanderling's short beak is designed to snap up food at the surface rather than to probe the sand as other waders do.

Sanderlings sometimes forage with the similarly sized dunlin, but the sanderlings are marked out by their distinctive black shoulder patch, and, in flight, a broad white wing-bar with a dark leading edge.

The gulls you are most likely to see on beaches in autumn are the familiar herring gull and the larger great black-backed gull. When you see them together, you will appreciate the massive build of the great black-backed gull, but if you stop and watch it you'll see what bursts of speed and agility it can put on in pursuit of prey.

The secret of success for all gulls is versatility. They can and will eat almost anything, from carrion to food scraps dropped on the ground or from rubbish dumps. The great black-backed also catches live food, ranging in size from a puffin down to a flying ant.

Youngsters out and about

In autumn you will see many juvenile shore birds, which can be distinguished from the adults by their plumage. Strikingly different plumage in young birds seems to be a hallmark of the most aggressive species, especially those that nest in colonies. This is because adult gulls, which normally attack one another to gain territory, will leave the different juvenile birds alone, knowing that they do not pose a threat.

Notice, too, how young gulls tend to stay close to the shore: they seem to be much less skilful

Growing birds *First-year gannets (above) are all black above, except for a white 'V' on the tail, but as they moult, the black feathers are replaced by white ones. This three-year-old (right) has another year to wait for its full adult plumage – white, with black at the wing tips.*

than their parents at fishing in the open sea. Their dark colour – which saves them from attack on land – makes them more visible to fish and makes it difficult for them to surprise their prey. This is why young gulls usually search for food on and around the beach instead.

Passing through

Autumn is the season for migrations. Passage birds such as chats, cuckoos, flycatchers and warblers often spend some days feeding and sheltering on dunes, especially when their departures are delayed by onshore winds or drizzle. Search for them where there is cover, especially around marram grass and bushes.

Berries on east coast dunes are eagerly sought by redwings and fieldfares arriving from Scandinavia. A favourite is sea buckthorn, whose vivid orange berries often persist into winter.

Gull or skua? *Young herring gulls (left) have a mottled brown plumage quite unlike their parents (above), which can make them look more like skuas.*

HOW DO PLANTS SURVIVE ON THE AUTUMN BEACH?

If you walk along the foreshore in autumn you will soon come across a late-developing plant, orache, which grows in a narrow zone along the strandline. Why is it so restricted? Because the orache's seeds are dispersed by sea water: washed away by the out-going tide and swept back on shore as it returns.

On the strandline orache finds a good supply of organic matter from decaying seaweed and just enough fresh water for it to survive. There are several species of orache, but the two best adapted for living on the beach are grass-leaved orache and frosted orache (above right).

Sugar-like coating Frosted orache is silvery white, and reflects the strong light from the sun at the coast. But its triangular or diamond-shaped leaves also reveal another survival attribute: they have a kind of 'frosted' coating, created by waxy scales that help to reduce water loss.

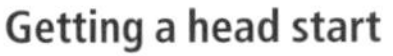

Getting a head start

With the return of cooler weather, moist nights and morning dews, mosses – which have lain dormant throughout the hot dry summer – are much easier to find. In dune hollows they can be the most dominant plants. One prominent moss, especially in lime-rich dunes, is *Camptothecium lutescens*, which has feather-like shoots with a shiny golden sheen. It can grow through a light burial of sand, so helps to stabilise the sand surface.

Look in rabbit scrapes and on sheltered banks and you will almost certainly find many tiny rosettes of young leaves. The seeds produced by annuals such as chickweeds and cresses in the spring are now starting to germinate, but the rosettes will not produce flowers until next spring. By germinating in autumn, the plants are ready to take advantage of the first spells of mild weather in the new year to flower and produce seeds before they succumb to drought or shade from taller dune plants in spring.

Rejuvenated moss The secret of survival for *Camptothecium lutescens,* is that it spends the dry summer shrivelled up, ready to come back to life when wetter weather returns.

A mushroom on the dunes? Sand dunes seem like an unlikely place to find fungi, but several species have adapted to the dry, unstable conditions and are found nowhere else. *Agaricus bernardii*, a relative of the field mushroom, has a thick skin and a long stalk, which is half buried in the sand and is one of the few large fungi that can tolerate salt spray.

Another sand-dweller is the dwarf earthstar, *Geastrum schmidelii*, which is often found in the moss-covered regions of the stabilised sand dunes. The fruiting body begins life below the sand, but as it matures the inner puff-ball structure is thrust upwards as the outer star-like lobes bend backwards. It takes its nutrients from dead vegetation, fruiting when the dunes become more moist in autumn.

In the rubble *Some of Britain's best fossil sites are at the foot of cliffs, such as this one in Lyme Regis (above), particularly where the rock is limestone. You would barely have to hunt to find the huge ammonite on the boulder in the foreground, but ammonites are often only the size of a penny and are found massed together (left).*

Close-up on Fossils

Fossils, our greatest clues to past life forms, lie all around us, even on city streets. Portland limestone, a popular building stone, is formed almost entirely of fossils and shells or is peppered with holes where the shells once were. For novice fossil-hunters, beaches are good places to start, because wave action is constantly breaking open rocks and exposing fresh specimens, but inland you will also find fossils in quarries, natural rock exposures and some caves.

Most fossils represent only the hard parts of an animal, such as bones, teeth and shells, or tough fragments of plants, like seeds or woody stems. The preservation of a plant or animal as a fossil is most likely if its decay is halted by burial in a sediment, such as at the bottom of a lake or ocean. So extinct corals and sea creatures, such as ammonites, are among the most common fossils to find. In contrast, fossils of land-based dinosaurs are rare, not just because the creatures were less numerous, but also because, to be preserved, they would have had to fall into water or be buried quickly by soft sediments.

HUNTING GROUNDS

Fossils are often more resistant to weathering than their surrounding rocks, and so they may protrude slightly from the surface, making them quite easy to find. Fossilised shells can be found lying on a beach as if they had only just been washed ashore, and they are useful as clues to where you might find less common fossils, such as sharks' teeth.

It is usually easier to find fossils by sifting through loose debris below a rock face than by scouring the cliff face itself. The upper part of the beach is equally good, since the sea will have helped to sort the stones into groups of roughly the same size and weight.

Some whole rock formations consist mainly of animal or plant remains. Chalk and flint, for example, are made from the shells of microscopic animals, while coal is derived from the crushed remains of plants, preserved in a swampy environment. Some limestone ridges, such as Wenlock Edge in Shropshire, are the remains of ancient coral reefs. All these rocks are likely to yield fossils.

Tools for the job

Do your homework before going in search of fossils. The map opposite shows the likely areas, but study a geological map, too, to find out what rocks are present and take the right equipment. For hard rocks you will need a geologist's hammer and for softer rocks, a stiff brush may be useful for removing loose dirt. Fossils collected from the coast often contain salt, which can damage the exposed specimen so soak them in fresh water for a day and then rinse them thoroughly.

Always obtain permission from the landowner before collecting fossils. Some sites have restrictions, which should be respected, but in any case, never take more than you need. Try to leave an area as you found it and beware of eroding or undermining cliffs.

HISTORY REVEALED IN THE ROCKS

The fossils found in an area give you clues about what was living on Earth when the rocks were formed. The best fossil sites are where the land was once under water, and may be far from today's coast, such as Dudley in the West Midlands.

Older than 670 million years
Fossils unlikely in rocks this old

670-439 million years old
Fish and crustaceans appear

439-362 million years old
Land plants start to appear

362-290 million years old
Swampy conditions cause plants to fossilise

290-208 million years old
Desert climate led to mass extinction and formation of sandstone. Dinosaurs appear, but few fossils preserved

208-65 million years old
Most of Britain was under water

Younger than 65 million years
Fossils found close to the surface

Igneous rocks
Rocks formed from lava
No fossils

670-439 MILLION YEARS OLD So-named because their skeletons are divided lengthways into three lobes, **trilobites** look like giant wood lice, although they lived in the sea. The round compact ones lived on the sea bottom but the more streamlined, spiny ones could probably swim. They are most common in very old rocks, such as in **north-west Scotland**.

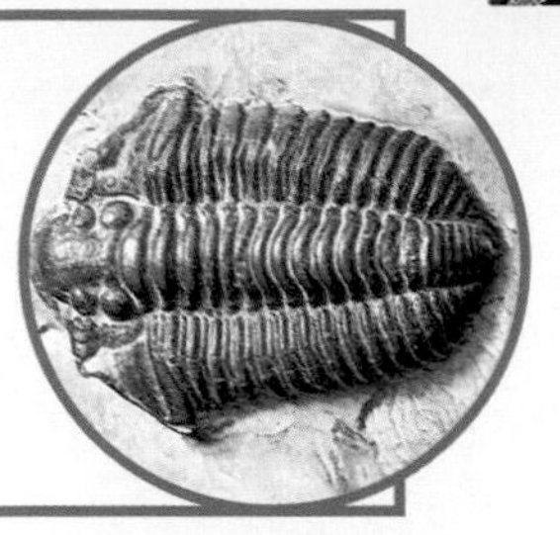

362-290 MILLION YEARS OLD The shape of ancient **corals** varies, but a common one is circular, the size of a 50p piece and looks like a half orange. They are common in limestone rocks, such as in the **Peak District**. When the corals were alive, what is now Britain was beneath a shallow sea in the tropics.

439-362 MILLION YEARS OLD Living **graptolites** were floating, comb-like organisms, about 5cm (2in) long, unlike anything alive today. These delicate fossils look rather like pencil marks, and are best preserved in fine shales and limestones, such as at **Wenlock Edge**. They are important clues, which help scientists to date rocks.

208-65 MILLION YEARS OLD Around ploughed fields in chalky districts, such as in **Northern Ireland**, look for roundish stones slightly smaller than a tennis ball. If five pairs of lines radiate from the centre, you have found a fossil **sea urchin**, very similar to the modern heart urchin.

208-65 MILLION YEARS OLD Dark bullet-shaped fossils are cuttlebones of **belemnites**, squid-like animals related to ammonites (see opposite page). Where you find them, such as on the **South Downs**, look also for shells and corals, for you are probably on an ancient coral reef.

362-290 MILLION YEARS OLD You can occasionally find fossilised **ferns** – or very rarely whole trees – perhaps preserved in a coal seam, such as in **South Wales**, but whole plant fossils are rare. They are normally found in pieces – leaves, branches, cones, bits of bark or just their seeds or stems.

YOUNGER THAN 65 MILLION YEARS Whole fish fossils are quite rare, but look carefully and you might find bony **sharks' teeth** in shales and limestone, such as in bays in **Dorset**. Though small, they are black and shiny, and so stand out. The fish these teeth came from lived in freshwater lakes, and not, as today, in the sea.

An autumn of activity for urban wildlife

Plants and animals prepare for the coming winter shutdown

As the nights become longer than the days there can be no doubt that autumn has arrived. The strident screams of swifts have been replaced by the subdued autumn songs of the robins. Late butterflies bask on walls and fences in the weak sunlight, while flocks of starlings fly in from the countryside in late afternoon and jostle for space in their urban roosts. The entire city landscape is smothered by drifts of dead leaves, and ripe fruit and nuts fall to the ground. For animals, autumn is a time of preparation for winter. Hedgehogs feed up before hibernating, while squirrels bury nuts as an insurance against leaner times. In parks the deer rut is under way – an annual contest between males for mating rights.

Parkland deer

Wild deer are wary animals, but in parks the open landscape offers them few places to hide and allows you a clear view to watch them. The deer are particularly interesting to observe during autumn when the males are in their finest condition, with fully grown antlers, ready to take on their rivals.

Most parkland herds consist either of fallow deer, such as these in Richmond Park in Surrey (above), which were introduced to Britain by the Normans, or of red deer – a native mammal, and the largest of all our deer. The colour of fallow deer varies, from chestnut brown dappled with pale spots to almost black all over. Some specially bred ornamental fallow deer are all white.

Like most deer, adult bucks keep away from the loose groups of fallow does and their young for much of the year. However,

Fallow deer are easy to identify from behind. They have dark tails, the longest tails of all the deer in Britain, which divide the white heart shape on their rump.

during late August or early September, the rutting season begins and things start to change. Loud groans echo around the park: the noisy challenges of bucks, competing for dominance over a patch of ground where they stand the best chance of attracting females to their side. Keep well away from any fighting bucks or you could be seen as just another rival and attacked – in fact, it is best never to get too close to deer.

The autumn harvest

In the countryside, autumn is the proverbial time of mellow fruitfulness, but there is also an autumn harvest in towns and cities. Part of this harvest consists of fruit grown in gardens, such as the apples in this garden in Cardiff, South Wales (above). But for urban wildlife an equally useful food supply comes from the ornamental apple trees which line many city streets.

Some of these trees, such as the Japanese crab apple, have prolific flowers in spring, but their autumn crop consists of apples not much bigger than peas. Other varieties, including the popular John Downie crab apple, have fruit up to the size of a golf ball – large enough to make a substantial meal for birds and insects. This unofficial harvest also includes a wide variety of other fruit, including that of dozens of different varieties of rowans and whitebeams – all common roadside trees – and the berries of firethorns or pyracanthas, which are often grown up garden walls.

As autumn progresses different fruits are eaten in succession. Crab apples and pyracantha berries are very attractive to birds and the fruit soon disappears from these plants. White snowberries are less appealing and their fruit can linger until midwinter.

Grey squirrels are known for hoarding and eating nuts in autumn but they will also make a meal of fallen fruit, which is plentiful in urban gardens.

Across the length and breadth of Britain, garden sheds offer animals a refuge against the cold weather. While gales strip leaves from the trees, and the rain beats down, these mini-habitats stay snug, warm and dry. It is not just the inside of the shed that has sights and clues to offer the detective. Many small animals will make their winter quarters in the space under the floor, or in piles of wood or old flowerpots that have built up outside. Even if you don't spot the creatures themselves, you will often find clues in autumn to who is at home.

Inside the garden shed

Out of harm's way *Many hibernating insects shelter in sheds for winter. Butterflies, such as this small tortoiseshell (left), often lodge in the angle between wall and roof whereas wasps (below) may cling to the roof.*

As winter approaches, many flying insects take refuge in holes in old trees. Wood is an excellent insulator against the worst of the cold, and garden sheds appeal to these creatures for this reason.

Take a close look at your shed's roof. By the time the first frosts make their mark, most of these flying squatters are already well installed and you may see lacewings scattered just above your head. They have slender green or brown bodies and delicate lacy wings which they fold like tents over their bodies.

Most butterflies die with the end of summer, leaving their offspring to survive the winter as eggs or in chrysalises. But the comma, peacock and small tortoiseshell butterflies all overwinter as adults. You will have to look carefully to spot them sheltering in your shed, as their wings are well camouflaged against timber.

A less welcome visitor for most shed-owners is a queen wasp, recognisable by the way she tucks her legs under her wings when she settles. Her priority is to find somewhere to hibernate and there is little risk of her stinging as long as you are content to observe but not disturb. When spring arrives she will fly off to start a new nest.

A permanent abode

Spiders are among the few year-round residents of garden sheds. They don't even have to venture outside to find food, as meals fly in every time the door opens. In sheds, their prey includes midges and other small flies but during the winter, very few insects are on offer. This isn't a problem for the spiders because they can go for weeks, or even months, without food at this time of year, since they are not very active themselves.

The house spider is the most common large species in sheds, where it spins its hammock-like webs in corners. At first glance these webs often seem to be littered with dead spiders, but if you take a closer look you will see that these are actually the owner's empty skins, shed each time it moults.

Q **I've woken up a butterfly – what should I do with it?**

A On mild autumn days butterflies often flap about in sheds if they are disturbed – leave it alone and it should eventually settle down again.

Don't be tempted to usher the butterfly outside because it is unlikely to survive once the weather turns cold again. However, if it gets tangled in a spider's web, as often happens, you will need to take action. Using a thumb and forefinger, gently pick it up by the wings, pull the web away and then put the butterfly in a corner.

ROOM DOWN BELOW

The space under a shed attracts different animals from those you find inside. It is a favourite location for hibernating toads, and for mammals which are active during winter, such as mice, the brown rat, and even foxes if there is room.

Sitting it out In the damp shelter beneath a shed a toad joins the snails for the winter (below). Mice are more difficult to spot, since they are mostly nocturnal, but you might find evidence of them, such as hoards of food (right), inside your shed.

Piles of earth around your shed are a sure sign you have foxes beneath, but they are unlikely to find their way inside. Rats and mice are another matter – if they live under the shed, they will almost certainly have explored the interior as well.

You might find signs of rats and mice during the autumn clear-up: corners nibbled off bags and scattered droppings, for example. Rat droppings are thin oval pellets, about 1cm (⅜in) long, while mouse droppings are smaller.

If you keep finding fresh droppings it is a sign that these rodents have taken up winter residence inside the shed rather than under it – their usual choice. Other evidence, such as piles of torn-up paper or shredded foam from the padding of garden chairs tell you that they have nested in the shed. By October, nests are empty, but their former occupants are unlikely to be far away.

Safe shelter *Many creatures, such as slow-worms use compost heaps as winter hideaways. You might also find hedgehogs and hibernating ladybirds in the pile.*

HOLD YOUR FIRE

No matter how big your garden shed, some things always seem to end up on the ground outside. Pieces of wood, cracked flowerpots and empty seed trays attract wildlife by providing a refuge for the winter months.

Snails often commandeer flowerpots, while upside-down seed trays make a useful roof for moths which are dormant in the winter. But for most animals, the biggest attractions are piles of old branches and prunings.

However, this is exactly the kind of refuse that often gets burned or thrown away in autumn so if you are planning a bonfire, spare a thought for the hedgehogs and other creatures which may be hiding there.

Rather than disturb them, it is better to leave your piles of prunings alone until spring. If you must have a bonfire, move the wood before setting it alight, then you can spot any sheltering animals and put them safely aside. They will move off to find somewhere else to hibernate.

IDENTITY PARADE – Mice

Three species of mouse are commonly found in garden sheds. The house mouse and wood mouse live all over the British Isles, but you will only find the yellow-necked mouse south of a line from Merseyside to The Wash.

House mouse Bags and old boxes make homes for house mice, which nest above ground. Their fur is grey-brown on top and slighter lighter below, and they have a pinkish tail.

Wood mouse Wood mice like to burrow. They have bigger ears than house mice, and are white on their underside. Their tail is black on top and white below.

Yellow-necked mouse This mouse has a white underside and a yellow band between its front legs. Like wood mice, the yellow-necked mouse often carries away food from where it finds it, to eat it later under cover.

Going into hiding

By October, most of Britain's swallows have already flown south, leaving the resident creatures behind, preparing to face the most testing time of the year. Many of these creatures – including birds, foxes and rodents – remain active throughout winter, living on whatever food they find, but others hibernate, shutting down altogether until the arrival of spring. Both survival techniques require careful preparation and autumn offers a chance to watch creatures making ready as winter draws near.

Survival strategy *Most predators will overlook an inconspicuous chrysalis, such as those of the elephant hawk moth (above), hidden in the leaf litter, or of the large white butterflies (right) on the bark of a tree.*

Even as late as November, you can spot hover flies and other insects visiting the last garden flowers. If you approach them, you will find that these late fliers are slow and sluggish – it's quite easy to catch one in your hand.

The reason for this grogginess is that insects are cold-blooded. When the outside temperature falls, their body temperature drops as well, until their muscles can hardly work. The exceptions are insects such as moths, which have bodies that are insulated by furry-looking scales. Moths use their muscles as heaters, shivering to warm themselves up until they are ready to fly. Some bumblebees can warm themselves up by generating heat chemically, as well as through muscular activity.

Bedding down

You will rarely see insects after autumn, since most die with the first frosts. By this time their work of reproducing has been done and their young spend the winter in an inactive state, as eggs or in chrysalises.

A few insects overwinter as adults; many shelter indoors, but some go underground. If you pull up any old plants in autumn, look out for aphids near their roots. Tucked away in the soil, these will often survive through into spring.

PREPARING FOR SHUT-DOWN

In Britain's temperate climate, many mammals can be seen out and about in even the coldest months. They may become less active, but if you know where and when to look, you still have a good chance of seeing them, or the signs they leave behind.

In autumn, suddenly squirrels seem to be everywhere. During the summer they find all they need in the trees but at this time of year squirrels come out into the open. They are busy all day in parks and gardens collecting nuts and acorns, which they bury in the ground. Once winter sets in, they will emerge for just a few hours each day to feed on these hidden stores.

Out of sight

Hedgehogs and dormice disappear completely in late autumn. During hibernation, their body processes slow down almost to a standstill, and their temperatures fall so low as to be only a few degrees above their surroundings. This state is more than just a deep sleep. A hibernating hedgehog's heart beats only 20 times a minute – one

Q **How do animals know when to hibernate?**

A Falling temperatures, declining food supplies and changing day length all tell animals that winter is approaching – although day length is not an issue for nocturnal creatures, such as hedgehogs. These signals encourage hibernators to gorge on food, so that they build up a store of body fat: fuel that will keep them alive throughout the winter months.

The changing length of days also helps to keep animals that do not hibernate in step with the seasons. But in towns and cities, where streetlights give off a lot of artificial light this natural timekeeping system may go awry. This is why you sometimes hear city birds singing in winter, and it is also why trees near streetlights tend to keep their leaves longer than ones in unlit parks.

Opportunist feeder *Urban squirrels will take food where they find it, but make their own stores of buried nuts, too.*

Stocking up *A common dormouse gorges on hawthorn (left) before hibernating. Then, like the fat, or edible dormouse (inset), it will live off its fat deposits.*

tenth of the rate when it is fully active. Unlike a sleeping animal, a hibernating one cannot wake up in a hurry, even if its life is in danger. This is why hibernating animals take care to hide themselves away and why they are rarely seen.

Winter quarters for bats

Bats are also preparing for hibernation, but because they feed on flying insects, they can find food only in fine weather. On mild afternoons well into November you may spot our smallest bat, the pipistrelle, hunting late-flying insects.

Bats hibernate in a variety of places, including tree holes, caves, attics and cellars – sometimes in groups. Pipistrelles normally choose outbuildings or trees, but bats wake easily and often, and if they get too cold they may come indoors.

If you accidentally disturb a hibernating pipistrelle it may fall to the ground, as if dead: until it has warmed up, it cannot move.

MARATHON SLEEPERS

The common dormouse beds down from the end of October onwards and does not usually reappear until April, roughly six months later. Dormice live only in southern Britain, where they are busy in autumn, feeding up on beech mast and hazelnuts.

Dormice make ball-shaped nests of leaves, moss and the stems of climbing plants in hedgerows or undergrowth, at or just below ground level.

If you think you have found an occupied nest, or if your dog sniffs one out on a walk, always resist the temptation to look inside and disturb the occupant. If a dormouse is aroused from hibernation – for example, by having its nest opened up – it runs the risk of starvation later on in winter.

Roman delicacy

The common dormouse is not the only dormouse that lives in Britain. In 1902, the fat, or edible dormouse was introduced from the Continent. With its thick grey fur and bushy tail it looks very much like a squirrel, although it is only about half the squirrel's size.

Edible dormice get their name from the habit, in Roman times, of rearing them in captivity for the pot. They are common in parts of mainland Europe and can be a nuisance where they raid gardens and outhouses for fruit.

In England, edible dormice are found only in the Chilterns, where the survivors of the original Edwardian immigrants live in woods and also in people's houses.

CREATING A WILDLIFE HAVEN Not all creatures hibernate for winter, and there are many things you can do to make your garden a haven for them in the cold weather and harsh times. Resist the temptation to tidy up all the fallen leaves, as they offer shelter and warmth to insects such as beetles, and slugs and snails. Leave **seed heads** on plants after their flowers have finished as they will provide food for birds such as this **goldfinch** (below) and try growing winter-flowering varieties of honeysuckle and other shrubs, and early flowering bulbs, such as snowdrops, to attract insects. Collect windfalls from fruit trees and store them in your shed or garage to put out through the winter and always choose plants with red berries over varieties with more unusual colours. Birds know that a berry is ripe by its colour, and red is the most familiar signal.

Close-up on
Urban hedgehogs

The hedgehog is one of Britain's best-loved mammals. Its prickly coat and portly profile make it instantly recognisable as it explores gardens and hedgerows in search of food. Hedgehogs naturally live in broad-leaved woodland, hedgerows and pasture, three habitats that have all diminished in area in the past 50 years, but they thrive in towns and cities and are increasingly animals of suburban parks and gardens as much as the open countryside. Urban areas suit them because shrubberies, lawns and flower borders mimic conditions along woodland edges, providing places to hide close to open spaces where they can forage for food.

Scaling heights Despite their tubby frame, hedgehogs are quite agile: garden fences present no problem to them and they are also capable of climbing trees. Coming down is not so easy but a hedgehog's spines help to cushion it if it falls. Hedgehogs can cover more than a mile in their nightly search for food – although males travel farther than females – visiting a dozen or more different gardens.

PATTERN OF LIFE

Hedgehogs make daytime nests in grass, covered with leaves, quite separate from the nest, or hibernaculum, where they will spend the winter (see opposite page). An adult male will use the same daytime nest for a few days then move to another one, sometimes returning to an old nest later.

Even in winter, though, you might see a hedgehog on the move. During its six-month hibernation a hedgehog may wake up several times, and it will usually move to a new hibernaculum at least once.

Hedgehogs start mating in May and the female gives birth to one or sometimes two litters a year. There will normally be between four and six young. The 'hoglets' are born – blind and without spines – usually from early June onwards, but are weaned, and ready to leave the nest within six weeks. For young hedgehogs, feeding is the first priority. To survive hibernation, they must weigh at least 450g (1lb) by autumn, and late litters might struggle to reach this target in time.

The search for food

Hedgehogs are nocturnal and hunt in the dark, so find their food mainly by smell. Beetles, earthworms and caterpillars make up most of their diet, along with slugs, snails and carrion. Hedgehogs will also occasionally take the eggs and chicks of ground nesting birds. They have devastated the population of dunlins in the Hebrides by preying on their eggs but eggs do not form a significant proportion of their regular food.

If you find a young undersized hedgehog in your garden in November, it stands little chance of surviving the winter, even if it looks healthy. You can improve its chances by putting it in a box with some hay or old newspapers to keep it warm, and feeding it indoors.

Bread and milk, though the traditional offering, is not the best diet for hedgehogs. They are carnivorous creatures and, what's more, cow's milk will probably give them diarrhoea.

Tinned cat or dog food is a far better choice, and if you are feeding up an undersized hoglet for hibernation, add some unsweetened fibrous cereal as well.

Q **I found a hedgehog foaming at the mouth. Was it ill?**

A Surprisingly, it was not. It was probably 'self-anointing', a curious habit that is not fully understood. The hedgehog covers its spines with frothy saliva, and then leaves them to dry. One theory is that this helps to deter predators; another is that it deters parasites. Hedgehogs are notorious for being infested with fleas, but in fact they have no more than a similar-sized rabbit and, despite their spines, can groom themselves surprisingly well.

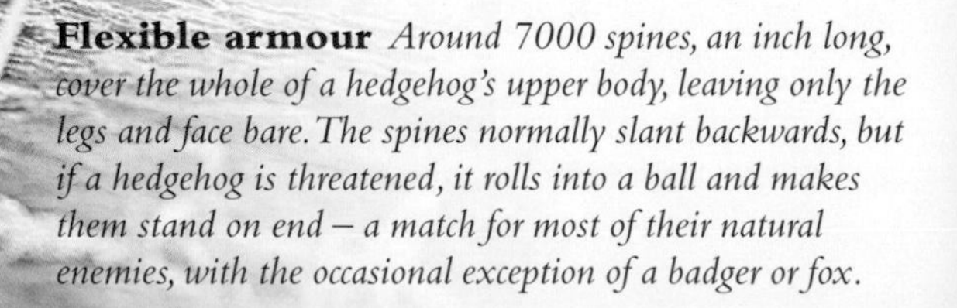

Flexible armour *Around 7000 spines, an inch long, cover the whole of a hedgehog's upper body, leaving only the legs and face bare. The spines normally slant backwards, but if a hedgehog is threatened, it rolls into a ball and makes them stand on end – a match for most of their natural enemies, with the occasional exception of a badger or fox.*

Water hog Hedgehogs are excellent swimmers, but many drown in garden ponds and swimming pools because they cannot haul themselves up a vertical edge out of the water. To make ponds less lethal, give them a gently sloping edge and for swimming pools, some chicken wire nailed to a frame makes a lifesaving ramp.

WINTER QUARTERS Hedgehogs build winter nests under garden sheds, piles of wood and prunings or in rabbit holes. Once it has chosen its spot, a hedgehog makes a **hibernaculum** from dead leaves, grass and twigs, then settles down for the winter. You can make a box (right) or buy one to encourage hedgehogs to hibernate in your garden.

SURVEILLANCE TIPS

Hedgehogs are rewarding subjects for the countryside detective because, compared with most of our native mammals, they are remarkably untroubled by being watched. Unless you actually touch a hedgehog, it is likely to wander nonchalantly away from you without much noticeable change of speed, confident in its spiny protective coat.

If you think you have a hedgehog in your garden, the best time to look for it is at dusk, when it will come out into the open to search for food. Hedgehogs are creatures of habit and tend to follow the same route at the same time each night, so if you spot a hedgehog once, you can be ready for it the next day.

The click of turning on a torch or a light in the house can send it scuttling away in alarm, so be in place in plenty of time. Hedgehogs seem less sensitive to red light than white, so try taping some clear red plastic over your torch.

The best time to see young hedgehogs is from the end of June onwards, when females start escorting their families on night-time forays for food. The party usually sets off after dark, but if you are around in early morning, you may see them trooping back to the nest in single file, the young shepherded by their mother.

LOOKING FOR CLUES Most people discover they have a hedgehog when it walks past an outside light, or across the road. In gardens, noisy foraging and snorting calls also help to give hedgehogs away, particularly during the courtship season in spring, but even if you don't see or hear these nocturnal visitors, you can find telltale clues that reveal where they have been.

The most obvious signs are hedgehog **droppings** (right), which are black, sausage-shaped and shiny, and up to the size of your little finger. If you look at them closely, you will probably be able to make out the wing-cases of beetles.

Other clues to watch for are meandering trails through wet grass, where the hedgehog has followed its nose like a dog, looking for food. In wet mud, or after a fall of snow, look for their **tracks** (left) – like tiny hand prints.

Autumn spiders and their webs

Spiders' webs are as distinctive as fingerprints, and there is no better time to investigate them and to learn to identify the maker than early on a cool autumn morning, when droplets of dew cling to the silk like jewels. Having fed all summer long, many spiders are now at their maximum size, and their webs – also as big as they get – are strung out over supports of all kinds, from grass blades to window frames. Some build disc-shaped webs, known as orb webs, others weave their silk into sheets, and a few species build no webs at all.

The glistening of sunlight on dew is not the only reason why morning is the best time for looking at webs. Orb webs are damaged by struggling insects and by rain as the day progresses and are rewoven by the spider every day around dawn. If you are in the garden this early you may see a spider at work.

Return to the web when the air has warmed up and insects are on the wing and you may see a victim caught in its sticky mesh. Some spiders hang on their webs, but more often they lurk out of sight. If you gently tickle a web with a piece of grass, imitating the struggles of a trapped insect, you may bring the owner out of hiding.

Britain's biggest orb-web spider is the garden spider, whose natural habitat is actually gorse-covered heath and woodland. In autumn the white cross-shaped markings on the spider's back are very clear, showing the origin of its two alternative names – the garden cross or diadem spider.

Watch the weaving process

Garden spiders take only about an hour to make their webs, so if you have the time to spare you can witness the entire process. The foundation of a web is a horizontal strand stretched between two supports. Once this is in place, the spider will hang a loop of silk beneath

Traps set *The garden spider waits for prey in the middle of its web (left) while a spider belonging to the genus* Zygiella *only comes out onto the web when something is caught (inset right): you can recognise the webs of spiders in this group – they have a gap occupied by a thicker strand of silk (below), which leads to the spider's lair.*

Heavily pregnant *In September, female orb-web spiders are swollen with eggs (left) but by late October they will all have disappeared. Once they have laid their eggs – protected by a layer of yellow silk – in out of the way places, such as this gate catch (above), they die.*

it, and then pull the loop down to make a 'Y'. The fork becomes the centre of the web and once more spokes have been added the spider fills in with spirals.

Look closely and you will discover that this part of the operation is more complex than it seems. First, the spider builds a temporary spiral of dry silk, working its way outwards from the middle. Once this spiral is complete it backtracks, eating the original silk and replacing it with a much finer spiral of sticky silk as it goes.

Dozens of spiders make their webs in gardens, and on the outside of walls and windows. Not all build orb webs, like the garden spider; some weave sheet webs, like domes or hammocks.

The money spider weaves domed sheet webs in bushes and hedges. Unlike orb webs, these are haphazard and untidy, and the spiders patch them instead of weaving new ones. If you touch a money spider's web you will find that it is not sticky. Instead, prey gets tangled in the mass of strands and the spider catches it before it escapes.

Body language *Spiders and harvestmen may look alike, but they are easy to tell apart. If the creature has a pear-shaped body, it is a harvestman (left); if it has a 'waist', or a segmented body, it is a spider. Harvestmen don't make silk, and rarely come into houses but are closely related to spiders, as you can tell by their eight legs.*

Q **Do spiders come up the plughole?**

A No, they don't, because spiders cannot get through the water trapped in the waste pipe's U-bend. If you find a spider in a bath, it will have fallen in from above. Once there, it is trapped by the bath's slippery sides. If you lay a towel over the edge of the bath, the spider will climb up it and run away.

SPIDERS IN THE HOUSE

No matter how regularly you do the housework, cobwebs never seem to go away. This is because as soon as you brush away a spider's web it sets about making another one in its place.

House spiders build webs shaped like hammocks in out-of-the-way places, such as dark corners in garages and cellars. They have a legspan of up to 6cm (2½in) – the females can be even larger – but are quite harmless.

These spiders are mainly active at night and on autumn evenings the males may cause panic as they scuttle across floors in search of a mate – it is these that often fall into the bath. Once a male house spider has mated, he remains with his partner for several weeks until he dies – providing her with a meal. The female then hides with her egg sac until the spiderlings disperse in spring.

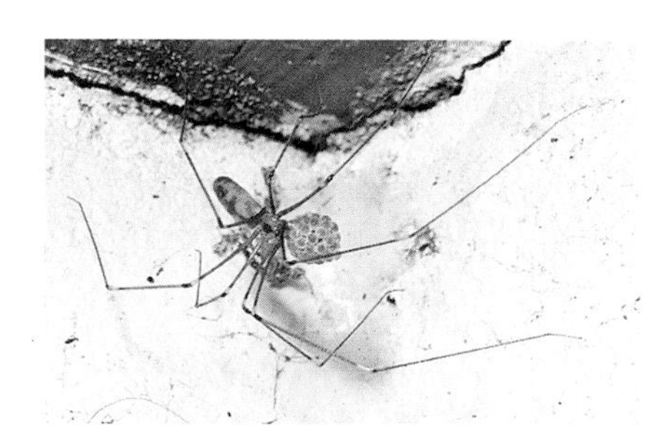

A clutch of eggs *Daddy longlegs spiders, or rafter spiders, always live indoors. The females are easy to identify in autumn because they hold their eggs in their jaws, like a bunch of tiny grapes.*

Shoe lair *The inside of an old shoe is a perfect quiet spot for a house spider to weave its web. This one has trapped a passing wood louse.*

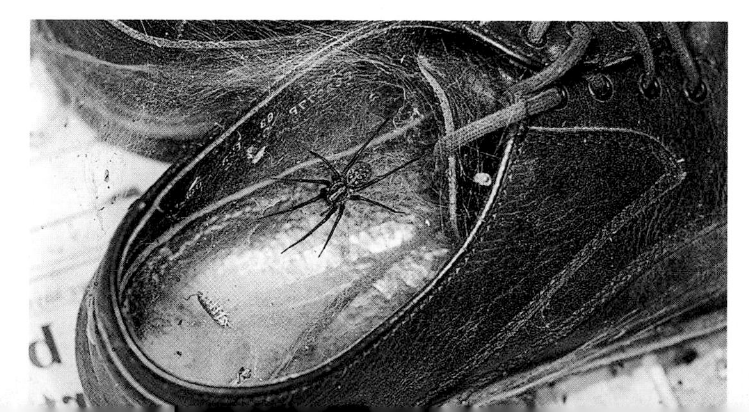

Flowers and fruitfulness

As the sun weakens, plant growth slows and nature's food supply begins to decline. But as long as the frost holds off, animals have time for one final feast. There are two courses on offer: ripening fruit and nectar from late flowers, with gardens and wasteland offering generous helpings of both. As you watch this end-of-season banquet, you can see how some animals earn their food by helping plants to spread, while others simply burrow into the things that they eat.

The flesh of soft fruit is merely a wrapper surrounding the seeds. Making this wrapper is an energy-intensive business for a plant, but it ensures the seeds are dispersed. When an animal eats a fruit the flesh is digested, but the seeds pass through in droppings, some distance from the parent plant, where they may have a better chance of germinating.

Look along fences and walls in towns, or on the roofs of cars parked under trees and you will often see bird droppings that are blue-black, not white. This is a sign that birds have been feeding on elderberries. If the ground underneath is damp, you may find elder saplings, growing from the seeds.

Fruit and berries change colour as they ripen – a signal to hungry animals and humans that the fruit is ready to eat and the seeds are mature. If you have autumn raspberries in your garden, have a close look at those that have been pecked by blackbirds. You will find that the deep red raspberries have attracted most attention; pale under-ripe ones are ignored.

Having a feast *Blackbirds cannot resist fallen apples, particularly when frozen ground makes worms inaccessible. They chisel out the juicy flesh, leaving the hollowed out skin.*

Given a head start *Birds often peck at fruit on the tree, and a wasp might enlarge the peck mark to reach the flesh inside.*

UNEXPECTED WINDFALLS

As autumn wears on and gales become more common, fruit often tumbles to the ground. These windfalls include apples, pears and plums in gardens and also ornamental wild fruits, such as crab apples, which are often planted in streets. Crab apples are small and rubbery, with a sour taste quite unlike cultivated eating apples.

Fallen fruit makes a welcome meal for animals that cannot climb. If you examine the remains of apples scattered under a tree, you can often work out what has eaten them. Foxes and badgers chew the fruit as they feed, often dropping pieces on the ground. Muntjac deer, which are increasingly common in gardens in East Anglia and central southern England, do the same. Mice are much tidier eaters: where they have been at work, you should be able to pick out teeth marks in the skin, as well as narrow gouges in the apple's flesh. They also eat the seeds as well as the pulp.

If you leave fallen fruit on the ground you may find that your garden is invaded by wasps. They are attracted to the decaying fruit because it is packed with sugar – just the food they need as the days shorten and grow cold. They track down food by its smell, which is why they buzz to and fro before settling down to eat. Queen wasps go into hibernation in early autumn, so if you see wasps in the garden after this, they will be workers.

Late lunch *Small tortoiseshells feed at Michaelmas daisies (above) and red admirals on rotting fruit (right) – the last food of the year.*

AUTUMN BUTTERFLIES

During the autumn, butterflies converge on rapidly waning supplies of food. If you have late-flowering plants or fallen fruit in your garden, watch for these autumn stragglers as they eat and bask in the fading warmth of the sun.

Michaelmas daisies, buddlejas, ice plants (sedums) and strawberry trees are particularly good for attracting butterflies because they produce nectar when most other garden flowers have finished for the year.

Small tortoiseshell butterflies overwinter as adults, and they must stock up with food before hibernating. Many of them will look as fresh and bright as in spring. This is because they are from the year's second brood and have only been on the wing since mid October.

Red admirals fly south in autumn – a few even make it across the Channel. Most of them eventually hibernate, but in Britain only a few will survive until spring because they hibernate in the open and are vulnerable to winter weather.

AT HOME INSIDE FRUIT For young insects fruits offer both protection and a supply of food. You need a keen eye to spot insects laying their eggs in early autumn but their grubs are easier to detect. If you find an apple or pear with a hole in the skin and a tunnel to its core, it is likely to have hosted the **caterpillar of a codling moth** (right). The caterpillar develops inside the fruit before crawling out in August or September to pupate under the bark of the tree.

A swollen pear that has fallen before it is ripe is a sign of the pear midge. If you cut open an affected pear before it drops, you will find the midge's yellowish white grubs.

Raspberry beetles often go unnoticed until the white grubs crawl out from a pile of picked fruit. Left on the bush, they eventually wriggle out of the fruit and complete their development in the soil, pupating in underground cells.

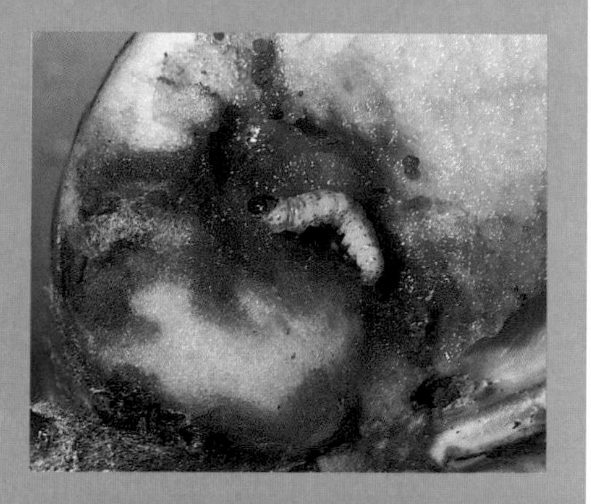

Close-up on
Traffic victims

Every year, millions of wild animals are killed as they cross the road. Some of these deaths occur when creatures scared by something in the undergrowth dash into the path of an oncoming vehicle, but most happen because animals have no road sense and misjudge the traffic. Unfortunate though these accidents are, they reveal a lot about the wildlife living in an area and by noting when and where an accident happened you can often piece together the story behind a life lost on the road.

Apart from the innumerable insects written off on windscreens and headlights, huge numbers of amphibians, birds and mammals also end up as traffic victims – even if you have never seen a living hedgehog, fox or badger, you will probably have spotted a dead one beside the road.

Peak periods for casualties

If you regularly drive along a route you'll notice that the road toll varies during the day, and during the year. Recently hit bodies are most common in the morning, because most of our wild mammals are nocturnal, and so are hit at night. The number of squashed hedgehogs rises in April: a clear sign that hibernation has ended and spring is under way. Six months on, autumn sees another high casualty rate among the new generation of badgers and foxes. You may be able to identify these vulnerable young animals – which have little experience of traffic – by their size, but by late autumn most are fully grown.

On the sidelines Look along the verge for accident victims, such as this fox, lying where they have been thrown clear of the traffic or have crept to die. These victims are easier to identify than ones squashed flat on the road.

CROSS WITH CARE

Some stretches of road see many more animal casualties than others. If you study these accident black spots as you drive through them, you can sometimes work out why they claim so many lives.

A wooded verge can obscure the road, encouraging animals to stray onto its surface, while a gap in a fence will channel creatures straight out onto the road. Cuttings are also problem areas, because birds often fly straight across between trees and, if they are low enough, will fly unwittingly into the path of the traffic. But some black spots occur in places where a road cuts across a traditional migration or foraging route.

This is a particular problem for toads in early spring, when they cross roads to reach their mating ponds. Badgers follow set routes when they feed – even if it means stepping out in front of traffic.

One sign that a stretch of road is particularly hazardous to wildlife is the presence of warning signs, or tunnels (see page 94), which allow animals to cross the road in safety.

The silver lining *The first sign of a dead animal ahead is often the hunched shape of a scavenging bird – usually a member of the crow family, like this magpie – on the road.*

The quick and the dead *Despite its white markings, you might not see a badger dash across the road at night, perhaps because it is so squat. A spot of blood on its head is the only visible evidence that the robin was hit by a car.*

PERILS OF ROADSIDE LIVING FOR BIRDS

If you watch a crow at its unsavoury work of feeding on a roadside corpse, you'll see that it flies up in front of a car only at the last minute. Inevitably, a crow will occasionally misjudge the traffic and end up a victim itself.

If you come across a corpse that looks intact, be prepared for a gruesome discovery. Crows and their fellow scavengers, magpies and rooks, all lack the special adaptations that birds of prey have for dealing with this kind of food. They have no trouble feeding if the victim's body is squashed, but find it difficult to peck their way through skin so you may find that they have eaten the only accessible part – the eyes.

The buzzard, a bigger but much less common roadside scavenger, can tear through skin with its hooked beak and will often carry a carcass away in its feet.

Although they risk getting hit themselves, all these scavengers make an effective clean-up squad preventing our roads from being littered with animal remains.

Low-flying birds

When a blackbird flies in front of your car at windscreen-height it seems reckless. But blackbirds have little choice since low-level flight is part of their instinctive behaviour. Being ground-feeders, they naturally keep low, sweeping upwards at the last moment as they land in trees and bushes.

If you examine birds that have been hit by cars, you will find that several other species are also vulnerable to low-level collisions, including sparrows, wrens and robins.

Like blackbirds, robins fly up to a perch from underneath, but this is a dangerous strategy if it includes flying across a road. The corpses of small birds are usually completely flattened by traffic but distinctively coloured feathers – from the robin's red breast, for example – will help you to make a post-mortem identification.

Much larger birds also get squashed. Flattened pheasants are a common sight in areas where they are raised for the shooting season. Barn owls are also vulnerable as they hunt at head-height along grassy verges, putting themselves in grave danger the moment they stray over the road.

Pigeons often suffer for their habit of standing in the road. They do this because in the morning the tarmac is warmer than the surroundings, but also because they need grit in their diet to grind up their food and roads are often the best source.

ACCIDENT BLACK SPOTS Where accidents are common, some simple pieces of equipment can help to reduce the death toll. **Reflective posts [1]** reflect light from the headlamps of passing cars into woods at night to deter deer from venturing onto the road. Where squirrels are often killed on a road separating two parts of a wood, a **rope bridge [2]** slung high above the traffic – and 'baited' by putting a feeding station at one end – provides a safer crossing.

But traffic is not the only hazard – cattle grids are lethal traps for small animals because their bars are far enough apart to let wandering hedgehogs and other creatures fall through, but the sides too steep to allow them to escape. Some cattle grids have a sloping ramp so that trapped animals can climb out, but if you cross a grid on foot, look down to make sure that nothing is struggling to get out.

The quest for food and shelter never ceases

Even in the dead of winter there is still plenty to investigate

Winter in the grasslands can seem bleak and desolate, with little to investigate. But a snow-covered landscape holds many clues. Footprints, especially, show up well. Try to identify them, so you know which animals are out and about.

The winter sun is rarely strong enough to melt all the snow, but some of its warmth will filter through the top few centimetres. Gradually the ground beneath warms up, melting the snow at the very bottom. Push your hand carefully down and you will find a narrow airspace just above the earth. Here you may find plants that have thawed out. These can offer a handy meal, so watch out for rabbits and deer scraping away the snow to graze on the exposed vegetation.

Clues in the snow

In the harsh winter scenery of Swaledale in Yorkshire (above), the shape of a farm is clearly outlined, with stone walls, buildings, hedges and spinneys standing out boldly against the contrast of the snow-covered fields. The low rays of the winter sun falling on frosted fields may reveal clues to past farming activities by highlighting the foundations of old field boundaries or evidence of the way land was once worked.

Early morning and evening are the best times to watch the fields for animals venturing into the open to feed, as they are less likely to be disturbed by human activities at these times. Use binoculars to scan the snow-covered landscape for hares, rabbits, pheasants and partridges, and to examine the bare branches of trees and hedgerows for perching birds.

Sheep, such as these Swaledale ewes (left), are hardy animals. Their thick coats and ability to live on scant grazing allow them to remain in the fields all winter.

You may be lucky enough to catch a glimpse of a stoat or weasel running along a stone wall, or a fox trotting across a field. However, you are more likely to come across their pawprints, and those of other mammals, especially by gaps in walls and near gateways. Look too for places where the ground is clear of snow or where fodder has been put out for farm animals, because birds will gather there to feed.

Refuge at the farm

Farms in the milder southern counties, like this one in Wiltshire (above), are criss-crossed by trim hedges and fences. Here many of the old sheep-grazed grasslands have been replaced with plantings of winter cereals. Generally they are not good places for watching wildlife, although the crops will attract some animals.

Large flocks of birds regularly show up on the wide fields. Fieldfares, gulls, jackdaws, lapwings and rooks are frequent visitors. And you are highly likely to see wood pigeons and, in some areas, geese and swans, descending in their thousands to feast on any tender, young shoots – much to the distress of farmers.

A better place to observe wildlife is around the farm buildings, where there are often old grassy paddocks and clumps of trees offering refuge. You should be able to spot a variety of birds visiting the farmyard: seed-eating sparrows, finches and buntings come to feed on spilt grain, and insect-eaters, such as wagtails, attracted by flies that swarm around the warm, steaming dung.

Even stark modern barns are a source of food and shelter for some animals, especially rats and mice, and these, in turn, attract owls and other predators.

Cattle are often kept indoors for the winter. This is because, on muddy ground especially, their heavy bodies can churn up the earth, ruining good pasture.

Running for cover

When the leaves have fallen and growth has died down, the chance of spotting small mammals or clues to where they live increases. Early winter is a good time to seek them out, when populations are still high after breeding and before food shortages lead to many deaths. Keep watch near rough verges and hedgerows where there is still some cover and perhaps a few seeds and berries to eat, as well as insects and other small prey. Remember to look up, too: squirrels are very visible on bare branches. And on not-so-chilly evenings, if there are enough insects about, you may see the odd bat.

After a good breeding season, field voles – sometimes called short-tailed voles – can be quite common. You may even see one scurrying through the long grass at your feet in rough pasture, or on verges and dunes, although you are unlikely to get more than a fleeting glance as one dashes by.

If you can't detect the actual animal, look for clues to where it has been. Find a patch of thick, matted grass and tease it apart. You may uncover voles' runways, some leading to a nest with bits of nibbled grass inside.

You might also find piles of olive-green droppings – about 5mm (¼in) long with rounded ends – along the runways. It is likely that bits of chopped grass will have been scattered over these droppings and possibly around the runway entrances.

It is always worth lifting any sheet of corrugated iron, log or plank you come across, because voles also build nests under such shelters, and you may discover one underneath. If you do this quickly and sharply, you might even spot the vole itself before it disappears. Always remember to replace carefully anything you move so that the animal and its home are not damaged.

Field voles have many predators, including foxes, stoats, weasels, buzzards, harriers and kestrels, and barn, tawny, and long and short-eared owls. It has been estimated that nearly a million field voles are killed and eaten every year in Britain, making them a sort of furry sausage for other wildlife.

But intensive cropping and tidying-up of the countryside have led to the loss of large areas of the dense, undisturbed grassland that field voles love. Consequently the field vole population has dropped, and some of its predators have suffered from food shortages as a result.

WHO'S BEEN DINING HERE?

Other common mammals are more elusive than the field vole. Hedgehogs, for instance, hibernate in winter, although you may find their droppings (see page 271) – proof that they do emerge for short periods if it is warm enough. Wood and yellow-necked mice do not hibernate but only come out at night, and shrews tend to stay under cover in thick grass.

Try looking in the hedges for signs of where animals have been feeding. If there are hazels in the area, search for empty nut shells and examine them. Neat holes in the shells

Hunter and hunted *Keeping a low profile in long, dense grass will not protect a field vole (left) from such a fierce and fast-moving predator as the stoat (top left). Stoats hunt by scent and have no trouble sniffing out prey. Voles have many predators, but are fast breeders and can quickly re-establish themselves in an area.*

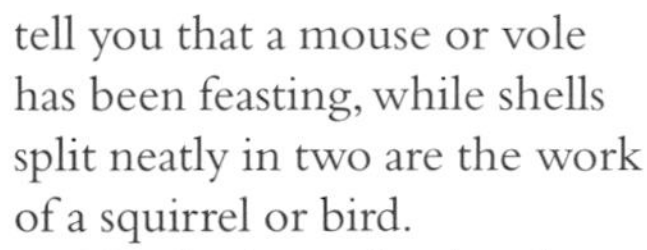

tell you that a mouse or vole has been feasting, while shells split neatly in two are the work of a squirrel or bird.

Wood mice and voles also use old, abandoned birds' nests as feeding platforms, so if you come across one, look inside – you may find the remains of a berry feast. Wood mice eat the seeds of hips, haws, blackberries and elderberries and leave the flesh behind, while voles eat only the flesh, leaving the seeds.

Old bird nests may also contain the remains of snails that have been eaten by mice. Look for toothmarks on the central pillar of the broken snail shell.

UNDIGESTED CLUES

Another way of discovering which small mammals live in the neighbourhood is to search for owl pellets, so you can take a good look at what they contain (see page 299). The best places to track them down are under nests and favourite roost sites. The barn owl's are the easiest to find, since they are deposited in old barns and sheds, where they are also likely to lie intact.

Pellets can be carefully broken open on the spot, although it is probably a better idea to take them home to examine. Soaking them in soapy water will help loosen the fur, making it much easier to tease out any bones.

You may find the skull of a small mammal, or occasionally of a bird, inside. If you do find a mammal's skull, take a close look at the teeth. A small gap – the diastema – between the front teeth and the cheek teeth will tell you that the skull belonged to a rodent – a mouse, rat or vole. If you have found a narrow skull, with no diastema, and all the teeth have sharp reddish points or cusps, you are looking at the skull of a shrew.

Dinner and after *The barn owl on the right will swallow its prey – a vole – whole, but cannot digest the fur or bones, which are regurgitated as pellets (right). Identifying what you find in owl pellets will tell you what animals are around.*

Blooming early Towards the end of winter, pinpoints of colour among the withered remains of last year's growth tell you that spring is not far away. Some plants that normally bloom in spring produce a few earlier flowers that will attract visits from similarly early insects, particularly flies and bees. Chickweed **[1]** and shepherd's purse **[2]**, for example, germinate in autumn, then overwinter in a dormant state, but they will burst into flower if there is a warm, wet day as winter moves towards spring. Coltsfoot, too, often provides patches of brilliant colour at this time of year.

Old homes on view

Nests, abandoned once the business of breeding and rearing the young is over, are now clearly visible, silhouetted against the winter sky. Identifying the builders of these nests can tell you which birds live in an area, at a time of year when you might be less likely to see the birds themselves. The most rewarding time to look for old nests is in early winter, before they are wrecked by wind and rain, and when you can be certain that they are no longer in use.

Many birds, such as blackbirds and collared doves, produce several clutches of eggs a year, building a new nest for each clutch. This means that even an area with only a few birds can hold a surprising number of nests. And don't just hunt for nests that are easy to spot. Take the time to search out those that are more difficult to locate.

Robins and wrens are noted for building their nests in places where they are likely to remain well hidden. This is why you often find them among the dense, evergreen foliage of ivy, or tucked into a crevice or hole between the roots of a large tree.

Also, take a careful look over any old, abandoned tractor or other discarded farm machinery you happen to come across. Robins are famous for building nests on such items, and you might discover one tucked into some nook or cranny.

Who lived here?

You will have no difficulty distinguishing a wren's nest from a robin's – a wren builds a ball-shaped nest, while the robin's nest is cup-shaped. But many similarly shaped nests, found in the same area, are easily confused (see right).

Usually what a nest is made of tells you which bird made it. But sometimes a nest contains the remains of dead nestlings or addled eggs, and these may offer you more clues to the nest-builders' identity.

SPOT THE DIFFERENCE

Song thrush or blackbird?
Blackbirds and song thrushes make similar, solid-looking nests of grass, leaves, twigs and mud. The best way to tell them apart is by taking a careful look at the way they have been lined. A song thrush will give its nest a smooth mud lining (left), while a blackbird lines its nest with leaves and chopped up pieces of fine grass.

Chaffinch or greenfinch?
It is easy to confuse the nests of chaffinches and greenfinches. Both make a deep cup and line it with a mixture of feathers, fur, hair and roots. But the chaffinch decorates the outside with moss and lichens (left). A greenfinch's nest lacks this and is larger: 12cm (4½in) in diameter compared with the chaffinch's 9cm (3½in).

Wren or long-tailed tit?
A wren's nest (left) is a hollow ball of leaves, moss or grass, with a side entrance and feather lining, which is similar to that of the long-tailed tit. But if you look closely at the tit's nest, you will spot spiders' webs and hair woven into it. The tit's nest also has a more elongated shape and the outside is often decorated with lichens.

Telltale signs *The white blobs are bird droppings. Wherever you see them on the ground, look up. You may spot roosting birds.*

Badly built? *This looks like just a loose bundle of twigs, but it is in fact a wood pigeon's nest and is much stronger than it appears. Many survive in the treetops, long after the pigeon family has moved out.*

High-rise housing

Although nests high up in trees are usually highly visible, they are more difficult to examine. Many, however, can be readily identified from a distance.

A rookery, for instance, with its collection of large nests made of sticks is unmistakable. But you may be fooled when a pair of rooks has decided to nest away from the flock.

Then it is easy to confuse a rook's nest with one made by the solitary crow. However, if you are able to get close enough to see into the nest, a glance at the lining should tell you which bird built it. Rooks line their nests with a mixture of grass and leaves, while crows line theirs with hair and wool.

When scanning the treetops, keep an eye out for magpie and pigeon nests, too. A magpie builds a cup nest, lines it with mud and fine roots, then contructs a dome of twigs over it, leaving a small opening in one side. Pigeons construct a flimsy-looking platform of fine twigs with no roof or lining.

A health warning!

Remember that if you handle a nest in the course of your investigations, you must always wash your hands thoroughly afterwards. Old nests are often infested with fleas, lice, mites, ticks and even fly larvae, all of which can cause illness if they make contact with any food you might prepare or eat.

CLUES UNDERFOOT

Remember to look down, too, when locating birds in winter. Telltale white droppings and feathers under a tree may signal that you have found a roost site.

These clues are very obvious under the trees in which wood pigeons roost, and you are also likely to see them near ivy and the dense conifer foliage, where many small birds like to roost. Also look near crevices and holes and under nest boxes. Birds need secure roosts that offer shelter from the wind and freezing night air, and will make use of most places offering these conditions. Even bare branches can provide a suitable perch. Rooks, for instance, will roost in leafless trees, but choose the side of the tree that faces away from the direction of the wind.

WELL HIDDEN Most small mammals build nests, but usually in concealed places. Many are underground and are only seen if they are dug up. Mice and voles also make nests under sheets of corrugated iron or planks of wood.

The **harvest mouse**, however, tends to nest in more accessible places. It builds different summer and winter nests. In early winter, you may still find an old summer nest (see page107) of tightly woven, shredded grass in a hedge or overgrown verge, or among brambles or reeds. A winter nest (right) is similar, but it tends to be nearer the ground: try searching for one in rough grass or among straw.

It is also worth scanning the trees for squirrels' nests, or dreys. Look for balls of twigs about 30cm (12in) across, often with leaves attached (see page122).

Close-up on Tracks

Shortly after a fresh fall of snow, when the sky has cleared and the snow surface is still fairly fresh, take the opportunity to hunt for tracks and other signs of animal activity. The best impressions are made in damp, shallow snow which holds its shape. Remember that as time passes snow melts and as it does, any tracks will then look much bigger than when they were freshly made. This can give a false impression of an animal's size.

Even in winters when there is little or no snow, you can still look for tracks. Search for them after a hard frost, or in damp, muddy places: near puddles, or along the edges of fields where there is often fine silt, or around gates to fields where animals graze and there is regular traffic. Sandy areas, such as beaches, dunes or golf bunkers, are also good for tracks, especially when they are damp.

Focus your search where animals are likely to pass by. This includes gaps in fences and the banks of steep-sided ditches where animals need to get a firm foothold. On fences you may also find evidence in the form of hair snagged on barbed wire. Look at the structure of any hair you find. If it is coarse, it may be from a badger, if it is fine, from a fox and if it is stiff and brittle, from a deer.

WHO PASSED THIS WAY?

The first thing to do when you find footprints is to decide what type of creature made them. Was it an animal with paws, an animal with hoofs, or a bird?

Remember that in any trail of footprints you will probably only find a few that are clearly identifiable. One reason is that a four-footed animal puts its hind feet almost on top of the prints of the forefeet; this is known as registering. A clear print is most likely to be found where the animal has broken step or changed its gait.

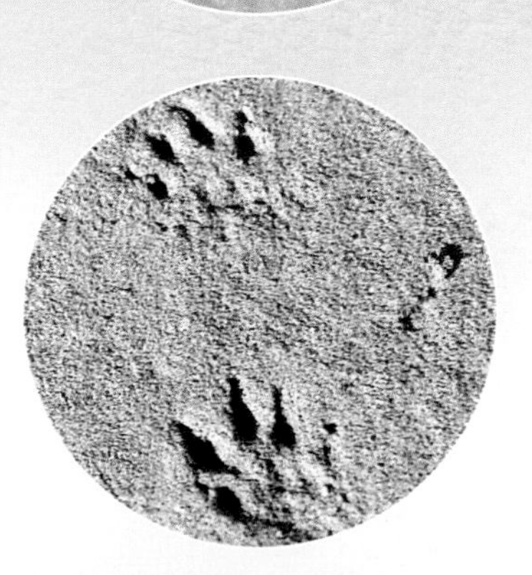

PAW PRINTS When footprints have been made by an animal with paws, you will see four or five toe marks.

The prints of a **cat** (top left), dog and fox show four distinct toes on each foot. Fox and dog prints are similar – both leave claw marks – but the fox's are longer and thinner. Cats leave no claw marks and their toes are well spread out.

Rabbit and hare prints will also show four toes, but often they are not very distinct. The best way to identify their prints is to look at the relative position of the feet: the long hindfeet are set down side by side in front of the rounded forefeet, which are placed one in front of the other (see opposite page).

Which rodent?

If you come across a set of footprints that have obviously been left by one animal, but some have four toe marks and some five, they have been made by a rodent: rodents have four toes on their front feet and five on their rear feet.

The prints of most small rodents are usually indistinguishable by species. However, if they are very small, there is a good chance they were made by a **wood mouse**. You may also spot the thin trail (centre left) which is often left by the mouse's tail. Where the tracks show clear claw marks, you can be fairly certain they were left by a squirrel.

When the prints all show five toe marks, they belong to a member of the Mustelidae family: a badger, mink, otter, **stoat** (bottom left) or weasel. Knowing this will stop you confusing a badger's prints with those of a large dog, which have just four toe marks (see page 39).

HOOF PRINTS A hoofed animal's print will show what appear to be either one or two large toe marks. Those with one will have been made by the circular hoofs of a **horse** (top right) or pony and those with two by a cloven-hoofed animal, such as a **deer** (centre right), goat, pig or sheep.

A deer's prints (called slots) are pointed at the front – the dew claws (rudimentary toes) do not show except in soft ground.

Goats, pigs and sheep leave prints that are rounded at the front. Pig prints usually have clear dew-claw marks, but goat and sheep prints do not.

BIRD PRINTS 'Arrowhead' footprints, with three, long, thin toes facing forwards and one backwards are unmistakably those of a bird, though you are unlikely to be able to tell which bird made them.

However, the bird's size should be obvious and the position of the prints will offer a clue to the way it moves. Footprints positioned one in front of the other were made by birds that walk. Prints that are side by side were made by hopping birds: most small birds, such as blackbirds and song thrushes, do this.

Any webbed prints you find will have been left by water birds, such as ducks, geese, **swans** (bottom right) or gulls.

WHAT HAPPENED HERE?

Fox tracks [1] are easy to find when they follow the line of a hedge or cross an open space. Look out for droppings left in prominent places along the trail as markers, or for places where the trail suddenly alters its course. This is likely to be where the fox spotted a rabbit or mouse and decided to follow it. You may find traces of the prey's trail to confirm this, and there may even be the signs of a scuffle where the fox attacked its victim.

Wherever you come across bird prints, search for **wing prints [2]** as well. These will tell you where a bird took off, perhaps to escape a predator. A large bird, such as a pheasant will leave particularly good, clear wing marks in snow, due to its stiff wing feathers.

TRAILS At first glance you may think a well-worn trail of footprints leading out across the snow was made by a human being, but look again. If the trail passes under low fence wires and brambles, it must have been made by an animal, probably a **badger** (below right) or hare. Follow the trail and you may even spot the animal itself, hunting, feeding or returning to the safety of its home.

Snowy conditions offer the best chance of following trails to find out where an animal has been and what it has been doing. If you find a squirrel's trail and follow it, you may come across the spot where the animal has dug up some nuts that it buried in the autumn. A **hare's trail** (below left) may lead to its form, a depression in the snow: droppings, and perhaps some hair, may help you confirm this.

Where you see small tracks disappearing into holes in the ground or under the snow, they are likely to be those of a small rodent. If the prints become more widely spaced, it suggests that the animal has increased its speed – maybe because it is in danger. Look for the tracks showing that a predator – a weasel or stoat – was in pursuit.

Uniting to beat the chill

Once they are no longer competing for a mate or nesting site, many birds become less territorial and adopt a more communal lifestyle. Not only do they find safety in numbers, it is also easier as a group to track down increasingly scarce supplies of food. As native birds gather in the fields, their ranks are swollen by migrants from the frozen lands to the north. An especially large number of visitors indicates a harsh winter in their home country.

Take the same walk regularly and you will start to notice how the bird population of an area can vary greatly from day to day. This is because some flocks are nomadic and roam about the country in their search for food.

If you find a hedgerow still laden with berries, keep an eye on it, as it will probably be plundered at some point by one of these roving groups. A crop of haws, for instance, that has been overlooked by local thrushes, may suddenly be invaded by fieldfares or redwings that move in and strip the bushes clean.

What's on the wing?

The waxwing is another winter visitor that can suddenly appear in an area. It is probably attracted to British fields and hedgerows by the availability of one of its favourite foods – rowan berries. Invasions vary greatly from fewer than 50 birds to more than 12,000. When large numbers flood in, it is said to be a 'waxwing winter'.

You should have no trouble recognising waxwings: they are the only buff-brown birds seen in Britain that have a crest. Look at them through binoculars, and see if you can spot the unusual waxy-looking, red tips along the edge of the upper wing, which give the birds their name.

Another wanderer to watch out for is the lapwing. Lapwings are becoming rarer, but you may still spot the occasional flock flying across the country in a long, straggling band. In the air, their floppy, erratic wing beats and black-and-white plumage twinkling in the winter sun make them easy to identify.

FEARED BY FARMERS

You may come across fields of winter crops that have been damaged or even destroyed completely. If the young shoots have not just been nibbled but squashed flat, it tells you that large flocks of geese have been about. Native Canada and greylag geese, as well as winter visitors, such as barnacle, pink-footed and brent geese, often feed on crops, trampling them with their large webbed feet.

The wild goose population is protected, and is now growing rapidly in some parts of the country. This is excellent news for some, but many farmers are not so happy about it.

Wood pigeons pose another problem for farmers, as flocks of them abandon the woods in winter to search for food elsewhere. They will descend on any field where they can spot a good meal – cereals and green leafy vegetables are favourites.

Once one flock has landed, others seem to follow. But what is the farmer's loss will offer the

What are these birds eating? *The pink-footed geese shown below are feasting on freshly sprouted winter wheat. They will have already flattened the crop with their webbed feet and are now nibbling their way through it.*

countryside detective a good opportunity to observe some interesting aspects of the way wood pigeons behave.

Wood pigeons are wary birds, constantly on the lookout for danger. If you happen to spot any in a field, stop and take the time to study them carefully – ideally through binoculars.

Can you see their white wing bars? If you can, it means the birds have been disturbed in some way and have, therefore, lifted their wings slightly, so that they are ready to take off at a moment's notice.

They may also be anxiously scanning around them, heads held high to display the white patches on their necks. Various experiments have indicated that the displaying of these patches and the wing bars could be a way that wood pigeons warn each other of potential danger.

Lunchtime *This wood pigeon will quickly polish off the sprouts it is perched on. Many winter crops are destroyed by huge, roving flocks.*

WHAT CAN YOU HEAR? When you are out and about in winter, don't forget to listen as well as look. Though we think of birds as starting to sing in spring, many begin much earlier and a few sing all winter long.

Starlings sing when they are about to enter or leave their winter roosts. Next time you are near a starling roost, listen for their chorus of jumbled squeaks and whistles rising to a crescendo, suddenly cutting off, then a few seconds later starting up again as the flock takes to the air once more. This singing is possibly how these birds co-ordinate group manoeuvres.

You may also catch the clear, warbling notes of a flock of skylarks hovering over an open field. And you will regularly hear bursts of song coming from great tits, nuthatches, **robins**, wrens and tawny owls, roosting in the winter hedgerows. All these birds are singing to defend their territories, which the males – and in the case of robins, both sexes – hold on to throughout the winter.

IS THAT THE SAME BIRD? At the end of the mating season, many birds moult their feathers and lose their often striking breeding plumage. The result is a new look for winter.

If you are familiar with the **golden plover** (top right) in summer, when the adult male's black belly contrasts strikingly with its gold-speckled back, you may be surprised by its much duller winter attire: a more uniform golden-brown with a white underside.

You could also be forgiven for not immediately recognising a **black-headed gull** (bottom right) in winter, as it loses its distinctive deep chocolate-brown head feathers. The only traces that remain are a tiny, dark spot behind each eye.

The change is less dramatic in many other species that gather in the winter fields. The only difference you will notice in lapwings is that there is slightly less black on the head and neck of the males, and that some have a scaly appearance – these are birds in their first winter.

Other birds undergo changes in plumage without moulting. After breeding, you will notice starlings gradually becoming a more uniform black, spangled with white spots.

Then, over the course of the winter, the tips of the starlings' feathers slowly wear away to reveal the inner parts of the feathers underneath. Eventually the shiny black spring plumage – shot through with a greeny violet sheen – is once again in evidence.

This same gradual abrasion of the feather tips during winter affects male chaffinches, bramblings, reed buntings and yellowhammers. All of them gradually look brighter and more colourful, greatly increasing their chances of attracting a mate when spring finally arrives.

Bare trees reveal the woods' winter survivors

Evergreens flourish, but animals have fewer places to hide

Winter is the least colourful and often the quietest time of year in a wood. The prevailing colour is a hazy greyish brown, with the odd splash of green from a holly or yew, or an ivy-covered stump. Most trees have shed their leaves, which have now rotted into a black mulch, but you can also find delicate lace-like leaf skeletons, if you search for them.

At first glance everything seems to be dormant, but the leaf litter and the canopy help to insulate the woodland floor from the worst of the winter frost. This allows invertebrates to stay alive and fungi to carry on fruiting; it also means that microbes in the soil are still active, so that the process of decomposition and nutrient recycling can continue.

Caledonian pine woods

The bright winter sun lights up the bunched needles of an old Scots pine in Glenmore Forest, near Aviemore (above), while in the distance – on the slopes of the snow-covered Cairngorms – lies a forestry plantation, with its man-made straight boundary. Some of Britain's most extensive remaining natural pine forests are here. They are known as the Caledonian pine woods in the belief that they are descended from the original wild forests of Caledonia, as the Highlands were known in Roman times.

Such old trees have rounded crowns, unlike the more common pyramidal conifer shape, furrowed bark and long twisting branches with needles at the tips. In winter their upper crowns bear ripe cones, whose seeds are prised out by the pinewood's most characteristic bird, the Scottish crossbill.

Pine needles have pores running along the needle so that the tree can 'breathe'. The pores are set deep in pits, reducing water loss in frosty weather.

The spaces between the trees are often a patchwork of heather, bilberry, juniper and cushions of moss, kept open by grazing animals, especially red deer which shelter and feed there in bad weather and at night. At these altitudes, snow often covers the ground between December and April, and on a bright day like this the woods are alive with red squirrels and black grouse. You may even spy a golden eagle passing overhead.

Rich mixed woodland

Much of the history of a wood is laid bare in winter. These New Forest oaks (above) have the tall trunks and narrow crowns typical of trees growing close together, and the twisted branches and knarled trunks of mature oaks. An understorey of holly is a consequence of a history of grazing domestic animals in the forest, which avoid the holly's prickly leaves.

Occasional snowy days offer clues to the present life of the wood. Firm snow is ideal for following animal tracks, and evidence like droppings, pellets and leftover food stand out against the white.

Despite the lack of flowers, there are attractions for the plant-lover. Mosses and leafy liverworts expand like sponges in the damp conditions. Some fungi, particularly those growing on wood, are fruiting, while tree trunks are green with powdery algae.

One of the pleasures of walking in woods in late winter is in detecting the first signs of spring. By the new year, great tits will be in full song, to be joined by a gradually swelling chorus as spring approaches. By the end of February violets and celandines will be appearing, and hazel bushes will be dancing with yellow lambs'-tail catkins. Make a note of any especially early sightings – they may herald a change in climate.

Jelly fungi form bright blobs of colour in the bare woods of midwinter. They grow on dead branches, and look (and feel) like folds of partly set jelly.

Staying green in winter

While most of our broad-leaved trees shed their leaves in autumn, one – the holly – is green all year round. Britain's three native conifers, the Scots pine, yew and juniper, are all evergreen trees, but the larch is a deciduous exception, turning yellow and shedding its small needles in autumn. Some other evergreens, such as mistletoe and ivy, attach themselves to deciduous trees and add a splash of colour to otherwise bare woods in winter.

For a plant, the main advantage of staying green in winter is that it can go on photosynthesising, meaning it can continue to store food and to grow. This helps understorey plants, such as holly, to survive beneath shady trees like beech and oak: they take advantage of the period when the trees above them are leafless.

But how do evergreen leaves survive the winter frosts when broad-leaved trees must shed theirs? The answer is that most have a tough leathery texture, plus a protective waterproof layer of wax – and conifers also have an 'antifreeze' in their sap. However, no leaf can afford to be completely sealed by wax, since it is through their leaves that plants take in and expel the necessary gases: carbon dioxide and oxygen.

Holly leaves are dull on their underside, with tiny pits in the surface – look at one through a lens. These are gaps in the waxy coat, allowing the tree to breathe.

The narrow shape and small surface area of pine needles help to reduce water loss from the tree. Their pores are also set deep in the needle, sheltering them from the worst drying conditions. This is particularly important to Scots pines: these grow in soil that is often frozen and so cannot draw water from the soil through their roots.

Energy conservation

Their small surface area makes conifer needles less efficient for photosynthesis than broad leaves. But, unlike a deciduous tree, a conifer does not need a sudden burst of energy to grow a new set of leaves in the spring.

Instead, there is a constant process of renewal – look underneath an evergreen and you will find thick piles of fallen leaves – so a slow, but steady supply of energy is sufficient. The leaves are shed when they are three or four years old and shaded by new growth.

Plants such as holly, ivy and mistletoe produce berries in winter, providing sustenance for

IDENTITY PARADE – Twigs and their buds

Towards the end of summer, trees begin to put out new growth from their twigs. These are the buds, which contain tiny new shoots protected from the winter frost and wind within tough scales. Their shape and the way they are arranged on the twig can help you to identify a tree in winter, even in the absence of leaves – look for the slender twigs and long spindle-shaped buds of the beech. Further clues are to be found in the colour and texture of the bark, and the profile of the tree, but these both change with increasing age. Buds, on the other hand, are the same whether the tree is young or old.

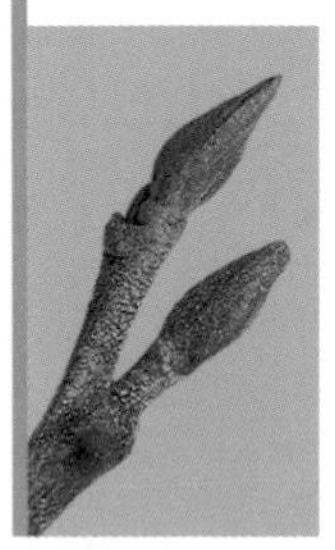

Alder buds are on short stalks and have a purple waxy bloom. The shiny twigs are reddish brown and, in winter, bear purple catkins and cones containing flat brown seeds.

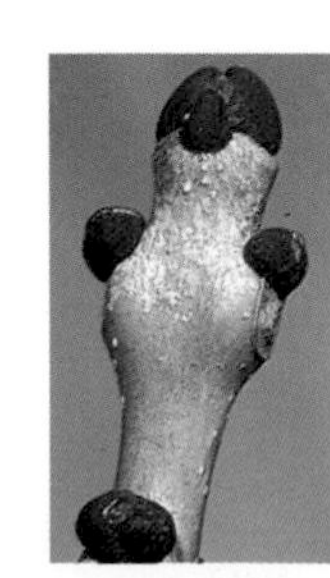

Ash has neat black buds, arranged in pairs, with the largest one right at the end. The tips look a bit like deer hoofs, and are extremely small compared with the size of the leaf.

Horse chestnut buds are large, and sticky – a deterrent to hungry birds and invertebrates. Look for the horseshoe-shaped leaf scars beneath the buds which give the tree its name.

Oak has clusters of pale brown buds borne at the tip of the twig, a large terminal bud and smaller side buds arranged alternately below. Older twigs are often lumpy and contorted.

birds and animals when food is scarce and so ensuring their seeds reach new sites in the creatures' droppings.

Brightly coloured berries attract the attention of thrushes and other birds, but not all hollies or mistletoes have them. The main reason is that holly and mistletoe plants are either male or female, and only the female bears berries. In the case of mistletoe, the two sexes look slightly different (the male has broader leaves), but with holly the presence or absence of berries is the only clue.

There may be other reasons for a plant lacking berries: a heavily grazed bush is unlikely to bear fruit, and a poor summer might have meant that not many flowers were pollinated.

Hard life in the pine forest

A Scots pine does not produce cones until it is about 16 years old, and the thickest crops are found on mature trees of 60 to 100 years old. This is why you are more likely to spot Scottish crossbills – which feed on the seeds in the cones – in native pinewoods than in managed plantations, where trees are usually felled before they can bear their best crops.

The vegetation beneath close-growing evergreens is normally sparse. This is partly because the ground is shaded all year round, so there is no interval in spring when plants can grow and flower. But another reason is that the waxes and resins in the needles makes the leaf litter slow to break down and produces a layer of very acid humus in which few plants are able to grow.

A SIGN OF CHRISTMAS

Mistletoe is one of our most unusual plants. It grows in ball-shaped tangles of leaves and stems on the upper branches of trees. If you see what looks like a rook's nest from a distance, move closer and have another look at its colour, it may be mistletoe. Unlike the twiggy brown nests, mistletoe is always green.

The plant is a partial parasite, but seems to do no harm. It is introduced to the tops of trees in the droppings of roosting birds, particularly mistle thrushes, which have eaten the sticky white berries on another plant.

Lime and crab apple are mistletoe's main hosts, but you can also find it on hawthorn, poplar, sycamore, maple and ash and on some orchard trees (see right), particularly along the Welsh border. It is very rare to find mistletoe on oak; probably the oak's chemical defences are too strong.

Double crop *Some farmers grow mistletoe in their orchards to give them two crops: apples or pears in autumn; mistletoe in winter.*

Sign of the season *High up in trees in winter, mistletoe, anchored with sucker-like roots, penetrates its host tree for water.*

Architecture of a wood

There are many different types of natural woodland in Britain. Some, such as the pine and birch forests of the Scottish Highlands, or the beech woods of the Chilterns, consist mostly of tall trees. However many long-established lowland woods have two distinct layers: a canopy formed by tall trees like oak and ash, and an understorey of smaller trees and shrubs. This layering is partly the result of past management. While tall oaks, known as standards, were left to mature for timber, the understorey met the everyday needs of a parish for firewood or fencing.

FOOD AND SHELTER Loose bark and cushions of moss on an ancient coppiced stool form miniature lawns and jungles for small invertebrates. In the middle there may be a thick mulch of damp, half-rotten debris being consumed by scavenging beetles, such as the **stag beetle** (right).

BIRD HAVEN Birds also find food and shelter in coppices. The many small invertebrates provide sustenance for birds such as this **wren** (below) or the treecreeper, while the rotting wood can be excavated for nesting. Mature coppice in the south of England is the best habitat for nightingales.

These two-layered woods are called 'coppice with standards'. Woodmen maintained a continual supply of new growth by cutting different parts of the underwood on a regular cycle, a practice known as coppicing.

Most native trees respond to cutting by producing a mass of new shoots from around the edge of the stump. As a result, repeated cutting at intervals of 10 to 20 years produces a kind of shrub, with a stump in the middle called a stool and a thicket of young branches growing from it. The size of the stump will give you a clue to the age of the tree, which may be much older than its height suggests. Very roughly, stumps increase in diameter by 30cm (1ft) every 100 years, so that a 1.8m (6ft) wide stump may have been alive in the Middle Ages.

Many of these coppiced stools are, in fact, older than the tall standard trees and provide many opportunities for wildlife. The stump may be completely hollow in the middle, or there may be crannies and rot holes with soft wood, which can be excavated by nesting tits.

Recognising the trees

Hazels and willows are among the most common coppiced trees, but some naturally tall, spreading trees can exist quite happily as coppice. Many old coppice stools are of ash, which is easily recognised in winter by its smooth grey bark and tight black buds.

In some woods, especially in central England and East Anglia, look for coppiced lime, which on well-drained sites is often cut flush with the ground so that all you will see is what looks like a circle of dark branches.

Oak coppice is becoming less widespread, but the gnarled branches, often hung with lichens, have a wonderfully primeval look.

Oak was coppiced in upland woods during the 18th century to supply fuel for the early

The end product *The strong whippy sticks of coppiced hazel are ideal for building light hurdle fences, once used to fold sheep at night and now popular in gardens.*

Shapely story *Pollarding raises tasty new growth out of the reach of grazing animals, but creates trees with a curious-shaped trunk, like a raised clenched fist.*

Industrial Revolution. Later, conifers were planted, which grow faster and are more profitable. But traces of former oak coppices, which have grown into tall trees (far right), survive on the fringes of Dartmoor and in western Scotland.

READING THE SIGNS OF OLD WOODLAND

Pollards (above) tell you that an area was once grazed by animals, which would have destroyed the low-level green shoots of coppice. You are most likely to find them in open park-like woodland, or at the edge of a wood where it meets a field. Beech and hornbeam are still pollarded in Epping Forest.

If you find a few scattered old trees standing in a thicket of younger ones, you may be looking at former parkland, which has turned to woodland through a lack of grazing.

The type of soil as well as the use of the land influences the look of a wood. One common kind of wood found on clay soils, often on hilltops in southern England, has tall standards of oak and ash, and a coppice layer of ash, hazel and a few field maples. On poorer soils, ash does not grow so well, and the shrub layer may be more gappy, with birch and holly replacing hazel.

Clues from a bank

As you walk through a wood, look out for banks. They often border footpaths, especially near the edge of the wood, and may be lined on at least one side by a shallow ditch. Such banks form a vital clue to the history of the wood. They reveal its original extent and may also show how the wood was subdivided into compartments, since the banks would originally have marked a boundary.

Sometimes a hedge was planted on top of a bank, and this may since have grown up into a line of trees. Look for signs of former hedge cutting and layering in the form of connecting and misshapen trunks which have developed from hedge shoots.

What made that hole?

Some woods contain large holes in the ground. A shallow crater often marks where a large tree has fallen, pulling up the roots and exposing a pit, which may have filled with water. Vertical 'plates' of earth and tangled roots were a feature of many woods in southern England after the gales of 1987 and 1991.

Another cause may be an underground stream that has produced a depression known as a swallow hole. But holes may also be man made.

Look out for the remains of a quarry or marl pit; a former pond; or even an archaeological feature like a saw pit or a sunken hearth, where sticks were burned to produce charcoal. Less often, a wood may preserve a bomb crater – particularly in woods that are close to industrial areas, such as Sutton Park, near Birmingham. Search for clues to the origin of the hole nearby, such as fallen trunks or an old spoil mound.

Mystery pit *Animal skins would be soaked for several weeks with oak bark, twigs and galls in a tanning pit like this to turn them into leather.*

MAPPING YOUR WOOD

If you really want to get to know your local wood, try plotting its banks and hollows on a large-scale map (1:10,000 is ideal). This may reveal all sorts of unseen treasures: moated banks around a former homestead; ridges-and-furrows showing an area which was ploughed in medieval times; platforms revetted into the slope where cut branches were baked into charcoal; and a multitude of other things which have turned the wood into what it is today.

Signs of old ways *If you see what looks like several mature oaks growing very close together, look again – it could be an old, neglected coppiced oak, in which several trunks have grown from a broad base.*

Close-up on
Deer

Head of the harem *Male red deer bear magnificent branched antlers during the rut, when a dominant stag, like this one in the Cairngorms, will claim mating rights over a large harem of hinds.*

Seven species of deer live wild in Britain. Red and roe deer are native, the fallow deer was introduced in Norman times, and muntjac, sika, reindeer and Chinese water deer were introduced or escaped from parks during the 20th century, and have established themselves in the wild. The best time to look for woodland deer is at dawn or dusk, but the most you normally see of roe deer, the most widespread species, is a glimpse of a white rump as the animal dashes for cover. The muntjac is even harder to spot, since it is only about 60cm (2ft) high at the shoulder and can hide in tall grass. Deer parks offer the best opportunities for spotting these shy animals, but even there, the cover of trees or a vehicle will help.

A question of scale *Large deer, such as red and fallow deer, and the similar-sized sika, prefer open woods and parks, while the nimble roe deer and small muntjac can live in dense woodland.*

IDENTIFICATION CLUES

All male British deer have antlers, except for Chinese water deer, which have tusks. Antlers are for display, and for fighting rival males at rutting time, but their size and shape (see below left) can help you to determine the species. Fallow deer antlers are flat, or 'palmate' and are the easiest way to distinguish them from the similarly sized sika deer, whose antlers have up to four points.

Deer produce antlers in their second year, and these grow in proportion to size and age, so that the oldest deer have the most substantial sets, although even mature muntjac deer have only short spikes. Antlers are at their most impressive for the rutting season and are shed each year at the end of winter. A new pair starts to grow almost immediately, initially covered in soft furry skin, called 'velvet'.

The colour of the coat is also a good clue to identification, although fallow deer vary in colour (see page 264).

EVIDENCE OF DEER

Woods with a **browse line** (see picture opposite) – where there is little or no foliage near the ground – tell you that there are large numbers of deer present. In spring, when young leaves are rich in nutrients, look for new shoots that have been snipped off. Deer also prune bushes, stunting their growth or creating a kind of topiary, with the bottom nibbled back, but a bushy top where the deer cannot reach.

In conifer woods, look for **young trees with two leaders** growing at the top instead of one (above) – the original top was probably bitten off by a hungry deer. In winter, patches of cleared snow might indicate where a deer has been grazing on the grass beneath, or searching for fallen acorns.

Frayed bark (right) is an easy clue to detect. Where you see long strips of bark torn off a springy young tree, around waist height, it is almost certainly where a deer has been rubbing its antlers.

Deer do this for two reasons. In late summer, rubbing helps them to get rid of the velvet that covers their antlers. Later – during the rut – the deer thrash saplings and rub against them to spread scent from glands in their face. During this period young trees are often severely damaged.

The roebuck also frays bark to mark its territory. Lower down the trunk other animals cause fraying, such as a badger scratching with its claws.

Muddy signs of the rut

Deer mate during their rutting season, which varies from late July and August for roe deer to October for red and fallow deer and lasts about a month. Muntjac have no particular rutting season. During the roe deer's rut, you may find bare circular paths, often around trees. These are 'roe rings', worn in the ground when the buck chases the doe during courtship.

In soft ground in or near woodland you may find a muddy wallow made by red and, less often, roe, deer during the rut. If you think you have found one, look for hoof prints to confirm it. Listen for nearby deer, too: males are more vocal during rutting than at other times – red and fallow deer make a loud groaning roar, while roe and muntjac bucks have a shorter, dog-like bark.

Deer damage *Where a deer has thrashed at a tree with its antlers, you might also find broken twigs and branches lying around the base.*

Height restriction *Bare trunks show how high these fallow deer in Bushy Park, London, can nibble away branches. Fences protect the tender interplanted saplings from damage.*

WHO GOES THERE?

Woodland deer roam along familiar trails so that they can escape quickly if in danger. These narrow paths are easy to find and often have tracks: clues to the deer that are in a wood. Other good places to look for deer prints are in the mud around ponds, and where they leap over ditches.

Deer have cloven hoofs, called slots, which are curved on both sides and narrow sharply towards their tips. Size is a good clue to the species that made the prints. Red deer prints (see page 64) are just larger than a tablespoon; fallow and sika deer prints are about dessertspoon sized; roe deer and Chinese water deer the size of a teaspoon and muntjac prints about half as big as that. Muntjac also have unequal slots: the inner slot is smaller and less distinct than the outer one.

Following the trail

If the prints form a continuous track, such as in snow, sand or soft mud, you can deduce how the animal was moving. When a deer moves from a walk to a trot, the length of stride increases and, as the animal gathers speed, the hind feet land farther and farther in front of the fore feet. A really deep print, with the hoofs splayed, shows where a deer has jumped. You may find faint marks where two small claws at the back of the deer's foot (known as dew claws) have left their mark.

DROPPINGS

Fallow deer droppings (above left) and those of red deer (see page 64), and sika are hard to tell apart, but **roe deer droppings** (above right) are distinctively shiny, black and oval-shaped.

Deer droppings are dark pellets: quite small for the size of the animal. The droppings of sheep (see page 64) or goats can look very similar, but are more often clustered together and are slightly larger.

Droppings are a good clue to search for because herbivorous animals like deer have to eat a lot of food to stay alive. In winter, they need even more, since the food is less nutritious. This means their droppings are frequent and easy to find. Look for them where the animals rest or feed, such as under dense foliage, or in thickets.

Gallop in the snow *The deer that left these tracks was galloping, putting its hind feet well ahead of its front feet.*

Buried treasure *Squirrels emerge for just a few hours each day in winter to dig up a meal from their buried stores of nuts.*

Beating the cold in the woods

Animals and birds will only survive the winter if they can beat the cold and find enough to eat. Many woodland mammals get through these months by reducing their activity. A few, such as bats and dormice, go into full hibernation. But some woodland birds face a further challenge: they establish their territories in winter, in order to be ready for courtship and nesting as soon as the weather gets warmer.

A bright sunny winter's day is a good time to go birdwatching. Not only are the birds easier to see on bare branches, but many species forage in large, noisy flocks. Tits and finches often feed on the ground, looking for nuts or seeds. Others find their sustenance mainly in the canopy. Look for siskins and redpolls systematically probing alder and birch cones for their seeds.

If you can't see a foraging bird, you might still hear its calls. Listen out for the monotonous *teach-er, teach-er* of the great tit, or the *dzweee* of the colourful brambling, an immigrant from northern Europe.

Anywhere with berries makes a good place to look for flocks of feeding thrushes, especially along the edge of a wood or in a surrounding hedgerow. Berries also attract the many redwings and fieldfares, which visit Britain every autumn. They stop to strip rosehips and other red fruits from hawthorn bushes and holly before moving on.

Mistle thrushes are resident all year round, but are easier to detect in winter, when they fly from tree to tree in small parties chattering noisily. You will start to hear the loud song of the male mistle thrush, an early nester, from February onwards.

Nuthatches commonly jam nuts into a bark crevice while they peck them open to reach the kernel inside (see page 42); if you find the remains of a nut, watch a while, because the nuthatch often uses the same tree over and over again.

Other woodland birds, such as jays and tits, hide stores of nuts: watch the birds as they search for them on the woodland floor in winter. Those they fail to find may germinate in spring.

Finding food *Tits, such as the great tit (below left), feed on berries or fallen nuts and seeds. The crossbill (below) extracts seeds from cones before they are dropped.*

Who lived there? Winter is the best time to spot old bird's nests in the wood. The easiest to see are the twiggy platforms of wood pigeons, rooks, jackdaws and crows, or the bulky nest of the blackbird, made of dry grass and moss. The similar nest of the mistle thrush can be found in the fork of a tree – look for the scraps of paper or rags with which it decorates its home.

Most woodland birds nest in thick cover, and you are more likely to find one if you take part in conservation work in winter, cutting back brambles and other growth. A particularly beautiful nest is the long-tailed tit's nest – domed, completely lined with thousands of feathers and coated with mosses and lichens.

Late fruit *Two late-fruiting winter fungi are the scarlet elf cup (above) and winter fungus (top).*

MUSHROOMS OUT OF SEASON

Some species of fungi continue to appear well into winter. One that sprouts in tufts from tree stumps around Christmas time is the winter fungus or velvet-stem toadstool, so called from its dark, velvety stems.

From the new year onwards, look for the beautiful scarlet elf-cup, which usually grows attached to moss-covered sticks, especially where there is hazel. The pale, scurfy underside of the cup contrasts with the brilliant red fertile layer.

If a shaft of sunlight has filtered through to strike the cups of the scarlet elf cup, put your ear close to the fungus and listen – you may hear a faint crackle as the spores are explosively discharged.

FLOWERS IN THE SNOW

Some woodland plants, like aconites and snowdrops, flower very early in the year, when there is less competition for light from trees, grasses and tall herbs, and less demand for insect pollinators. But how do they manage it?

There are two strategies for winter growth: plants either use food stored in underground organs – tubers or bulbs – or they are evergreen, like spurge laurel and hellebores. They must also be specially adapted to function at low temperatures and during short days.

The snowdrop, aconite and lesser celandine store food in tubers, but how do their underground stores know when to sprout? There are no cues from changing day length and ground temperatures are still low, so the underground parts must have an internal, chemical clock, like an egg timer.

Snowdrop bulbs multiply from underground buds, producing such large masses that little or no room is left for other plants to become established.

Snowdrops are probably not native to Britain, so if you find them in a wild wood, try following the snowdrop trail. Very often it will end in a cultivated place such as an old garden or churchyard, from where a plant once escaped.

Winter growth *Stinking hellebores have evergreen leaves and take advantage of the absence of competition to grow in winter. The yellowish green flowers appear from February onwards, and give off a pungent scent.*

Moss balls Mosses are prominent in winter, but most are difficult to recognise. One, though, is easy: a large cushion moss, *Leucobryum glaucum*, which forms tight greyish green hummocks 5-10cm (2-4in) across. Look for it in southern beech woods, or on acidic soil under oak or conifers. Sometimes they become detached, yet continue to grow, and may turn into moss balls (right).

Pushing through *Snowdrops have hard-ended chisel-like leaves – try feeling them – which help them to push through the hard frosty ground in winter.*

Close-up on Owls

SECRET OF STEALTH The upper surface of an owl's wing is very soft – almost furry – and deadens the sound as it swoops. If you look through a hand lens at the edges of a primary feather, you will see a **comb-like fringe**, which smooths the airflow, silencing the owl's flight even more.

Winter is a good time to look for owls: not only are the leaves off the trees, but the owls are hungry so that even barn and long-eared owls – both normally strictly nocturnal – may be forced to hunt during the short period of daylight to obtain enough food, especially in the north. Often the only clue to the presence of these stealthy hunters is the sound of their calls, especially in spring and autumn: tawny owls and little owls can be very noisy, but the others mostly stay silent outside the breeding season.

Knowing which owl you are likely to find in a particular habitat will help you to know where and when to look for one. The tawny owl is a bird of woodland, including city parks and gardens, while the long-eared owl is found mainly in overgrown hedges and among small areas of conifers, except in Northern Ireland. There it often breeds in broad-leaved woodlands too, probably because there are no tawny or little owls in Ireland to offer competition. The short-eared owl breeds mainly in the north on moorland and in young forestry plantations, but spreads out in winter to marshes, rough grassland and sand dunes. In open country with a mix of grassland and hedges look for barn owls and little owls.

IS IT AN OWL, OR IS IT A THRUSH?

Most owls hunt small mammals and birds but the **little owl** (below) – Britain's smallest owl, at only the size of a portly thrush – also catches insects. It may hover clumsily when hunting, but also runs after insects and worms on the ground. The species was introduced to Britain in the 1880s and is often out and about in broad daylight, although it hunts mainly at dusk and dawn. Blazing yellow eyes and prominent white eyebrows give it an angry, frowning 'expression' and it chooses prominent perches, from where it bobs its head comically at intruders.

Look for little owls in trees, where they nest in holes, or on the ground, as they also make use of abandoned rabbit burrows. They have a bounding flight, shared by the similarly sized green woodpecker and mistle thrush and are very vocal, with a loud, mournful ***keeeooo*** song, often given as a duet by a pair, as well as a ***kip-kip-kip*** or yelping ***werrow*** of alarm.

FEEDING THE FAMILY Barn owls patrol slowly, low over the ground in search of rodents, alert to the slightest sound, often altering direction and sometimes hovering before dropping down onto their prey. Barn owls nest in holes and ledges in **barns** (above) or other old buildings, or even in tree hollows and crevices in cliffs or quarries. As with all the species of owls, the male hunts while his mate sits on the eggs. Later, he helps to bring prey for the young owlets, too.

FINDING FOOD CLUES Unlike birds of prey, owls usually swallow their prey whole, but cannot digest bones, fur, feathers, beetle wing-cases and some other hard parts, and these are regurgitated as pellets, at the rate of about two a day. Look for pellets under roost sites. Barn owls tend to use a single sheltered roost, such as a beam across the inside of an old barn, so this is a good place to start. Other owls use several roosts, so their pellets are more scattered. At first, you may mistake a fox dropping for an owl pellet, but fox droppings are usually found singly, and are distinctly twisted, with at least one pointed end. Any food remains in a dropping lie parallel to the long axis, but in a pellet they are mixed up. Finally, when fresh, a fox dropping smells strongly.

What have the owls been eating?

For the serious nature detective, dissecting owl pellets can provide fascinating information about the creatures that live in a habitat and form part of the owl's diet. This dissected **short-eared owl pellet** (right) contains the fur and bones from two pygmy shrews, two short-tailed voles and two wood mice. Even without dissecting the **little owl's pellet** (inset above) you can guess that its favourite food includes beetles, whose shiny indigestible wing-cases are clearly visible.

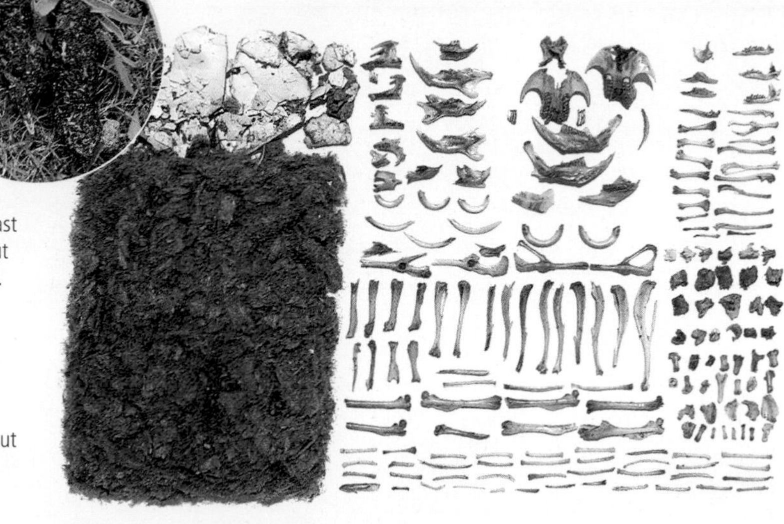

FAMILY LIFE

Owls court and form pairs at different times from autumn to spring. Listen for their calls, as this is when they are most vocal. Tawny, barn, little and resident long-eared owls pair for life, or several years at least, but short-eared owls are great nomads, and usually take a new partner each year.

Owls generally use the same nest site for life. This may be a hole in a tree, cliff or building or the empty nest of a magpie, squirrel or rabbit, although the short-eared owl nests on the ground, in a mere scrape sheltered by heather, other shrubs or clumps of grass. The **long-eared owl** (below) roosts in groups in trees. At rest these owls look plump and relaxed, but in their alert state they look like a different species: tall, exaggeratedly thin and upright.

Adopted nest *The long-eared owl takes over the nests of large birds such as crows, magpies and sparrowhawks.*

SIGNS LEFT BEHIND

If you find a ghostly **powdery imprint** of a bird's head and wings on a windowpane (right), it may have been made by an owl – although the collared dove is another common clumsy culprit.

Like herons, hawks, pigeons and some other birds, owls have special down feathers that break down slowly to form a fine white powder, called powder down. This is thought to help to keep the plumage clean and in tiptop condition by absorbing dirt.

Owls are quite prone to colliding with windows at night, and the mark they leave is made by this powder down.

Hunting for owls in winter

If the ground is carpeted with snow, go out in early morning, before it is disturbed. You might be lucky enough to find tracks and the patterns left by an owl's wings and tail, where it has swooped down on prey during the night.

Owl footprints are distinctive because they show two toes pointing forward and two backward, but a feather on the ground can confirm that owls are around. Feathers are moulted from early summer to winter – although the barn owl moults all year round. But a lost feather may also be the result of an owl brushing against a tree on a cloudy, moonless night, when it relies on spatial memory alone to find its way.

A lost feather could also signal that an owl has been in a tussle with prey or a predator such as a sparrowhawk, kestrel, or a tawny owl, which attacks other owls.

Dusk vigil *The tawny owl is a strictly nocturnal hunter, but you may spot one perched on a branch, out-building or television aerial as it waits for night to fall. The tawny is our noisiest owl: listen for its* ***kewick*** *calls and quavering hoots.*

Life goes on hold in the dim and chilly depths

Rationed light and severe cold put a brake on the food chain

As the days shorten and midwinter approaches, freshwater life slows down. There is still plenty to see along the banks of canals, rivers and lakes – particularly now that few leaves block the view – but in the water itself little moves. Most fish skulk near the bottom, often going without food for weeks on end, and smaller inhabitants, such as insect larvae, seem to have vanished without trace. Cold alone is not responsible for the shut-down – although the water feels chilly, it is usually warmer than the air. Animals are far more affected by limited daylight, which results in water plants growing very slowly, so the whole food chain is affected; in response, many creatures become inactive or hibernate.

Stirred water

In lakes, especially deep ones like Loch Laggan (above), in Invernesshire, subtle changes are occurring in the grip of winter.

During the summer, sunshine heated the water near the surface, but even on the hottest days this warm layer extended only for a metre or so below the surface. Deeper down, the water remained sharply colder, with the two layers not mixing. Life concentrated itself in the warm layer, using up the food supply there far faster than that lower down.

From autumn on, however, the surface starts to cool until, by midwinter, the temperature of the water is the same from the surface to the bottom of the lake. This change is vital for the lake's life, because as the temperature evens out the water mixes thoroughly, so that nutrients from the depths

Greylag geese roost on Scottish lochs all year round, but in winter their ranks are swollen by migrants fleeing the freeze-up in the Arctic lands farther north.

are carried to the surface, where they are in short supply. By the time winter is over and the surface starts to warm up once more, it is recharged with fresh nutrients, which will support the explosion of plant and animal life when spring arrives.

Winter winds ruffling the surface of the lake and turning it choppy also help to stir up the water and ensure a good supply of food for waterlife in the coming year.

Temporary lakes

Floods are more common in winter, but only partly because there is usually more rain than in summer (in some eastern areas the reverse is the case). An equally important factor is the slowdown in evaporation rates as the ground and the air grow colder.

Flooded fields often mean economic losses for farmers and inconvenience for others, but for the countryside detective they are a golden opportunity because waterfowl and waders can turn up almost anywhere that is temporarily under water.

The types of birds which take advantage of these temporary stretches of water are as unpredictable as the floods themselves. The Somerset Levels (above) and the Ouse Washes in the Fens attract large winter populations of waders such as dunlins, redshanks and snipe, some from nearby estuaries, but many from much farther afield. And you might see such species as the Bewick's swan and golden plover, both of which fly south from the Arctic and Scandinavia to winter in Britain.

Even the subsiding floodwaters are fascinating, with their muddy bequest of footprints and holes showing where birds have waded and probed with their bills as they searched for food.

You are more likely to spot a snipe in winter, when the breed is more numerous and widespread – they turn up almost anywhere that is waterlogged.

Surviving the freeze

Three centuries ago, winter fairs were held in London on the frozen Thames. In today's milder climate, iced-over rivers are a rare sight, but the still waters of canals and lakes do freeze if the thermometer stays below zero for longer than a day or two. The ice shuts off aquatic plants and animals from the outside world, but also protects them from some of the creatures that would normally consume them. If there is then a dusting of snow, you may find the footprints of animals that have ventured out to search for food.

Refugees *Icy conditions force the heron (above) and water rail (right) into new feeding grounds.*

A patch of clear ice close to the edge of a pond provides the countryside detective with a window into the waters below. You might spot a few brightly coloured water mites, sculling about on their feathery legs, or a victim of the freeze-up – a dead dragonfly nymph, for example – trapped in the ice. A tap on the surface of the ice could disturb any motionless insect larvae and set them wriggling around in their enclosed world.

Where life congregates

There is no need to break the ice: none of these creatures, nor any fish or amphibians in the pond, are going to suffocate, because they require far less oxygen in the depths of winter – a consequence of being very inactive. And because life gravitates towards the bottom of the pond as the temperature of the water drops, creatures are in little danger of freezing either. This is because water, unlike most liquids, expands (and so becomes lighter) as it nears freezing point. The result is that the coldest water sits just below the ice, and the warmest, heaviest water lies along the bottom, where it stays at around 4°C (39°F) – not exactly warm, but at a temperature that is high enough to sustain life.

An icy grave *This water boatman (below) probably didn't move fast enough to escape as the water froze over.*

WATCHING BIRDS' REACTIONS

A freeze-up poses real problems for birds that live on and around water. Ice can cut them off from their food, and they react to this according to where they feed in the waterside habitat. Herons fish in the shallows, the part of the water that freezes first. They will simply seek new feeding grounds, perhaps where there is a current stopping or slowing the formation of ice.

Ducks and swans feed in deeper water, and you might see them paddling on the surface to impede the spread of ice. But after dark, when the birds are roosting and temperatures are at their lowest, patches of water often freeze over, crowding the birds into an increasingly smaller area. If the water freezes over entirely, these birds fly away or resort to searching for food on the adjoining land.

The freeze-up drives reed-bed birds out into the open, presenting perhaps the best opportunity of spotting the water rail, a bird which normally eats insects and molluscs, but which will be driven by hunger into the fields to hunt for other birds, mice and voles.

Q **Why don't ducks get frozen feet when standing on ice?**

A If you watch ducks resting on ice, you will see that they often stand on one leg, keeping the other warm by tucking it up close to the body. Also, the feet can function at low temperatures because they contain little apart from skin, tendons and bone, fed by a blood circulation that is specially adapted to limit heat loss. The muscles that move the feet are high up the leg, under an insulating layer of feathers.

Crowding in *Encroaching ice forces Canada geese and other birds into a dwindling patch of water.*

HOW WATER PLANTS SURVIVE

When you look at ponds and canals in winter, you will notice that there are very few plants floating on or near the surface. This is very different from the situation in summer, when patches of water are often covered with a thick carpet of growth. The plants' disappearing act is not, however, quite as complete as it seems, because the plants have not died but merely retreated from sight.

Ice is potentially deadly for frogbit and other floating plants, and they survive by producing winter growth that sinks to the bottom of the water, out of harm's way. For both frogbit and greater duckweed, this growth consists of starch-enriched buds that are shed by the parent plant, which then dies back. The buds lie dormant on the bottom until spring, when they float back up to the surface and start to grow. Common duckweed remains intact: the whole plant fills up with starch and sinks from sight.

Water soldier – one of the largest but rarest floating plants found in Britain – also sinks as winter approaches, weighed down by chalky deposits that its leaves gradually absorbed from the surrounding water during the summer. This is why it can only grow in hard water, which is rich in the mineral calcium.

WHY THE ALDER DRAWS BIRDS

Look carefully at any alders you spot growing along the water's edge. You should notice that their leafless branches are peppered with dark brown and black oval cones, making them stand out from other waterside trees. These cones are full of seeds, an important winter food for siskins and other small-beaked birds. Stand quietly and watch, and you may see a few coming to feed.

If birds do arrive, you'll notice that they focus on the brown cones and ignore the black ones. This is because the black ones are old – left over from previous years – and contain no seeds.

Although it may seem a long time until spring, alders often get the new year off to a rapid start. In January, their catkins develop a purple tinge, and then, from February on, start to lengthen, turning a yellowish green as they flower and shed their pollen into the chilly air.

You might see some alders with peeling bark and only a few cones or catkins. These are the symptoms of a fungal disease – alder blight – which first appeared in the early 1990s.

Searching for seeds *A male siskin, distinguishable from the female by his black crown, perches on a wintry alder branch.*

Paradise for birdwatchers

On a blustery winter's day, marshes and flooded meadows may not seem to be ideal places to explore. The wet ground can make walking difficult and, because there is usually little or no cover, you are likely to experience the full blast of the icy wind. But wetlands can offer an unmissable opportunity to see waders and wildfowl in spectacular numbers, so it's well worth paying them a visit. The birds can turn up wherever there is standing water, but the best birdwatching spots are managed, to help both the birds and the watchers.

Many areas are so quiet in winter that they offer little for the countryside dectective to investigate, but the Ouse Washes in East Anglia are an exception. Visit this long, thin strip of land – about 1km (½ mile) wide and 22km (14 miles) long – in summer, and you will see a patchwork of small, low-lying fields, grazed by cattle to produce the kind of rough grassland favoured by ground-nesting waders, such as lapwings and ruffs. But return in winter and you will find the whole area transformed – by controlled flooding – into a vast watery paradise for migratory wildfowl.

As the water spills in, so do thousands of ducks, including wigeon, pintails and teal, as well as Bewick's and whooper swans. Because the Washes are not entirely flat, the depth of the water varies, and you will see all these birds, regardless of size, feeding side by side.

The area lies between two artificial rivers – the Old and New Bedford Rivers – which were created in the 17th century to take up flood water drained off the surrounding farmland. The Washes were designed to hold any overflow from these rivers, particularly in the wetter, winter months.

Viewing hides

Today much of the land is owned by the Wildfowl and Wetlands Trust (see page 339), which manages it in the interests of wildlife. At Welney, in the Norfolk section, and near Manea, in the Cambridgeshire section, there are hides from which you can observe the huge gatherings of birds.

Settling in *The flooded pastures of the Ouse Washes offer an ideal winter home to ducks and swans from the icy north.*

IDENTITY PARADE – Swans

At the Ouse Washes and other wetland reserves, such as Slimbridge in Gloucestershire, winter offers the rare chance to see three different species of swan in one place. The mute swan lives in Britain all year round, but the whooper and Bewick's migrate from the Arctic, with the same birds returning to the same places each winter, year after year.

Mute swan You should have no problem identifying this familiar bird by its orange bill, with a black knob or 'berry' at its base, and the graceful curve of its head and neck. In flight, the wing beats are deliberate and powerful, making a loud throbbing hum, which has been likened to the sound of horses galloping over hard ground.

Whooper swan This bird is the same size as the mute swan, but its beak is yellow and black, and slopes down in a straight line from its forehead. Instead of the loud wing beat of the mute swan, you will only hear a gentle swishing sound as a whooper swan flies by. Whooper swans come to Britain in winter from their breeding grounds in Iceland, Scandinavia and Siberia.

Bewick's swan At a glance you might confuse this with the whooper swan, as it also has a black and yellow beak. However, the yellow patch is usually smaller and rounder than that on a whooper's beak, and the bird itself is smaller and stockier. It breeds in the Siberian Arctic, and often touches down on British lakes and reservoirs on its journeys north and south.

THE SOMERSET LEVELS

During the winter, floodwater often spreads over the Somerset Levels. Like the Ouse Washes, the Levels consist largely of pasture, and the flooded fields attract a wide variety of waders and waterfowl, including species that fly in from the nearby coast. You are highly likely to find Bewick's swans there, along with curlews, golden plovers, lapwings, mallards, pintails, redshanks, shovelers, snipe, teal, whimbrel and wigeon.

The small roads that crisscross the Levels traverse one of the strangest landscapes in south-west England. The ground will feel spongy underfoot and, if you look out across the fields, you will notice that they are regularly interspersed with areas where peat is being dug out of the ground to supply garden centres and the horticultural industry. If you look closely into some of the deeper peat cuttings, you may spot pieces of blackened wood – these can be several thousands of years old, and come from a time when the area was covered by reeds and scattered trees.

Future in the balance

Although the Levels are rich in plant and animal life, many of the species that live here depend on wet conditions to survive. Since the 1970s, however, an increasing amount of the land has been drained, so that crops can be grown on the highly fertile, peaty soil.

A similar kind of agricultural change destroyed much of the wetlands in East Anglia, and it remains to be seen if this unique corner of the West Country can escape this fate.

Conflicting demands *Countless years of flooding have resulted in rich peat deposits on the Somerset Levels, economic demands for which often compete with those of conservationists seeking to preserve the wildlife.*

Close-up on
The otter

On the ground *The otter leaves its droppings, or spraints (left), as territorial markers. Fish scales and bones are often visible in the deposits. An otter's paw prints (below left) usually occur in pairs – a pattern created as the animal bounds along.*

Most people think of otters as being river animals, but they are equally at home on rocky coasts (below) as long as there is fresh water close by. River otters face the greatest threat of disturbance from humans, which explains why they are generally nocturnal and why you are unlikely to spot one out and about. Coastal otters tend to live in isolated areas and consequently are abroad in daylight. But you don't have to actually see otters to discover where they live and how they behave. Although they are among our most secretive mammals, they leave a wealth of clues to their activities.

Also, your chances of tracking down this delightful and fascinating animal are on the increase. Thirty years ago, because of pollution and disturbance by humans, the British otter population was in rapid decline. It had vanished completely from some areas, particularly in central and south-eastern Britain. Only in the Highlands and Islands, with their abundant food supplies and sparse human population, did the otter continue to flourish. But now there is good news: careful conservation work has reversed the trend, and although Scotland remains the best place to spot an otter, the population elsewhere is definitely on the up.

CLUES TO LOOK FOR

The first clue to the presence of otters that you are likely to encounter is their tarry black droppings, known as spraints. You will find them in small piles or, more often, smeared on prominent objects near the water's edge, such as grassy tussocks, rocks, fallen trees, and the piers beneath bridges.

Otters leave their spraints in such conspicuous places to mark out their territory. To underline their claim they will coat spraints with a jelly-like secretion that gives them a distinctive, sweet, oily smell, quite unlike the odour of other carnivores' droppings. Knowing this will enable you to distinguish them from the similar but much more foul-smelling droppings of mink.

Paw prints and leftovers

In mud or damp sand near the water's edge, you might spot a second clue to resident otters – their pawprints. The place you are most likely to find these is under an overhanging tree or bridge where they have been preserved from the rain. The prints of a mature animal are about 7cm (2¾in) long, almost circular, and have five teardrop-shaped toe marks. Also, all four feet are webbed. By contrast a mink's pawprints are about half the size and display no signs of webbing.

Food leftovers, if you find them before a scavenger does, often consist of the backbone and tail of a fish or a small pile of mussel shells, broken open and emptied of their contents.

Levels of security *The gnarled bole of a fallen tree (top), surrounded on three sides by water, makes a safer, less conspicuous place for an otter's holt than a bankside burrow with a signposting of nest debris (above).*

Resting places and holts

Patches of flattened vegetation among the tall grasses and reeds along a riverbank could be the 'couches', or resting places, regularly used by otters.

Look also for the openings to a female otter's breeding den, known as a holt. Like a couch, a holt entrance will be close to the water's edge, often among boulders or the roots of a tree. Sometimes, however, holts lie below the waterline, to protect the litter of two or three cubs, born blind and helpless, from the gaze of predators.

A nursing female is highly sensitive and can be easily upset by any kind of noise or movement near her holt. So if you think you have found one, don't get too close. Remember that you can be prosecuted for disturbing a holt.

It is possible to find quite a few holts along a single stretch of riverside, all belonging to the females from the harem of a single male, whose territory can stretch up to 10 miles along the bank. The male plays no part in rearing the young, so if you see an adult with cubs, you will know it is a female.

Mud slides

A broad, muddy furrow on the bank could be an otter slide. Otters are renowned for their playfulness and the slides are created by adults as well as young as they repeatedly launch themselves down a slippery bank, front legs tucked in and hind ones splayed out. If you find a slide, try returning at night; with luck, your patience may be rewarded by the sight of otters at play.

MINK OR OTTER?

In England and Wales, many sightings of 'otters' are actually glimpses of a related animal, the North American mink. In fact, you are much more likely to see mink, because they are generally active during the day, and less inclined to run off when people are about.

There is no real evidence that the two species compete for food, as was once thought. However, where otter numbers have declined, mink will often move in and colonise an area.

Originally raised in captivity for their fur, mink have escaped periodically over the years or been deliberately released, and are now firmly established in the wild. They are voracious, and eat a wide variety of prey, including rodents, rabbits, fish, birds and eggs. Mink have now reached the west coast of Scotland,where they have wiped out many sea bird nesting colonies.

What to look for

At a glance, it is quite easy to confuse the two waterside animals. Both are long-bodied, but the mink is only about 70cm (28in) long – smaller than the average domestic cat – while an adult otter is twice as big. Mink are usually dark, with glossy, brownish black fur, though some pale coloured mink have also escaped. They are less streamlined than otters and have thick, hairy tails. The otter is mid brown with a pale, grey-white underside and its long tail has short hairs and a thick base that tapers towards the tip.

But it is in the water that appearances differ most: if you can see the animal's head, neck and back above the surface, it is almost certainly a mink; otters usually swim with only their heads above the water.

On dry land *The mink (above), whose chocolate-brown fur looks almost black at a distance, catches much of its prey on land. In contrast to the otter, you are as likely to see one hunting in fields for rabbits and other small animals as swimming in a river.*

Surface view *The mink (above right) holds more of its body out of the water than the otter (right). Notice, too, how the heads of the two animals differ in shape – the otter's being much broader, with widely splayed nostrils on its flatter muzzle.*

Stone-shattered heights

The bleak summits surrounding Scotland's Rannoch Moor (above) are an inhospitable winter environment, with the peaks offering no protection from the worst that winter can bring to the Highlands. On a fine day, you might see a golden eagle patrolling the ridges, silhouetted against the sky as it does the rounds of its territory or pursues a flicker of white against the blue – a ptarmigan attempting to outfly the bird of prey. But even the eagle is forced to fly lower altitude missions on most days, hunting for hares crouching in the heather, or searching for carrion to eke out the winter rations.

For other predators, too, lower ground offers a better chance of a meal. Though food is in short supply, they remain wary, but when snow covers the ground, you

Time to stage a retreat or prepare for a siege

Wildlife finds ways of coping as winter's icy grip tightens

As temperatures plummet across Britain's high country, animals and plants respond in different ways. Birds such as the redpoll and siskin, and mammals such as red deer move to lower altitudes as conditions grow more severe and food more scarce on high ground. A few creatures, however, such as the ptarmigan and mountain hare, stay put, braving the severe weather and never going far below the snowline in their search for food.

Dense evergreens that lie flat or form cushions, like juniper, resist wind chill, and are soon covered by a protective blanket of snow. They can also photosynthesise on sunny days – so their growth gets off to an early start when spring finally arrives.

Although it can fly to great heights, you may also see a golden eagle swooping low in the sky, ready to drop silently on an unsuspecting hare or ptarmigan.

might spot a fox or pine marten as it hunts for small rodents or rabbits – the colour of its fur made more conspicuous by the white background.

Most elusive of all is the wild cat: just finding the pawprints of one in snow, then maybe following them to an abandoned rabbit burrow, heap of boulders or hollow tree containing the animal's den, would be a first-rate piece of detective work.

Frozen falls

When cascades like those along Sourmilk Gill in the Lake District (above) become locked in ice, wild creatures go thirsty, and may die if the freeze-up continues and they do not head downstream, where the cold is less extreme. The dipper, which also relies on finding its food supply in water, is doubly at risk. It needs clean water, with boulders, overhanging branches or shingle banks as perches. That's why the rare sight of one hunting in a lowland river or estuary in winter for the aquatic insects it feeds on is a sure sign of severe cold high up.

Freezing winds sculpt trees such as hawthorns, mountain oaks and rowans. A moment's observation tells you from which direction the prevailing winds blow: shoots on the windward side of trees are damaged by freezing winds and die; those on the leeward side are shaped by the wind, giving the overall tree a lopsided look. Branches are gnarled and twisted, pruned into weird shapes by frost, and by animals biting shoots and tender twigs for food.

Much of the soft vegetation that grows high up – plants like the moss campion and saxifrages – have low, cushion-like shapes or rosettes of ground-hugging leaves, which help them to avoid wind damage.

The cells of many mountain plants contain chemicals that act as an antifreeze, allowing them to survive the rapid thaws that can kill plants.

Strategies for survival

On rare winter days when not a breath of wind disturbs the summits, the high country is intensely silent and seems devoid of animal life. In truth, few creatures are about. Many small mammals, such as voles, rarely emerge from under the ground. Insects that have not flown are also passing winter in the soil, where there is less risk of freezing – often as chrysalises, in transition from one stage of their life cycle to the next. Still, there are a few creatures which are active, having successfully adapted to the harshest time of year in the mountains.

Watch the rocks *Keep an eye on any rocky outcrops poking above the snow. They may provide a lookout point for a stoat as it seeks it's prey, but the exposed stones also provide a coloured background which makes it easier to spot the creature's white winter coat. Crevices among the outcrops also provide the stoat with dry, secure winter quarters.*

Among the places worth watching in the mountains in winter are the edges of belts of trees. Many animals, including red deer, spend much of the winter sheltering under tree branches from the cold, but on fine days they emerge into the open. If you see a squirrel quartering the slope near the trees, it is probably looking for a cache of nuts that it buried in autumn. A noisy screech ringing from the trees signals that a jay, which also buries stores of food, has spotted you.

USEFUL WINTER COATS

Red deer and squirrels grow thick winter coats to insulate them from the cold. But beyond the treeline there are two animals – one a predator (the stoat), the other its prey (the mountain hare) – whose fur also changes colour, becoming white to match the winter landscape.

If these transformations were complete, and if a blanket of snow was a permanent feature of the upland winter, they would be virtually impossible to detect against the white background. But because this is often not the case, their winter camouflage can give them away.

Problem patches

Over most of Britain, stoats become piebald in winter. The amount of white fur that they grow is related to the coldness of the surroundings, and inherited and hormonal factors. Patches of fur that remain brown show up against a snow-covered background, while the white fur makes them stand out when there is no snow. Even in the coldest areas, such as the Highlands, an ermine, as a stoat in complete winter white is called, keeps the black tip to its tail – a small brush stroke clearly seen against the snow.

Like the stoat, the mountain hare, an animal midway in size and build between a brown hare and a rabbit, also turns wholly or partly white in winter. As with stoats, you are more likely to see completely white animals the farther north you go.

The closer a mountain hare is to the southern limit of its range (the Pennines), the more likely it is to have brown patches showing among the white. This mixed colouring camouflages the animal when the country is partly covered with snow, but at other times it can make it more conspicuous to a predator – and easier for you to spot.

In Northern Ireland, where there are no very high mountains and where snow usually thaws very quickly, mountain hares tend to stay brown throughout the year.

Almost invisible *A mountain hare bounds up a snowfield in the Scottish Highlands. Its tracks, up to 6cm (2½in) long with four small claw marks, are usually the only clue to its existence you will find.*

WHITE PLUMAGE IN SNOW

White feathers help a bird to conceal itself on a snowy mountainside. The ptarmigan, found only above 600m (1970ft) on Scottish mountains, is the only British bird to turn white in winter. This makes it very inconspicuous in snow unless you are really close. Fortunately for the countryside detective, the ptarmigan shares the reluctance of most gamebirds to take to the air, so getting near to one is possible.

Best vantage point

Ski lifts are the quickest way to reach the ptarmigan's habitat, and they also give you a vantage point. You may spot one of these birds as it crouches to conceal itself, or scurries into a hole in the snow – dug by the bird as a secure, warm place to roost. If you can use binoculars to scan the ground, this will increase your chances of seeing the bird and observing details, such as the black face patches of the male.

Walk quietly and keep your ears pricked, because a ptarmigan sometimes betrays itself with a noise: listen for the scratch of a claw or the clink of a stone being dislodged. As long as the bird has been aware of your approach, it is likely to just walk away when it is spotted, although fine winter days encourage the male to fly up, displaying his brilliant white plumage and uttering his dry, belching calls.

FLOCKS ON THE HIGHLANDS

The Scottish mountains in winter are the best place to see the snow bunting, although the bird also occurs farther south – along England's North Sea coast, and around the coast of Northern Ireland. You will need binoculars to spot details, like the feathery 'shorts' around the top of the snow bunting's legs. Other features, such as the contrasting black-and-white wings of the male, are easy to see with the naked eye.

On cloudy days, the creamy white breast and tawny or black upperparts of snow buntings enables them to vanish among patches of scree and snow. When a flock of them flies up, however, their rippling, tinkling trills and deeper *tew* calls will enable you to identify them, even if they are hidden by mist.

Levels of concealment A female ptarmigan (below), crouches in the snow, her plumage camouflaging her more effectively than that of the snow bunting (inset), although the smaller bird is hard to spot when the snow cover is incomplete.

Q **I thought I saw reindeer in the Scottish Highlands. Was I right?**

A If you were on the Cairngorm plateau south of Loch Morlich at the time, then you probably did see reindeer. They were introduced to the region in the 1950s and look very different from the native red deer. They have much heavier bodies and heads, and paler greyish or whitish coats – featuring a thick mane of neck hair in the case of bulls (below). Both sexes have flattened, crescent-shaped antlers. Reindeer leave characteristic crescent-shaped cloven hoofprints like those of deer (see page 284), with the separate indentations of the dew claws showing if the tracks are made in snow or muddy ground.

The feeders on carrion

For predators of moorland and mountain, such as the fox and buzzard, prey is scarce in winter. Creatures like voles and rabbits conserve their energy, rarely appearing, and starvation stalks the carnivores unless they supplement their diet with carrion. Most do just that, joining those more regular scavengers, the hooded crow, carrion crow, magpie and raven, wherever there is a carcass to be stripped. For these carrion eaters, recent decades have been a time of comparative abundance because of increases in the numbers of livestock, sheep and red deer especially, being kept on higher land.

Pecking order *A solitary buzzard stakes first claim to a dead ewe. Once it has opened up the carcass, some of the magpies will distract the bird of prey while others seize pieces of flesh and entrails.*

The body of a dead animal may smell appalling but it provides a great opportunity for some detective work. By finding a place nearby to shelter and stay concealed, it is possible to see some of the creatures that eat carrion, and to observe the pecking order among them.

Crows are likely to be the first callers at a fresh corpse. Even if they spot you from the air, they are unlikely to be deterred by a watcher who is considered to be at a safe distance, but if they don't settle, try creeping slightly farther away.

Which members of this bird family you see will depend on which part of Britain you're in. In England, Wales and southern Scotland, the carrion crow and magpie are the commonest crows on carrion. Farther north in Scotland, in Ireland and the Isle of Man, it is largely replaced by the hooded crow – a similar-sized bird with a grey back and underparts. Watch how a carrion crow, magpie, or hooded crow tackles a carcass, and you will see it has to get into it by pecking at one of the weak points – the eyes or eye sockets, or the rear end. This is because these birds lack the sharp, hooked, tearing beak of a true bird of prey.

A stronger beak

The biggest of the crows, the raven, however, has a stouter beak than its cousins and will lunge at the back of the skull of a dead animal, as well as probing and pecking at the soft spots. The raven occurs, over much of western and northern Britain and is always top of the pecking order among the feathered feasters on carrion. It uses its superior size and strength to drive away other crows and gulls from a carcass and reserve the carrion for itself, but in the Highlands it is supplanted by the golden eagle.

Stay hidden

The chances of seeing Britain's most majestic bird of prey feeding on a carcass on the ground are remote unless you are well wrapped-up and prepared to stay hidden from aerial view for a long time. A more likely sighting is that of a pair of golden eagles in the air, where their huge up-curved wings and finger-like pinion feathers are unmistakable.

Catching sight of a fox, biggest of the carrion-eating mammals, also demands patience and luck. It will brave mobbing crows to compete for carrion, although it won't stand its ground against the attacks of a golden eagle.

Bones to pick *A hooded crow, or hoodie as the bird is called in Scotland, perches on the carcass of a sheep, already stripped to the bone.*

Tracking the red kite's return If you see a bird of prey with a small coloured square fluttering from its wing, it is likely to be a red kite, tagged as a chick so that the extent of its flight in search of a territory can be recorded. The species has been brought back from the verge of extinction over the past few decades, and the dispersal of young birds and release of imported ones mean you might see a kite flying over places as far apart as Inverness and the Chilterns.

The hills of Mid Wales, however, remain the red kite's main stronghold. Here, its taste for carrion is catered for at feeding stations, and visitors to places such as Tregaron, south-east of Aberystwyth, and Gigrin Farm, near Rhayader, can see kites close-up. It is easily distinguishable from other birds of prey by its forked tail, often twisted and fanned as a rudder, its mainly reddish plumage and the way its long wings are flexed independently in flight.

CARRION OFF THE MENU

Some birds of prey will not readily eat carrion. The merlin and male sparrowhawk, for example, appear to resort to it only when exceptionally hungry, although the larger, female sparrowhawk is more ready to feed on a carcass. The hen harrier, too, alights on carrion only occasionally.

The bird that appears to rely most exclusively on live kills is the short-eared owl, possibly because it has a sense of smell – a rare attribute in a bird. Research has shown that the short-eared owl will readily eat fresh liver, but reject the meat if it is 'off'.

When winter approaches, and many of the creatures the owls feed on disappear from the uplands, these birds of prey respond by abandoning the bleak moors and becoming more widespread over heaths, coastal marshes and farmland. There they find greater numbers of small mammals and birds on which to feed, and so survive the months of cold.

Cold predator *A short-eared owl fluffs out its feathers to keep warm in winter as it scans the ground for prey.*

SPOT THE DIFFERENCE

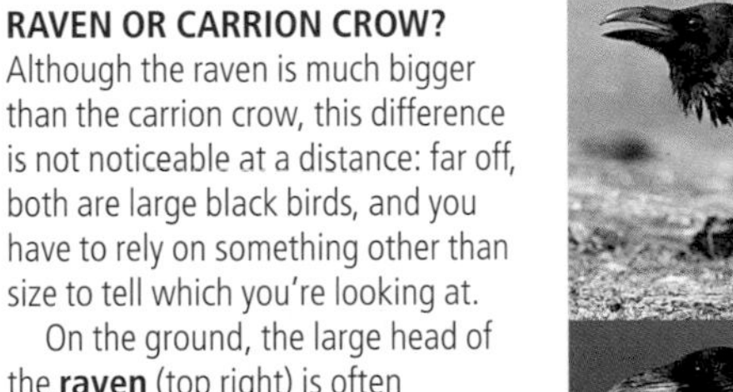

RAVEN OR CARRION CROW?

Although the raven is much bigger than the carrion crow, this difference is not noticeable at a distance: far off, both are large black birds, and you have to rely on something other than size to tell which you're looking at.

On the ground, the large head of the **raven** (top right) is often accentuated by a shaggy beard of throat feathers, especially when it calls. The **carrion crow** (bottom right) has smooth neck feathers and is less animated when calling. Its guttural ***kaarr*** is often repeated three times, where the raven utters a deep ***prruk***, or ***kronk***. But it is the beaks which really differ. The raven's beak is heavy, black and arching, the carrion crow's is less stout, dark grey in colour and only slightly curved.

With its long, broad wings and diamond-shaped tail, the raven is a master of the air. It soars and swoops with its wings angled, and frequently performs a unique roll-over, flying upside down for a moment before flipping the right way up again. It is also able to hover against a strong headwind. By comparison, the carrion crow is a plodder in the air, flapping laboriously along, soaring little and typically maintaining a straight course – hence the expression 'as the crow flies'.

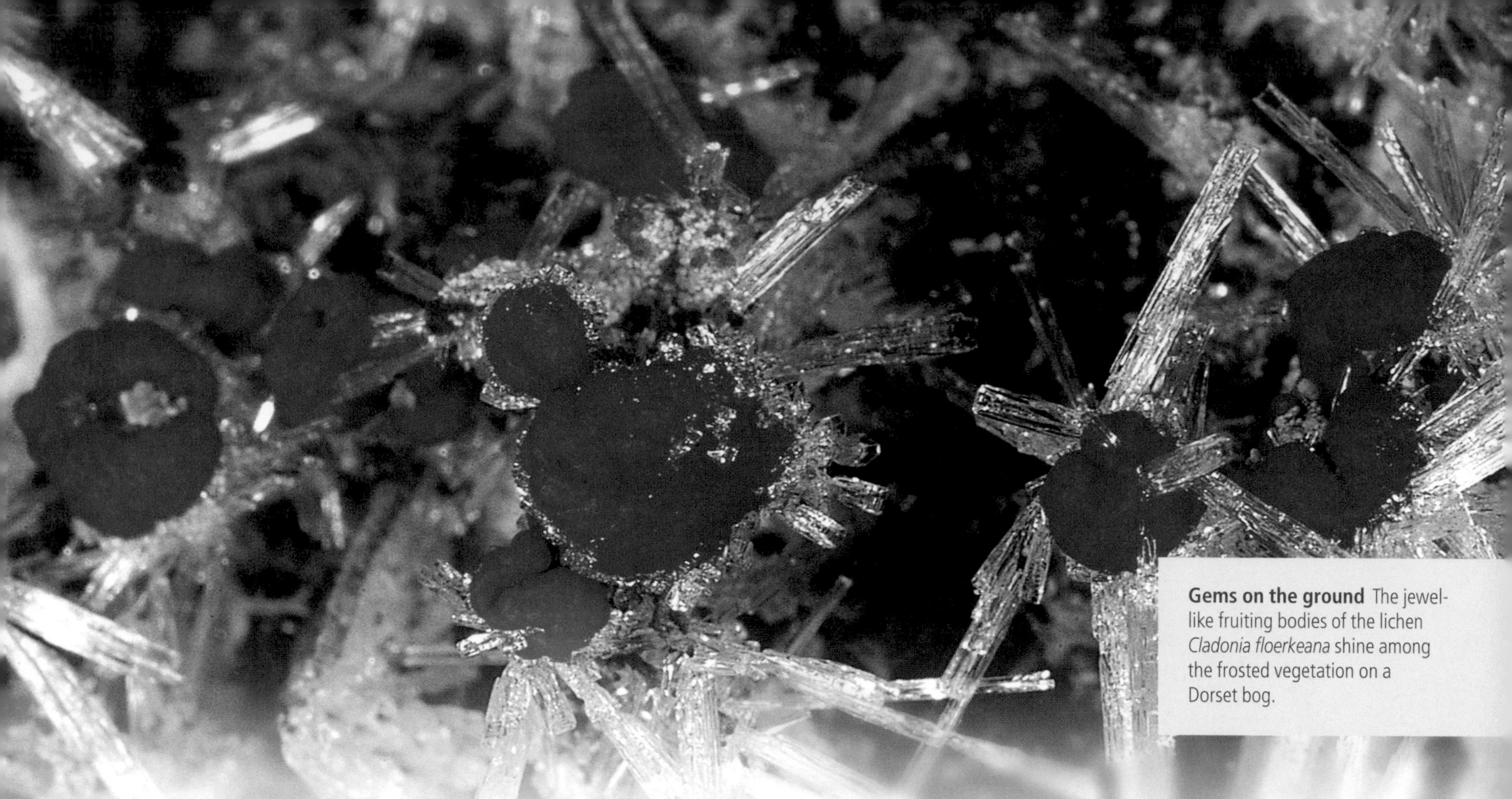

Gems on the ground The jewel-like fruiting bodies of the lichen *Cladonia floerkeana* shine among the frosted vegetation on a Dorset bog.

Miniatures revealed

The winter shades of moorland and heath are subtle and few compared with the vibrant colours of summer and autumn. Subdued browns and greys give the vegetation a lifeless look. The dead heather flowers cling persistently to the plants, but they are bleached and bone-grey. The bracken is a tangled mass of stems and shrivelled fronds – heavy, dark and pliant after a soaking. Yet a closer look, preferably with the help of a magnifying glass, reveals that there is still life in this plant world.

Heather may look dull and dormant, especially where old plants have grown leggy and open, but the plant is an evergreen – its stems still carry small triangular leaves, though not so densely packed at this time of year.

The freezing temperatures and biting winter winds are the equivalents of summer heat and drying breezes, and the heather responds in the same way to prevent moisture loss. Look at the foliage through a magnifying glass and you will see that the edges of the leaves curl down to form small tubes. This means that any moisture released through the pores on the underside of the leaf is trapped inside this sheltered environment. Unroll a leaf, and you will see that the underside is covered with a fine layer of hairs, which also help to conserve moisture.

While looking at heather, you might also see mosses and lichens, low-growing plants that are easily overlooked in summer, but which are more prominent once the vegetation dies back.

Lichens are very sensitive to pollution, so if you find grey lacey shawls of the species *Hypogymnia physodes* covering heather stems, it is a good indication of clean air.

Several of the most common lichens growing on peaty soils, rocks and tree trunks in moor and heath habitats belong to the Cladonia group, characterised by their intricate, branching structures. Among the most common of these on heather moors is *Cladonia impexa*, whose low, silvery grey cushions look like scouring pads. Easy to spot, because of the incongruous bright red of their fruiting bodies among the dull hues of winter, are *Cladonia coccifera* and *Cladonia floerkeana*.

Pixie cups *A glance is enough to tell you how the lichen* Cladonia fimbriata *got its common name.*

High tolerance *The moss* Racomitrium lanuginosum, *here shown on a mountain top, tolerates high metal content in the soil and so is also found on spoil heaps.*

TRADEMARK MOSSES

Mosses need damp conditions because without a film of water on the plant's surface the male sperm would not be able to 'swim' to the female structures and fertilise them. Apart from this basic requirement, however, many mosses are specialists, and you can often identify them by where you find them growing.

Scottish mountaintops are often covered with the shaggy, grey-green woolly moss, *Racomitrium lanuginosum*. At the opposite end of the country, neat blocks of the bright green moss, *Ceratodon purpureus*, and clumps of the bushier *Hypnum jutlandicum*, often grow among heather on southern heaths.

High up on blanket bogs, sphagnum mosses are abundant. They become waterlogged because their leaves are full of hollow cells, rather like sponges, and this enables them to absorb many times their own weight in water.

One moss found on the hills and moors of the north and west has an extra requirement – *Splachnum ampullaceum* grows only on the dung of grazing animals. The spores are dispersed by the wind, and so many are produced that some inevitably land on a favourable site.

Look at a patch of moss and you may still find the spore capsules attached to it in winter, even though they are empty. These come in a variety of shapes, but can be recognised because they crown slender, colourful stalks growing from the body of the moss.

Lifting the lid

With the aid of a magnifying glass, you can see how the spores are spread. In some cases, the capsule shrinks as it dries, causing the lid to pop open and allowing the spores to blow out.

Other mosses have a spore capsule with a toothed ring around the top. When humidity is low, this curls open and allows spores to escape, then closes up again when the atmospheric moisture levels rise.

EVIDENCE OF SCOTS PINE UNDER THREAT

Few images could be more evocative of winter in the mountains than a snow-laden Scots pine. Yet the tree is also found on southern heaths, where it has been introduced. In both habitats, however, its future is threatened.

If you look for young Scots pines in the Highlands, you are likely to find only nibbled and dying seedlings. This is because there are many more deer on the mountains than in the past, and the young Scots pines are being browsed and ultimately killed before they can become established. On the heaths of southern England, the opposite is the case: there are not enough livestock, so faster-growing birch becomes established at the expense of the slower Scots pine.

The **cones of the Scots pine** (right) take two years to develop, and if you examine them you can distinguish small, green, year-old cones and mature woody ones, from which winged seeds fall in spring. Many empty three-year-old cones can be found too, but most of these soon fall off.

The seeds germinate easily on ground that has been burned, and once established, their leathery needles and **thick insulating bark** (inset) enables them to survive the regular **burning of heather** (below).

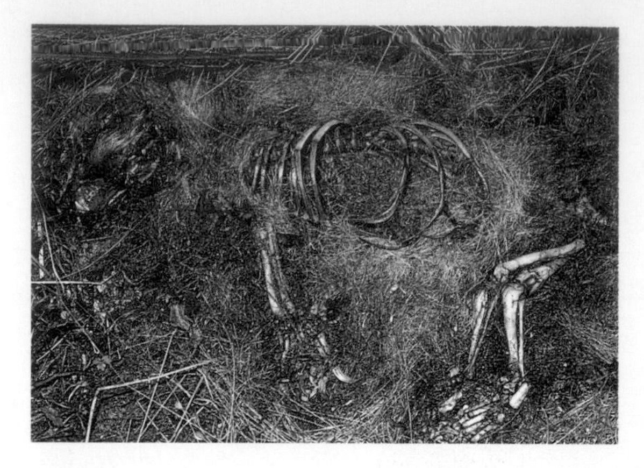

Vanishing evidence *In the four weeks since it died, this badger (left) has been reduced to a skeleton and wreath of fur. Soon the fur will blow away and the skeleton will fall apart, allowing scavengers to carry off many of the bones.*

IDENTIFYING A CARNIVORE

Long, pointed fangs (the canine teeth) and eye sockets on the front of the head identify a skull as being from a carnivore, such as a **fox**. The canines overlap, so a creature seized in them has little chance of escape. The animal's forward-facing eyes provide about 180° of vision **[1]** in total and a wide field of binocular vision **[2]** for spotting prey and assessing how far away it is.

Close-up on Bones

A skeleton or collection of bones provide many clues about a dead animal. They can tell you whether the creature was a bird or mammal, whether it ate plants or flesh, and sometimes even enable you to identify the animal's exact species. But time is the enemy of such detective work. Decomposition and scavengers see to it that entire skeletons rarely survive for more than a few weeks.

Once the binding ligaments and sinews have rotted or been gnawed through, bones become separated at the joints and the smallest are soon carried off by scavengers, or lost in undergrowth. Big bones, however, survive longer and may lie around for years. It is these that you are likeliest to come across – limb bones and, most vital of all in the clues they provide, skulls. Bones make interesting items on a nature table. If you want to take them home, protect your hands with a polythene bag or rubber gloves when you collect them, then clean and whiten the bones by boiling them in water containing a little chlorine-free bleach before exhibiting them.

WHICH CARNIVORE?

Identifying which species of animal a carnivore skull belonged to can be difficult. The mink, pine marten, polecat, stoat and weasel are all related and have similarly shaped skulls. Telling one from another depends on relating the size of the skull to that of the whole animal. Even then, it is hard to tell a weasel's skull from a stoat's, while it takes an expert to differentiate those of the mink, pine marten and polecat.

By contrast, it is relatively easy to distinguish a fox's skull (above) from that of a badger.

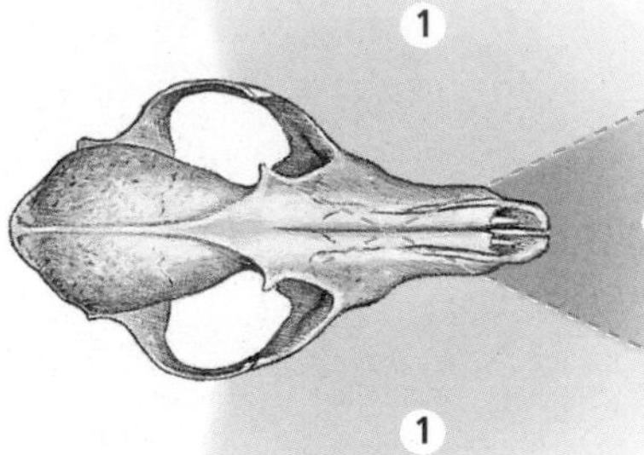

The fox's has a flat forehead, tapering nose, and is about 13cm (5in) long. A badger's skull is about the same length but broader, and the canine teeth are shorter. If the lower jaw is missing, the skull cannot be a badger's, because this is jointed in such a way that it cannot become detached.

BIRD OR MAMMAL? Even when the feathers or fur have gone, there are ways of distinguishing the skeleton of a bird, such as the **puffin** (left), and a mammal, like the **rabbit** (right). A bird's skull contains no teeth and, like other parts of its skeleton, is far lighter than a mammal's. This is because it contains air chambers – an important evolutionary development for a creature that takes to the wing. A bird's backbone is shorter than a mammal's, bringing its centre of gravity farther forward so that it can support its weight on its legs when on the ground. And a bird's front limb bones are elongated to support the wings. The sternum, or breastbone, so conspicuous in the dead puffin, has developed into a big, flat blade-like bone for the attachment of the flight muscles, quite unlike its much smaller equivalent in mammals.

IDENTIFYING A HERBIVORE

A long toothless gap (diastema) between the front incisor teeth and the back molars, and sideways-facing eye sockets distinguish a skull of a herbivore, such as a **rabbit**. The flat, chisel-like incisors, which exist only in the lower jaw in deer and sheep, enable it to cut through grass and tough, woody shoots. They also jut forward, so that the animal can nibble short grass. The position of the eyes gives a wide angle of view **[1]** – good for spotting predators approaching from behind – but a narrower field of binocular vision **[2]** than the fox.

1
2
1

Grass grinders When you find a herbivore's skull, look at the molar (back) teeth. You will see that they have complex ridges – as in this roe deer's jaw. This is because they are made up of alternating hard and soft layers which wear at different rates. The resulting rasp-like surface is ideal for shredding grass and liberating its nutritious contents as the animal moves its jaws from side to side.

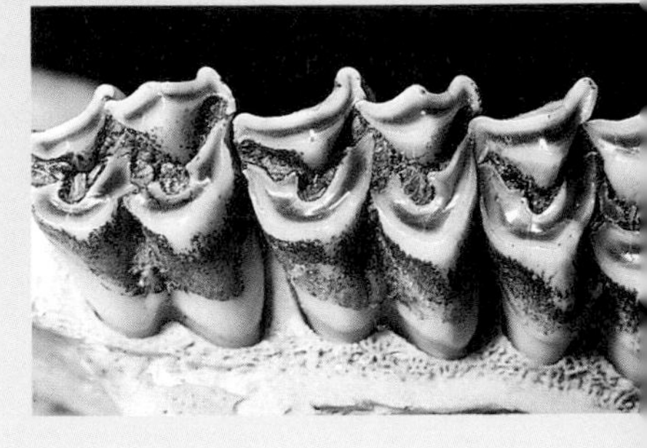

Positive identification *Incisor teeth, separated from the molars by a gap, and eye sockets on the side identify this skull as a herbivore's. The restriction of incisors to the lower jaw narrows it down to a deer or sheep, but the tusks and back-swept antler supports leave you in no doubt that it belonged to a muntjac deer.*

WHICH HERBIVORE?

The number of incisors in the upper jaw of a herbivore's skull will help you to determine what species of animal it belonged to.

Four upper incisors – a large front pair with a smaller second pair immediately behind them – mark out the skull as that of a rabbit or hare. Rabbits – and therefore their skulls – are far more common than hares, but always look for other evidence in the surrounding area, such as the presence or absence of rabbit burrows, before reaching a conclusion.

The biggest skull you are likely to come across will belong to a sheep or deer, and it will have no upper incisors. Other features will help you to determine which of the two animals it belonged to. Horns instantly identify a skull as a sheep's, and antler supports as a deer's. But if there are no horns or antlers to help you, look at the shape of the skull: a sheep's skull is heavy and thickset, a deer's lighter and more tapered.

Tell-tale tusks

You can take your detective work a little further by measuring the skull of a deer. A fully grown red deer's skull is about 30cm (12in) long, that of a mature fallow or sika about 25cm (10in) in length, and one belonging to a roe or muntjac, 20cm (8in).

There are other clues to help you to narrow the possibilities, including the prominent tusk-like teeth that you would see in the upper jaw of a male muntjac and Chinese water deer – these are about 2cm (¾in) long in the case of a muntjac, but can reach 8cm (3¼in) in a Chinese water deer.

The smallest herbivore skulls belong to rodents – rats, mice, voles and squirrels. You can recognise one of these by its single pair of upper incisors, which are usually yellow or orange on the front surface, something not found in other herbivores.

With the exception of a squirrel, the skull of which measures about 5.5cm (2¼in) long, most of these animals are so small that their bones are unlikely to survive for long. However, you might find their skulls preserved in discarded bottles and other containers where they have become trapped (see page 197).

SIGNATURES ON BONE

Always examine bones and bony structures like **antlers** (right) for clues. Often bones have been bitten, pecked or gnawed and, if you know what to look for, you can identify the culprit by the signs left behind. A fox leaves twin grooves where it has gnawed; small rodents make ragged holes and scored patches when they nibble. A bird of prey leaves triangular notches on bones – these are most usually found on the breastbones of small birds.

Rich pickings left after high tide retreats

Waves pound the beach, bringing opportunities in the debris

Winter can be an exciting time at the coast. Estuaries and bays teem with birds feeding in the soft mud exposed at low tide. Among them are gulls, the most opportunistic of shore birds; waders, whose bills probe down for food such as worms; geese and swans arriving at dusk to roost on flats and sandbanks; and ducks, such as wigeon and shelduck. Bright days offer excellent birdwatching and you may be spoiled for choice as flocks of dunlin or knot wheel through the chilly air and skeins of wild geese pass overhead. Sandy shores are quiet, but rock pools still contain seaweeds, and you can only marvel at the endurance of mussels and other sedentary animals as winter storms lash their rocky homes.

Shallow estuaries

Estuaries take on a bleak beauty in winter as the low light is reflected on sheets of shallow water or produces a greyish blue haze when filtered through low cloud. Between the moored boats stranded at low tide on the Thames estuary (above), flocks of wigeon and brent geese feed on the exposed eelgrass and green seaweeds.

With the naked eye, these winter visitors from breeding grounds on the Arctic tundra appear as little more than small shadows, but with binoculars they become individual birds, bursting into colour and life as the light strikes them.

Scouring the mud or probing into it with slender bills are other small greyish or brownish birds: waders, looking for shells, crustaceans and worms on or near the surface. Like the geese, they feed in flocks,

Wigeon are grazing ducks, which flock on large estuaries in huge numbers. The males' high whistle is one of the most evocative sounds of the winter coast.

and frequently take to the air in tight, often vocal formations. They search for food hidden in undisturbed mud, alerted by clues such as wormcasts or burrows.

As you watch the flocks of birds you can begin to recognise the individual postures of these often very similar birds – the hunched, rather dejected look of the grey plover, contrasted with the manic, stitching action of our most common wader, the dunlin.

Crashing waves

North Sea breakers pound the shore on a typically grey overcast winter day (above). The force of the waves will scour the seabed, tearing up weak or broken seaweeds and casting them ashore in piles – often far up the beach – along with floating objects such as driftwood. Only the best adapted animals can defy the full brunt of a winter storm. Limpets and barnacles cling tightly to the rocks, while beds of mussels stay firmly fixed by strong anchoring threads.

Storms also create new opportunities for wildlife. The debris cast ashore provides rich pickings for foraging birds, and even attracts roving mammals, such as foxes or hedgehogs. For the human beachcomber, the strandline is full of clues to life offshore, from the empty egg cases of dogfish or whelks to shells, bones and driftwood, and even castaway 'treasure' such as water-polished minerals or tropical pods washed up on our Atlantic shores.

Many fish move offshore in winter to deeper waters both calmer and warmer than the shallow seas. Others move into deep and sheltered rock pools on the shore, or hide in cracks and crevices. Clingfish and some other shorefish have suckers, which help them withstand the battering of the waves.

Gulls are strong birds capable of powerful, sustained flight. Even in stormy seas, they ride on the eddying wind, alert for any floating food carried by the waves.

The mud flat spectacular

One of the great wildlife spectacles of winter is the congregation of thousands of wading birds and wildfowl in estuaries. At first sight the ground may seem to be alive, as the feeding masses move across the mud flats exposed by the retreating tide. Countless grey or brown birds may take to the air as one, flashing white bellies and wing bars, then whirr across the water in formation and settle somewhere else, filling the air with piping calls.

Closing ranks *At high tide, knots huddle together to conserve warmth when they settle to roost. The birds pack themselves together so tightly that, from a distance, the effect is of a patterned grey carpet.*

One of the first things you will notice when watching waders in an estuary is that most will be feeding close to the water's edge. This is because the small molluscs and worms that they feed on are found close to the surface where the mud is wet. As the tide goes out and the mud dries, the prey will burrow deeper in search of moisture, and will soon be out of reach of the birds' probing bills.

What will strike you most forcibly as you watch waders is that most of them feed, fly and roost in large flocks. Why is this? The reason is that there is safety in numbers. Mud flats are bare and exposed, with few places to hide, and so feeding waders are visible to birdwatchers – and predators – from some distance.

Putting their heads together

While a solitary bird has only one pair of eyes, a large flock has thousands, and so is far less likely to be surprised by a swooping merlin or peregrine. Moreover, when faced by a flock of birds suddenly taking to the air, the predator is offered a confusion of targets.

Probably one reason why many waders have white bars on their wings, tail stripes and other contrasting markings is that they help to break up each bird's profile in the air, and confuse a predator still more.

The effect is increased by the waders' rapidly whirring wings and incredible agility as aerial acrobats. Only starlings can match waders as masters of synchronised flying.

Flocking cuts down on the time individual birds would need to spend locating good feeding sites, since the birds exchange information on the most profitable sites. In turn, this increases the flock's potential feeding time.

Waders are good at spotting individuals that are feeding well, and less successful birds rush to join them. Watch how quickly a flock of small waders gathers when one bird hits a spot rich in food and starts probing the mud like a sewing machine needle.

Taking a dip *A bar-tailed godwit goes into the water to feed, wading belly-deep in the shallows and immersing its head to sift the wet mud.*

Standing alone *Solitary waders at rest, like this redshank, keep warm by withdrawing their necks and sometimes one leg and tucking their bills under a wing.*

The characteristic swirling flights of flocks of waders are not necessarily a sign that the birds are alarmed, but represent a systematic group search for feeding grounds. Most waders feed only by day, and by working together they can maximise their feeding time – a vital consideration when winter days are short and often wet, and when worms and crustaceans can take some finding.

How do waders keep warm?

Conserving heat is a crucial factor for small birds that spend the winter on windswept estuaries. Their small bodies lose heat quickly, but flocking together during roosting enables them to keep warm.

Waders that do not live in flocks must find other ways of staying warm. If you see a redshank, for example, notice how it always faces into the wind when roosting. By aligning itself in this way the bird presents the least possible resistance to the wind and does its best to prevent its feathers being ruffled.

Knots, medium-sized greyish waders with short black bills (see opposite page), congregate in huge numbers – sometimes many thousands of birds – on large estuaries in England, Wales and eastern Scotland. They remain at close quarters when feeding, and move slowly across the mud as one.

If you see a flock of knots feeding, wait a while to see the birds take to the air. They give wonderful displays of close-formation flying: twisting and turning in unison, with their feathers seeming to alternate between grey and silver. From a distance a flock can look like swirling clouds of smoke.

The diversity of flocks

The benefits of flocking mean that most waders, such as knot, dunlin and golden plovers, are rarely seen singly in winter. They also associate with other birds with similar feeding requirements and it is common to see mixed flocks. So if you spot dunlins out on the mud flats, look for sanderlings and grey plover, too.

If you hear the sad whistling call of a golden plover, or catch sight of a flock passing overhead, glittering silver as the light reflects off their feathers, look around for lapwings and black-headed gulls nearby.

SEA-GOING DUCKS

While waders feed in mud exposed at low tide, high water is the time to watch fish-eating estuary birds: cormorants, grebes and sea-going ducks. No season can match winter for watching ducks. They are back in their finest colours, following their moult in early autumn, and many are living in large flocks.

If you see a pair or small group of sleek ducks with wispy crests at the back of their heads and most un-duck-like slender bills, they are likely to be red-breasted mergansers. These ducks work together to herd shoals of small fish into shallow water, where they can be seen more easily. Then they dive to seize their slippery prey with serrated bills.

Most other sea-going ducks have broader, more general-purpose bills, a clue that they are less specialised feeders. One to look out for in large estuaries is the pintail, a relatively silent duck. Its quiet nature helps to distinguish the pintail from the equally elegant male long-tailed duck, which has a loud and frequent yodelling ***a-ahulee*** call. This earned it its folk-name, 'calloo'. Look for long-tailed ducks on northern coasts, particularly in Shetland and on the west coast of Scotland.

The eider duck, whose feathers are used to stuff pillows and eiderdowns, is found mainly on northern shores and both sexes have a distinctive call. Listen for a loud crooning ***ah-aooh*** from the piebald male and a guttural ***gok-gok-gok*** from the brown female, like the chugging of a distant fishing boat.

Duck parade *The eider duck (top) uses its heavy bill to break open mussels and crab shells, and often leaves the debris as evidence. The common scoter (right) usually stays well off shore, where it occurs in large flocks, while red-breasted mergansers (below) are seen in smaller flocks or pairs.*

Wintering wildfowl

Skeins of geese threading across the sky in a straggly line or in V formation are a sure sign of approaching winter. Nearly all of the thousands of geese that congregate on the British coast from autumn onwards have come from nesting sites on the Arctic tundra, as far away as Greenland or Siberia. Also arriving on estuaries and coastal marshes at the same time as the geese are migratory duck, such as wigeon, and beautiful wild swans from the far north. Take your binoculars in mittened hands, focus on the feathered masses and try to decipher the action.

Why do geese fly in formation? The main reason is to reduce air resistance and save energy. The wing beats of the leading bird create a slight suction in the air, which helps to lift and pull the bird behind, and this effect continues along the line (see page 211). From time to time, the leader falls back into the slipstream to recover, while a new leader takes over. The geese manage to stay in formation, even in low cloud and poor visibility, because they honk continually as they fly to maintain contact.

Geese are primarily grazers: look at one closely and you'll see that it has a powerful bill with serrated edges to grip and yank out grass. Geese also pull up clovers, reeds and sedges to get at the nutritious creeping stems (stolons) and roots from beneath the surface.

In winter, you may see other grazers, such as the wigeon, mingling with a flock of feeding geese. This attractive duck feeds at low tide on tender eelgrass and green seaweeds, sometimes in huge flocks. At high tide, the flocks move to dry ground to roost, bunching closely together. The wigeon is a whistling duck: listen for the male's *whee-oo*.

Taking a gander at the geese

Britain's smallest species of goose, and the one you're most likely to see at the coast, is the brent goose. Look for flocks of a dark stocky bird no bigger than a mallard paddling in water at low tide and listen for their distinctive call: a guttural *krrook*.

Brent geese fly in from late October – you can tell where they came from by the colour of their bellies. Dark-bellied brent geese, which winter mainly in south and east England, have flown from Russia; pale-bellied ones, wintering at Lindisfarne in Northumberland, or Strangford Lough in Northern Ireland, hail from Spitsbergen, in the Arctic.

Low growls coming from a flock of feeding geese will tell you that you are observing barnacle geese, distinctive with their black necks and white

Mixed meal time *A flock of geese, such as these barnacle geese, will feed happily alongside other birds, like the all-black coots.*

Arable grazers *If you are on the east coast in early morning from September onwards, you may see a noisy flock of pink-footed geese flying inland. These geese roost at night on water, but feed in fields by day.*

faces (see opposite page). The growl grows to a cacophany of noise as the birds take flight. From October to April flocks of barnacle geese from Greenland visit western Scotland, while others from Spitsbergen are found in the Solway Firth area.

If you are in the Severn Estuary in winter you might hear the sounds that signal the arrival of white-fronted geese. Their high-pitched call has been compared to yelping dogs and also, when they are flying, to laughter. If you hear it, scan the sky for a flock of dark birds with white fronts to their faces.

THE KILLERS FLY IN

Just as geese and small waders are attracted to estuaries by their abundant supplies of food, so too are hungry birds of prey in search of an easy meal. Wherever you see flocks of birds on mud flats, look up into the sky to see if you can spot a predatory merlin or peregrine (see pages 160-161) on the look out. Both birds are falcons, with narrow wings and powerful feet perfectly evolved for chasing and catching birds in flight.

Signs of agitation among the wader and wildfowl flocks on the ground give you a clue that a bird of prey is threateningly close. The merlin is a tiny falcon: the male not much bigger than a thrush, and the female smaller than a male kestrel. It will dash low over an estuary to ambush small birds, which it takes back to its regular plucking post.

The peregrine normally takes larger prey, such as ducks and pigeons, stooping on them at tremendous speed from above. The strike, with outstretched talons, often kills the prey instantly; indeed, at a speed of up to 180mph (290km/h) – it is the fastest creature on earth – a peregrine can easily knock its victim's head clean off.

Great estuaries *The winter influx of migrant birds and wildfowl to our coast is one of the greatest wildlife events of the year. Here are some of the best estuaries to witness this phenomenon. Many have a nature reserve where you can observe the birds more easily, sometimes at close quarters from a hide.*

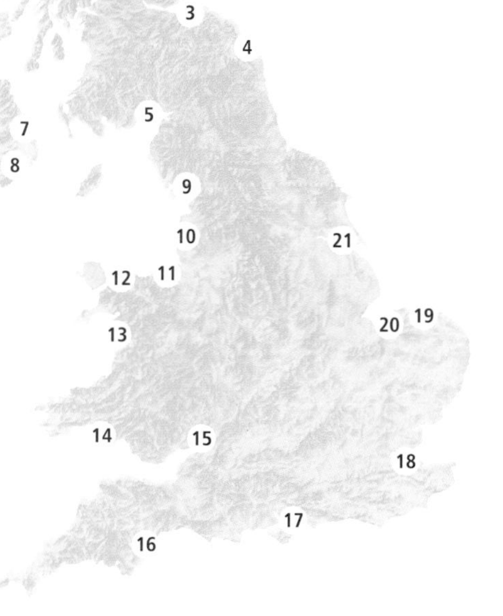

1. **River Nairn *R*** at Culbin Sands
2. **Ythan Estuary *SN*** at Sands of Forvie
3. **Aberlady Bay, Firth of Forth**
4. **Lindisfarne *SN***
5. **Caerlaverock *SN*** at Solway Firth
6. **Lough Foyle *R***
7. **Belfast Lough *R***
8. **Strangford Lough *W*** at Castle Espie
9. **Morecambe Bay *R***
10. **Ribble Estuary *N*** at Marshside and Lytham St Anne's
11. **Dee Estuary *R*** at Point of Air
12. **Conwy Estuary *R***
13. **Dyfi Estuary *R*** at Ynys-hir
14. **Burry Inlet *W*** at Llanelli
15. **Severn Estuary *W*** at Slimbridge
16. **Exe Estuary *R***
17. **Langstone Harbour *R***
18. **Thames Estuary *R*** at Elmley Marshes
19. **North Norfolk coast *N*** at Holkham, ***R*** at Titchwell Marsh
20. **The Wash *R*** at Snettisham
21. **Humber Estuary *N*** at Spurn Peninsula, ***R*** at Blacktoft Sands

KEY

N English Nature reserve
SN Scottish National Heritage reserve
R RSPB reserve
W Wildfowl and Wetland Trust reserve

Contact numbers: page 339

On guard *Watch a flock of feeding geese, like these white-fronted geese, and you will see some birds popping their heads up and looking around. They are acting as sentries for the flock, allowing the other birds to feed in safety.*

Close-up on
The strandline

The strandline is the narrow zone high on the shore, where debris washed in by tide and waves is left high and drying. The best time for beachcombing on the strandline is after a winter storm, when an amazing amount that is worthy of investigation is left piled on the beach: driftwood, seaweeds, shells and many other remains that offer clues to the life offshore.

Even when the weather has not been stormy, spring tides, which have the largest ranges of all tides, sweep debris high up the beach and also expose great expanses of the lower shore, where delicate red seaweeds grow in abundance. Lots of red seaweed in the strandline tells you that it is the season for spring tides.

Stranded on the shore *Any floating objects, including litter thrown into the sea, are likely to end up on the strandline (above), together with torn-up seaweeds and animal remains, such as moulted crab shells (right).*

A FERTILE STRIP On rocky beaches you may see a bright green strip running from the land to the sea between normally brownish seaweeds. This usually marks a **sewage outlet** (left), or a stream enriched with sewage. These brackish, phosphate-rich conditions are the ideal habitat for green seaweeds such as gutweed (*Enteromorpha*), sea lettuce (*Ulva*) or the filamentous blanket weed (*Cladophora*). Rub some blanket weed between your finger and thumb and you will find it is rough and gritty, not slimy like most seaweeds. This enables tiny organisms to cling to the rough surface and colonise it – you can just make out some of them with a hand lens, but to see the beautiful detail you will need a microscope.

WHAT'S BEEN WASHED UP ON THE BEACH?

Kelp seaweeds routinely shed their fronds in winter, but the storm-driven currents also detach old or weakened plants and churn up the seabed, exposing both live burrowing animals and empty shells. All this loose material is driven onto the beach by the crashing waves. Occasionally a ship's cargo, washed overboard in a storm, will also be washed up.

On sandy shores, this rotting debris provides food and a habitat for small crustaceans and insects, from shore crabs to sand hoppers and kelp flies, which feed on dead remains and help to break it down.

In winter, look for the turnstone, an attractive grey and white, plover-like bird with orange legs. It gets its name from its habit of turning over stones or shells with its strong, wedge-shaped bill to look for food items beneath. Small flocks of turnstones tend to work an area, then fly out to sea, wheel back and resume feeding farther along the beach. Listen for their dry, rattling ***tuk-a-tuk*** call.

Seaweeds on the shore
Saucer-sized, but bulky and elaborately branched objects, each with a thick stalk attached, are kelp 'roots', or holdfasts, and are firm evidence that there are kelp beds offshore (see page 176). These beds are among the richest marine wildlife habitats, so examine the beached holdfasts for sponges, sea squirts and limpets.

Another seaweed you can often find on the strandline is the slimy, bootlace weed or mermaid's tresses, whose long

Floating platforms *Driftwood attracts marine animals in search of shelter or support. Bivalves of the piddock family bore holes into wood (above) or soft rock; goose barnacles (right) just need a firm base to cling to, such as this bottle, which has been drifting at sea.*

hollow fronds are vulnerable to storm winds. On sheltered shores, you might discover japweed with its small flat 'leaves' and divided stalk. This invader from the Pacific is a nuisance on the south coast, because it smothers native eelgrasses and seaweeds and fouls boat engines. A useful clue to identifying this seaweed is to hold up a long piece from either end. The side branches hang down like washing on a clothes line.

Signs of animal life

Study the mass of weed on the strandline for clues to the animal life in the water and on the beach. What may look like a papery, buff-coloured seaweed could be hornwrack, a colony of tiny bryozoans or sea mats (see page 177). Look through a hand lens and you'll see that the 'weed' is made up of tiny rectangular boxes. When the bryozoan was alive, a single tentacled animal inhabited each box.

You might also find empty crab shells on the strandline, complete with legs, feelers and eye coverings. These are not the remains of dead crabs but are entire shells moulted by the crustaceans – a process vital for growth for a creature like a crab, which is encased in an inflexible shell.

DRIFTWOOD DRIFTERS

Look out for pieces of ships' timber riddled with small holes made by shipworms. Despite appearances, these long worm-like animals are molluscs, and sometimes leave their saw-toothed shells inside the wood.

If you find a piece of wood with thumbnail-sized holes (see above), break it open and look for the elongated white shells of the piddock inside. At sea, the piddocks extend siphons, or feeding tubes, out of the hole to filter morsels from the water.

Freshly beached timbers or fishing floats are often covered by whitish or bluish grey triangular shells supported on a tough black stalk. These are goose barnacles (inset above). Their shells make them look like molluscs, but, in fact, they are crustaceans. Goose barnacles filter-feed in the sea by creating currents using the whirring motion of their modified legs, known as 'cirri'.

Young goose barnacles develop with the floating plankton. They only colonise driftwood and other floating objects in the water as they mature, and attach themselves to any firm object they find. The structures of piers are another favourite place.

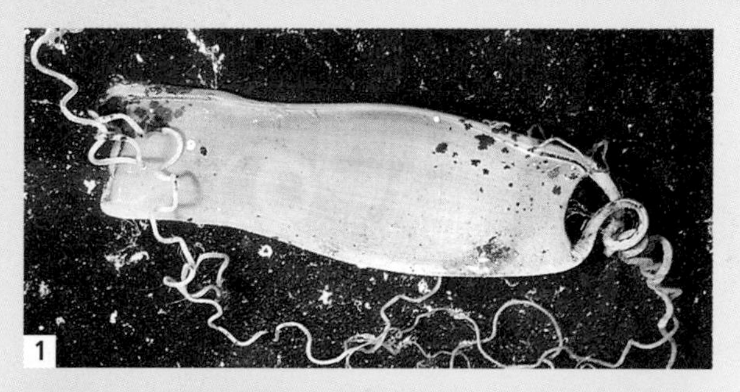

1

2

STRANGE SHAPES ON THE STRANDLINE Many of the odds and ends you may find as you comb the strandline are neither animals nor their remains, but are their egg cases. Dark oblongs with 'horns' at each corner, commonly called mermaid's purses, are the egg cases of skates and rays. Similar, but paler brown and with long tendrils, are the related **dogfish egg cases [1]**. The tendrils anchor the egg cases to seaweed but, when empty, they float away and, being tough and resistant to rotting, they accumulate on the shore.

If you are on a rocky beach you may see round papery bundles of empty cases, rather like weathered bubble wrap **[2]**. These are the eggs of the whelk and are known as **sea wash balls** because of the way they bounce along the beach as they are blown by the wind.

For one whelk, the dog whelk, there is another sign to look for. Dog whelks feed on barnacles and mussels by boring neat holes through their shells with file-like tongues and special chemicals. Look at the tops of barnacles – if there is a hole instead of a closed door, the barnacle is dead and has probably been eaten by a dog whelk.

Living on the winter beach

How does life on the shore survive being battered by blizzards and stormy breakers during the bleak winter months? Fish and mobile invertebrates move to deeper waters, where they will be less vulnerable to storms, but sedentary animals, such as barnacles and limpets, are fixed to the rocks and must survive where they are. Fortunately there is still plenty of plankton in the water for these filter-feeders. Also, at low tide, shells protect their inhabitants from frost and wind as effectively as from the air.

Winter rations *A black-faced sheep in Scotland makes a meal of seaweed at low tide, while the kelp flies (inset) will feed scavenging birds.*

In winter, the extraordinary ability of mussels to hang on to even the most storm-tossed rocks is easy to see. Their secret is the strong but flexible shank of nylon-like threads, called the byssus, which binds the shells to the rocks and to one another (below right). These threads are secreted by the mussel when it is young. If its position is not satisfactory, it can reabsorb the threads and move slowly to a more favourable place.

Once the mussels have found a suitable spot, they stay put. High up on the shore, mussels can live for 15 years or more, and gradually become encrusted with other sedentary animals, such as barnacles, tube worms and sea mats.

Because they are protected by a slimy covering, frost-damaged seaweeds are rare. Piles of seaweed create their own microclimate, slightly warmer and more humid than the surrounding air: a home for flies and tempting food for hungry cattle and sheep.

The seaweed washed ashore during storms often has dead creatures caught up in it, providing food for scavengers such as shore crabs, which shelter from the worst of the weather in rock crevices.

WHERE ARE THE FISH?

Peer into a rock pool at low tide in winter and you will find fewer fish than there were in the summer. You might still spot a butterfish: a yellowish fish that spawns in winter and lays sticky clumps of eggs in empty shells or fissures in the rocks. Butterfish will dart away if they

A STABLE ENVIRONMENT
A rock at the bottom of the beach provides a solid base for **mussels** (top left) to cling to in the face of crashing waves. Their shells offer protection, but some animals without shells make their own – a hard tube of calcium carbonate or sand.

The **honeycomb worm** builds golden masses of 'honeycomb' on rocks on the lower shore, with a single worm living inside each cell (far left). The **keel worm** fixes its white, triangular tube shelter to any solid object it can find, such as this razor shell (below left).

spot you, but if you net one you will discover the reason for the fish's name: butterfish are extremely slippery.

The plump warty lumpsucker is also still around in winter, especially in the north-east. It spawns from late winter, and the black-and-red male clings to a nearby rock with its sucker to guard the eggs. This habit makes the fish vulnerable in storms, when lumpsuckers are often washed ashore in large numbers. Look for the pink egg masses in large pools on the lower shore. Dyed and pickled, they are sold as mock caviare, or lumpfish roe.

Silvery shoals offshore

You often see shoals of silvery fish in harbours and estuaries in winter. Among them may be grey mullet, striped fish which suck at the algae on pier pilings and rocks.

Smaller fish are probably either the deep-bodied sprat, which looks like a small herring, or the slender sand smelt. A good clue to identifying sand smelt is that the shoals often remain still, unlike other small silver fish which seem to be in constant motion.

WINTER TREATS FOR HARDY BIRDWATCHERS

Countryside detectives prepared to face the bracing winter winds are often well rewarded. On soft shores on the east coast, look for parties of pale finch-like birds feeding on the strandline. You may see them as they take off in a flurry of white wing and tail markings. These are snow buntings, regular coastal visitors from the Arctic. They are often remarkably tame, and let you have a close view – you can even try feeding them with bird food or crumbs.

Another winter visitor is the shore lark, often overlooked in a flock of finches and buntings. Listen out for its distinctive call, a high, rippling *tsee-sirrp*, and if you hear it, look again. November is the best time to see shore larks at their regular stops, such as at Gibraltar Point, near Skegness, or on the Norfolk coast.

Purple piper *On rocky shores look for the purple sandpiper foraging on the kelp. At first glance a dull brownish grey wader, the bird has a deep slate sheen on its back.*

WHO'S BEEN WALKING ON THE BEACH?

Winter is a good time to look for tracks of animals and birds on the shore for two reasons. Shores are often deserted by tourists at this time of year so tracks are less likely to be disturbed, and the sun is low in the sky, casting shadows that help to make tracks more distinct.

Among the more easily recognised bird tracks are the large webbed prints of shelduck on muddy estuaries, and marks from the long narrow pronged feet of the heron, which fishes around sheltered coasts in winter. Gull prints (inset below) usually have a distinct claw mark on each toe, and the web curves in between each toe, unlike ducks' webs, which are fuller and somewhat straighter. If you find oval clawed prints, similar to a small dog's, but narrower, they could have been made by a fox, or even an otter in northern Scotland and its islands. Hard weather sometimes attracts these and other unexpected visitors to the beach in winter in the hope of finding something to eat.

Spot the footprint Gull prints (inset top) are the most common prints on the beach, but look out for more unexpected tracks in winter. Large deep prints show where a brown hare has bounded off the beach (centre), while small close prints showing toes and claws (above right) record the passage of a scurrying rat.

Wildlife seeks board and lodging in the city

Gardens and rooftops offer a welcome refuge from the cold

Britain's gardens form the country's largest nature reserve. From hanging baskets in small backyards to the grounds of stately homes, they provide a wide range of habitats. Wild animals visit gardens to feed and breed all year round, but in winter, when nature's food supply is at its leanest, they can offer hungry birds their best chance of survival.

For wildlife, built-up areas have other advantages as well. The temperature in towns and cities is often a few degrees warmer than in the surrounding countryside, and buildings provide places to bed down and shelter from the winds. The reward of coping with urban noise and bustle is a greater chance of pulling through the harshest season of the year.

Sanctuary in the suburbs

Changes in countryside management mean that built-up areas are more important to birds than ever before. When fields were not ploughed until spring, birds could forage for spilt grain throughout the winter. But today, ploughing tends to occur straight after the harvest, so opportunities for gleaning a living in this way have gone. What is more, hedgerows and field edges are generally kept much tidier, and with fewer weeds, there are fewer wild flowers, and that means fewer insects, spiders and seeds for birds to eat.

This steep decline in sources of winter food has forced birds to look elsewhere for nourishment. Blackbirds are common visitors in urban gardens (above) in winter, but other farmland birds, such as linnets, are increasingly following them. Put out a mixture of oil-rich seeds and nuts and you

During the barren winter months, starlings are frequent visitors to urban gardens. This one has a birdfeeder all to itself, but it is unlikely to be long before other members of its flock join the feast.

may lure them to your patch. You may also spot siskins, small yellow-green, woodland finches, hanging upside down as they feed.

Other winter visitors are the blackcap and chiffchaff. These warblers normally migrate south in autumn, but – perhaps as a result of the trend towards warmer winters – some now stay in Britain. The blackcap can be quite aggressive: you may see it driving other birds away from the bird table.

Up on the roof

Birds have a higher body temperature than humans, and burn up a great deal of energy simply staying warm. In winter, warmth – or the lack of it – plays a crucial part in daily life, explaining much of their behaviour.

If you are out and about in the morning, look up at the rooftops. If the sun is shining, you are likely to catch glimpses of city pigeons sunbathing in the near-horizontal light. There is not much heat in winter sunshine, but pigeons, such as those on Pulteney Bridge, in Bath (above), know how to get the best of it. You may notice that they often congregrate on ledges and roofs that face south-east, where they catch the first of the sun's rays. They are also particularly fond of slate roofs, because these absorb warmth well, releasing it throughout the night like outdoor storage radiators.

For humans, a brisk walk is a good way of warming up, but birds don't exercise simply to stay warm. Instead, they keep fluffing up their feathers to trap more insulating air. If there is no reason to move, they stay still to avoid wasting energy. The chance of food is one of the few things that has them rushing into action, although as dusk falls they will remain firmly in their roosting places, ready to face up to 16 hours of darkness.

Warmth from heated shops and offices in city centres spreads through the stone of the walls to reach the pigeons perched on the roofs and ledges outside.

Seeking sanctuary

Although many of the birds that breed in Britain migrate to warmer climates in winter, most – about 140 species – stay to face the challenge of finding food when it is scarce and of coping with low, often freezing, night temperatures. Many seek the shelter of urban gardens, especially where food is put out. Others find sanctuary on reservoirs, rubbish tips and sewage farms. Built-up areas also offer country birds an overnight roost, where they enjoy some much-needed warmth, before flying out of town again at dawn.

Birds have been quick to exploit the many reservoirs that now dot the British landscape. Some of the biggest urban reservoirs, such as those along London's Lee Valley, are among the best places for seeing water birds during the winter months.

Try to take a walk around such a site in winter. Your local water authority will tell you if there is a good reservoir for birdwatching near you and if it welcomes visitors. You should spot quite a variety of birds – a mixture of natives and winter migrants. However, with many species, such as teal and tufted ducks, it's impossible to tell which are the 'home-grown' birds and which are the new arrivals, because they look exactly the same.

If you are in the south-east of England or East Anglia between November and March, look out for the smew, a small, diving duck that turns up in limited numbers on reservoirs in these areas in winter.

Another diving duck, and a more common visitor to British waters, is the goldeneye. It is mainly white, but the females have a brown head and the males a greenish black one with a white spot on each cheek. Look for goldeneyes from September to April, although in Scotland some stay on to breed.

It may seem strange for a bird to fly to the British Isles for the coldest time of year, when many native species are heading for the sunny south. But compared with central European and Arctic Circle countries, Britain in winter is mild. The smew and goldeneye breed in northern Asia, Russia and northern Scandinavia, so an urban British reservoir makes a convenient residence when their summer home is frozen over.

Smart dresser Shy, and fast-moving you may see little of the smew (left) on its winter visits to Britain, but you will have no difficulty identifying the male. His snow-white and jet-black plumage makes him one of the handsomest birds around.

TIP-TOP DINNERS

For the opportunists of the bird world, rubbish tips, where food scraps are dumped along with other waste, are like giant restaurants. So take your binoculars along to one and see what you can spot wheeling about in the sky overhead.

More birds are attracted to rubbish tips in winter because food is scarce elsewhere. Look for herring and black-headed gulls that may have flown in from the coast. They will usually be squabbling noisily with other birds over food.

Near hilly areas, especially in Wales and Scotland, the gulls' main rivals are ravens, but elsewhere you will find them joined by rooks and jackdaws, both on the tip and following the refuse trucks.

You may be lucky enough to spot a rare red kite on tips in the Midlands and Scotland, where it

A bird banquet *Like all members of the crow family, these hooded crows (above), spotted on a Sunderland refuse tip, will exploit any source of food available. They descend with relish as each new load arrives at the tip, joining the frenzied free-for-all of feasting birds.*

has recently been re-introduced. But you are more likely to see this magnificent bird of prey scavenging on tips in central Wales, the home of the original, native population.

Mini wetlands

Your local sewage farm is another good place to observe different birds in winter, because it, too, offers a wide range of food. Gulls, waders, pied wagtails and starlings can be seen foraging for insect larvae and other small animals that thrive in the damp ground.

In some sewage farms, the treated effluent runs through beds that are stocked with water plants, which help to trap any nutrients before the water is discharged into a river. Where you come across these small-scale wetlands, look out for mallard, teal, snipe, lapwings and other waders, moorhens and even water rails.

FLYING FROM THE FREEZE

On winter nights, the city can be up to 3°C (5.5°F) warmer than the countryside around it. Warm clothes and heated homes mean this difference has little impact on us, but for birds it is important. Severe cold can be lethal to them, and the chance of escaping it often makes it worth the effort of commuting into town to roost.

Nightly commuters

Starlings are renowned for flying up to about 50km (30 miles) every night from their country feeding grounds to roost in city centres. Look out for them in the late afternoon, as chattering flocks converge on a roosting site – some parkland trees, a town square, an office block or the girders beneath a bridge. Before they settle down, they often perform spectacular aerial displays (see page 211).

Pied wagtails also fly in to the city to roost at night. Sometimes you will spot them in trees, though you are more likely to find them grouped on the roofs of large buildings or on greenhouses, attracted by the warm air rising from below.

If you have a nest box in your garden, try to peep inside after dark one night in winter, taking great care not to create too much disturbance. You may see what looks like a feathery ball. This could be a group of roosting wrens. These normally solitary birds seek warmth on cold nights by packing closely together in tree holes and nest boxes. This stops them losing as much heat as they would if they roosted alone.

Festive fuel *Remember that Christmas lights are not just decorative, they usually give off quite a lot of heat, warming the air around them. So look out for groups of birds, such as pied wagtails (above) roosting nearby.*

Q **Why don't all birds migrate?**

A The idea of enjoying two summers a year might sound appealing, but migration is not necessarily an easy option. Migratory birds not only face many hazards on their journey, but have to find a nesting site very quickly on their return. Birds that stay put conserve energy by avoiding the long journey, and can set up their breeding territories before spring begins, but they face the hazards of bad weather.

Close-up on Urban foxes

Highs and lows *Foxes find food and shelter in built-up areas. But unlike these specimens, many urban foxes look thin and shabby, either because they are moulting at the end of winter or because they have picked up mange.*

Foxes are so common in towns and cities that you are more likely to come across one here than in the countryside. These scavengers eat almost anything, making it easy for them to take advantage of the endless supply of food available all year round. In the country, finding a meal is affected more by the seasons and new farming methods have made this increasingly difficult over the past 50 years. With the expansion of many urban areas during the 1950s, foxes moved along roads and railway embankments into leafy suburbia, and from there into city centres.

Because foxes are generally wary and nocturnal, you may have difficulty spotting one. But if they are in your area, you will find plenty of evidence that they are about. Tracks and foxy scents point the finger of suspicion, as do disappearing toys, vanishing shoes, and, most alarming of all, shrill, spine-chilling screams at the dead of night in January – thought to be a signal from the vixen that she is ready to mate.

WHERE DO THEY LIVE?

If you think there are foxes in your neighbourhood, check your garden for signs of a lair. Search for a hole leading underground, among the roots of a tree or beneath a garden shed, and also look under any piles of wood.

Occasionally you will see a fox out during the day, but generally they stay in their lairs until darkness falls, when they emerge to search for food.

Foxes tend to live in family groups – one dog, one vixen, their cubs and sometimes one or two female 'helpers' from a previous litter. Each family will have a number of lairs and one or more breeding dens. These will be scattered over a home range of up to 20ha (50 acres), so the lair in your garden will be one of many in the area.

Family life

While lairs are usually small, breeding dens, or earths, are much more substantial. A favourite place for them in city parks and gardens is beneath Leyland cypresses, whose dense, evergreen foliage comes right down to the ground, providing excellent cover.

Other popular sites that offer similar shelter are under garden sheds or in clumps of brambles. Foxes have even been known to get through airbricks and make an earth in the cellar or walls of a house.

To distinguish an earth from a lair, look for heaps of excavated spoil that tell you where the entrance holes are – earths tend to have several entrances while each lair has only one.

These heaps are often littered with food remains and droppings, and if an earth is occupied, soil nearby will be trampled flat by passing paws.

Litters of four to six cubs are born between March and May. You might spot them when they start playing outside the earth at about six weeks old. But before this, you may catch an entire family on the move – probably as a safety measure. If you see a fox carrying a cub by the scruff of the neck, it is likely to be on its way to a new earth.

Stocking the larder *Foxes don't like to waste food, and will bury any leftovers (below left) to eat later. But they often do this badly. So if you spot something, such as the pheasant below, sticking out of the ground, it could indicate a fox's cache. Urban foxes don't just bury food. Old crisp packets, toys, shoes and golf balls have been found in their caches.*

Tucking in *Dustbins (above right) offer the urban fox an endless range of gourmet treats.*

NO-FUSS EATER

In town, you are unlikely to come across the scene of a fox's kill, although they do prey on small mammals, when they can, and on earthworms and insects. But ready-prepared food is so abundant that up to half of their daily intake consists of things that people leave outside or throw away.

In winter you might be lucky enough to catch foxes taking scraps off garden bird tables, but the most likely places to spot them after dark are anywhere rubbish is left out for collection, especially behind cafés and restaurants.

Studies of the stomach contents of dead foxes have revealed potato peelings, fish bones, runner beans and the remains of takeaway meals.

Left-over clues

Even if you don't actually catch sight of foxes feeding in your garden, you may find the evidence of where they have been scavenging. Look out for overturned bins, torn refuse bags and the chewed remains of their contents, such as gnawed meat bones, strewn across the lawn.

Look out also for patches of freshly scraped earth with odd bits of half-buried food sticking out. This is a fox's cache and is a reminder of the animal's country origins – killing a rabbit or pheasant would usually provide more food that the fox could eat at one sitting, so the surplus was saved for future meals. Foxes have a very good memory for cache sites, and will return over a period of days to finish off the remains.

Who passed this way? *Foxes and dogs leave similar footprints, but a close look should enable you to tell them apart. A fox's footprints (above left) are a slender diamond shape, with front claws close together, while a dog's (above right) are almost round with widely spaced front claws.*

Q **Will foxes harm my cat?**

A No – foxes generally ignore cats. If one did get into a serious confrontation with a cat, it would almost certainly come off worse. Foxes do, however, prey on smaller mammals, such as guinea pigs and rabbits, which is why you should keep such pets in secure cages. Fox cubs have also been seen playing with dogs, but adult foxes are wary of them and tend to give them a wide berth.

Who left these? *The twisted point at one end and grey colouring should tell you these are fox droppings. During summer and autumn the remains of beetles and berries can often make them almost black. You will usually find them in prominent places – on tree stumps and large stones, because they mark territory, so the fox wants them to be noticed.*

The urban dinner table

Animals have to be resourceful in their hunt for food in winter as missed opportunities can mean the difference between survival and starvation. Those creatures that have made a life for themselves in town have a distinct advantage. Take a close look at a city street: there will be lunchtime leftovers hidden in litter bins, tiny crumbs on the pavement, apple cores chucked into the undergrowth, snack debris littering the ground by bus stops or where crowds flow in and out of cinemas and stadiums. Yet you will probably miss much of the food that urban animals, with their keen senses, have learnt to track down.

A change of menu *Animals must seize any sort of food they can in the city. A grey squirrel discovers dropped lunchtime crumbs (above). Blue tits (below) and great tits found that the shiny tops of milk bottles signalled cream beneath and learnt to peck through them. The switch to semi-skimmed, and to cartons, is making it harder for them to find food this way.*

Many animals live in towns because they exploit the food we throw away. Without us, rats, foxes, pigeons and starlings would not be as common as they are. What we eat – and where we eat it – is of great importance to these creatures.

Our recently acquired fondness for fast food, and for eating on the move, has been good news for many animals, because it produces a steady stream of edible remains that often end up on the street.

You will see pigeons and sometimes house sparrows gathering in places where people regularly eat lunch outside, and close to crowds and queues, looking out for any dropped morsel.

Midnight feasts

Wait until dark and in many cities you may spot a fox or feral cat scavaging in a litter bin, or tearing open a black plastic bag, which smells of food.

But animals are also at the mercy of our changing habits. For example, old-fashioned dustbins were easy for foxes and badgers to tip over, scattering their contents. Modern wheelie bins are much harder for them to get into.

Mice make their homes in urban buildings, and feed at night. A clue that you have one in your house is the contents of bags of cereal or rice rapidly diminishing. Look, too, for mice droppings in the bag and near the wall. These mark runs that may lead to their nest.

Be our guest *Tourists who scatter a regular supply of seeds for the city pigeons help to preserve them through the worst months.*

FOOD FOR WORMS

Many small animals seem to disappear in winter, but you will see earthworms on the move all year round, except when it is very dry or very cold. Even in towns, the common earthworm is an amazingly abundant animal – one that many others use as a winter food.

Earthworms, together with fungi, are nature's most efficient and important recyclers. They eat their way through the soil, digesting any decaying organic matter and, in doing so, release minerals that plants can use.

Worms also feed on fallen leaves: if you look carefully into the garden at night, you might see dead leaves sticking out of the ground and slowly disappearing as they are dragged beneath the surface. This is a sign that earthworms are at work, and are busy gathering food. By breaking down the leaves, they again add plant nutrients to the soil.

Worm at work *A coil like muddy toothpaste shows where a long worm is munching through the soil and squirting its waste onto the lawn.*

Every year, the worms living in the average garden create several miles of tunnels as they feed. These help to improve drainage and the circulation of air in the soil. Common earthworms eliminate processed soil from their rear ends as they move along, but the long worm leaves its worm casts on the surface. They are particularly easy to spot on damp mornings.

What's eating the worms?

Earthworms are an important source of protein, particularly in winter, for many animals that forage in the city. The blackbird is probably the best-known urban earthworm eater, because it is such a regular garden visitor. Watch a blackbird at work: you will see it cocking its head to one side as if it were listening for the sound of movement in the ground below. This was how it once was thought to hunt, but it is now known that it is actually looking not listening for worms. A blackbird's eyes face sideways, so with its head tilted to the side it is scanning the ground closely for signs of its prey.

Watch other birds too: robins, song thrushes and even kestrels and tawny owls can also be seen feeding on earthworms, and many small mammals feast on them. Moles eat little else, and hedgehogs also like them, but the other animal you are likely to see foraging for earthworms in town, mainly after dark, is the fox. If you find small holes in your lawn, the size of a small teacup, it shows where a fox has been digging for worms.

Q **Why do worms come to the surface after rain?**

A Many worms spend their entire life underground, but the worm that you will see on the surface after rain is the common earthworm. It comes to the surface to collect leaves and you may be lucky enough to see a leaf being dragged down by a worm (below) to nibble. Earthworms can eat only wet leaves, because dry ones get stuck, so when they sense rain, they take the opportunity to surface for a leaf-collection expedition. Strangely, common earthworms will also surface if they are given a succession of jolts. To test this, try stamping on some damp ground – if there are any earthworms nearby, you will see them emerge from the soil then wriggle away.

Worm's end *Look closely and you'll see not all worms are the same. The sturdy one with the flattened tail tip (below left) is the earthworm; the skinny worms enjoying the rich compost heap (below right) are brandlings. The blackbird prefers the earthworm.*

Close-up on
Ivy

One of Britain's most widespread and successful plants, ivy also arouses mixed feelings. For some, it looks dark and sombre, particularly when it shrouds old gravestones and crumbling buildings. Even harder for many to tolerate is the way it swarms up bushes and trees, apparently choking them to death.

In reality, ivy is one of the most valuable plants around, particularly for wildlife in towns. Study a patch of ivy through the seasons, and note the wide variety of birds and insects that visit it. Its dense evergreen foliage offers shelter at any time and a meal for the caterpillars of the holly blue butterfly and swallow-tailed moth in autumn, while its winter flowers and berries are a welcome source of food when other supplies are becoming scarce.

GETTING A GRIP

Ivy is renowned for its very tenacious grip on whatever it is using as a support. Pull a large strand of ivy from a dead tree or old wall and you are quite likely to bring some bark or brick with it. This is because ivy has short roots growing along its stems, that will lock onto anything rough and solid.

The roots reach into cracks and crevices, and their tips then swell up, jamming them in position. With the help of these sturdy anchors, stems stay firmly in place.

It is interesting to compare the way ivy clings onto its support with the methods used by other woody climbers. Look at a honeysuckle and you will see how it simply winds its way around other plants, spiralling up towards the light. Or you may spot how clematis hangs on by wrapping its leafstalks around anything solid. Neither method gives the firm hold of ivy's aerial roots.

Perhaps you have noticed that ivy can grow to great heights. Its strong grip helps by keeping it securely in place, but more significantly ivy is tough and continues to grow year after year, rather than dying back like many other climbers.

A tight grip *The 'beard' found on ivy stems is in fact a row of aerial roots. Their fierce grip fixes the stems to their support.*

Changing shape

If you gather ivy to use as a Christmas decoration, notice the way the shape of the leaves varies from those on young stems to those growing on more mature parts of the plant.

Ivy is one of the few plants that changes in this way as it grows older, and there are other alterations too. When young, ivy plants lie flat against the ground or a support, but as they age they develop bushy tops, and begin to partly support themselves.

This bushy growth appears at any height – on a low wall or in the top of a tree – but usually where there is full daylight, and it is a sure sign that the plant is ready to flower. Also, it is the bushy nature of older ivy that enables birds to nest in it.

Young or old?
Leaf-shape changes as ivy gets older. The leaves on new growth are almost triangular (above left), but older stems bear narrower, diamond-shaped leaves (above right).

Q **Is the ivy killing that tree?**

A Almost certainly not. Ivy may, however, weaken a tree by competing with it for water, nutrients and light, although it rarely overgrows the tree's canopy. The main problem with ivy growing on a tree is that, being evergreen, ivy keeps its leaves in winter and they add to the tree's weight, making it more susceptible to being felled by very strong winds. On the other hand, old ivy stems, which can be as thick as your thigh, often help to support frail tree trunks through their old age.

Making a meal of it *Without the nectar of ivy flowers many insects, such as the fly above, would starve in winter.*

WHAT CAN I SMELL?

If you walk past ivy, particularly on a sunny winter's day, you might detect a pungent, slightly oily smell, and you may hear a sudden buzzing, produced by a flurry of insects taking to the air. Both are clues that the ivy is in flower. It flowers late in the year – sometimes as late as December – and you will have to look carefully in order to spot the greenish yellow flowers. They grow in sizable clusters, but their colour means they tend to blend in well with their surroundings. The insects you heard – flies, midges and sometimes a few late wasps – feed on nectar and pollen from the ivy flowers. For them, these flowers are a valuable source of nourishment when other food is hard to find.

If you look closely at the flowers, you will see that they are shallow, so are accessible to all comers, both long and short-tongued insects.

This insect activity helps with pollination and by blooming so late, when few other plants are in flower, the ivy has the services of these insect visitors more or less to itself.

FOOD AND SHELTER

Once its flowers have been pollinated, ivy starts to produce clusters of small, round berries. As the new year begins – surprisingly for such a cold time of the year – you will start to see them ripen, gradually turning a conspicuous purplish black by late February or early March. Ivy plants then become centres of noisy activity, as birds descend on them to feast on this succulent harvest.

What birds can you hope to see on ivy? The list of the berry-feeders is long, but you are most likely to spot flocks of fieldfares and starlings, as well as solitary blackbirds, song thrushes and robins. As with yew berries, the seeds inside ivy berries are poisonous, but they, too, pass undigested through birds' intestines and are scattered in their droppings. With luck, some will fall at the foot of a tree or a wall, which will offer support for the seedlings that grow from them.

Safe, warm and dry

Thick, shiny and tough, ivy leaves can withstand the worst of the winter weather, throwing off water like tiles on a roof – which is why old ivy stems often feel dusty and dry.

Many animals exploit this waterproofing by using ivy's dense, evergreen foliage as a weatherproof shelter. You will sometimes see brimstone butterflies hibernating beneath ivy leaves with their wings folded over their backs, and on cold winter nights, you may catch a glimpse of birds roosting in it.

By late winter, birds will start to explore the ivy for different reasons. The thick leafy canopy now provides the perfect cover against prying eyes, and the tangled stems create an ideal support for small nests. Keep a lookout for robins and pied wagtails. They book their nest-sites well before winter is over.

Watch these birds at work and notice how they try to throw predators off their trail – foxes and hedgehogs will climb up ivy in search of eggs and baby birds. Robins are particularly canny. Instead of flying straight towards their nest, they usually take an indirect route, fluttering into it only when the coast is clear.

Bed and breakfast *Ivy plays host to a wide variety of feathered guests during the winter months. Many, including the blackbird (above left), will drop by regularly to snack on the berries, but others, like the robin (above right), often prefer to take up residence.*

Gazetteer of
Places to investigate

The best place to begin an investigation of the countryside is in a public landscape where access is encouraged and the habitat is cared for. The countryside detective will be welcome both in the large National Parks and in many small nature reserves. In some nature reserves you will find that there are wardens to guide you to the more interesting features, or self-guided trails and maps that you can follow. Local reserves often hold special events, such as a nightingale evening or a fungus foray, to help you to hone your detective skills (see addresses opposite and overleaf).

Around a fifth of the land in the UK is protected by legislation. While some of this land is owned by wildlife bodies, much relies on the cooperation of private landowners. Designated nature conservation areas may overlap: for instance, many National Nature Reserves are located in National Parks and all of them are listed as Sites of Special Scientific Interest. In addition, some rare species of wild plants, animals and invertebrates are protected by law, which makes it illegal to disturb, move, sell or destroy them.

AREAS OF OUTSTANDING NATURAL BEAUTY

There are over 50 Areas of Outstanding Natural Beauty in England, Wales and Northern Ireland, and 40 similar National Scenic Areas in Scotland. AONBs enjoy limited protection under planning laws but there is no statutory provision for overall public access.

NATIONAL PARKS

The aims of National Parks are to conserve the landscape and to promote the quiet enjoyment and understanding of these areas by the public. Ten parks have been set up in England and Wales under the National Parks and Access to the Countryside Act 1949 (there are none in Scotland). Two other areas, The Broads and the New Forest, have equivalent status.

Because most of the land remains in private ownership, access to National Parks is generally along footpaths and roads, with a more general right to roam over some open areas. ***Details from*** the information service of individual National Park Authorities (see map and box, right).

Brecon Beacons Dramatic hill country separating mid and south Wales. Tel: 01874 624437
The Broads Shallow lakes, rivers, reed beds, wet woodlands and marshes. Tel: 01603 610734
Dartmoor High boggy plateau, with rocky tors, cut by the River Dart. Tel: 01626 832093
Exmoor Moorland scored by wooded valleys and bordered by coastal cliffs. Tel: 01398 323665
Lake District England's highest mountains loom over a score of lakes. Tel: 01539 724555
New Forest Ancient forest and heath. Tel: 023 8028 4244
North York Moors A plateau dissected by valleys and bordered by cliffs. Tel: 01439 770657
Northumberland Wild border country of moor and forest. Tel: 01434 605555
Peak District Peat moorlands, a millstone grit escarpment and limestone plateaus. Tel: 01629 816200
Pembrokeshire Coast Coastal cliffs, islands, estuaries and a high moorland plateau. Tel: 01437 764636
Snowdonia High mountains with glaciated valleys and lakes, a coast of dunes and sandy bays. Tel: 01766 770274
Yorkshire Dales Upland limestone country with cliffs, gorges, screes and pavement. Tel: 01969 650456

BUY A BOOK With the help of a good field guide, you can identify the plants and wildlife you discover in the countryside and start to learn more about them.

Nature Lover's Library published by Reader's Digest is a series of six books at £12.50 each: *Field Guide to the Animals of Britain, Field Guide to the Birds of Britain, Field Guide to the Butterflies and Other Insects of Britain, Field Guide to the Waterlife of Britain, Field Guide to the Trees and Shrubs of Britain* and *Field Guide to the Wild Flowers of Britain.*
Country Walks and Scenic Drives, £29.99, also published by Reader's Digest, guides you through some of Britain's most beautiful countryside.
These books can be ordered through RD customer services, tel. 0990 113366 or through the RD web site: www.readersdigest.co.uk. They are also available in good bookshops and in various garden centres.
Top Wildlife Spots*: the best 200 places to see wildlife in the UK,* £6.99, HarperCollins, profiles some important Wildlife Trusts reserves.

SITES OF SPECIAL SCIENTIFIC INTEREST

Sites (or in Northern Ireland Areas) of Special Scientific Interest are designated by the national conservation bodies as the most important wildlife habitats or geological features in the country. There are over 6000 SSSIs, many of them nature reserves with public access.
Details from the appropriate national body (below).

NATIONAL NATURE RESERVES

National Nature Reserves comprise land of national importance, which is managed by the national conservation authorities, or by others, such as the National Trust, on their behalf. There are over 300 NNRs in the UK.
Details from the appropriate national body (below).

National organisations responsible for NATURE CONSERVATION

English Nature Northminster House, Peterborough PE1 1UA. Tel. 01733 455 000 www.english-nature.org.uk
Countryside Council for Wales Plas Penrhos, Ffordd Penrhos, Bangor, Gwynedd LL57 2LQ. Tel. 01248 305500. www.ccw.gov.uk
Scottish Natural Heritage 12 Hope Terrace, Edinburgh EH9 2AS. Tel. 0131 447 4784 www.snh.org.uk
Department of Environment for Northern Ireland Clarence Court, 10-18 Adelaide Street, Belfast BT1 2GB. Tel. 028 9054 0540 www.nics.gov.uk/env.htm

OTHER GREAT PLACES TO LOOK FOR WILDLIFE

Local Nature Reserves (LNR) are areas set up by a local authority for the enjoyment of the general public. There are over 600 LNR'S in England, Wales and Scotland, but none in Northern Ireland.
Details from local authority environment offices.

The National Trust owns many properties of importance for wildlife, including large areas of Snowdon, the Lake District, the Peak District and 620 miles of coastline.
Details from 36 Queen Anne's Gate, London SW1A 9AS. Tel: 020 7222 8251. www.nationaltrust.org.uk

The National Trust for Scotland owns 72,000 hectares (180,000 acres) of land, including mountainous areas.
Details from 28 Charlotte Square, Edinburgh EH2 4ET. www.nts.org.uk

The Wildlife Trusts manage over 2070 nature reserves. Some have wardens though most are managed by volunteers, and public walks or leaflets of self-guided walks are often available. Your nearest branch office can provide details of local reserves.
Details from The Wildlife Trusts, The Kiln, Waterside, Mather Road, Newark NG24 1WT. Tel: 01636 677711. www.wildlifetrust. org.uk
Scotland: Scottish Wildlife Trust, Cramond House, off Cramond Glebe Road, Edinburgh EH4 6NS. Tel: 0131 312 7765. www.swt.org.uk

The Woodland Trust owns over 1000 woods across the UK which are open to the public, some with guided walks.
Details from Autumn Park, Dysart Road, Grantham, Lincolnshire NG31 6LL. Tel: 01476 581111. www.woodland-trust.org.uk

The Forestry Commission has 46 Forest Nature Reserves and many arboretums in England, Scotland and Wales of particular interest for woodland wildlife, with public access.
Details from Forest Enterprise, 231 Corstophine Road, Edinburgh EH12 7AT. Tel: 0131 314 6373. www.forestry.gov.uk

The Royal Society for the Protection of Birds (RSPB) manages 158 nature reserves, most with excellent facilities.
Details from The Lodge, Sandy, Bedfordshire SG19 2DL. Tel: 01767 680551. www.rspb.org.uk
N. Ireland Tel: 028 9049 1547.
Scotland Tel: 0131 311 6500.
Wales Tel: 028 2035 3000.

The Wildfowl & Wetlands Trust maintains nine important wildfowl reserves in England, Scotland and Wales.
Details from The New Grounds, Slimbridge, Glos GL2 7BT. Tel: 01453 891900. www.greenchannel.com/wwt

The Ministry of Defence owns 204 SSSIs and publishes a booklet outlining wildlife walks open to the public at some of its sites, though access may be restricted at times.
Details from MOD Press Office, Whitehall, London SW1A 2HB. Tel: 020 7218 7931. www.mod.uk

Marine Nature Reserves around Lundy island, off north Devon, and Skomer island, off the coast of Pembrokeshire, have wardens, guided walks and snorkelling trails. A third designated reserve at Strangford Lough in Northern Ireland offers boat trips. There are also Voluntary Marine Conservation Areas around the coast.
Details from Marine Conservation Society, 9 Gloucester Road, Ross-on-Wye, Herefordshire HR9 5BU. Tel: 01989 566017.

Where to see

Special features

If you want to take a closer look at some of the very special flora and fauna described in *The Countryside Detective,* here are some of the best habitats to explore.

NNR National Nature Reserve
LNR Local nature reserve

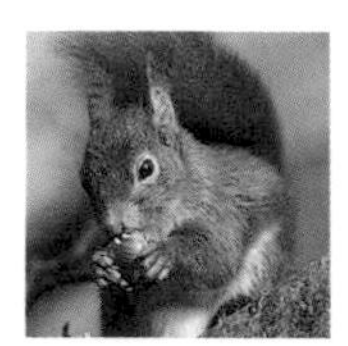

RED SQUIRRELS

Pages 122-3

England

Brownsea Island, National Trust. Boats visit from Poole, summer only.
Cragside, Northumberland, National Trust.
Formby Red Squirrel Sanctuary, Merseyside. National Trust reserve open all year, with a 'squirrel walk' in which close-up views are possible.
Isle of Wight: good areas to look are Osborne, and the woods at Newtown and Parkhurst Forest.

Scotland

Abernethy Forest: RSPB reserve at Loch Garten with full access.
Speyside: Landmark Centre at Carrbridge; Scottish Natural Heritage NNR at Loch an Eilein.

Northern Ireland

Belvoir Forest Park, Belfast: close-up views are possible.

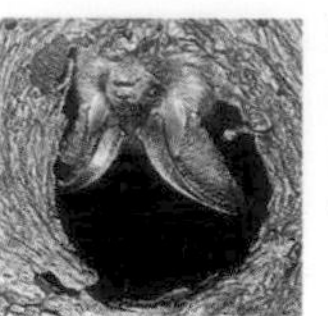

WOODS AND PARKS WITH FINE OLD TREES

Pages 126-7

England

Berks: Windsor Great Park, access to designated areas and on paths.
Bucks: Burnham Beeches, freedom to roam.
Birmingham: Sutton Park NNR with full facilities.
Cumbria: Borrowdale, National Trust.
Dorset: Powerstock Common, Wildlife Trust reserve with access along paths.
Essex: Epping Forest, freedom to roam.
Hatfield Forest, National Trust with full facilities.
Hampshire: New Forest, freedom to roam.
London: Royal Botanic Gardens, Kew.
Richmond Park, freedom to roam.
Norfolk: Felbrigg Great Wood.
North Yorkshire: Duncombe Park NNR.
Notts: Birklands LNR in Sherwood Forest, with visitor centre and trails.
Somerset: Horner Wood, National Trust with informal walks.
Surrey: Staffhurst Wood LNR with full access.
Sussex: Kingley Vale NNR with access along paths.
The Mens, Wildlife Trust reserve with access along paths.
Wilts: Savernake Forest, Forest Enteprise with informal walks and picnic sites.

Wales

Snowdonia oak woods: many are National Trust or NNRs with access along paths.

Scotland

Perth & Kinross: Black Wood Forest, Rannoch, NNR with access.
Highland: Abernethy Forest, RSPB reserve at Loch Garten, good facilities and choice of trails.
Glen Affric: NNR with open access.

JOIN A CLUB You can continue to improve your detective skills by joining a group that will teach you more about your favourite creature or plant, or that involves you in caring for the habitat they need. These all encourage members to be actively involved.

Amateur Entomologists Society runs a Bug Club for young people. Organises field trips during the summer, which all are welcome at. AES, PO Box 8774, London SW7 5ZG. Tel: 07788 163951 www.theaes.org

Bat Conservation Trust encourages the public to monitor local roosts. 15 Cloisters House, 8 Battersea Park Road, London SW8 4BG. Tel: 020 7627 2629 www.bats.org.uk

British Dragonfly Society organises local field trips in summer, organises surveys and offers autumn talks. The Haywain, Hollywater Road, Bordon, Hants GU35 0AD. Tel: 01420 472329

British Lichen Society runs conservation groups monitoring lichens in churchyards, using lichens to check pollution levels and holding field meetings. BLS c/o The Natural History Museum, Cromwell Road, London SW7 5BD. Tel: 020 7942 5000 www.argonet.co.uk/users/jmgray

British Trust for Conservation Volunteers runs a voluntary field force, the National Conservation Corps, who devote spare time to practical conservation chores. Age 16 and over. 36 St Mary's St, Wallingford OX10 0EU. Tel: 01491 839766 www.btcv.org

British Trust for Ornithology asks volunteers to monitor local bird populations to aid conservation. The National Centre for Ornithology, The Nunnery, Thetford, Norfolk IP24 2PU. Tel: 01842 750050

Butterfly Conservation organises guided walks and conducts surveys during the butterfly season. In winter, there are conservation activities and talks. PO Box 222, Dedham, Colchester, Essex CO7 6EY. Tel: 01206 322 342

The Conchological Society of Great Britain and Ireland promotes the study of slugs, snails and seashells through newsletters and field meetings. c/o 1 Court Farm, Hillfarrance, Taunton, Somerset TA4 1AN. Tel: 01823 461482

Council for the Protection of Rural England is the main independent lobbying body for the preservation of rural countryside, with branches in every county. Warwick House, 25 Buckingham Palace Road, London SW1W 0PP. Tel: 020 7976 6433 www.greenchannel.com/cpre

Countryside Restoration Trust links farming, rural and wildlife conservation and manages a number of farm reserves. Barton, Cambridge CB3 7AG. Tel: 01223 843322

Froglife uses volunteers to conserve frogs, toads, newts, lizards and snakes, and runs projects such as toad patrols. Triton House, Bramfield, Halesworth, Suffolk TP19 9AE. Tel: 01986 784518 www.froglife.co.uk

The Herpetological Conservation Trust, conserves habitats for amphibians and reptiles. 655a Christchurch Road, Boscombe, Bournemouth BH1 4AP. Tel: 01202 391319

LIMESTONE PAVEMENTS

Pages 162-3

Many limestone pavements are fragile and access is discouraged, but the following are open to visitors:

Cumbria: Gait Barrows NNR: footpath access only.
Hagg Hill Top, Kendal.
Homepark Fell, National Trust, near Burton-in-Kendall.
Hutton Roof Crags NNR.
North Yorkshire: Winskill Stones, Winskill Farm Visitors Centre, Settle.

SEA BIRD CITIES

Pages 180-1

England

Cumbria: St Bees Head, RSPB reserve.
Devon: Berry Head LNR.
Lundy Island, boats from Ilfracombe, facilities on island.
Dorset: Durlston County Park, Swanage.
St Alban's Head LNR.
East Riding of Yorkshire: Bempton Cliffs, RSPB reserve.
Isles of Scilly.
Northumberland: Farne Islands, National Trust.
South Tyneside: Marsden Bay.

Wales

Anglesey: South Stack, Holy Island, RSPB reserve.
Gwynedd: Bardsey Island.
Pembrokeshire: Skomer NNR, Martin's Haven and Castlemartin Ranges.

Scotland

Aberdeenshire: Fowlsheugh RSPB reserve.
Borders: St Abb's Head.
Dumfries and Galloway: Mull of Galloway, RSPB reserve.
East Lothian: Bass Rock.
Fair Isle.
Fife: Isle of May NNR.
Highland: Handa and Caithness Cliffs.
Orkney: Hobbister on Copinsay; Marwick Head; RSPB reserves at North Hoy and Noup Cliffs.
Shetland: NNRs at Noss, Fetlar and Herma Ness.

Northern Ireland

County Antrim: Rathlin Island.

CHALK STREAMS

Pages 234-5

These are some of the best chalk rivers. But note that in many cases you will only see typical chalk stream features along the upper reaches.

Berks: Lambourn.
Bucks: Chess, Misbourne.
Dorset: Frome, Piddle.
East Riding of Yorkshire: Hull.
Hants: Allen, Itchen, Meon, Test.
Herts: Beane, Gade, Lea, Mimram, Ver.
Kent: Great Stour.
Norfolk: Nar.
Wilts: Avon, Kennet, Wylye.

DOLPHINS, SEALS, SHARKS AND WHALES

Pages 256-7

England

Farne Islands: grey seal.
Humberside: common seal.
South Cornwall and Devon: basking shark, common dolphin, grey seal, porpoise.
The Wash: common seal.

Wales

Cardigan Bay: bottle-nosed dolphin.
Pembroke coast and islands: dolphin, grey seal.

Scotland

Hebrides: basking shark, dolphin, grey seal, minke whale, otter, porpoise.
Moray Firth: bottle-nosed dolphin, seals.
Orkney and Shetland: dolphin, fin whale, otter, seals.

Northern Ireland

Strangford Lough: porpoise, seals.

The Mammal Society has local groups which carry out surveys, runs a National Mammal Week of walks and talks and also runs mammal identification skills workshops. 15 Cloisters House, 8 Battersea Park Road, London SW8 4BG. Tel: 020 7498 4358 www.mammal.org.uk

Marine Conservation Society records marine wildlife sightings by the public, organises Beachwatch (a good beach survey) and welcomes volunteers at its conservation sites. 9 Gloucester Road, Ross-on-Wye, Herefordshire HR9 5BU. Tel: 01989 56601 www.mcsuk.org

The National Federation of Badger Groups is the central body for local badger groups which monitor badger setts, sightings, road victims and badger persecution. 2 Cloisters House, 8 Battersea Park Road, London SW8 4BG. Tel: 020 7498 3220

The Otter Trust has sites in Cornwall, County Durham and Suffolk open in the summer, and works with Wildlife Trusts volunteers to restore habitats. Earsham, Bungay, Norfolk NR35 2AF. Tel: 01986 893470

Plantlife specialises in plant protection and manages a number of nature reserves where volunteers can become guardians of rare species. 21 Elizabeth Street, London SW1W 9RP. Tel: 020 7808 0100 www.plantlife.org.uk

Royal Society for the Protection of Birds encourages members to be involved on the RSPB reserves. It also runs a Young Ornithologists Club for 6-13 year olds and RSPB Phoenix for teenagers, offering a magazine, wildlife fun days and holidays. Details on page 339.

Sea Watch Foundation co-ordinates a network of volunteers to monitor cetaceans in British and Irish waters. 11 Jersey Road, Oxford OX4 4RT. Tel: 01865 717276 www.seawatch.org.uk

Tree Council promotes the planting and good cultivation of trees and coordinates the National Grid Tree Warden Scheme working with local communities and tree specialists. 51 Catherine Place, London SW1E 6DY. Tel: 020 7828 9928 www.treecouncil.org.uk

The Wild Flower Society encourages knowledge of wild flowers with field meetings and by keeping a wild flower diary. 68 Outwoods Road, Loughborough, Leics LE11 3LY.

The Wildlife Trusts, President David Bellamy, encourages volunteers to get involved and also runs Wildlife Watch, a club for young environmentalists with the emphasis on activity. Details on page 339.

The Woodland Trust organises tree planting events from mid Nov-March. Details on page 339.

Index

c

d

g

h

ijk

l

m

no

pq

r

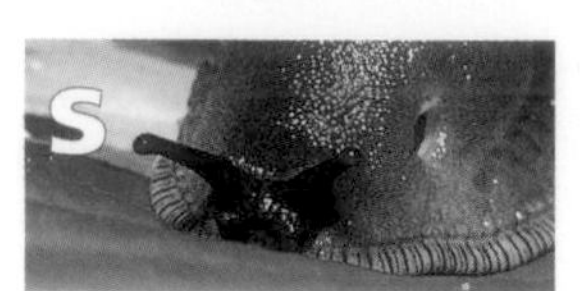
s

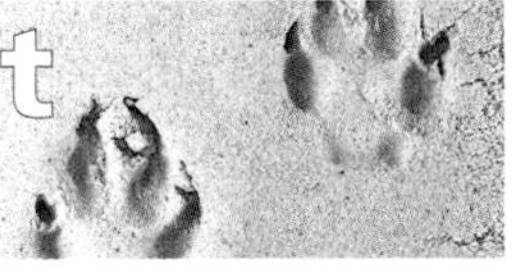

t

uv

wxyz

Acknowledgments

The sources of the illustrations in this book are listed below. Agency names have been abbreviated as follows: AL = Ardea, London, AQI = Aquila Wildlife Images, BBC = BBC Natural History Unit Photo Library, BCL = Bruce Coleman Ltd., NI = Natural Image, NSP = Natural Science Photos, OSF = Oxford Scientific Films, PEP = Planet Earth Pictures and PW = Premaphotos Wildlife. All pictures marked © RD, are copyright of The Reader's Digest Association Ltd.
The following abbreviations indicate the position of a picture on the page, **B** = bottom, **C** = centre, **L** = left, **R** = right and **T** = top. Where more than one picture occupies the same part of the page, their relative positions are shown by extra letters in brackets, as in **TL(L)** and **TL(R)**. Where photographs from more than one source have been combined to form a single image, the positions of the different parts are given and where necessary, their subjects.

Front cover TL (**wood**) PEP/Geoff du Feu **TL** (**deer**) OSF/Mark Hamblin **TR** (**lake**) NHPA/Stephen Dalton **TR** (**heron**) BCL/William Paton **BL** (**hedge**) NHPA/E.A. Janes **BL** (**rabbits**) PEP/Neil McIntyre **BR** (**snow**) Biofotos/Heather Angel **BR** (**fox**) © RD **Spine** OSF/G.A.Maclean **Back cover T** BCL/Dr.Scott Nielsen **C** Photo-Works, Middlesbrough **BR** OSF/G.A.Maclean **Endpaper** NHPA/Roger Tidman **1** Chris & Helen Pellant **2** PEP/Colin Weston **5** © RD/All Andrea Jones except for Woodland icon Jason Smalley **7** Photo-Works, Middlesbrough **8 L** © RD/PCGraphics (UK) Ltd **TC** © RD/Andrea Jones **TR** © RD/Andrea Jones **BR** © RD/PCGraphics (UK) Ltd **9 TC** © RD/Jason Smalley **CL** © RD/Andrea Jones **C** © RD/Andrea Jones **CR** © RD/Andrea Jones **BL** © RD/PCGraphics (UK) Ltd **BR** © RD/PCGraphics (UK) Ltd **10** BBC/Geoff Dore **11** OSF/Chris Knights **12 TR** OSF/Richard Davies **BL** Biofotos/Heather Angel **BR** AQI/Jonathan Need **13 TL** BCL/Jane Burton **BL** AL/Bob Gibbons **BR** OSF/Harold Taylor **14-15** BBC/Niall Benvie **16-17** Tim Woodcock **17 T** NI/Bob Gibbons **TL** (**swifts**) AL/Anthony & Elizabeth Bomford **BL** AL/John Daniels **BR** OSF/Gordon Maclean **18 BL** AQI/A.T.Moffett **BR** NSP/R.C.Revels (**bee**) PW/Ken Preston-Mafham **18-19** (**background**) © RD/Jason Smalley (**flight patterns**) © RD/Mike Langman/Wildlife Arts **19 TL** (**lark**) NI/Mike Lane **CR** NHPA/Bill Coster **BR** AQI/Mike Wilkes **20 TL** AQI/C.S.Milkins **BL** AL/Jack A.Bailey **BC** Nature Photographers/R.T.Smith **20-21** © RD/Jason Smalley **21 TL** Chris & Helen Pellant **TR** BCL/Kim Taylor **CL** NSP/Richard J Brigham **CR** NSP/Richard J Brigham **BL** AQI/Peter Castell **BR** BBC/Rico & Ruiz **22 TR** AQI/Mike Lane **C** © RD/Jason Smalley **BL** © RD/Jason Smalley **BR** © RD/Jason Smalley **22-23** © RD/Jason Smalley **23 CL** (**rabbits**) PEP/Neil McIntyre **CR** © RD/Jason Smalley **BL** BBC/William Osborn **BR** OSF/Mark Hamblin **24 TR** © RD/Jason Smalley **BL(L)** AL/Bob Gibbons **BL(R)** AL/R.F.Porter **BC** PW/Ken Preston-Mafham **BR(L)** NSP/Richard Revels **BR(R)** Biofotos **25 TL** PW/Ken Preston-Mafham **TR** BCL/Hans Reinhard **BL(L)** OSF/Barrie Watts **BL(R)** Martin & Dorothy Grace **BR** PEP/Georgette Douwma **BL** NSP/Richard Revels **BC** NI/Peter Wilson **BR** AL/D W Greenslade **B** (**background**) © RD/Jason Smalley **27 T** AL/John Daniels **BL** BCL/Sir Jeremy Grayson **BR** Pat Morris **28 T** © RD/Jason Smalley **CR** © RD/Jason Smalley **BC** PW/Ken Preston-Mafham **BR(L)** PEP/Nigel Downer **BR(R)** © RD/Jason Smalley **29 TL** © RD/Jason Smalley **TR** © RD/Jason Smalley **BC** AL/A.P.Paterson **BR(L)** PW/Ken Preston-Mafham **BR(R)** AQI/Ivan West **30** Nature Photographers/E.A.Janes **30-31** PEP/Colin Weston **31** © RD/Jason Smalley **32** PEP/Geoff du Feu **33 TL** NSP/Richard Revels **CL** PW/Ken Preston-Mafham **CR** AL/Bob Gibbons **BR** PEP/Nigel Downer **34 C & TR** NSP/Richard Revells **BL** NI/Peter Wilson **BR** NI/Peter Wilson **35 TL** BBC/David Kjaer **TR** © RD/Jason Smalley **CL** Biofotos/Heather Angel **CR(T)** NSP/Richard Revels **CR(B)** © RD/Jason Smalley **BL** Biofotos/Heather Angel **BR** © RD/Jason Smalley **36 CL** © RD/Jason Smalley **C** © RD/Jason Smalley **CR** © RD/Jason Smalley **BL** © RD/Jason Smalley **BC** © RD/Jason Smalley **BR** © RD/Jason Smalley **36-39** © RD/Jason Smalley **37 TR** PEP/Rosemary Calvert **BL** NSP/W. Cane **BC** AL/John Mason **BR** PW/K.G. Preston-Mafham **38 TL** AL/R.J.C.Blewitt **TC** Biofotos/Heather Angel **BL** Frank Lane Picture Agency/R.Tidman **BC** OSF/M.J.Coe **38-39** AQI/R.T. Mills **39 TL** Biofotos/Heather Angel **TC** OSF/M.J.Coe **TR** AL/R.J.C.Blewitt **C** AQI **BL** Pat Morris **BC** BCL/Gordon Langsbury **40 CL** OSF/Irvine Cushing **C** AQI/J.Lawton Roberts **BL** OSF/Tony Tilford **BR** PEP/David Kjaer **41 TL** OSF/Tony Tilford **TC** BBC/Nigel Bean **CL** AL/Chris Knights **C(L)** OSF/Richard Packwood **C(R)** © RD/PCGraphics (UK) Ltd **CR** OSF/Jos Korenromp **42 TR** AQI/Mike Wilkes **BL** © RD/Jason Smalley **BR(T)** NI/Michael Woods **BR(B)** NI/Bob Gibbons **42-43** © RD/Jason Smalley **43 TL** AL/J.B.& S.Bottomley **TC** AL/Denis Avon **TR** BBC/Mike Wilkes **CL** AQI/R.Thomas **CR** OSF/Terry Heathcote **BC** © RD/Jason Smalley **BR** NI/Bob Gibbons **44 C** (**vole**) Biofotos/Heather Angel **44-45** NHPA/David Woodfall **45 T** Biofotos/Heather Angel **BL** AL/Ian Beames **BR** Biofotos/Heather Angel **46 BL** © RD/Jason Smalley **BR** © RD/Jason Smalley **46-47** Background © RD/Jason Smalley **47 TC(T)** © RD/Jason Smalley **TC(B)** © RD/Jason Smalley **CR** OSF/Scott Camazine **BR** OSF/James Robinson **48 CL** Biofotos **CR(T)** © RD/Jason Smalley **BL** Angling Times **CR(B)** © RD/Jason Smalley **BR** Angling Times **49 T** © RD/Jason Smalley **C** OSF/David Thompson **CR** © RD/Jason Smalley **BC(T)** OSF/David Thompson **BC(B)** OSF/David Thompson **50 TR** PEP/John & Gillian Lythgoe **C** BCL/Andrew Davies **BL** Biofotos **51 T** Biofotos **C** OSF/G.I.Bernard **CR** OSF/G.I.Bernard **BC** OSF/G.I.Bernard **BR** AQI/Abraham Cardwell **52 TL** Chris & Helen Pellant **CR** BCL/Kim Taylor **BC** © RD/Jason Smalley **BR** AQI/C.S.Wilkins **52-53** AQI/E.A.Janes **53 TC** Biofotos/Heather Angel **CL** NSP/Richard Revels **CR** Biofotos **BL** AQI/Mike Lane **BC** OSF/L.M.Crowhurst **BR** NSP/D.Yendall **54 TL** BCL/Dr.Scott Nielsen **BL** NSP/Richard J Brigham **BC** BBC/Mike Wilkes **BR** AQI/Mike Wilkes **54-55** © RD/Jason Smalley **55 L** PEP/John **R** Bracegirdle **TR(L)** BBC/William Osborn **TR(R)** © RD/Jason Smalley **CR(L)** © RD/Jason Smalley **CR(R)** © RD/Jason Smalley **BR** AQI/M.C.Wilkes **56 L** AL/Zdenek Tunka **R** AQI/E.K.Thompson **57 TL** BBC/Brian Lightfoot **TC(T)** BBC/Dietmar Nill **TC(B)** OSF/Gerald Thompson **BR** PEP/Neil McIntyre **58 TL** AQI/M.C.Wilkes **TR** AQI/R.Glover **CL** BCL/George McCarthy **59 CL** BBC/Tom Vezo **R** OSF/Michael Leach **BL** AQI/M.C.Wilkes **60 CR** (**hare**) BCL/Gordon Langsbury **60-61** OSF/Alastair Shay **61 T** NHPA/David Woodfall **BL** BCL/Gordon Langsbury **BR** Chris & Helen Pellant **62 TC** OSF/Geoff Kidd **TR** AL/Ian Beames **C** PEP/Mike Reid **BL** PW/Ken Preston-Mafham **62-63** © RD/Jason Smalley **63 C(L)** Chris & Helen Pellant **C** Nature Photographers/Colin Carver **CR** BCL/Andrew Purcell **B** BBC/Graham Hatherley **64 CL** Nature Photographers/Andrew Cleave **C** PW/Ken Preston-Mafham **64-65** © RD/Jason Smalley **65 TL** AL/Ian Beames **C** Chris & Helen Pellant (**sheep print**) © RD/Jason Smalley **CR** AQI/S.Phillipps (**deer print**) AQI/A.P.Walmsley **BL** Biofotos **BR** AQI/Mike Lane **66 C** BBC/Niall Benvie **BC** PEP/Steve Hopkin **66-67** © RD/Jason Smalley **67 TL(T)** NI/Bob Gibbons **TL(B)** OSF **TR(T)** PEP/Jan Tove Johansson **TR(B)** NSP/Steve Downer **CL** AQI/Richard T.Mills **C** OSF/Barrie E.Watts **BC** PW/Ken Preston-Mafham **BR** PW/Ken Preston-Mafham **68 L** AQI/D.Green **TR**(**snipe**) AL/John Daniels **TR** AL/D.Green **68-69** OSF/Mark Hamblin **69** BBC/David Kjaer **70** NHPA/J & M Bain **70-71** © RD/Neil Holmes **71 BR** © RD/PCGraphics (UK) Ltd **72 TC** NI/Bob Gibbons **BL** PEP/Antony Joyce **72-73** (**grass**) OSF/Mike Slater (**roots**) © RD/Stuart Carter **73 TL** BBC/Jason Smalley **TR** NI/Bob Gibbons **CL** Pat Morris **CR** NI/Bob Gibbons (**rabbits**) AL/Stefan Myers **BR(T)** The National Trust/Kevin J. Richardson **BR(B)** The National Trust/Kevin J.Richardson **74 TR** BBC/Premaphotos **CL** NI/Peter Wilson **BL** BBC/Brian Lightfoot **74-75** AQI/E.Soothill **75 TL** NI/Peter Wilson **CL** PW/Ken Preston-Mafham **CR** AQI/C.Smith **B** OSF/Martyn Chillmaid **76 C** OSF/G.I.Bernard **BL** OSF/G.I. Bernard **BC** OSF/G.I.Bernard **76-77** Biofotos/Heather Angel **77 TC(T)** Biofotos/Heather Angel **TC(B)** OSF/G.I.Bernard **CR** AL/P.Morris **BC** NSP/D.B.Lewis **BR** Biofotos/Heather Angel **78 L** Collections/Paul Watts **BC** Biofotos/Heather Angel **78-79** Biofotos **79 TC** Biofotos/Heather Angel **TR** AL/Pat Morris **BL** Biofotos/Heather Angel **BC(L)** OSF/C.E. Jeffree **BC(R)** Biofotos/Heather Angel **80 CL** PW/Ken Preston-Mafham **BL** Biofotos/Heather Angel **BR** AQI **81 TC** (**all**) © RD/Jason Smalley **BL** Biofotos/Heather Angel **BR** Biofotos/Heather Angel **82-83** OSF/Anna Walsh **83 T** NHPA/E.A.Janes **BL** NSP/Richard Revels **BR** (**flowers**) Chris & Helen Pellant **BR** (**tit**) AQI/Abraham Cardwell **84 C** NI/Bob Gibbons **BL** OSF/G.A.Maclean **84-85** © RD/Jason Smalley **85 CL** PW/Ken Preston-Mafham **C** AQI/A.J. Bond **CR** NSP/Richard Revels **BR** PEP/Andrew McGeeney **86 CL** BBC/William Osborn **CR** Martin & Dorothy Grace (**brimstone**) BCL/George McCarthy **BR(T)** AL/C.J.A.Bailey **BL** PEP/Geoff Trinder **BR(B)** NI/Alec S.Harmer (**background**) © RD/Jason Smalley **87 CR** AL/Bob Gibbons **BL** AL/John Mason **BC** AQI/M.C.Wilkes **BR** AQI/Mike Wilkes **88 TC** AQI/M.C.Wilkes **CL** OSF/Tony Tilford **CR** BCL/Colin Varndell **88-89** © RD/Jason Smalley **89 CL** Nature Photographers/Paul Sterry **C(L)** Nature Photographers/Paul Sterry **C(R)** AQI/Robert Maier **CR** OSF/Jos Korenromp **BR** OSF/Jos Korenromp **90 L** OSF/Okapia **BC** PEP/A.P.Barnes **BR** AQI/M.C.Wilkes **91 TL** AQI/M.C.Wilkes **CL** BCL/Dr.Scott Nielsen **CR** AL/Wardene Weisser **BR** AL/George Reszeter **92 TR** AL/Bob Gibbons **CL** AQI/D.Meredith **C** NI/Bob Gibbons **CR(L)** AL/I.R.Beames **CR(R)** Biofotos/Heather Angel **92-93** NSP/Richard Revels **93 TR** AL/Denis Avon **CL(L)** Rentokil Initial **CL(R)** Rentokil Initial **BL** Martin & Dorothy Grace **BC** Biofotos/Heather Angel **94 TL** BCL/George McCarthy **BR** OSF/Rodger Jackman **94-95** BCL/George McCarthy **95 TL** AL/Ian Beames **TC** AQI/Abraham Cardwell **TR** NSP/P.H.& S.L.Ward **CL** NSP/Ian West **BL** AL/John Clegg **BR(T)** AQI/M.C.Wilkes **BR(B)** AQI/M.C.Wilkes **96-97** © RD/Jon Wyand **97 TR** Tim Woodcock **BL** NI/W.Cane **BR** NI/C.Blaney **98 BL** © RD/Jason Smalley (**map**) © RD/PCGraphics (UK) Ltd **98-99** © RD/Jason Smalley **99 C(L)** PW/Ken Preston-Mafham **C** NI/Bob Gibbons **C(R)** NSP/Ian West (**spotted orchid**) NSP/Richard Revels (**heath spotted**) NSP/Richard Revels (**bee orchid**) NSP/Richard Revels (**cleavers**) NSP/Richard Revels (**wall barley**) AL (**green winged orchid**) PEP/Allan Parker **100 TC** PW/Ken Preston-Mafham **TR** Biofotos/Heather Angel **C** AL/David Dixon **CR** NSP/Andrew Watts **100-101** © RD/Jason Smalley **101 TL(L)** Martin & Dorothy Grace **TL(R)** PW/Ken Preston-Mafham **CL** NI/Bob Gibbons **CR (T)** NSP/Ian West **CR (B)** PW/Ken Preston-Mafham **BL** NI/Bob Gibbons **BR** NSP/Richard Revels **102** (**background**) © RD/Jason Smalley **BR** (**foxes**) AL/John Daniels **103 TR** BCL/Kim Taylor **CL** NHPA/Roger Tidman **BL** PEP/F. Millington **BC** PEP/Martin King **104 CL** AL/Ian Beames **CR** PW/Ken Preston-Mafham **BL** NSP/Richard Revels **BC** NSP/P.H.& S.L.Ward **BR** AL/I & L Beames **104-105** © RD/Jason Smalley **105 TL(T)** NSP/Richard Revels **TL(B)** NSP/Richard Revels **TR** NSP/Richard Revels **CR** AL/Bob Gibbons **BC** NI/Peter Wilson **106 L** (**background**) Holt Studios Ltd./Sarah Rowland **CR(T)** Holt Studios Ltd./Nigel Cattlin **CR(B)** Holt Studios Ltd./Nigel Cattlin **BL** Holt Studios Ltd./Nigel Cattlin **BC** Holt Studios Ltd./Nigel Cattlin **BR** Holt Studios Ltd./Nigel Cattlin **107 TR** Holt Studios Ltd./Nigel Cattlin **CR** Holt Studios Ltd./Nigel Cattlin **BL** (**nest**) OSF/David Thompson **BR** (**beet**) NSP/Richard Revels **BL** (**background**) © RD/Jason Smalley **BR** (**background**) Holt Studios Ltd./Gordon Roberts **108 C** Holt Studios Ltd./Nigel Catlin **BR** PEP/Steve Hopkin **108-109** © RD/Jason Smalley **109 TC** AL/John Mason **TR** AQI/M.Lane **CL** AL/John Daniels **BR** NHPA/N.A.Callow **110** (**short-eared owl**) PEP/J.Bracegirdle **110-111** (**background**) AL/Chris Knights **111 T** BCL/Jane Burton **BL** AL/John Daniels **BC** AL/John Mason **112 C** NSP/P.H. & S.L. Ward **BC** PW/Ken Preston-Mafham **BR** (**cow pat**) © RD/Jason Smalley **112-113** © RD/Jason Smalley **113 TL** (**jackdaws**) AL/Chris Knights **TL** (**background**) © RD/Jason Smalley **BL** AQI/Mike Lane **BC** (**artwork**) © RD/Stuart Carter/Widlife Art **BC** (**photo**) © RD/Jason Smalley **114-115** OSF/Terry Heathcote **115 T** Martin & Dorothy Grace **TR** (**bird**) AL/Chris Knights **BL** PEP/Hans Christian Heap **BR** AL/Chris Knights **116 BL** © RD/Jason Smalley **116-117** © RD/Jason Smalley **117 T** AL/John Mason **B** NSP/P.H. & S.L. Ward **118 TR** PEP/Steve Hopkin **C** PEP/Georgette Douwma **BL** PEP/J. Bracegirdle **BC** NSP/Andrew Watts **118-119** © RD/Jason Smalley **119 TL** NSP/Ian West **TC** NHPA/Stephen Dalton **C** NI/David Element **CR** AL/Ian Beames **BL** (**foxglove**) Martin & Dorothy Grace **BR** NSP/Richard Revels **120** AL/Liz & Tony Bomford **120-121** © RD/Jason Smalley **121 TL** NSP/Richard Revels **TC** PW/Ken Preston-Mafham **CR** NHPA/Stephen Dalton **BL** PW/Ken Preston-Mafham **BR** PEP/Mark Mattock **122 C** NHPA/Laurie Campbell **CR** NHPA/Eckart Pott **BR** NSP/Richard Revels **B** (**background**) © RD/Jason Smalley **123 TR** (**background**) © RD/Jason Smalley **CL** NHPA/Laurie Campbell **CR** (**squirrel**) NHPA **BL** AL/Liz Bomford **124 TL** AQI/M.C.Wilkes **TR** PEP/Frank Blackburn **125 TC** NI/Michael Woods **TR** Pat Morris **BL** NSP/G. Kinns (**nuts**) AL/John Mason **BR** AL/Elizabeth & Tony Bomford **126 L** © RD/Jason Smalley **CL** NHPA/Yves Lanceau **BR** AQI/David Owen **127 TL** NSP/Richard Revels **TR** NSP/Richard Revels **BR** NI/Peter Wilson **128 C** © RD/Jason Smalley **CR** © RD/Jason Smalley **BL** OSF/Barrie Watts **BR** OSF/D.J.Saunders **129 TL** © RD/Jason Smalley **CR** NSP/Richard Revels **BL** AQI/Abraham Cardwell **130 TL** PEP/Trevor Risi **TR** © RD/Jason Smalley **CL** PEP/Georgette Douwma **BL** NHPA/Stephen Dalton **BR** NHPA/Jane Gifford **131 TR** AL/Jean-Paul Ferrero **CL(T)** BBC/Duncan McEwan **CL(B)** PW/Ken Preston-Mafham **R** © RD/Jason Smalley **BL** PW/Ken Preston-Mafham **132 TC** (**swans**) BCL/George McCarthy **132-133** NHPA/David Woodfall **133 T** PEP/Thomas Broad **CR** (**frog**) Biofotos/Heather Angel **BL** BCL/George McCarthy **BR** Biofotos/Heather Angel **134 TL** AQI/Abraham Cardwell **C** PEP/Nigel Downer **BC(L)** OSF/George Bernard **BC(R)** Martin & Dorothy Grace **135 TL** NHPA/E.A. Janes (**scum**) Biofotos/Heather Angel **C** OSF/G.H. Thompson **CR** Biofotos/Heather Angel **BC** AQI/Heather Angel **B** AQI/A.P.Walmsley **136 TR** BCL/Sir Jeremy Grayson **BL** OSF/Bob Fredrick **BC** AQI/David Owen **136-137** © RD/Jason Smalley **137 TR** AQI/Jonathan Need **CL** OSF/Larry Crowhurst **C** OSF/G I Bernard **CR** BCL/Kim Taylor **BL** OSF/Irvine Cushing **BC** OSF/Marshall Black **138 TR** AL/G.K.Brown **C** NHPA/Stephen Dalton **BR** AQI/Richard T.Mills **138-139** © RD/Jason Smalley **139 TC** BCL/Kim Taylor **TR** OSF/Hans Reinhard/Okapia **CL** NHPA/Stephen Dalton **C** BBC/Dietmar Nill **CR** AQI/Steve Downer **BR** AQI/Mike Wilkes **140 CR** OSF/Colin Milkins **BR** BCL/Andrew Purcell **140-141** © RD/Jason Smalley **141 CL** BBC/Tim Martin **CR** OSF/Richard Davies **BC** Biofotos/Heather Angel **BR** OSF/Fredrik Ehrenstrom **142 TR** OSF/Mark Hamblin **CR** Rentokil Initial/David Cropp **BL** AL/John Daniels **BC** BCL/Geoge McCarthy **BR** BCL/Geoge McCarthy **142-143** Background © RD/Jason Smalley **143 TL** OSF/Press-Tige Pictures **TC** AQI/Mike Lane **C** Biofotos/Heather Angel **BR** AQI/Mike Wilkes **144 L** BCL/Gordon Langsbury **C** AQI/J.J. Pearson **BL** OSF/Ben Osborne **BC** OSF/Ben Osborne **BR** OSF/Ben Osborne **145 TL** Martin & Dorothy Grace **TR** PW/Ken Preston-Mafham **CR(T)** NHPA/Stephen Dalton **CR(B)** PW/Ken Preston-Maffham **BL** AQI/M.C. Wilkes **BR** PW/Ken Preston-Mafham **146 CL** NSP/Richard Revels **C** NI/Bob Gibbons **CR** Biofotos **146-147** © RD/Jason Smalley **147 TL** Biofotos **TR** AL/P.Morris (**toad**) Biofotos **148 TL** AQI/M. Lane **TC** AQI/M.C. Wilkes **CR(T)** © RD/Jason Smalley **CR(B)** © RD/Jason Smalley **BR** © RD/Jason Smalley **149 TL** The Wildfowl & Wetlands Trust/Ichuro Kikuta **TR** AQI/Wayne Lankinen **BL** OSF/Terry Button **BR** The Wildfowl & Wetlands Trust/Joe Blossom **150 TC** PW/Ken Preston-Mafham **C(T)** AQI/Sawford/Castle **C(B)** NHPA/David Woodfall **BL** AQI/Kevin Carlson **BR** PW/Ken Preston-Mafham **150-151** Robin Chittenden **151 TR** AQI/Hans Gebuis **BL** BBC/Hans Christoph Kappel **BC** Biofotos/Heather Angel **152 TC** (**deer**) NSP/Andrew Watts **152-153** Biofotos/Heather Angel **153 T** John Cleare/Mountain Camera **C** (**pipit**) PEP/Mike Read **BL** NSP/Andrew Watts **BR** PEP/Mike Read **154 T** (**all**) © RD/Jason Smalley **BR** PEP/Alan Barnes **155 TL** AL/Bob Gibbons **TC** (**bell**) © RD/Jason Smalley **TC** (**heath**) NI/Bob Gibbons **TR** NSP/M Chinery **CL** Biofotos/Heather Angel **CR** AL **BR** AQI/Mike Lane **156 CR** NSP/P.H.& S.L.Ward **BL** NSP/Ian West **BR** PEP/Frank Blackburn (**background**) © RD/Jason

Smalley 157 C AL/Jean-Paul Ferrero BL AL/John Daniels BC © RD/Paul Kenward BR PW/Ken Preston-Mafham 158 (background) NI/Bob Gibbons (goat) PEP/William S.Paton 159 TL NI/Bob Gibbons TR NI/Peter Wilson CL NSP/Richard Revels C NI/Bob Gibbons BL AL BR © RD/Neil Holmes 160 TL NHPA/Silvestris Fotoservice TC AL/R.F. Porter TR NHPA/Stephen Dalton BL AL/R. Blewitt 160-161 © RD/Jason Smalley 161 TL(L) AQI/Richard T.Mills TR(R) OSF/Gordon Langsbury TC OSF/Mark Hamblin TR(L) RSPB Images/C.H.Gomersall TR(R) OSF/Denis Green C NHPA/Alan Williams BL BBC BR AL 162 CR © RD/Jason Smalley B © RD/Jason Smalley 162-163 © RD/Jason Smalley 163 TR AL/Bob Gibbons CL © RD/Jason Smalley CR © RD/Jason Smalley 164 TL AL/Bob Gibbons CR NI/Bob Gibbons BL AL/Bob Gibbons 164-165 AL/John Mason 165 TR Chris & Helen Pellant BC NSP/Ian West BR NI/Bob Gibbons 166 TR Chris O'Toole CR Chris O'Toole BL PW/Ken Preston-Mafham BC PW/Ken Preston-Mafham 167 TL(T) Martin & Dorothy Grace TL(B) NI/Bob Gibbons CR(B) PW/Ken Preston-Mafham CR(B) NI/Bob Gibbons BL PW/Ken Preston-Mafham BR NI/Bob Gibbons 168-169 AA Photo Library 169 TR NI/Bob Gibbons BL Biofotos BR AQI/M.Lane 170 T NHPA/E.A. Janes CR(T) NHPA/N.A. Callow CR(B) PEP/David George BL OSF/Paul Kay 171 TL PW/Rod Preston-Maffham TR(T) AL/Pat Morris TR(B) AL/Pat Morris BL NI/Bob Gibbons BR OSF/Paul Kay 172 TR PEP/Lythgoe BL OSF/G.I. Bernard BC(L) OSF/G.I. Bernard BC(R) Biofotos/Heather Angel BR Biofotos/Heather Angel 172-173 © RD/Jason Smalley 173 TL PEP/Jim Greenfield TC Biofotos/Heather Angel TR OSF/Paul Kay BL NSP/D.B. Lewis BC(L) PEP/Linda Pitkin BC(R) NHPA/Gerard Lacz BR PEP/Jim Greenfield 174 TR NHPA/Morten Strange (plover) OSF/Barry Walker (plover detail) OSF/Barry Walker (godwit) OSF/Barry Walker (godwit detail) OSF/Barry Walker BL PEP/Keith Scholey (avocet print) Nature Photographers/Roger Tidman (gull) NHPA/Laurie Campbell (gull detail) NHPA/Laurie Campbell 175 TC © RD/Jason Smalley BL AL/J.B.& S.Bottomley BC AL/Peter Steyn BR Nature Photographers/Andrew Cleave 176 PEP/Georgette Douwma 177 TL(T) NHPA/Roy Waller TL(B) PEP/Jim Greenfield CL PEP/Jim Greenfield C NHPA/Trevor McDonald CR NHPA/Laurie Campbell BC(T) PW/Dr. Rod Preston-Mafham BC(B) PW/Dr. Rod Preston-Mafham BR PEP/David George 178 CR Martin & Dorothy Grace BR NI/Bob Gibbons 178-179 Nature Photographers 179 TR NHPA/E.A. Janes CR OSF/William Paton BL(T) Nature Photographers/Paul Sterry BL(B) OSF/Larry Crowhurst BR AL/A.Greensmith 180 L OSF/David Tipling C OSF/Doug Allan BR NSP/Richard Revels 181 TL BBC/Adrian Davies CR AL/David & Katie Urry BR AL/Dave & Kate Urry 182 L NI/Bob Gibbons TR Martin & Dorothy Grace C PW/Ken Preston-Mafham CR Chris & Helen Pellant 183 TC NSP/Richard Revels TR PW/Ken Preston-Mafham C PW/Ken Preston-Mafham BL NI/Bob Gibbons 184-185 Biofotos/Heather Angel 185 TR NHPA/Michael Leach BL AQI/Mike Lane BR NSP/David Jackson 186 © RD/Guy Edwardes 186-187 © RD/Guy Edwardes 187 TR Biofotos/Heather Angel CR © RD/Guy Edwardes BL AL/Liz and Tony Bomford BC NSP/Richard Revels BR Biofotos/Heather Angel 188 TL OSF/Harold Taylor TC OSF/G.I. Bernard TR AQI/C.S. Milkins BL © RD/Jason Smalley 189 TL PEP/Steve Hopkin TR OSF/G.I. Bernard CL OSF/Peter Gould CR(T) OSF/Barrie Watts CR(B) NSP/P. Bowman BR BCL 190 TC PW/Ken Preston-Mafham TR AQI/Abraham Cardwell CL (beetles) OSF/Bob Fredrick BL OSF/Bob Fredrick 190-191 © RD/Jason Smalley 191 TL BCL/Kim Taylor TC OSF/G.I.Bernard TR (bee) PW/Ken Preston-Maffham TR (poppies) Biofotos/Heather Angel BR BBC/Geoff Dore 192 TR OSF/David Boag BL BBC/Barrie Britton BC Biofotos/Heather Angel 192-193 OSF/Michael Leach 193 TR NHPA/Joe Blossom BR OSF/C.M.Perrins 194 TR BCL/William Paton CL Biofotos/Jason Venus BL PEP/Geoff du Feu 195 TC NI/Mike Lane TR NHPA/Stephen Dalton BL AQI/M.C. Wilkes BR AQI 196 TC AQI/Mike Wilkes C AQI/Mike Wilkes BL BCL/Kim Taylor BR BCL/Kim Taylor 196-197 BCL/Kim Taylor 197 TR © RD/Guy Edwardes C © RD/Guy Edwardes BR Pat Morris 198 BL AL/Liz and Tony Bomford BR (fox) Biofotos/Heather Angel 198-199 © RD/Guy Edwardes 199 TC © RD/Guy Edwardes TR Biofotos/Heather Angel CL OSF/Steve Littlewood CR BBC/Niall Benvie BR © RD/Guy Edwardes 200 C Biofotos BL OSF/Niall Benvie 200-201 Skyscan 201 TL © RD/Jason Smalley TC Biofotos C OSF/Martyn Colbeck CR OSF/Press-Tige Pictures BC Chris & Helen Pellant 202-203 © RD/Jason Smalley 203 TR © RD/Jason Smalley BL AQI/M.C. Wilkes BR PEP/Nigel Downer 204 TR BBC/Mike Wilkes CR AQI/Kevin Carlson BC(T) PW/Ken Preston-Mafham BC(B) NI/Bob Gibbons BR(T) NI/Bob Gibbons BR(B) AL 204-205 © RD/Jason Smalley © RD/Jason Smalley 205 TL AQI/David Owen CL Biofotos/Heather Angel BR OSF/Roger Jackman 206 TR Martin & Dorothy Grace BL © RD/Jason Smalley 206-207 BCL/Andrew Purcell 207 C Pat Morris BR BBC/Angela Bird 208 CR AQI/Mike Lane BL (artwork) © RD/Peter D. Scott BR NSP/C. Seddon 208-209 © RD/Jason Smalley 209 TR OSF/Lon E. Lauber C (stoat artwork) © RD/Peter D. Scott BC AL/M. Watson 210 T AL/John Daniels BL BCL/William Paton BR AL/Chris Knights 211 TL BBC/William Osborn BR AL/R T Smith 212 TC AQI/R. Glover CR(T) AQI/R. Glover CR(B) BBC/Mike Wilkes BR BBC/Nigel Bean B AL/Chris Knight 213 TL AL/C. Lamb TR BBC/Mike Wilkes B AQI/Ulf Antonsson 214 TR(L) AQI/R.T. Mills TR(R) BBC/Mike Wilkes BL BBC/Artur Tabor 215 T PEP/Mark Mattock CL Biofotos/Heather Angel B OSF/Chris Knights 216-217 OSF/Niall Benvie 217 T AL/Bob Gibbons BL PW/Ken Preston-Mafham BR NHPA/Jane Gifford 218 CL © RD/Jason Smalley R © RD/Jason Smalley BL © RD/Jason Smalley 219 TR Biofotos/Heather Angel CL Biofotos/Heather Angel C © RD/Jason Smalley BL Biofotos/Heather Angel BC(L) OSF/Frithjof Skibbe BC(R) OSF/Deni Down BR PW/Ken Preston-Mafham 220 C © RD/Jason Smalley BR © RD/Jason Smalley 220-221 © RD/Jason Smalley 221 TC PEP/Mark Mattock BL OSF/Harold Taylor BC PEP/Mark Mattock 222 L Biofotos/Heather Angel TR AQI/Mike Wilkes BC PEP/Paul Stevens 223 TL PEP/Heather Angel TR BBC/William Osborn BL PEP/Mike Read BR AQI/Richard Mills 224 TL OSF/M. Lanfranchi TC Biofotos/Heather Angel TR BBC/Duncan McEwan C NSP/Richard Revels 224-225 © RD/Simon Turvey 225 TC © RD/Jason Smalley C OSF/Richard Packwood BR AQI/R.T. Mills 226 T AQI/John Burnham CL NSP/Richard Revels C(L) BBC/E.C. Bignell C(R) AQI/Mike Lane 227 BL(T) PW/Ken Preston-Mafham BL(B) Martin & Dorothy Grace BL(R) PEP/Nigel Downer BR NHPA/Jane Gifford 228 TR AQI/M. Lane C © RD/Mike Langman CR BBC/Niall Benvie B (all) Trustees of the British Museum (Natural History) 229 L © RD/Jason Smalley CR AQI/Richard Mills BR AQI/Mike Wilkes B Pat Morris Tom Mackie 230-231 R (ducks) AL/Chris Knights 231 TR John Cleare/Mountain Camera BL AL/Chris Knights BR Chris & Helen Pellant 232 CR (hawk) NHPA/Stephen Dalton R (background) AL/David & Katie Urry 233 TL OSF/Tony Tilford CR NHPA/Melvin Grey BR NHPA/N.A. Callow 234 C AL/Bob Gibbons B © RD/Jason Smalley 235 TL OSF/H.L. Fox TR AL/John Mason CR OSF/Terry Heathcote BL AL/John Mason 236 (map) © RD/PCGraphics (UK) Ltd (background) OSF/Keith Ringland BR NHPA/Laurie Campbell 237 TC PW/Ken Preston-Mafham BL AL/Pat Morris BR NHPA/Stephen Dalton 238 TL (background) PW/Ken Preston-Mafham TL (inset) PW/Ken Preston-Mafham C PW/Ken Preston-Mafham BL NI/Bob Gibbons BC AL/Pascal Goetgheluck 239 TC PW/Ken Preston-Mafham CL AL/Bob Gibbons CR NI/Peter Wilson BL NSP/M.Chinery BC PW/Ken Preston-Mafham BR PW/Ken Preston-Mafham 240-241 NHPA/Laurie Campbell 241 TR Biofotos BL AQI/Mike Wilkes BR OSF/Barrie E.Watts 242 CR Martin & Dorothy Grace BL AQI/S & B A Craig BR BBC/Mike Wilkes 242-243 AQI/Abraham Cardwell 243 CR AQI/J.Lawton Roberts BC Biofotos BR AL/Ian Beames 244 (red grouse) Biofotos/Heather Angel (ptarmigan) BBC/David Kjaer (black grouse) Pat Morris (capercaillie) BBC/Niall Benvie B Biofotos/Heather Angel 245 CL(T) BBC/Duncan McEwan CL(B) Biofotos/heather Angel CR BBC/John Free BL OSF/Irvine Cushing BR OSF/Terry Heathcote 246 TC BCL/Sir Jeremy Grayson TR BBC/Niall Benvie C Biofotos/Heather Angel CR Martin & Dorothy Grace 246-247 BBC/Niall Benvie 247 TR AQI/Abraham Cardwell C OSF/Frithjof Skibbe BL AQI/Mike Lane BR Biofotos/Heather Angel 248 BL BBC/Nigel Bean BC Biofotos/Heather Angel 248-249 © RD/Jason Smalley 249 TR © RD/Jason Smalley CR © RD/Jason Smalley BR Biofotos/Heather Angel 250 TC OSF/Mark Hamblin BL Biofotos/Heather Angel BC NSP/R.A. Powell BR AQI/R. Glover 250-251 NSP/Richard Revels 251 TR Windrush Photos/David Cottridge BL AL BR Biofotos/Heather Angel 252 TR (falcon) BCL/Mike Freeman 252-253 Woodfall Wild Images/David Woodfall 253 T AL/Liz & Tony Bomford BL BCL/Mike Freeman BR OSF/Mark Hamblin 254 BL(L) BBC/Niall Benvie BL(R) BBC/Dan Burton 254-255 NI/Bob Gibbons 255 TL Biofotos/Heather Angel TR NI/Bob Gibbons 256 TR BBC/Tom Walmsley CR AQI/Kevin Carlson BL NSP/B. Cranston BC NSP/B. Cranston 256-257 Chris & Helen Pellant 257 TL BBC/Michael Pitts TR Chris & Helen Pellant CR PEP/Robert Canis BR BBC/David Tipling 258 TL NI/Mike Lane C Biofotos/Heather Angel BC OSF/Rodger Jackman 259 TL AQI/Gary Smith BL BBC/Alan James BC OSF/G.I. Bernard BR NSP/Paul Kay B (background) Biofotos/Heather Angel 260 TL AL/David and Kate Urry B AQI/M.C. Wilkes 261 TL(T) AL/Pat Morris TL(B) AQI/Mike Wilkes TR PW/Ken Preston-Mafham BL(T) NI/Bob Gibbons BL(B) AQI/Ross Macleod BR PW/Ken Preston-Mafham 262 TL AL C Chris & Helen Pellant 263 TR(T) Chris & Helen Pellant TR(B) Chris & Helen Pellant (map) © RD/PCGraphics (UK) Ltd CR OSF/W.J. Kennedy BL(T) AL/Bob Gibbons BR(T) Biofotos/Heather Angel BL(B) Chris & Helen Pellant BR(B) NSP 264-265 AQI/Mike Birkhead 265 T © RD/Jason Smalley CR (squirrel) BBC/Angela Bird BL BBC/David Tipling BR BBC/Angela Bird 266 CL NSP/Richard Revels C NI/Peter Wilson 266-267 © RD/Jason Smalley 267 TR Biofotos/Heather Angel C(T) NSP/Ian West C(B) BCL/Jane Burton BL OSF/Barrie Watts BC(L) NSP/C. Blaney BC(R) AQI/Johan de Meester 268 CL AQI/Richard Mills C Chris & Helen Pellant BR AQI/Stephen Basset 269 TL Biofotos/Heather Angel C AL/M. Watson BR BBC/David Kjaer 270 TR NSP/Richard Revels CR BCL/Jane Burton BL Biofotos/Jason Venus 271 TL BBC/Fabio Liverani TR NI/Bob Gibbons BC AL/Liz & Tony Bomford BR Pat Morris 272 CR BBC/Adrian Davis BL NI/Bob Gibbons BR OSF/Harold Taylor 273 TL OSF/Alastair MacEwen TR PW/Ken Preston-Mafham CL Biofotos/Heather Angel CR PW/Ken Preston-Mafham BL BBC/Paul Johnson BR PEP/Steve Hopkin 274 L BCL/Sir Jeremy Grayson BR PEP/Susan & Allan Parker 275 TL OSF/G.A. MacLean TR AQI/Abraham Cardwell CR NI/Alec Harmer BC NSP/Richard Revels 276 L BCL/William Paton BL Biofotos/Heather Angel 277 TL AQI/R.T. Mills TR Biofotos/Jason Venus CR Biofotos/Heather Angel BC © RD/Jason Smalley BR © RD/Jason Smalley 278-279 OSF/Mark Hamblin 279 T Holt Studios Ltd./Nigle Cattlin BL Holt Studios Ltd./Wayne Hutchinson BR Holt Studios Ltd./Nigel Cattlin 280 CL OSF/Prestige Pictures BL OSF/G.I. Bernard 280-281 PEP/Geoff du Feu 281 TC NI/Bob Gibbons TR NSP/Richard Revels BC AQI/G.W. Ward BR OSF/Dennis Green 282 CR(T) © RD/Jason Smalley CR(B) © RD/Jason Smalley BR BCL/William Patton 282-283 © RD/Jason Smalley 283 TR © RD/Jason Smalley CL AQI/P.K. Lucas BR OSF/Michael Leach 284 C(T) OSF/Jack Dermid C(B) OSF/Michael Leach BC AQI/Richard Hems 284-285 OSF/Larry Crowhurst 285 TR AQI/Richard T. Miles C(T) OSF/Jack Dermid C(B) OSF/Micael Leach CR NSP/Richard Revels BC Biofotos/Heather Angel BR(L) OSF/Richard Packwood BR(R) Pat Morris 286 AL/Chris Knights 287 TL AQI/B. Speake TR NI/Mike Lane C NSP/M.W. Powles CR AQI/Mike Lane BC BCL/george McCarthy BR BBC/Niall Benvie 288-289 Tom Mackie 289 T Biofotos/Heather Angel BL NSP/Andrew Watts BR NSP/Andrew Watts 290 CL BCL/Dr. Eckart Pott C OSF/David Fox BL © RD/Jason Smalley BC(L) PEP/Peter and Tristan Millen BC(R) Biofotos/Heather Angel BR BCL/Kim Taylor 291 TR PEP/Wayne Harris BR BBC/Adrian Davies 292 TL PEP/Margaret Welby TC Martin & Dorothy Grace TR BBC/Torsten Brehm BR NI/Bob Gibbons 293 TL AL/Bob Gibbons CR AL/Bob Gibbons BC Martin & Dorothy Grace 294 T OSF/William Patton CR BBC/Brian Lightfoot BL © RD/Stuart Carter 295 L OSF/Terry Heathcote TR Pat Morris CR(L) OSF/Barrie Watts CR(R) NI/Bob Gibbons BC OSF/Terry Heathcote 296 TL NSP/Mike Powles BL AL/M. Watson BC AL/M. Watson 297 TL AL TR NSP/W. Cane CL PEP/Paul Stevens BL PW/Ken Preston-Mafham BR BBC/William Osborne 298 L Biofotos/Jason Venus TC OSF/G.I. Bernard BR AL/J. A. Bailey 299 TC BCL/Kim Taylor TR AL/S. Roberts C AL/Ian Beames CR OSF/S. Roberts BL BBC/Paul Hobson 300 TR (goose) AL/M.D. England 300-301 Biofotos/Heather Angel 301 TR NHPA/Jane Gifford C (snipe) BBC/Geoff Dore BL AL/M.D. England BR BBC/Geoff Dore 302 TR(T) AQI/David Chapman TR(B) BBC/David Kjaer BL NSP/P.H. & S.L. Ward BR Martin & Dorothy Grace 302-303 NSP/Richard Revels 303 PEP/Frank Blackburn 304 BL BBC/John Cancalosi BC AQI/Anthony Cooper BR AL/Ian Beames 304-305 Biofotos/Heather Angel 305 Pat Morris 306 TC BBC/Niall Benvie C BBC/Geoff Dore 306-307 AQI/Mick Durham 307 TL AQI/Mike Birkhead TR NI/Mike Lane CL AQI/Mick Durham CR AQI/Mick Durham BR Biofotos/Jason Venus 308 TC (eagle) BBC/John Downer 308-309 David Paterson 309 T BCL/Peter Hinchliffe BL BBC/John Downer BR BCL/Peter Hinchliffe 310 TR PEP/Elio della Ferrera 310-311 PEP/Neil McIntyre 311 CR OSF/Mark Hamblin R BBC/David Kjaer BL OSF/Richard Packwood 312 TR AQI/Mike Wilkes BL AQI/S. Phillipps 313 TL OSF/Richard Packwood CL(T) BBC/Rico & Ruiz CL(B) AQI/Mike Lane BR (background) Chris & Helen Pellant 314 T NI/Bob Gibbons BR Biofotos/Brian Rogers 315 TL(L) Martin & Dorothy Grace TL(R) BBC/Duncan McEwan TR AL/John Mason CR Biofotos/Heather Angel BR Biofotos/Brian Rogers 316 TL AL TR (fox head) © RD/Simon Turvey TR (skull overlay) OSF/Alastair Shay CR © RD/Simon Turvey BL Chris & Helen Pellant BR OSF/G.I. Bernard 317 TL (rabbit head) © RD/Simon Turvey TL (skull overlay) OSF/G.I. Bernard TR Pat Morris CL © RD/Simon Turvey CR OSF/Terry Heathcote BR Pat Morris 318-319 Biofotos/Heather Angel 319 T NHPA/Laurie Campbell TR (gull) AL/Stefan Meyers BL PEP/Susan & Allan Parker BR AL/Stefan Meyers 320 T AQI/Guy Huntington BR OSF/Lon Lauber 321 TL AL/Chris Knights CR(T) AL/K. Fink CR(B) AQI/B. Wright BR BCL/Dr. Scott Nielsen 322 AQI/Hans Gebuis 323 TL AL/Chris Knights TR © RD/PCGraphics (UK) LTD BR AL/Chris Knights 324 TR PEP/Geoff du Feu CR BBC/Niall Benvie BL PEP/J. Bracegirdle 324-325 AL/John Mason 325 TL OSF/Jack Wiburn C OSF/Colin Milkins CR(T) AL/Pat Morris CR(B) Biofotos/Heather Angel 326 TR(T) OSF/Ben Osbourne TR(B) Biofotos/Heather Angel BL (background) Biofotos/Heather Angel BL (inset) OSF/Colin Milkins BR(T) Biofotos/Heather Angel BR(B) Biofotos/Heather Angel 327 C AQI/S. Phillips (hare track) AL/Bob Gibbons BL AQI/Simon Rowlands BR Pat Morris 328 TR (feeder) © RD/Andrea Jones 328-329 © RD/Andrea Jones 329 T BCL/Dr Stephen Coyne CL © RD/Andrea Jones BR PEP/Peter Gasson 330 BL AL/Liz and Tony Bomford BC AQI/Mike Lane 330-331 AL/Jack A.Bailey 331 TR AL/Chris Knights CL AL/Richard Vaughan 332 T AQI/Mike Birkhead CR Biofotos/Jason Venus 333 TL PEP/Edward Coleman TR OSF/Robin Redfern CL AL/Ian Beames CR(L) OSF/David Cayless CR(R) OSF/Jack Demid BR NSP/Richard Revels 334 TL AL/John Daniels BL BCL/Kim Taylor BC OSF/Mike Birkenhead 335 TC OSF/Kathie Atkinson C AQI/Mike Lane CR PEP/Steve Hopkin BL OSF/David Thompson BR AQI/Gary Smith 336 L AL/Johon Mason C Biofotos/Heather Angel 336-337 PW/Ken Preston-Mafham 337 CL PEP/Andrew Mac Geeney BC AQI/Mike Wilkes BR OSF/D.J. Saunders 338 © RD/PCGraphics (UK) Ltd 340 TC NSP/Richard Revels CL NHPA/Laurie Campbell 341 TL © RD/Jason Smalley TC AL/John Mason TR BBC/David Tipling CL NSP/Richard Revels 342 TL PEP/Trevor Risi TC OSF/G.A.Maclean 343 BL PEP/Georgette Douwma CR AQI/Kevin Carlson 344 T Chris & Helen Pellant B OSF/Doug Allan 345 TL AL/Dave & Kate Urry TR Biofotos/Jason Venus 346 CL AL/Zdenek Tunka C BBC/Niall Benvie CR PW/Ken Preston-Mafham 347 T © RD/Jason Smalley C Biofotos/Heather Angel 348 L BBC/William Osborn R Biofotos/Heather Angel 349 BCL 350 T AL B OSF/Press-Tige Pictures Endpaper NHPA/Roger Tidman

The publishers would like to thank the following for their assistance in the preparation of this book:
Dr Heather Binney, Bill Burroughs, Allerton Research Educational Trust, Friends of the Lake District, English Nature, Royal Society for the Protection of Birds, The Wildlife Trusts, Woodland Trust

Book Production Manager Chris Reynolds
Assistant Book Production Manager Fiona McIntosh
Pre-press Manager Howard Reynolds
Pre-press Support Kathy Brown, Martin Hendrick, Jane Holyer, Jim Lindsay
Origination Colour Systems Ltd, London, England
Paper Townsend Hook Ltd, Snodland, England
Printing and binding Brepols Graphic Industries NV, Turnhout, Belgium

40-958-02